MAKING A
KILLING

MAKING A
KILLING

HOW AND WHY CORPORATIONS USE **ARMED FORCE** TO DO BUSINESS

MADELAINE DROHAN

RANDOM HOUSE CANADA

www.randomhouse.ca

National Library of Canada Cataloguing in Publication

Drohan, Madelaine
Making a killing : how and why corporations use armed force
to do business / Madelaine Drohan

Includes bibilographical references and index.
ISBN 0-679-31197-1

1. Corporations—Corrupt practices. 2. Mercenary troops. 3. Politics, Private.
4. International business enterprises. I. Title.

HD2755.5.D76 2003   338.8'8   C2003-902643-4

Text design by Daniel Cullen

Printed and bound in the United States of America
10 9 8 7 6 5 4 3 2 1

FOR FRANK

CONTENTS

Africa

SUDAN

SIERRA
LEONE

NIGERIA

CONGO

ANGOLA

UGANDA

MOZAMBIQUE

SOUTH
AFRICA

INTRODUCTION

WE ROCKETED ALONG THE THIN STRIP OF PAVEMENT THAT PASSED FOR a highway in northeastern Angola, heading for a diamond mine located in what was, until recently, rebel-held territory. The drivers in our small convoy of cars and trucks were either extremely careless or terrified. Feet to the floor, they careened around potholes and washouts, their juddering vehicles protesting with metal shrieks and groans. We held on as best we could. At the front and back of our group were pickup trucks filled with men cradling AK-47 knock-offs. The men somehow managed to stay in place, despite being precariously seated on two rows of plastic lawn chairs lined back to back down the centre of each truck bed.

It was 1998 and Angola was at war, but we—a motley collection of business journalists, investment analysts, potential investors and tight-lipped mystery men—had been assured that this part of the country was peaceful, so peaceful that a number of mining companies had begun operations there. The company that had organized this investment tour, DiamondWorks Ltd., had wined and dined us the previous evening at the Sandton Hilton in Johannesburg and filled our heads with tales of giant gemstones just waiting to be plucked from the earth. This morning they had flown us on a Million Air charter jet to the Angolan capital, Luanda, and then on to Saurimo in the northeast of the country. We were now making the last leg of the journey by road, to the region near the Congo border that was famous for the quality of its diamonds.

More gun-toting men came out to greet us at the site. It was a mine in name only. Here and there, the buffalo grass had been scraped away by bulldozers to expose the iron-red earth of Africa. But the real action was on the Luo River, which ran through the property. There, miners were using a simple but effective machine to suck gravel from the riverbed and extract from it the alluvial diamonds that had travelled downstream on the current. DiamondWorks planned to divert the river from its course to enable a more thorough search.

A group of us were handed over to the care of a soft-spoken Angolan mine employee, who painted an impossibly bright picture of the area as he drove us around. Not only were there no human predators lurking nearby, there were also no crocodiles or hippopotamuses in the river and no large snakes in the bush. The investment analysts in our group nodded approvingly when told that three levels of security surrounded an iron cargo container that served as both a sorting area and a storage space for recovered gems. "Diamonds bring out the worst in people," a DiamondWorks representative confided to us as he wrestled with the three massive padlocks on the container. "They are evil. They are the only thing in the world this small"—he made a gesture with two fingers—"that can pay for your family's future." The diamonds on the sorting tables ranged from brilliant white to dark brown. They looked like fish tank gravel.

That afternoon, we dined on lobster flown in for the occasion and on bread baked by the camp cook over an open fire. The food might have been appetizing were it not for the hordes of flies that rose when flicked away by the serving men, only to descend again. Still, the company had done its utmost to create a civilized atmosphere. And it all seemed rather peaceful until I excused myself to use the toilet facilities. Four men, one heavily armed, escorted me to a concrete cubicle in the bush. At the door, I was handed a padlock to secure it from the inside. I looked at the lock in my hand, puzzled. Why, if the area was so safe, was there so much emphasis on security?

At the end of the day we retraced our steps—another hair-raising ride to Saurimo and then onto the Million Air flight to South Africa. It had cost DiamondWorks CDN$100,000 to organize our visit, but the company thought it was well worth it. They knew they could raise millions on the stock exchange back home if we—journalists, analysts and money men—reported to our various audiences that the mine was operating and secure. Which is what we did. Their methods may not have been the most sophisticated in the world, but they were finding diamonds with their giant vacuum, even if they were harvesting them behind a wall of guns.

Several months later came news that put my armed escort to the lavatory in perspective. Rebels, thought to be from the National Union for the Total Independence of Angola (UNITA), had overrun part of the DiamondWorks operation, killing eight people and dragging another ten into the bush. The rebels looted the mine, and when they were done, government forces arrived and looted it again. The hostages were still missing and presumed dead.

I had first encountered DiamondWorks and its majority shareholder, Tony Buckingham, a former Special Services officer from Britain, three years earlier while I was working as a foreign correspondent in London for the Canadian newspaper the *Globe and Mail*. DiamondWorks was nominally Canadian—it was registered in the Yukon and raised money on the Vancouver Stock Exchange—and the newspaper wanted coverage of its activities. Specifically, my editors wanted to know if the rumours linking DiamondWorks with a group of mercenaries out of South Africa called Executive Outcomes were true.

Through my investigation, I learned that Tony Buckingham had been making a practice of introducing Executive Outcomes to weak and unstable governments in need of armed support. These governments often hired the mercenaries to retake prime resource areas in their countries— diamond mines in particular—from rebel forces. Once these areas were back in a government's control, mineral concessions were awarded to multinational corporations. When it was revealed that some of these corporations were associated with Buckingham, he was accused of employing armed force to acquire mineral riches, much as the imperial chartered companies had done a century before. Buckingham never talked to the media, but his spokespersons insisted that there was no connection between the introductions Buckingham had made to the governments of Angola and Sierra Leone and the subsequent arrival of DiamondWorks in those countries.

I became interested not just in Tony Buckingham and DiamondWorks, but in companies like DiamondWorks that combined their search for profit with some form of armed force. Until then I had been focusing on more prosaic topics, such as multilateral trade talks and global investment agreements. Passions had certainly run high during those negotiations—there was much at stake—but I had yet to hear of anyone being killed for the sake of a favourable clause in a final agreement. What would drive a company, I wondered, to sanction the use of armed force, knowing that lives would be lost?

This book traces the route I took in trying to answer that question. It begins with Cecil Rhodes and the British South Africa Company, which blazed a trail that other corporations are still treading. Rhodes was looking for the fabled gold mines of King Solomon when he raised his own private army and invaded what has since become Zimbabwe and Zambia, seizing land and resources. Buckingham has sometimes been compared to Cecil Rhodes. From Rhodes, I moved on to King Léopold II of Belgium and the rubber companies he set up to exploit the Congo at the point of a gun. The head of diamond giant De Beers, Sir Ernest Oppenheimer, added a twist to the pattern set by Rhodes and Léopold when he hired the former head of MI5 to set up an international spy organization to safeguard his gems. In the 1960s, Union Minière tried to protect its copper empire in the Congo by funding an armed insurrection. The mercenaries who were hired with Union Minière money were so brutal they were collectively known as *les affreux*, or the horrible ones.

As my research progressed, I found companies that had benefited from the use of armed force without actually having to raise private armies of their own. Instead, they made special arrangements with national armies, government militias or police forces to ensure that their corporate interests were met. Both Royal Dutch/Shell in Nigeria and Talisman Energy Inc. in Sudan elected to use the security arms of repressive regimes to protect their commercial assets. Roland "Tiny" Rowland of Lonrho PLC channelled funds to rebel movements in Mozambique to keep his oil pipeline operating, and Salim Saleh of Uganda combined many of the tactics used by corporations in the past to expand and protect his commercial enterprises in the Congo.

What links all these examples together is the fact that each company or corporate leader benefited from the aggressive use of armed force. In each instance, I tried to uncover what special circumstances within the company and outside it contributed to the lethal outcome. I looked at why the checks and balances designed to prevent such behaviour did not work. Why didn't those who had the power to intervene—company directors, national governments and the reigning global powers—do so? Finally, I looked at what can be done to prevent similar corporate abuses in the future.

Though this book could have included accounts of companies that have used armed force in the former Soviet Union, Latin America, Asia or anywhere else where resources are found in combination with weak or non-existent governments, I chose to focus on Africa for ease of research and because that beleaguered continent offers up more than enough examples to satisfy the purposes of my inquiry. Over the course of four years, I travelled to Angola, Sudan, South Africa, Mozambique, Uganda, Kenya, Nigeria and Zambia, sometimes visiting the same country more than once. I interviewed business leaders and visited mine sites and production platforms. I spoke to government officials and bankers, sat down with warlords, mercenaries and retired guerilla leaders and asked charitable groups and ordinary citizens for their views. This book contains the answers I found.

LUSAKA

ZAMBIA

Zambezi R.

LIVINGSTONE

HARARE
(Fort Salisbury)

Victoria Falls

ANGOLA

Zambezi R.

NAMIBIA

ZIMBABWE

BULAWAYO

MASVINGO
(Fort Victoria)

BEIRA

MOZAMBIQUE

BOTSWANA

Limpopo R.

WINDHOEK

GABORONE

PRETORIA

JOHANNESBURG

MAPUTO

Swaziland

Natal

Orange R.

KIMBERLEY

Lesotho

SOUTH AFRICA

DURBAN

Atlantic Ocean

Orange R.

Indian Ocean

N

▪▪▪▪ International Boundary
▬ ▬ Regional Boundary
+++ Railway
—— River

Port Elizabeth

CAPE TOWN

| 0 km | | 400 |
| 0 mi | | 400 |

CHAPTER ONE

CECIL RHODES AND THE BRITISH SOUTH AFRICA COMPANY

IN THE PANTHEON OF BUSINESSMEN WHO THROUGH THE AGES HAVE resorted to military solutions for corporate problems, Cecil Rhodes stands head and shoulders above the rest. He amassed a great fortune in diamonds and gold and then used those riches to raise a private army with which he seized and occupied a huge swath of southern Africa. Within twenty years of his arrival on the continent as a cash-strapped parson's son, he stood at the helm of a commercial empire that began with De Beers Mining Company, continued with Consolidated Goldfields of South Africa and culminated with the British South Africa Company, which bore a royal charter. Timing had played an important role in his amazing commercial success. The diamond rush at what is now called Kimberley was in its infancy when he first arrived in Africa, and the great gold discoveries at Witwatersrand were about to be made. But it was Rhodes's ruthlessness, his utter conviction that nothing, and certainly no man, must stand in the way of his mission to expand the British Empire, that led to his success.

History has been kind to Rhodes. He ensured his posthumous respectability by endowing the University of Oxford with a magnificent library and prestigious scholarships that still bear his name. Do the eager young scholars who flock through the carved doors of Rhodes House each fall connect their educational windfall with its tainted roots? "Behind every great fortune, there is a crime," said French novelist Honoré de Balzac. In the case of Rhodes, there was more than one.

He was born in July 1853 at Bishop's Stortford, a market town northeast of London where his father was vicar for the Church of England. Young Cecil was a sickly but pleasant child. A former governess described him as good-looking, with fair hair and an agreeable way of speaking. Because of his health, he was not sent to boarding school as his brothers were; instead, he attended the small local grammar school. When he graduated in 1869, his plan was to attend university and become a barrister, despite his father's wish that he enter the Church. Rhodes fell ill before he could accomplish his goals. The doctor, fearing Rhodes was suffering from consumption, prescribed a long sea voyage. Rhodes was packed off to Natal in southern Africa, where one of his elder brothers, Herbert, was growing cotton. In the late nineteenth century it was not unusual for young Englishmen, particularly second or third sons, to head off to the far reaches of the empire to seek their fortunes. They had a wealth of places to choose from; Queen Victoria's empire, which was then approaching its zenith, encompassed 372 million people in an area ninety-one times the size of Great Britain.

Rhodes arrived at his brother's cotton farm to find that Herbert had already departed for the newly discovered diamond fields in the southern African interior. At the time, there were four regions in southernmost Africa that were settled by whites: Cape Colony and Natal, which were controlled by the British, and Orange Free State and Transvaal, which were controlled by descendants of Dutch settlers known as the Boers. The diamond fields lay outside these regions in a no man's land known as Griqualand West. Diamonds had first been found in 1866 on the banks of the Orange River. Two years later, prospectors began finding diamond-bearing kimberlites nearby. Four of the richest of these—Bultfontein (1869), Dutoitspan (1869), De Beers (1871) and Kimberley (1871)—were within five kilometres of each other between the Orange and Vaal rivers.

The discoveries were transforming the rural backwater where farmers eked out a poor living into an area with a promising future, and the British and Boers began jockeying for control of it—a contest the British eventually won in 1902 after a bruising three-year war.

Rhodes stayed in Natal long enough to supervise the cotton harvest then trekked west into the interior to find his brother. Herbert was working three claims at the Kimberley mine when his brother Cecil joined him. In a letter to his mother, Cecil described the site: "Imagine a small, round hill at its very highest part only 30 feet above the level of the surrounding country, about 180 yards broad and 220 feet long; all round it a mass of white tents . . . It is like an immense number of ant heaps covered with black ants, as thick as can be, the latter represented by human beings." The entire area was staked out in claims, with narrow roads running between them. Digging Herbert's claims, Rhodes averaged thirty carats a week. He described the earth as having the composition of Stilton cheese, with the diamond-bearing soil being the blue bits between the white cheese. A diamond of over fifty carats was found at least once a day somewhere in the fields, although Rhodes had yet to find one so large. Over the next half-century, miners at Kimberley would dig a pit more than a kilometre and a half wide and so deep that it would become one of the few artificial formations on earth that could be seen from space.

Life on the diamond fields was rough. The lure of instant riches had attracted an estimated ten thousand prospectors to the general area within months. They included the young sons of British gentry such as Rhodes and his brother, military men, speculators and ne'er-do-wells. At Kimberley, the men lived in tents. Those who could afford it had African and Indian servants to do the heavy work and to forage for fuel and food. Water was so scarce that a man wanting to take a bath would often have to make do with soda water. The men shared their meals in various messes, with like-minded men grouping together for conversation and games. This was a very male world, something Rhodes preferred. While still a young teenager, he had vowed never to marry because he felt marriage would prove too much a distraction. He kept that vow, leading some later biographers to suggest that Rhodes was homosexual. "It was not that he was a woman hater," said Frank Johnson, one of the men who worked for Rhodes, "but he certainly feared women. Invariably, he was opposed to having any married man in his entourage. He always used to say that no one could marry a wife and also keep secrets." In his memoirs, *Great Days*, Johnson described Rhodes's reaction when one of his personal secretaries told him that he was engaged: "Rhodes raved and stormed like a maniac. His falsetto voice rose to a screech as he kept on screaming: 'Leave my house! Leave my house!' No small schoolboy or even schoolgirl, could have behaved more childishly than he did."

It was during his years at Kimberley that Rhodes met the men who would later help him build his empire: Charles Rudd, a Northamptonshire man who like Rhodes had come to Africa for his health, would become his partner; Alfred Beit, the son of a Hamburg Jew and a diamond expert, would become the financial brains behind Rhodes's operations; Sidney Shippard, the attorney general of Griqualand West and the face of authority in the rough community of diamond diggers, would become his protector; and Leander Starr Jameson, a young Scottish doctor who was a partner in the local medical practice, would be his trusted deputy.

About a year after Rhodes arrived in southern Africa, his brother Herbert left Kimberley to seek adventure elsewhere. He gave his diamond claims to Cecil, who continued to work them until he had raised enough money to attend Oxford—for he had never given up his dream of going to university. He set off for England in time to enrol at Oriel College for the fall session of 1873, leaving his claims to be managed by Rudd, who was now his partner. Rhodes's biographers have described this period for him as a curious double life. Over the next eight years, he travelled back and forth between Kimberley and Oxford, attending school for a term or sometimes two before returning to Africa to manage his diamond business. Rhodes loved university and read voraciously, although he rarely appeared at lectures. He was much taken with the teachings of John Ruskin, an English art and social critic who lectured at Oxford about the necessity of England's founding colonies "as fast and as far as she is able" in order to advance the power of England and to teach the colonized to be faithful to the Crown.

Rhodes had shown strong imperialist leanings even before attending university. His first will, which he wrote not long after arriving in Africa, left his estate, such as it was, to the secretary for the colonies in trust, to be used to expand the British Empire. Later wills—and there were many—expanded on this theme, leaving money to establish a secret society whose aim would be to extend the British Empire across the whole world. At the age of twenty-four he composed a stirring passage laying out his goals as a young Englishman. "It is our duty," he wrote, "to seize every opportunity of acquiring more territory and we should keep this one idea steadily before our eyes: that the more territory simply means more of the Anglo-Saxon race, more of the best, the most human, most honourable race the world possesses." Rhodes cited these grandiose plans as the motivation behind his commercial activities.

Originally, there were 430 claims at Kimberley, each of 31 square feet. Some were subdivided, resulting in about 1,600 separate holdings by 1872. One of the problems with this was that as the miners dug deeper into the soil, the roads between their claims began to collapse, causing arguments about boundaries and who could claim the debris. Rhodes recognized that the diamonds could be better exploited if the thousands of individual plots were amalgamated into one company. When the price of diamonds went down in 1875 as a result of a worldwide economic depression, Rhodes took advantage of the situation by buying claims that other miners were eager to abandon. Rumour had it that the mines were just about played out. As the miners dug ever deeper, they were reaching a layer of hard blue ground that was different from the softer yellow earth on top. Many believed this new layer would not contain diamonds. It would in fact prove to be far richer.

It was during this period of change at Kimberley that Rhodes gave an early indication of the questionable business tactics he was prepared to use if more legitimate means failed. In 1874, he successfully bid for and won a contract to pump water from the De Beers, Kimberley and

Dutoitspan mines. Although water was scarce on the surface of the land, flooding was a constant danger underground. There are several versions of what happened next. In one, Rhodes began the contract with old equipment, which broke down, necessitating the shipment of a replacement pump. In another, he had to import a pump from England before he could even start the contract. Either way, the pumping contract was given in the interim to a Mr. Huteau, who did the job so well that there was talk he should continue with it in place of Rhodes. Huteau's success, however, came to a sudden end one night when his equipment was sabotaged. Parts of the pump had been removed, ruining the engine and allowing the claims to be flooded. The miners were enraged.

In the ensuing court case, Huteau testified that Rhodes had offered him a bribe to damage his own equipment. Rhodes accused Huteau of perjury and sued for defamation. It was at this point that Attorney General Sidney Shippard made the first of his fortuitous interventions in Rhodes's life. Shippard, who had shared the same mess with Rhodes at Kimberley, dropped the case against Huteau, which if brought to its conclusion might well have established Rhodes's guilt. Rhodes made no further attempt to clear his name, which was surprising given the importance of honour to a Victorian gentleman. It was interpreted at the time as proof of his guilt.

Rhodes eventually got the pumping contract back, and it provided him with a steady source of income, supplementing the irregular payments from his diamond finds. There was an added advantage for him in controlling the pump: claims he left covered by water were cheaper to buy and cost less to maintain because licence fees were reduced as long as a claim could not be worked. Rhodes exploited this situation to expand his diamond holdings.

By 1880, he, Rudd and another partner, a man named Alderson, set up the De Beers Mining Company with an initial capital of £200,000 made up of 2,000 shares worth £100 each. By 1885, the original 3,600 claims at the four big mines—Bultfontein, Dutoitspan, Kimberley and De Beers—had been consolidated into ninety-eight claims owned mostly by De Beers and its competitors, such as Kimberley Central Mining Co., which was controlled by Barney Barnato. Rhodes mounted a fierce campaign that resulted in De Beers winning a virtual monopoly of the richest diamond fields. The £5,338,650 cheque Rhodes wrote Barnato for his Kimberley Central shares was the largest cheque ever written to that time. The money was furnished by the Rothschild banking family, whose solid reputation later smoothed Rhodes's path and helped him attract men of social standing to his company boards. The key players in the amalgamation—Rhodes, Beit, Barnato and F.S. Philipson-Stow, a lawyer—were made life governors of De Beers Consolidated Mines Ltd. and held among them 75 per cent of its shares.

While Rhodes was busy securing his grip on the diamond industry, Griqualand West was incorporated into the Cape Colony, opening up six new seats in parliament. Rhodes successfully ran for a seat—at the time, it was not unusual to combine a business and a political career. He was also making forays into the gold fields that were discovered in 1886 at what is now called Johannesburg. Although he came to the rush late, he still managed to build up a sizable position, which he then used to form Goldfields of South Africa.

With his fortune assured, Rhodes began to focus on his dream of extending the British Empire from the Cape to Cairo. Despite the misgivings of his fellow governors at De Beers, Rhodes wanted to give the company a sweeping mandate in its trust deed. He planned to use the company's resources to plant the flag of Britain in Central Africa, pursuing whatever business opportunities were available. Barnato was the strongest advocate for limiting the new company to the digging for and marketing of diamonds. His nephew, who attended one of the meetings where the trust deed was debated, accused Rhodes of wanting to pursue dreams that did not pay dividends. "No, my friend," replied Rhodes. "They're not dreams, they're plans. There's a difference." Rhodes won the argument.

The European scramble for African possessions began in earnest in the late nineteenth century, fuelled in part by the desire for rubber, ivory, diamonds and gold. It was in this atmosphere of profit and plunder that Rhodes pursued his expansionist plans. The British already had the Cape Colony, but the path north to Cairo passed through areas claimed by other European powers before reaching a region of quasi-British control in British East Africa (now Kenya and Uganda), Anglo-Egyptian Sudan (now Sudan) and Egypt. Most worrisome from the British perspective were the German holdings in South West Africa (now Namibia) and German East Africa (now Tanzania). The Germans were making noises about joining their possessions to create a territory spanning Africa from coast to coast. Had this Mittelafrika policy been successful, the British would have been shut into southern Africa, extinguishing any hope of the Cape-to-Cairo rail link. What further alarmed the British was the increasingly warm relationship developing between the Germans and the Boers, who had settled just north of the Cape.

The most direct route from the German possessions on the southwest coast of Africa to those on the east coast ran through the areas of Mashonaland and Matabeleland, which correspond roughly to present-day Zimbabwe. Similarly, those travelling from the Portuguese possession of Angola on the west coast to Mozambique on the southeast coast passed through this region. If either the Germans or the Portuguese decided to link their African territories by adding an interior bridge, Mashonaland and Matabeleland were attractive prospects. Rhodes knew he had to seize the area if he was to have any chance of building his railway and founding a new dominion. "If we get Mashonaland," he wrote a friend, "we shall get the balance of Africa." Adding to the allure of the area was the rumour spread by European travellers and hunters that somewhere within its boundaries lay the legendary Land of Ophir, the site of King Solomon's Mines. The Old Testament mentions six sources of gold—Havilah, Parvaim, Sheba, Midian, Uphaz and Ophir—but is vague about their locations. Ruins of a great civilization in Mashonaland encouraged specu-lators to believe it was the site of a new El Dorado.

Rhodes knew that if his plans were to be realized, he would have to deal with the ruler of Matabeleland and Mashonaland, the Ndebele king

Lobengula. Stories of Lobengula's brutal rule abounded. One trader said he had witnessed the punishment of a thief caught drinking royal beer; Lobengula ordered that first the thief's lips should be cut off for touching the beer, then his nose for smelling it, then the skin on his forehead peeled down over his eyes, which had looked on the beer, and that he should then be thrown to the crocodiles. Lobengula refused to be photographed, but the Europeans who met him described him as enormously fat and of regal bearing. He was usually clad in a kilt of monkey skins. Despite his fearsome reputation, Lobengula had tolerated the presence of small numbers of Europeans in his territory, including missionaries, whom he mistakenly believed could be trusted to give him disinterested advice.

In the summer of 1887–88, Rhodes went with Sir Sidney Shippard, now administrator of the British territory Bechuanaland (now Botswana), to see Sir Hercules Robinson, the British high commissioner in the Cape Colony. Rhodes wanted the British government to declare a protectorate in Matabeleland and Mashonaland. To that end, he and Shippard told Robinson that the Boers of the Transvaal were attempting to align themselves with Lobengula against the British. Robinson knew that the government would not agree to a protectorate, but as a compromise he gave Shippard permission to send one of his officials to persuade Lobengula to at least sign a treaty of friendship with the British promising not to cede any rights in his territory without British approval. Lobengula, who was becoming alarmed at the interest being shown in his territory by various European governments and businessmen, agreed to sign the treaty and throw his lot in with the British, if only to stave off the others. He made a point, however, of telling Shippard's official that he did not want the Great White Queen, Victoria, to send too many of her people to his land.

Despite the treaty, Lobengula made contradictory promises to various European suitors, creating confusion about his real intentions. Desperate to secure some sort of hold on the territory, Rhodes sent a delegation to see Lobengula, headed by his good friend and business partner Rudd. Pretending to be big game hunters, the delegation set out from Kimberley, carrying stocks of brandy, champagne and stout—they'd heard that Lobengula had acquired a taste for these beverages. It took them ten weeks to make the journey, and when they arrived at Lobengula's kraal, they found a throng of other Europeans, including representatives of German banks and of several competing exploration companies backed by British businessmen. What the king really wanted was to be left alone with his sixty-eight wives, vast herds of cattle and royal beer, but he realized that he would have to deal with the white men who were clamouring for mineral rights. He turned to one of the missionaries in his entourage, Rev. Charles Helm of the London Missionary Society, for advice. Unbeknownst to him, Helm was in Rhodes's camp. Helm suggested that the king do business with the strongest of the European groups, which happened to be that of Rhodes.

At this point Sir Sidney Shippard made another of his fortuitous appearances, helping Rhodes's case immeasurably. As British deputy commissioner for Bechuanaland, he was the accredited representative of the British government in Bulawayo, where Lobengula had his headquarters. Etiquette at Lobengula's court dictated that visitors squat in the dust before him and share a "feast" of undercooked meat and warm beer before conducting any negotiations. Shippard avoided this unpleasant ritual. Despite the intense heat of Bulawayo, he appeared in a black frock coat, complete with military decorations, kid gloves and patent leather boots. He arranged to have his own chairs brought so he would not have to squat. Then he got right down to business. Shippard put Rhodes's case to Lobengula, giving assurances that Rhodes had the blessing of the imperial government. Both Shippard and his superior, Sir Hercules Robinson, were rewarded for their support with shares and directorships in Rhodes's companies when they left the colonial service.

As extra insurance, the Rudd delegation promised Lotje, a key adviser to Lobengula, gifts if he would use his influence with the king. Lotje added his voice to that of Rudd, Helm and Shippard, publicly backing Rhodes. He would later pay dearly for his support.

Although Rudd was well aware that Rhodes's ultimate goal was absolute control of Matabeleland and Mashonaland, he knew that

Lobengula was unlikely to cede any of his land to the British. Rudd therefore negotiated only for mineral rights. In order that the concession cover as large an area as possible, Rudd and the company exaggerated the extent of Lobengula's reach, ascribing to him territory that in reality he did not hold. While Lobengula held absolute sway in Matabeleland with his army of fifteen thousand warriors, his control of Mashonaland, to the north and east, was not as secure. The borders of his kingdom shifted from year to year, sometimes from season to season, and were never as clear as Rudd suggested they were.

The final text of the deal between Lobengula and Rudd, later known as the Rudd Concession, gave the signatories a monopoly over mining and mineral rights in Lobengula's territory in exchange for £100 a month, one thousand Martini-Henry breech-loading rifles and one hundred thousand rounds of ammunition, plus either a steamboat with guns or £500. The deal did not mention occupation rights, an important point in light of what was to follow. Rochefort Maguire, a London-trained lawyer who had accompanied Rudd, drafted the concession. When Lobengula had trouble understanding the import of the legal text, Rudd gave an oral explanation, making many verbal assurances that were not included in the document that Lobengula signed. Chief among these was the promise that no more than ten white men would come to work in the area at any one time.

The other European competitors at Bulawayo were quick to tell Lobengula that he had been cheated. Although the king protested the deal, pointing out that he would hardly have sold monopoly mineral rights in his territory for so little, it was too late. Rudd took off within hours, bringing the signed document to Rhodes in Kimberley. Concession in hand, Rhodes left for England to apply for a royal charter. The unfortunate bribe-taking Lotje paid with his life for backing Rudd. Angry over being duped, Lobengula had Lotje and his household of three hundred put to death.

On learning of the Rudd Concession, Britain's imperial authorities grumbled—not about the way the concession was achieved, but because

Lobengula was to receive guns and ammunition as part of the deal. This contravened the General Act of the Brussels Conference of 1876, to which Britain was a party and which stated that Africans were not to be armed. But the grumbling never resulted in any action.

When Rhodes reached London in the spring of 1889, his application for a royal charter was looked upon with suspicion. Everything from the speed with which he had amassed his fortune to his friendship with prominent Boer politicians in the Cape Colony was cause for negative comment. And there were whispers about his involvement with the pump sabotage at the De Beers mine years before. Rhodes also had to contend with business competitors who had received contradictory promises from Lobengula. He squared as many of these as he could, paying them to discard their claims and recognize his own. But what really turned many people against him was the revelation that he had "donated" £10,000 to the Irish Nationalist Party, which was fighting for Home Rule in Ireland. In exchange, Rhodes received parliamentary support for his business schemes from those Irish Nationalist Party members who held seats in the British parliament.

Working against the tide of gossip and suspicion about Rhodes was his association with the banker Nathaniel, Lord Rothschild, who had financed his takeover of the Kimberley diamond mine and who also happened to be the father-in-law of Archibald Primrose, Lord Rosebery, soon to become prime minister. Sir Hercules Robinson also intervened on Rhodes's behalf with Henry Holland, Lord Knutsford, Secretary for the Colonies. Knutsford was initially skeptical, but he swung his support behind the charter. He persuaded the prime minister, Robert Gascoyne-Cecil, Lord Salisbury, that by granting Rhodes a charter, Britain would be able to extend its territories, with the British South Africa Company, not the government, bearing the expense. It was a winning argument.

Salisbury agreed to back the charter but suggested that since Rhodes and his fellow applicants were relatively unknown in London, it would be a good idea for them to add men of social standing to the board. As a result, the Duke of Abercorn, the Duke of Fife and Albert Grey were made directors of the new charter company. Abercorn had extensive estates in Northern Ireland and had been in the House of Commons for twenty years before inheriting the dukedom. Fife was the son-in-law of the Prince of Wales. Grey, who was to become the fourth earl Grey in 1894, was the prize acquisition, for he was the grandson of a former prime minister and was a well-known champion of African human rights. Before accepting Rhodes's offer, Grey approached Joseph Chamberlain, a leading politician, for his opinion. "I only know three things about Rhodes, and they all put me against him," said Chamberlain. "One, he has made an enormous fortune very rapidly; two he is an Afrikander [meaning he was a colonialist rather than an imperialist]; and three, he gave 10,000 pounds to Parnell [the Irish politician]." Grey chose not to listen to Chamberlain's advice. He met with Rhodes and was persuaded that the magnate was very much an imperialist. This was Grey's soft spot. He often wrote in autograph books, "The empire is my country. England is my home." With three illustrious names attached to an enterprise whose ambitions were dressed up in the proper imperial rhetoric, approval for the charter was finally granted on October 29, 1889.

A royal charter gave a company sovereign powers. The company could raise its own army, build forts, make treaties, govern territories, exercise criminal jurisdiction and even coin its own currency. The charter also legitimized the use of armed force for commercial gain. Since the seventeenth century, the English Crown had been using chartered companies to build the empire on the cheap, opening up Canada with the Hudson's Bay Company, acquiring India through the East India Company and settling the first American colonies with the Massachusetts Bay and Virginia companies. Once he had his charter, Rhodes lost no time in organizing the occupation of his new territory by settlers and miners tempted by the legend of the Land of Ophir. His goal was to secure the land both for short-term corporate profit and as part of his grander scheme of building the Cape-to-Cairo railway.

Frank Johnson, a former army quartermaster, was hired to organize a pioneer column and raise a police force to protect it. This force would eventually become the British South Africa Company's private army and would earn a reputation for brutality in the years ahead. Johnson's fee was 80,000 acres of land, twenty gold claims for each of twelve friends, whom he would nominate, and £94,000 (£6 million in 2001) to cover costs. Rhodes insisted that Johnson include in the column a number of sons from the leading families of the Cape Colony. He reasoned that if the group was attacked, the influential fathers of these men would put pressure on the empire to rescue them. When word went round that the British South Africa Company was looking for pioneers, a ragtag collection of farmers, artisans, miners, doctors, lawyers, engineers, builders, bakers, soldiers, sailors, cadets, cricketers, army deserters and men of the cloth assembled in Mafeking. They were each offered 3,000 acres of land and fifteen gold claims.

Lobengula kept abreast of these preparations. His people were split over whether they should allow the planned march to take place. While the young bloods wanted to attack and slaughter the column, the older advisers urged caution. Rhodes sent an old friend from his Kimberley mining days, Dr. Jameson, to persuade Lobengula not to attack.

It is worth saying a word or two about Jameson at this point, as he played such a large part in the Ndebele War that was to come and in Rhodes's eventual disgrace. The Scottish doctor was a small, dapper man whose background as a skilled surgeon and diagnostician seemed better suited to London than to the African wilds. But Jameson was a gambler and adventurer at heart. He arrived in Kimberley after answering a newspaper ad for a share in a medical practice and won early notoriety for the part he played in what became known as "The Great Smallpox War." Called out to see a sick African on a farm near the diamond mines, Jameson said the man was suffering from "a bulbous disease of the skin allied to pemphigus." Another doctor disputed the diagnosis and accused Jameson of fudging his report because the mine owners were afraid smallpox would scare the workers away. There were suits and countersuits, and the scandal went all the way to the Cape parliament before blowing over, but not without leaving an early stain on Jameson's reputation.

When the doctor arrived at Lobengula's kraal at Bulawayo, he offered to treat the king's various ailments. Morphine was a key ingredient in the medicine he prescribed, and, unsurprisingly, Lobengula's belligerence waned. When a message for the king arrived from the British government concerning the British South Africa Company, Jameson read the letter first. Feeling that its tone was not quite positive enough, he tore it up and wrote a new one, praising the chartered company and Rhodes. Still Lobengula wavered about the pioneer column. Jameson forced the issue by walking into a religious ceremony one day, interrupting the startled Lobengula in mid-sacrifice. Jameson reminded him of the promise he'd made earlier to allow the company men into Mashonaland. "Did the king lie?" Jameson asked. "The king never lies," Lobengula answered.

The settlers' march was on. In order not to put temptation directly in the path of Lobengula's restive warriors, the pioneer column of about one hundred settlers and five hundred police officers took a roundabout route from British territory in southern Africa toward Mashonaland, skirting Bulawayo and the heart of Matabeleland. Not long after they had set out, a political crisis erupted in Cape Town, forcing the prime minister to step down. Rhodes, who had done little in parliament for several years, preoccupied as he was with building De Beers and Goldfields and with organizing the settling of the north, was nevertheless persuaded by the British authorities to lead the new government. He hadn't sought the position, but he realized he could use his political powers to benefit his commercial schemes. Assembling a cabinet with members from most of the political parties, he pledged to conduct what he called a "South African policy" that would expand the Cape Colony north to the Zambezi River. Rhodes made this vow even as the pioneer column was already en route to accomplish the first step toward that goal.

Reaching Mashonaland without incident, the settlers raised the Union Jack on September 13, 1890, at what is now Harare. They began the long, arduous process of staking their gold claims and establishing a settlement, which the British South Africa Company called Fort Salisbury, after the British prime minister. Company officials mistakenly believed that the reason they had not been attacked was that the Shona, whose land they now occupied, recognized the supremacy of the white man. In fact, the Shona had held back because they thought the pioneers were a trading caravan just passing through. The pioneers used the Shona as a source of cheap labour in their mines and on their farms. This became an increasing source of friction between the settlers and the Ndebele, who regarded the Shona as their property.

During the first few months of the settlement, the pioneers saw some of the heaviest rainfall ever experienced in the area. Their shelters leaked, their boots and clothes rotted, and supplies were scarce because the rudimentary roads became impassable. While the settlers suffered in such conditions, insects flourished. Termites ate away at the huts, and mosquitoes were a constant irritant. Malaria and blackwater fever further debilitated the settlers, leading to plunging morale.

In March 1891, the British South Africa Company held its first annual meeting at the Cannon Street Hotel in London's financial district. Rhodes's personal copy of the company's annual meetings and reports is kept at Rhodes House Library at Oxford University. To open it up and read his personal annotations is to plunge into history. The collection contains copies of speeches he and others made at the meetings, as well as financial reports. Bound in burgundy leather, with the name of the great man in gilt, the tome makes fascinating reading for anyone interested in how easily shareholders and directors can be duped. In the meetings chronicled, the Duke of Fife stood up often to tell shareholders that he had never before sat on the board of a public company and would not have accepted Rhodes's invitation but for the fact that he was convinced "that this company has in view a great Imperial object."

The existence of the shareholders might have been expected to add an element of accountability to the enterprise, but this was not always so. The shareholders' chief interest, then as now, was profit. How those profits were made was seldom a cause for concern. London was a long way from the company's field of operations, and communication lines were weak. It took nineteen days for a steamer to reach London from Cape

Town. Even if unsavoury news did eventually filter through, it could easily be downplayed. The spirit of the age was such that actions taken in the name of the empire had a golden aura that obscured tawdry details. Shareholders were no more immune then than they are now to being bamboozled by a charismatic corporate leader whose optimistic forecasts carried them away.

Rhodes was not at that first meeting, where the company boasted of its vast enterprise, under which it was "administering for Britain" an area of 500,000 square miles, larger than France and Germany combined. "With these possessions, it will be recognized that the possibilities of future wealth are great, and that the large expenditure incurred in securing and maintaining the rights acquired has been fully justified," said the report. The directors downplayed accounts of hardship, starvation and disease among the pioneers, focusing instead on the great wealth that awaited the company in its new territory.

Then came some unpleasant news. It appeared that the Rudd Concession, which the shareholders thought they owned, was actually the property of a company called United Concession Company Ltd., whose directors included Rhodes, Beit and Rudd. Shareholders were told that United Concessions was willing to sell the Rudd Concession to the British South Africa Company in exchange for one million shares of company stock, valued at one pound each. This questionable agreement was never written down or dated and only came to light at this first meeting, causing some shareholders to protest. The directors agreed to let the matter rest until further discussion could take place.

The United Concessions affair was an indication that Rhodes was having difficulties in financing his various schemes. While he was enormously wealthy on paper—his fortune was estimated at £5 million in 1895 (£315 million in 2001)—he was having cash flow problems and was encountering unexpected resistance from De Beers shareholders in financing the occupation of the interior. Mashonaland was proving to be a disappointment. Gold was being found, but not in huge amounts, and mining royalties were well below expectations. Though De Beers was initially held by shareholders in southern Africa, many of whom Rhodes could influence, more London-based shareholders came on board as the company grew. By 1891, they represented the majority, and they were more interested in making a profit than in spending money on imperial expansion.

Rhodes had to find other ways to raise money, and the United Concessions scheme was one. Another was to sell diamonds. The cartel that would eventually control the majority of world diamond sales began taking shape after Rhodes had amalgamated the diamond mines in 1888. Known as the Diamond Syndicate, it had the contract to buy the bulk of De Beers's production, and it regulated the amount of supply available to outside buyers in order to artificially boost the price of diamonds. Rhodes chose to clandestinely sell some of De Beers's diamonds outside the syndicate to build up a cash reserve that he could use for his own purposes.

Rhodes also instituted the compound system at his diamond mines in an effort to make more money. African labourers were forced to live on site, away from their families, in order to reduce opportunities for diamond smuggling and to increase labour control. This inhumane system, which became a symbol of white oppression in southern Africa, was emulated by mine owners throughout the area.

In order to further lighten the financial burden of the British South Africa Company, Rhodes decided to shortchange the settlers on their security. In 1892, the company force was reduced to forty men, aided by thirty-five Africans. To make up the shortfall, a volunteer force of five hundred settlers was set up and every able-bodied man in the territory was told he would be called up if needed. This new arrangement reduced the company's security costs from £250,000 a year to £30,000 a year, but it left the new community feeling vulnerable at a time when threats to its continued existence were increasing.

These threats had begun with raids waged by the Ndebele warriors on the Shona who were working for the white settlers. Under orders from Lobengula, the Ndebele did not touch the Europeans, but they did invade their farms and mines and kill their workers or scare them away. The pioneers passed on reports of Ndebele warriors spearing Shona men, cutting off their genitals, disembowelling Shona women and roasting Shona children alive. The settlers protested vociferously to Rhodes when he visited the settlement. His attempts to rally their spirits by telling them they were working for empire and posterity were not well received.

Back in London, company officials told shareholders that the Ndebele raids were isolated events and that the situation was peaceful. At the second annual meeting, held on November 29, 1892, the Duke of Abercorn said the attacks had stopped. Investors were beginning to have doubts about the company, particularly after Lord Randolph Churchill, a former cabinet minister who had visited Mashonaland in 1891, published a book, titled *Men, Mines and Animals in South Africa*, in which he criticized the company police and the prospects for gold in the new settlement. To distract shareholders from the bad news, the directors outlined new projects that the company was undertaking, including the construction of a railway link between Beira, on the coast of the Indian Ocean, and company territory. In the annual report, the official estimate of the company's land was expanded from 500,000 square miles the previous year to 750,000 square miles. Rhodes was in attendance at this meeting, and he told shareholders that the biggest difficulty facing the company was not Lobengula but the concession hunters who were demanding compensation for land they claimed had been given to them before the Rudd Concession was signed. Rhodes had bought some of them off, while others he was fighting in court. He went on to tell the gathering that 400 miles of gold reef had been marked out in Mashonaland—a tantalizing indication that the area could indeed be the site of the Land of Ophir. The meeting broke up with loud cheers and applause.

Regardless of what he was telling shareholders, Rhodes realized that the situation with Lobengula was rapidly becoming unsustainable. His old friend Jameson had been appointed high commissioner of the settlement at the end of 1891 and had approved a punishing campaign of reprisals against any African suspected of killing a European or stealing goods. "I intend to treat them like dogs," Jameson confided to a colleague at the time. These punishments were carried out by Captain C.F. Lendy, a military man and the magistrate at the settlement known as Fort Victoria, which lay to the east of Bulawayo. Lendy burned compounds and confiscated cattle. In one instance, he surrounded a suspect's hut at dawn and opened fire with a Maxim, the forerunner of the machine gun, and a seven-pound cannon; twenty-one Africans were killed and forty-seven cattle were taken. On hearing of the activities of the company police force, Rhodes sent a note to Jameson, saying, "I am glad to hear that you are maintaining the dignity of the law."

Imperial authorities, however, were not pleased. They warned that if the public heard about such brutality, it would do incalculable damage to the British South Africa Company. "Lendy acted in this matter with recklessness and undue harshness," wrote Lord Knutsford, then secretary of the colonies, in a dispatch. But far from being disciplined by the company, Lendy was sent out on more patrols.

Matters came to a head in May 1893, when some 750 metres of copper wire were stolen from a telegraph line that Rhodes was building in Mashonaland. A local Shona chief, Gomalla, and his people were suspected of stealing the copper. When the company police came round to question him, he quickly handed over cattle in restitution. Because Lobengula technically owned all the cattle in his territory, he sent a group of Ndebele warriors to punish Gomalla and his people. Lobengula warned Jameson that this raid was about to take place and assured him that Europeans would not be targeted. Despite his orders, some of the Ndebele warriors entered European farms and houses to slaughter their Shona servants and take their cattle.

The raid provided the British South Africa Company with the excuse it needed to attack Lobengula. While the company's representatives protested publicly that they did not want war, they agreed privately that seizing Matabeleland would boost the value of their shares, which had flagged on the London Stock Exchange. The company needed to create a new expectation of profit and that meant acquiring new territory. It cranked up its public relations machine and began releasing letters that missionaries had written over the years detailing the savagery of

Lobengula and the Ndebele. Once public opinion had been appropriately swayed, the battle could begin.

On July 18, 1893, Captain Lendy and a small troop of thirty-eight armed men set out to hunt down and punish the Ndebele chiefs responsible for the raid. What the chiefs were doing when Lendy's patrol first caught up with them near Fort Victoria has long been disputed. Some reports say they were stealing cattle and attacking the local Shona. Others say the Ndebele were making their way home and showed no resistance to the armed company patrol. Accounts of the bloody encounter, written by the victors, had Lendy's small force bravely battling three thousand fearsome warriors. But the truth is not so glorious. There may have been thousands of warriors in the general area, but the encounter that day took place with only a handful of them. In addition, Lendy's men were mounted and armed with modern weapons, including the Maxim, while the Ndebele carried traditional iron-tipped spears known as assegai and shields made of hide through which bullets could easily pass. Though the Ndebele also had a sprinkling of single-shot Martini-Henry rifles, which had been provided by Rhodes as part of the Rudd Concession agreement, they did not know how to set the sights properly, and the guns were all but useless in their hands. Lendy's men mowed down between fifty and sixty warriors. The rest fled across the Tokwe River to their home in Matabeleland.

Lobengula was again caught between the desire of his warriors for revenge and his fear that the whites, with their advanced firepower, would almost certainly win the war. At the invitation of the British high commissioner in the Cape Colony, he sent a delegation to peace talks in Cape Town. But the delegates were murdered en route by whites who claimed it was a case of mistaken identity. Lobengula saw this as an act of treachery and declared war. Accounts of his declaration put him in full battle dress in front of his doomed warriors. He reportedly drove his spear so hard into the ground that the shaft broke: the battle was on. But it would prove to be short lived. When the Ndebele tried to wage traditional war, they were cut down by the Europeans' guns. They never even got close enough to the British South Africa Company troops to use their spears.

Lendy was given the task of raising a force of men, known as the Victoria Column, to invade Matabeleland and attack Lobengula in his home territory. Each man who took up arms was promised 6,350 acres of land, twenty gold claims and a share in any loot. A photograph from that period shows the men at Fort Victoria; some of them would have formed Lendy's group. They are a rough-looking lot, sporting unruly beards and assorted outfits that look durable, if not military. Lined up in front of one of the rough-hewn buildings in their fort, they appear to be on parade, although their uneven line and unsoldierly bearing would make a military man wince at that description. The photo could be mistaken for a scene from the Wild West, with cowboys instead of a corporate army getting ready to defend the town. British history painted this ragtag force as heroes fighting for the Empire.

While the Victoria Column was massing, Rhodes travelled from the Cape Colony up to an area near Salisbury, where he made camp in the bush and proceeded to go partridge shooting. His companions were bemused by his actions, until they realized that he had deliberately chosen the remote location so that he could not be reached by telegram in case the Colonial Office in London decided to order him not to attack Lobengula.

The war was over in a matter of months. In all, the British South Africa Company lost about fifty European employees, including Captain Lendy, and thirty African workers. The Ndebele lost an estimated five thousand people, most of whom were young men. The invasion provoked a storm of protest in Britain. Henry Labouchere used his magazine, *Truth*, to lambaste Rhodes personally. In an item published on November 30, 1893, he called Rhodes "the head of a gang of shady financiers who forced on a war with the man through whose kindness they have pocketed millions, conducted it on the principle that 'godless heathen' ought to be mowed down with Maxim guns if they happen to inhabit a country where there may be gold, and their envoys murdered in order that a rotten Company might be saved from immediate bankruptcy, and the financing gang might be in a position to transfer more money from the pockets of British investors into their own."

The public outcry prompted the British government to step in and negotiate peace with Lobengula. But Rhodes was determined that the imperial authorities should not intervene. An ugly confrontation was shaping up between the two sides when the Ndebele king took matters into his own hands and disappeared into the bush, taking his wives and treasure with him. While on the run, Lobengula tried to buy peace by sending a bag of gold sovereigns to the company troops pursuing him. With the sovereigns was the message, "White men, I am conquered. Take this and go back." But the white men had one final act of treachery in store for him. The two troopers who received the gold decided to divide the money between them and to not pass on Lobengula's final request. The king died shortly afterward. Various accounts put his cause of death at smallpox, poison or a broken heart.

With the death of Lobengula and the defeat of his forces, Rhodes was able to add Matabeleland to the growing list of British South Africa Company possessions. He immediately instructed Jameson to begin the settlement of the new area. "The men who had fought must have the farms and mining claims they had been promised," he wrote. A new township was laid out at Bulawayo, Lobengula's former headquarters, and settlers began to arrive. The British government sanctioned the new settlement in 1894, despite criticism from Labouchere and others, and declared its sovereignty over Mashonaland and Matabeleland. Rhodes's victory was complete. The British South Africa Company's claim now derived from the British Crown and not from the dubious Rudd Concession. Rhodes was a commercial colossus at the height of his formidable powers—not only the key figure driving the acquisitive British South Africa Company, but also chairman of both De Beers and Goldfields, and the prime minister of the Cape Colony. The business methods he had used to attain all this, however, ensured that more trouble was on its way.

As the victor in the war, the British South Africa Company laid claim to all the cattle and almost all the best land in Matabeleland. Ndebele warriors returning home found that their land and cattle had been given away. The theft of their land was both an economic and a spiritual blow:

they depended on cattle for their livelihood, and they were removed from the graves of their ancestors and other sacred sites. Nevertheless, they were forced to move to two reserves located on poor grazing land between the Guai and Shangani rivers. Lord Grey, a board director, protested to Rhodes that the reserves were "regarded by the natives as cemeteries, not homes."

The Ndebele had no way of supporting themselves or their families save by working for the victors. But the idea of working was foreign to their culture. They were warriors—it was the Shona who were labourers. The company sent its police to force the Ndebele to work. It also instituted a hut tax of 10 shillings a year so the Ndebele would have to find work in order to pay it. Land, cattle, enforced labour—grievances piled up in Matabeleland and Mashonaland. Then a series of plagues almost biblical in proportion hit the region. First locusts, then drought and finally cattle disease in the form of rinderpest caused widespread starvation and disease.

The festering anger of the Ndebele erupted in March 1896 when Jameson unwisely took the bulk of the company's police on an ill-fated raid into the Transvaal. In the absence of most of the company's security forces, the Ndebele began a mass slaughter of the settlers. The Shona followed the Ndebele's example. Within the course of a week, an estimated two hundred Europeans were killed. The panicked settlers retreated to Matabeleland's few towns for safety. Feelings ran high against the British South Africa Company, not for the brutal treatment of the Africans, which had caused the uprising, but for leaving the settlers undefended in order to invade the Transvaal in yet another piece of Rhodes's personal empire building.

The Transvaal, where the Witwatersrand gold strike had been made, was governed by Paul Kruger, a descendant of the Dutch colonists, the Boers, who had made the long trek from the Cape in order to establish their own republic free from British rule. Rhodes was unhappy with Kruger because he was squeezing the gold companies, including Goldfields, for higher and higher taxes. At the same time, Kruger was refusing to give outsiders the right to vote for fear of losing control over the settlement. The Boers were far outnumbered by the prospectors, businessmen, thieves and ruffians who had poured into the region in search of gold. Rhodes allowed the rebel leaders in the Transvaal, whose numbers included politicians opposed to Kruger, outsiders denied the vote and some gold company men, to use the Goldfields offices to plan an uprising and to smuggle arms into Johannesburg through De Beers. At the same time, he was wily enough to ensure that Joseph Chamberlain, who had been made British secretary for the colonies in 1895, was kept informed of the progress of the rebels' plan. While he still distrusted Rhodes, Chamberlain was in favour of extending British authority over the Transvaal if at all possible. Rhodes was in accord—as long as he was running the show.

But as the proposed date drew nearer for an uprising, timed to coincide with the arrival of Jameson and his men, the plotters in the Transvaal lost heart. Rhodes, too, became increasingly ambivalent. He told some that the raid was off, but he did not send direct instructions to Jameson until it was too late. His health was failing and he was growing impatient to achieve his grand ambition before he died. His biographers have speculated that it was this impatience that led him to take the foolhardy step of planning the invasion of the Transvaal in the first place and putting Jameson, who was unskilled in military action, in charge.

Though Jameson's forces had triumphed in earlier skirmishes with the poorly armed Ndebele and Shona, they were no match for Kruger's troops, who had modern guns and knew how to use them. Jameson's men were quickly defeated and the Transvaal rebellion sputtered out. The British government scrambled to dissociate itself from Rhodes. The raid was seen as a huge political embarrassment, both in the Cape Colony, where there was still a large community of Boers, and in Britain. Rhodes was forced to step down as prime minister and to relinquish his position as chairman of De Beers and Goldfields. He also had to give up his place on the board of the British South Africa Company for a time, though he was re-elected as a director in 1898.

Meanwhile, the uprising in Matabeleland and Mashonaland was threatening to bankrupt the British South Africa Company unless hostilities could be brought to a quick end. The British government, mindful of the negative publicity that had surrounded the previous battle between the company and the Ndebele, insisted on sending in some of its own troops at the company's expense. Sir Frederick Carrington was appointed by the imperial government to lead the force. With events threatening to capsize the company, Rhodes finally decided to take an active role in Matabeleland. Until this point, he had been a distant figure, controlling events from afar while he tended to his diamond and gold interests and to his political duties in the Cape parliament. Now that he no longer held political or corporate office, he had time on his hands. He decided to negotiate with the Ndebele directly, participating in several dramatic encounters with massed warriors and chiefs and winning the admiration of some Ndebele for his courage. They gave him the name Mla'mlakunzi, or separator of the fighting bulls.

Vere Stent, a journalist who accompanied Rhodes on one of these negotiating forays, wrote a highly romanticized explanation of why the great man had decided to negotiate in the first place. Rhodes was "cut to the heart" by the death of some of the British soldiers and wearied by the "cruel bloodiness of war," wrote Stent. "Soldiers of fortune, if you will; having their faults, not too overburdened with humane considerations; they asked for no quarter; they probably would have given none. But they were the men that Rhodesia wanted to smoothe her rugged ways, to break her in." Despite this moving rhetoric, Stent recognized that the war was about money, specifically that of the British South Africa Company. When a deal was reached between Rhodes and the Ndebele chiefs, Stent rushed to wire his agent in London, telling him to buy shares in the chartered company.

After the Ndebele settled, the Shona chose to fight on. The company force found it difficult to attack the Africans, who hid in the multitude of caves in the area. Then the soldiers decided to drop dynamite through the ventilation shafts that led to the hideouts. One of the soldiers described what happened next: "The fuse lit and we ran for safety. The explosion blew in the poles and rocks at the entrance and a rebel who must have been on guard there came staggering out. He was a terrible sight. He was skinned from top to toe but still grasping his rifle." Thousands of Shona were killed in this manner before the rebellion ended. That same year, the British government gave its permission to offi-cially name the territories administered by the company Rhodesia.

Carrington, who had led the imperial forces, wrote a report after the hostilities had ended. In it, he accused the British South Africa Company of putting the interests of its shareholders above those of the settlers: "The officials of the company, both in Rhodesia and in England, have— probably with a view to reassuring the stock market—systematically endeavoured to make the least of the dangerous aspects of the rebellion; and possibly from a fear of the Imperial government obtaining too strong a claim upon the country they have steadily opposed the bringing in of imperial troops and have belittled or ignored the work done by those troops when brought in." His report made a clear case against allowing companies to do the job of governments, because they tended to sacrifice public services, such as security, in the interest of greater profit.

Rhodes was to hear similar criticisms in London in early 1897 when he appeared before a select committee of the House of Commons set up to investigate the Jameson Raid and the administration of the British South Africa Company. But Rhodes had an ace up his sleeve: the telegrams to and from Chamberlain, which proved that the secretary of the colonies had known about the raid in advance and had at one point even supported it. Chamberlain, dreading the end of his political career, used all his powers to diminish official criticism of Rhodes. Much of the truth about the raid was kept from the committee members, not just by Rhodes, but by gov-ernment officials. In a rush to complete their work before Parliament ended its session, committee members ignored the second part of their mandate and looked only at the Jameson Raid. The report published in July 1897 was harshly critical of Rhodes, but he didn't care—the British South Africa Company was allowed to keep its precious charter.

In the last few years of his life, Rhodes was plagued by declining health but continued to work as a private individual on projects in southern Africa. He never realized his dream of establishing British rule in an unbroken stretch of territory from the Cape to Cairo. He died in 1902 from the heart condition that had first brought him to the African continent. His last words were purportedly "So little done, so much to do."

It is difficult to separate a man from his time. Many of the methods Rhodes used or sanctioned were seen as perfectly acceptable during the Age of Empire, given the appropriate imperial gloss and the right whiff of adventure. Many in Britain saw themselves as the natural ruling race, destined to bring the world the three Cs: commerce, Christianity and civilization. But even then questions were raised about the wisdom of allowing an enterprise that was accountable only to its shareholders to operate far beyond the reach of governmental control and to use military power to pursue its commercial ends.

A century later, Rhodes's legacy in Mashonaland and Matabeleland comes into even sharper focus. Like many of those who followed in his footsteps, his lasting impact on Africans has been negative. His use and abuse of power left a legacy of racial tensions in southern Africa and created the template for the exploitative use of African labour by major mining houses. The questionable means used to acquire the Rudd Concession and ultimately Matabeleland created a lasting distrust of whites in the area. The Ndebele and Shona uprising in 1896 left the white settlers traumatized and determined to suppress any further resistance on the part of the Africans. In the decades that followed, Rhodesia developed an oppressive and extensive police apparatus that fought African efforts for independence long after all the surrounding colonies had been granted theirs. In 1965, descendants of the white settlers seized power in southern Rhodesia in an effort to keep Africans from power. They held on until 1980 by brutally suppressing any and all opposition. Rhodes bears a measure of responsibility for that long and bloody fight. His effect is still being felt in Zimbabwe today, where President Robert Mugabe, struggling to maintain domestic support, has been taking land from white farmers, ostensibly to redistribute it to black Africans. The country is in an advanced state of political and economic collapse, with widespread starvation and violence.

On the fiftieth anniversary of the British South Africa Company in 1939, company president Dougal O. Malcolm wrote a paean of praise to Rhodes, comparing him to Sir Walter Raleigh and Sir Francis Drake. All three, according to Malcolm, displayed the "half-conquistador, half-commercial spirit of the merchant adventurer." Rhodes shared something else with these two: a belief that the end justifies the means, however brutal, and that laws were written for others to obey and for him to flout if necessary for commercial gain.

CHAPTER TWO

KING LÉOPOLD AND THE
RUBBER COMPANIES

As THE PASSENGER SHIP VOLTA STEAMED OUT OF THE PORT OF Liverpool, England, in 1883, the men on board thronged the deck to watch the city's dockyards slip away. They were headed for adventure in a new territory in Africa called the Congo. Among them was a nineteen-year-old office worker who was thanking his lucky stars for being included in their number. Edward James Glave had worked for months to win a place with the International African Association, a group headquartered in Brussels and charged with overseeing the peaceful development of the territory. He had bombarded the association office in Brussels with letters, finally succeeding in winning an interview with their London representative. Just four days before the Volta was to sail, he received word that he would be leaving on it.

Like many of his generation, Glave had grown up reading about the exploits of the great explorers who were attempting to fill in the massive blank spot at the centre of Africa on European maps. This was the era of David Livingstone, the missionary who survived thirty years in the African bush, and his contemporaries Richard Burton, John Speke, James Grant and Samuel Baker, who were looking for the source of the Nile. Their arduous expeditions took them through trackless jungles and new-found mountain ranges, and they wrote of their adventures in thrilling detail for readers back home. Glave's boyhood heroes were trappers, pioneers, big game hunters, explorers—men who had gone out to conquer the world. Chief among them was the journalist Henry Morton Stanley, who in 1871 had ventured into the African bush for his employer, the *New York Herald*, and successfully tracked down Livingstone, who had not been heard from in five years and was presumed dead. Glave eagerly devoured Stanley's books, *How I Found Livingstone*, published in 1872, and *Through the Dark Continent*, published in 1878, in which the journalist recounted his crossing of central Africa.

This was the life Glave dreamed of as he walked to and from the dreary office job he had taken on leaving school. Salvation beckoned when he heard that the International African Association was looking for young men to help with its work in the Congo. Glave did not know much about the association, only that several influential and philanthropic men had formed it in 1876 under the patronage of King Léopold II of Belgium. The organization had emerged from a geographic conference that Léopold had convened that year and to which he had invited the leading explorers of the day, including the Marquis de Compiègne of France, who had travelled the Ogowe River in Gabon, Gerhard Rohlfs of Germany, who had explored the Sahara, and Russian geographer Pyotr Semenov-Tianshansky, who had charted the Tyan-Shan mountains of central Asia.

Léopold had dazzled his guests with lavish banquets at his palace before getting down to the business of the conference. His goal, he said, was to help spread civilization to central Africa and to abolish the slave trade by setting up a chain of scientific posts across the continent along the Congo River. Each post, from which the taming influences of Europe would emanate, was to be staffed by professionals, including scientists who could teach skills to the Africans while at the same time collecting information about the flora and fauna of the territory. The conference delegates heartily supported the idea and voted to establish the International African Association. Léopold generously offered to be its chairman for the first year.

This, then, was the noble crusade that Glave had elected to join. But over the course of the next twelve years, he would bear witness as the philanthropic trappings that Léopold had so artfully erected at the conference gradually fell away, exposing a commercial enterprise so ruthless in its design and so pitiless in its implementation that it resulted in the mass extermination of millions of human beings. Under the guise of bringing civilization to Africa, Léopold used his outposts to collect ivory and squeeze competitors out of the trade. When ivory alone did not produce the riches he desired, he set up companies headed by his cronies and gave them exclusive rights to vast expanses of land. These corporate fiefdoms used armed force to pillage for ivory and rubber, enslaving the unlucky inhabitants and eliminating all resistance. By the time the rest of the world had fully woken up to the human catastrophe unfolding in the Congo, the men responsible for it had made their fortunes. They were never called to account. Léopold demonstrated the corporate advantage of linking the private sector with a state apparatus and dampening any criticism with a well-oiled public relations machine.

King Léopold II ascended the throne in 1865 after the death of his father. Belgium was a small country, dwarfed by its powerful neighbours, France and Germany. Léopold dreamed of playing a larger role on the world stage. He looked with envy at Britain, Spain and the Netherlands, with their far-flung possessions. While still a prince, he had travelled extensively, visiting the Balkans, Constantinople, the Aegean and Egypt. He went to Seville to learn about Spain's imperial expansion and then journeyed to Ceylon, India, Burma and China to see how the British ran their empire. He visited the East Indies, which at the time belonged to Holland, and admired how the Dutch had extracted the maximum wealth from their colony, repatriating the profits to the metropole. That the Netherlands, Belgium's small neighbour, had colonies of its own encouraged Léopold's imperial ambitions. He wrote that while Belgium was not large, "the sea bathes our coast, the universe lies in front of us, steam and electricity have made distances disappear, all the unappropriated lands on the surface of the globe may become the field of our operations and of our successes."

Léopold variously considered buying land in Egypt, on an island off South America and in Fiji, but none of these plans ever came to fruition. He offered to buy the Philippines from Spain in 1875, but the Spanish did not want to part with their overseas holding. Léopold decided to shift his focus to Africa, where large areas were still unclaimed by Europeans. The discovery of diamonds in southern Africa in the late 1860s hinted at the possibility of more mineral wealth in the region. And Léopold, too, had heard the theories that located the fabled King Solomon's Mines somewhere in central Africa. But he would have to move quickly if he hoped to stake a claim before the British, Germans, Portuguese and French, who were all actively exploring the African interior. His 1876 geographic conference and the establishment of the International African Association got his foot in the door. His next step was to find someone to help him realize his dream. Since there was no imperial lobby within Belgium—Léopold's subjects were more interested in internal political squabbles than in acquiring territory—he had to look outside his country for a partner in his venture. He found that partner in Henry Morton Stanley.

Like many Europeans, Léopold had been following Stanley's adventures in Africa through the newspapers. Before finding Livingstone in a village on the shores of Lake Tanganyika, Stanley had led a checkered existence. Born John Rowlands in Wales in 1841, he was an illegitimate child who spent time in a workhouse before sailing for America as a cabin boy on a packet ship. Rowlands reinvented himself in the United States. When he reappeared in England years later, it was as American journalist Henry Stanley, the roving correspondent for the *New York Herald*. At the paper's behest, Stanley spent two years trekking through the African bush in search of Livingstone. His account of their meeting, which was later challenged by the president of the Geographical Society in England, had him tracking the missionary to the village of Ujiji and greeting him with the phrase "Dr. Livingstone, I presume?" Livingstone died while still in Africa and was not able to corroborate Stanley's version of events.

In 1874, the *Herald* together with the *London Daily Telegraph* co-sponsored an expedition to be led by Stanley to trace the Lualaba River to its mouth.

Geographers of the day debated whether the Lualaba, which Livingstone had discovered, ran into the Nile or was part of the Congo River. Stanley set off from Zanzibar on the Indian Ocean and stumbled out of the bush three years later at Boma on the Congo estuary. By boat and on foot, Stanley and his entourage had crossed the continent, mapping the waters of the Lualaba as they flowed into the Congo and westward to the Atlantic Ocean. News of his great feat caused a sensation in Europe and the United States, and he received telegrams of congratulations from the US Congress and from many of his fellow explorers. Stanley had travelled about half the Congo's 4,800-kilometre length, enough to convince him that the river was a key access route to the African interior.

Once recovered from his journey, Stanley set out for London intent on persuading the British government to make the Congo basin a British colony. Léopold had other ideas. He prevailed on the US ambassador to Belgium, General Henry Shelton Sanford, to waylay Stanley when he landed in Marseilles en route to England. Sanford, who was also Léopold's friend, offered the explorer a job with the International African Association. Stanley turned him down. But in London he discovered that the British government had no appetite for taking on yet another expensive new colony. Britain had already repudiated a claim to part of the Congo basin made on its behalf two years earlier by Verney Lovett Cameron, the first European to cross Africa from east to west. Disappointed, Stanley reconsidered Léopold's offer and agreed to return to the Congo to set up the chain of scientific posts that had been envisioned at the geographic convention.

A letter Léopold wrote to his ambassador in London at that time makes clear that his intentions went well beyond the merely philanthropic. He wanted to make the Congo his colony, but he could not openly charge Stanley with taking possession of the region in his name without being stopped by the British. The British might not want the Congo for themselves, but that did not mean they wanted to see it colonized by another European power—"So I think I'll just give Stanley some job of exploration which would offend no one, and will give us the bases and headquarters which we can take over later on." Thus began Léopold and Stanley's long partnership. Both were men of gargantuan ego and ambition. Each, however, recognized the mutual advantages of an alliance: continuing fame for the journalist-explorer and a colony for the king.

Stanley returned to the Congo in 1879 with a five-year plan to establish posts along the river. He would start at the Congo's mouth, building a road to a settlement 400 kilometres upstream that he would call Léopoldville (now Kinshasa). The road, which would later be replaced by a railway, was needed to circumvent the cataracts that made the river impassable. From Léopoldville, Stanley would work his way into the interior, setting up posts and signing treaties with local chiefs who were willing to cede their sovereignty. The recalcitrant would be pacified.

Stanley and his men opened the original route by blasting through the mountains and the rocky, uneven terrain between Matadi and Léopoldville. This earned him the name Bula Matari, "breaker of rocks," an appellation the Congolese later used to describe the state apparatus in the Congo. He and his men used guns and steamboats to overwhelm and keep in thrall the Africans, who were armed with spears and travelled in dugout canoes. Once Stanley had built the road, Europeans wishing to journey into the interior could take a steamer from England to Matadi and then walk overland for about twenty days to reach Léopoldville, their supplies and equipment carried by thousands of porters. From the settlement they could board steamers travelling upstream.

Stanley was midway through the initial phase of his work in the Congo when Glave was hired by the International African Association. The *Volta* was at sea for forty-five days before the captain told his passengers they were nearing the mouth of the Congo. They landed at Boma, which was a busy trading settlement for merchants from England, France, Holland and Portugal. Glave later wrote about his experiences in the Congo in a book called *Six Years of Adventure in Congo-land*, which was published in 1893. His first night on land was a bad one. The mosquitoes made sleep impossible. Glave wrote, "We hardly recognized each other in the morning, so swollen and altered were our features." The party travelled upstream as far as the rapids and then marched overland to Léopoldville. It was there that Glave met Stanley, the hero whose accounts had brought him to Africa. "I recognized his masterly character immediately," recalled Glave, who caught sight of Stanley strolling up and down the veranda of his house. Stanley gave the new arrival a choice of two posts: one that was already established, and another about 500 kilometres upriver that had yet to be built. Glave chose the second and was delighted to hear that Stanley would accompany him upstream. Every night of their journey, they would sit down to a dinner of steamed goat and rice, and Stanley would regale his impressionable young companion with tales of his adventures: how he was attacked by cannibals, how he and his men survived a battle with a veritable armada of war canoes, how they bravely faced the gleaming spears of their adversaries. Glave was impressed that Stanley, who had risked his life hundreds of times, was prepared to do so again in an attempt to "make friends" with "the savages."

Eventually they reached Lukolela, the spot where Glave was to set up the post. They were greeted by "a large crowd of good-humoured savages" who swarmed around the steamer. Glave saw that the elders kept their distance, but decided their wariness could be overcome: "These simple-minded folk are easily convinced. Their opinions, fears, likes and dislikes, have but shallow formation, and the gift of a penny tin fork or a handful of beads will remove all of their false impressions." Stanley signed a treaty with the local chiefs, one of 450 he was to negotiate, giving the International African Association full rights to all the surrounding territory in exchange for beads, cloth, brass wire and metal ornaments. Like the Rudd Concession signed by Rhodes's representatives in Matabeleland, many of the treaties Stanley concluded were of dubious merit. It is unlikely that the chiefs knew what powers they were assigning with the pieces of paper. Stanley provided Glave with fifteen African soldiers and then steamed away, leaving the young, inexperienced office clerk alone in the bush.

Glave's assignment bore little resemblance to the scientific missions that Léopold had described. There were no scientists or artisans gathering data or instructing the Africans. Glave was the only European at the post, and he had a full-time job clearing the land with the help of local labourers. They succeeded in hacking back enough of the forest, which rose 60 metres up from the riverbank, to build a house flanked by huts. Glave passed his spare time hunting, and often brought back spare meat to the villagers. When Stanley stopped by the post some months later on his way downstream, he pronounced himself pleased at the progress Glave had made. "To know Stanley was satisfied in the way I had executed my duties," wrote Glave, "was to me the greatest satisfaction I had ever experienced in my life."

While Stanley was busy building transport routes and sending men like Glave out into the bush, Léopold was in Europe trying to reach the next stage in establishing a real colony, which was to secure international recognition of his claim. What made this step complicated was that other European powers were also interested in the area. The mouth of the Congo had been "discovered" by a Portuguese naval officer four hundred years before, and the Portuguese had built a fortress there at Cabinda in 1784. While the territory under direct Portuguese control lay along the coast, the Portuguese felt they also had a right to the hinterland. The French had been actively exploring the western reaches of the Congo River. French explorer Comte Pierre Savorgnan de Brazza secured for his country a piece of land directly opposite Léopoldville on the river. Worried by the French advances, Britain initially backed the Portuguese claim. The Germans, meanwhile, held territory to the north on the Atlantic Coast and were interested in maintaining trade routes into the interior. Chancellor Otto von Bismarck feared the area would be closed to German traders if either France or Portugal, with their protectionist bent, secured control. The United States also had interests to consider. Although it wasn't in the market for colonies, it could be a powerful ally or a formidable enemy when its trade interests were involved.

Léopold decided to move on several fronts. He asked his old friend Sanford to lobby the US government for support. Slavery was the lure with which he baited his hook. Europeans were no longer taking slaves from this part of Africa to North and South America because slavery had been abolished by all the major European powers and in the United States by the late 1880s. The Indian Ocean trade, however, which was carried out by Arab-African traders, still flourished. Léopold portrayed his campaign as a philanthropic mission to wipe out the Arab slavers and spread civilization throughout the interior. He insisted that he had no commercial objectives. Sanford succeeded in getting US President Chester Arthur to praise Léopold's work in the Congo in his annual message to Congress in 1884. That led to congressional support for the Belgian king and ultimately to US recognition of Léopold's claim.

Next, the king went to work on Bismarck, persuading the German chancellor that it would be better to have his philanthropic association controlling the Congo and allowing traders of all nationalities free access to the area than to see it fall to either France or Portugal. Bismarck reluctantly agreed. Léopold knew how to play to his audience. To persuade merchants, he promised free trade. To gain the backing of missionary groups, he promised to fight slavery. To win over powerful governments, he presented himself as a non-threatening alternative to rival powers. Léopold gained the backing of the powerful Manchester, England, business lobby by promising that the Congo would be a free trade zone. At the time, Manchester factories were busy churning out buttons and cotton cloth for the African market. These businessmen in turn helped shift the British government's support from Portugal to Léopold.

In November 1884, Bismarck convened a conference in Berlin to resolve the conflicting European claims to African territories. Léopold chose to stay in the background and have Stanley represent him. The explorer awed the delegates with his knowledge of Africa and with tales of his daring deeds, helping to turn opinion in Léopold's favour. By the time the conference ended in February, Léopold had secured the recognition he wanted, right down to the flag of his new state: one gold star on a blue background. Historians would later say that the rivalry of the powerful opened the door to the rule of the feeble.

The General Act of the Berlin Conference, signed by representatives of the fourteen countries, called for free trade in the Congo basin and a prohibition on import duties. Other provisions promised freedom of religion and a pan-European endeavour to wipe out slavery and improve the lot of Africans. In the body of the General Act, sovereignty was granted to the International African Association. But the international conventions concluded at the conference under which this sovereignty was conferred named the International Association of the Congo as the relevant party. This bit of confusion had been purposely created by Léopold as a means of securing power to himself. The International African Association, which had been set up in 1876 at the geographic conference, had by now largely faded away, replaced by the International Association of the Congo. Léopold had deliberately chosen the second appellation so that it would sound like the first and would obscure the fact that control had shifted from a philanthropic association to one that he controlled more directly. To add to the confusion, his new association used the same flag as the old association. The signatories at the Berlin Conference seemed unaware that they were handing the Congo over to an association that was merely a blind for Léopold himself. And the king had another surprise in store. On August 1, 1885, he gave notice that the new territory would be known henceforth as the Congo Free State and that he would be its sovereign. His takeover of a territory more than eighty times the size of Belgium was complete.

Léopold no longer needed to continue the sham of setting up scientific outposts, and so those that had no commercial potential were abandoned. Glave received word at Lukolela that the station he had laboured long and hard to construct would be closed. He was instructed to move to another station closer to the coast. In 1886, his three-year contract ended and he returned to England. But life at home held no excitement for someone who had survived on his own in the Congolese bush. Glave was eager to return as soon as possible. After only ten weeks in England, he once more boarded a ship bound for Africa. He had signed on as a member of the Sanford Exploring Expedition, a business venture set up by the former US ambassador to Belgium. While Léopold and his cronies still claimed that their official cause was the fight against slavery, they had privately stepped up efforts to explore the commercial potential of the king's new realm. Sanford received permission from Léopold to gather ivory and any other marketable products he could find in the Congo. This second trip was to be a very different one for the young Glave.

When Glave arrived in the Congo, he found that relations between Africans and Europeans had worsened considerably since his first trip. Traders could no longer count on a peaceful reception when they arrived in a village. While steaming slowly upriver, Glave reported passing a group of Africans "whose ominous sullenness was noticeable." At a given signal, the Africans rose up and hurled their spears at the passing boat. One barely missed Glave, splintering the wooden deck behind him. "We punished them by burning their village and capturing their stock," he wrote in his diary.

After its smooth birth, the Congo Free State was quickly running into teething problems. Léopold was using his personal fortune to build the colony, but the exorbitant costs were proving to be beyond even his considerable means. Roads had to be built, an army raised to secure and hold territory, officials employed for administration, and settlements established. In his haste to acquire a colony, Léopold had overlooked how expensive it was to administer one. In the first few years after the Berlin Conference, the costs incurred in the Congo vastly exceeded the colony's revenues. Léopold's much-professed humanitarian goals meant he couldn't enter into large-scale trade in liquor or guns. And while palm oil and groundnuts were in demand in Europe for machinery lubrication and soap, the infant colony lacked the infrastructure needed to produce and sell marketable quantities of those goods. Ivory, which was much in demand in Europe and the United States for making billiard balls, piano keys, knife handles and jewellery, appeared to hold the most promise. The profits that could be made from its trade were substantial. When Glave visited a post in the Congo interior, he noted that ivory was being traded for lengths of cloth, handkerchiefs, brass wire, tin spoons and forks, and beads. He estimated that the cost to the traders was about 25 cents per pound of ivory. In Europe, they could sell ivory for $2.50 per pound. At another post a year later, Glave bought 4,000 pounds of ivory for 2 cents a pound on behalf of Sanford.

Before Léopold and his business associates could fully exploit the ivory trade, however, they had to overcome two major obstacles. The first was the presence of Arab traders, who, as well as capturing and selling slaves, were collecting ivory to sell in India. Arab traders had been in eastern Africa for over a thousand years and did not look kindly on European attempts to get into the ivory trade. Because Léopold's forces were initially too weak to fight them, an uneasy co-operation began between the two. At one point, Stanley even teamed up with an Arab trader named Tippu Tip, who had built an empire from his base in Zanzibar on the proceeds of ivory and slaves. By the late 1880s, Tip controlled much of the eastern Congo and on several occasions supplied Stanley with porters. In 1887 he became governor of the eastern province of the Congo Free State at King Léopold's request. Glave met the Arab slaver and was impressed with his attire—a flowing white linen robe, a silk sash, embossed leather sandals and a silver dagger. After speaking with him, Glave pronounced Tip "very knowledgeable about European matters." Although Africa was remote, word got back to Europe that the new state was doing business with the very people the king's representatives were supposed to be fighting. Criticism of Léopold, however, was muted, and Tip continued to work with the Congo Free State until 1891. At that point, he realized that confrontation with the Europeans over ivory was inevitable. He led one last slaving expedition and retired with his fortune. That same year, all-out war broke out between the remaining Arab traders and the Congo Free State. It ended in 1893 with a state victory.

The second obstacle in Léopold's way was the presence of European competitors. In some ways it was more difficult for Léopold to deal with them than with the Arab traders. Since he had declared the area a free state, he couldn't stop them from collecting ivory in the region. If he tried, they could make trouble for him back home by influencing public opinion.

The General Act of the Berlin Conference also prevented him from tapping into their profits by imposing export and import taxes. He decided to gradually discard the undertakings he had made in the General Act while carefully preserving his humanitarian cloak.

In 1889 he called an anti-slavery conference in Brussels and argued that in order to raise funds to fight slavery, he should be permitted to impose duties on ivory. Once again, the king exploited the rivalry between the great powers to get his way. Germany backed the duties because it feared that if Léopold ran out of money he would sell the Congo to France. France was in favour because Léopold promised that his state officials would no longer directly trade in ivory. Britain supported Léopold's request so that he could fight the Arab slavers, a move popular with the British public.

In the end, Léopold got his way and imposed a duty of one to two francs on every pound of ivory bought from the Africans. The tax was enough to squeeze out most of the European competition. Less than a year after the anti-slavery conference, Léopold broke the promise he had made to delegates and issued a decree that not only gave his representatives in the Congo a monopoly on trade in ivory, but also made it clear that the paramount duty of state officials was to raise revenue. In decrees that followed, Léopold made it illegal for anyone but the state to trade guns with the Africans, which meant they would want to do business only with the state. Still, his financial situation remained perilous and he was forced to ask the Belgian government for a loan of £1 million. The government agreed, on condition that the king leave the Congo to Belgium in his will.

The relationship between the new colony and Belgium was a strange one, the only link being a personal one through Léopold himself. The Belgian government had no direct say in the colony, and Léopold did not inform the government of colonial affairs. The Congo Free State was run from Brussels by an administrative team hand-picked by the king. Léopold regarded the Congo as his private property, sometimes calling himself its proprietor. In Léopold's time, nation-states generally exercised control of colonies, not monarchs. The peculiar circumstances of the

Congo Free State meant that Léopold, and those he designated, stood to gain if the state made a profit. By the same token, the king was liable for all its costs. But he was able to defray those costs by borrowing from the Belgian government and willing bankers. The £1-million loan made in 1890 was only the first of many.

The ivory trade proved profitable at first. In 1890, 168,200 pounds of ivory were exported from the Congo. That amount increased to 601,230 pounds by 1895. Profits from these sales, while not vast, helped Léopold finance his colony. But it soon became clear that the elephant herds were being hunted to extinction. Léopold cast about for other ways to earn money from his colony. He decided that the growing trade in wild rubber was worth pursuing and turned his efforts in that direction. This opened the door to one of the darkest periods in the Congo's history. While the ivory trade required that Europeans stay on reasonably good terms with Africans who had the necessary skills to hunt and kill elephants, rubber gathering required no such bargain. There was little skill involved. The relationship between the Europeans and the Congolese shifted irrevocably to that of master and servant.

The European discovery of wild rubber has been attributed to the explorer Christopher Columbus, who saw the indigenous people on what is now Haiti playing with balls made of elastic material. No mass-scale uses for rubber were found, however, until English inventor Thomas Hancock discovered a method to shape it. He built the first rubber factory in England in 1820. Three years later, Scottish chemist Charles Macintosh used rubber to waterproof fabric. He achieved an immortality of sorts when his popular rainwear became known as a Macintosh. Next in the line of inventors working with rubber was Charles Goodyear, an American hardware merchant who in 1839 accidentally discovered vulcanization by spilling some sulphur into the rubber he was heating. The resulting material was elastic, yet tough enough to be used for industrial purposes such as hoses, tubes, washers and diaphragms.

The rubber tire was first patented in 1845 by English engineer and inventor Robert William Thomson, who concocted what he called "elastic bearings" for carriages, made from several layers of canvas saturated with rubber. John Boyd Dunlop, a veterinarian from Northern Ireland, further developed the idea with his invention of an inflatable rubber tire for his son's bicycle in 1887. He patented the design the following year. The timing was perfect. Two years earlier, a German by the name of Karl Benz had built the world's first automobile—a three-wheeled affair with a one-cylinder engine whose top speed was 13 kilometres an hour. Within a few years, automobile production took off and with it the demand for inflatable rubber tires.

At the time, rubber came from trees or vines growing in the wild. The highest-yielding trees were not in Africa but in Brazil, where the *Hevea brasiliensis* grew. In order to secure a reliable and plentiful source of rubber for themselves, the British brought Brazilian seeds to England in 1876. They propagated them and used the seedlings to start rubber plantations in British colonies in Asia, such as Ceylon, Malaysia and Singapore. But it would be another thirty years before the trees would mature to the point where large-scale rubber production was feasible.

Even as Léopold was making plans for the Congo's rubber, he was aware that production from southeast Asia would eventually come on stream. With their higher-yielding trees concentrated in plantations, the producers in Asia would have an advantage over those scavenging large areas in the wild. Léopold knew he had only a limited window of opportunity in which to exploit his rubber riches, which may partly explain why he pillaged the Congo with such ferocity. Rubber from southeast Asia began appearing in Europe in 1910, with a giant wave hitting the market in 1913. By that time Léopold had already left the Congo.

Because the king didn't have the funds to develop the rubber trade in his colony on his own, he decided to create a series of rubber companies that would be jointly owned by him and his financier friends. Several companies were given vast concessions in the Congo, to which they held exclusive development rights. The two principal companies were the Anglo-Belgian India Rubber and Exploration Company (ABIR) and the Société Anversoise du Commerce au Congo.

ABIR was formed in Antwerp on August 6, 1892. Among its earliest backers was British investor John Thomas North, whom Léopold had met at the racecourse in Ostend, Belgium. North, an illiterate Yorkshireman, had made his fortune speculating on nitrates in South America. He agreed to invest £40,000 in ABIR and brought with him other British shareholders. The company turned half of its shares over to the Congo Free State, which was Léopold by another name. In return, the company received a thirty-year concession on all the land within a 25-mile radius of eight designated posts. ABIR territory lay in central Congo, south of the Congo River. The Maringa and Lopori rivers, which join to form the Lulonga River, formed its northern and southern boundaries. The Congo Free State agreed to help the company set up its posts and to provide guns, ammunition and soldiers while the posts were being constructed. North's association with ABIR did not last long. He died of apoplexy in 1898, and his heirs sold his stocks to Belgian investors.

The financiers Léopold succeeded in attracting were risk-takers and gamblers—men well suited to the robber colonialism that ensued. In 1898, ABIR was reconstituted under Congolese law, allowing it to avoid Belgian taxes and, almost as important, Belgian justice. In the new shareholding structure, Alexandre de Browne de Tiège was the second largest shareholder after the Congo Free State. An Antwerp banker who had loaned money to Léopold in the past, de Browne de Tiège was also president of Société Anversoise du Commerce au Congo, the second largest rubber company in the Congo. It too was founded in 1892 and turned over half its shares to the Congo Free State in exchange for a concession north of ABIR land, but still south of the Congo River. De Browne de Tiège also had connections with many of the other concessionaire companies through shareholdings or directorships. Edouard Bunge, the administrator of Société Anversoise and the president of the Antwerp Chamber of Commerce, was listed among the major shareholders. And the rubber companies bought shares in each other, setting a pattern of corporate concentration in the Congo that was to last until it gained independence.

In 1896, Léopold secretly treated himself to a concession, creating the Domaine de la Couronne, an area larger than the ABIR and Anversoise territories combined. He kept all revenues from this concession for himself and used his Congo money to extend his palace at Laeken and to buy more real estate. In an effort to build support for his dynasty, he funded major public monuments, such as the Arcade of the Cinquantenaire in Brussels for the fiftieth anniversary of Belgian independence.

The rubber companies in the Congo all followed a specific model of operation. They divided their territories into zones, each with its own white *chef-de-zone* who supervised the managers of the posts. The managers ֥umbered between three and six per zone. They were paid very little in terms of salary but received a percentage of the profits made from rubber collected in their areas. The more rubber they collected, the richer they became. Some of the most violent excesses witnessed in the Congo can be traced to these financial incentives. Agents were paid between 1,800 and 2,100 Belgian francs per year, but there was no ceiling on their total bonuses. One agent for ABIR became famous among the agents in 1903 when he received a bonus of 16,800 francs, eight times his base salary.

The agents ran their posts with the help of African labour. Each had between 25 and 80 post sentries, armed with Albini rifles, which were the latest in European technology. The post sentries in turn controlled between 65 and 150 village sentries, who were armed with muzzle-loading rifles. This second tier of sentries lived in the villages to enforce the rubber regime. They usually belonged to a tribe from elsewhere. Like most of the other artificially created countries in Africa, the Congo held within its European-drawn borders a wide variety of ethnic groups, some of which were historical rivals. There were four main tribes in the Congo—the Mongo, the Luba, the Kongo and the Mangbetu-Azande—and an estimated 196 smaller ethnic groups. Officials for the state and rubber companies would play one group against another, taking men from one tribe to serve as sentries in the villages of traditional rivals, or transporting men across the country to serve in the colonial army, knowing the men would find it difficult to desert and find their way home. The village sentries were paid by the state or the rubber company but were fed by the villagers. There were numerous reports of their parasitical behaviour. Using their position to enrich themselves, they demanded housing, wives, goats and chickens from the villagers.

The agents also had about ten workmen at each post, seven house servants and about thirty paddlers for the post canoes. Without these Africans, the European agents could not have survived in the dense tropical forest, nor could they have performed their part in the rubber-collecting machine.

Villagers were compelled to gather rubber and were given numbered zinc discs to wear around their necks so that the company agents could keep track of how much each person collected. Those who did not meet the quota set by the company agent were flogged with a *chicotte*, a whip made from the hide of the hippopotamus, with edges so sharp it broke the skin after a couple of blows. Floggings ranged from twenty-five lashes for a minor misdemeanour to one hundred in extreme cases. Often the victims died.

Most of the rubber in the Congo Free State came from vines (primarily the liane *Landolphia*), which are more fragile than rubber trees. With care, trees can be repeatedly tapped, and even when tapped out they can be used again after a five-year wait. Vines are not as robust and their sap runs more slowly. As well, the vines in the Congo were relatively scarce, with only two to six per acre of forest. Rubber gatherers would have to move higher and higher up the vine into the forest canopy 60 metres above-ground to find sap still flowing. It took so long for the sap to fill the pots that it became a common occurrence for gatherers to fall asleep in the trees and fall to their deaths. As the Europeans became more and more ravenous for rubber, the Africans were forced to go farther and farther afield to fill the quotas arbitrarily imposed by the state or the rubber companies. The work necessary for their survival—cultivating and tending their subsistence crops, hunting, mending their houses—was left undone.

Some villagers desperate to fill their quotas would chop vines into pieces and squeeze the sap out. But this attracted swift retribution from the Europeans, because it ruined the resource forever. One district commissioner wrote to the official at the Inoryo post telling him that the locals were a "bad lot" who had cut down rubber vines: "We must fight them until their absolute submission has been obtained, or their complete extermination." Other ways the villagers tried to get around the quotas were to supply a substance that looked like rubber but did not have the same elastic qualities, or to add dirt to their baskets of rubber. Those caught were forced to eat their substandard load.

Before Léopold had acquired the Congo, Africans had voluntarily offered rubber to Europeans in exchange for cloth, beads and brass rods. In the early days of the rubber companies, the Congolese were paid for what they gathered, though it didn't add up to much. One post in Société Anversoise territory paid a penny per pound of rubber. The rubber would sell for hundreds of times that amount in Europe. Eventually, however, even this pretence of payment was discarded, and locals were forced at the point of a gun to collect rubber for nothing.

In order for this coercive system to function, vast numbers of soldiers were needed. The state army, called the Force Publique, was officially established in 1886. It attracted three kinds of soldiers: members of the Belgian army who were bored and poor, adventurers from across Europe and the Americas, and officers from the armies of smaller countries such as Switzerland and Italy and from Scandinavia. These men left their countries with the blessing of the Roman Catholic Church, which had endorsed the anti-slavery crusade but which openly supported Léopold long after the horrors of the Congo had been exposed.

Service in Léopold's newly created Force Publique offered Belgian soldiers adventure, romance, accelerated advancement and the possibility of glory. Colonial adventure spawned a series of books in Belgium that glorified brave Belgian soldiers who died in front of screaming black hordes. But historians L.H. Gann and Peter Duignan estimate that close to 40 per cent of European volunteers in the Congo forces died in the colony, many from disease.

Given the size of the Congo—roughly 1.7 million square kilometres— Europeans could not hope to control the colony alone. Their strength as a fighting force was further weakened by the fact that until 1904, officers in the Force Publique also had to perform non-military tasks. They built roads and houses, became foremen in the rubber operations, collected statistics for censuses and worked as ordinary constables. As a result there were never enough officers to command the army, which led to persistent discipline problems, including several mutinies.

Léopold turned to African soldiers to expand his occupying force. They were recruited in the thousands. The Force Publique went from 3,186 men in 1891 to 10,215 in 1894 and 19,028 in 1898. By 1904, the army had swelled to 30,000. This number did not include the armed forces in the pay of the rubber companies, whose exact numbers remained a corporate secret. Léopold also turned to neighbouring colonies to man his Force Publique, recruiting from British West Africa and Lagos. Recruits were paid a franc and a quarter per day, given free medical treatment and food, and promised a ticket home at the end of their three-year contract. Their appeal to the Congo Free State was that they were already adjusted to the African climate, they knew how to survive in the bush and they were familiar with the ways of the white men. The European soldiers answering Léopold's call, meanwhile, were unskilled in the guerrilla war tactics needed to fight in the dense vegetation of the Congo. They had been trained for the set-piece battles of Europe.

Léopold soon found he needed even more troops. He decided to recruit "volunteers" from within the Congo. These men were paid 21 centimes a day—a large savings over the franc and a quarter paid to the West Africans. Their term of service was seven years instead of three, and some of their pay was held back until the end of that period. Many of the recruits never made it to the seven-year mark, and the state pocketed their accumulated salaries.

A memo from the king's office laid out the bonuses that were to be paid to the Congo state agents for each recruit from their area. Healthy and vigorous men suitable for military duty earned the agent 90 francs, a youth was worth 65 francs, and male children, who had to be strong enough to march, were worth 5 francs each. The children were put in camps, where they were trained to be soldiers. Village chiefs were ordered to supply a certain number of men for the Force Publique or the armies of the rubber companies. The difference between the two types of forces was often blurred as Force Publique troops fought for the rubber companies and the companies supplied some of their soldiers to the Force Publique if necessary. The chiefs were supposed to receive payment for the men they supplied, but all too often they were shortchanged by European agents or African intermediaries who pocketed the money or goods. Increasingly, chiefs were browbeaten into supplying people for free. They responded by offering the most worthless men from the village or the troublemakers who challenged their authority. Together with the slaves, prisoners, criminals and the riff-raff of Europe, these formed the occupying force in the Congo.

Violence permeated most colonial conquest in Africa, but that of the Congo was on a different scale. People from ordinary backgrounds became bloodthirsty despots capable of the most abhorrent acts. One practice that leaked out to the wider world through missionary dispatches was the severing of hands by soldiers as proof that they had killed Africans resisting the rubber trade. Missionaries talked of seeing soldiers smoking scores of hands over fires in the bush in order to preserve them long enough to bring them into the closest post. For their part, the Belgian officials and soldiers justified their violence by exaggerating the supposed barbarity of the Africans. Cannibalistic practices were frequently reported, although on closer examination few of those accounts were first-hand. Eurocentrism and the need to justify their presence in Africa led explorers, missionaries and colonizers to spread such stories without any attempt at verification.

Glave himself made frequent mention of cannibalism in the diary he kept during his third and final trip to the Congo. He had returned just as the rubber companies were gearing up for full production in the mid-1890s. His bleak comments during this period stand in stark contrast to his early musings about the glorious endeavour he had embarked on with his indomitable hero Stanley. He wrote about coming across chain gangs of old women at one of the rubber posts. They had been reduced to skeletons by their captors yet were still being forced to work by the sentries. "Women ought not to be flogged," he wrote after seeing that many of them bore the welts and open wounds of the *chicotte*. At another post he came across a tree where a group of natives had been hanged. Further downriver, the boat he was travelling on stopped to take on a cargo of one hundred slaves, mostly seven- and eight-year-old boys suffering from disease and hunger. They were destined for a mission where they would be trained to be soldiers—if they survived the trip. "The state has not suppressed slavery, but established a monopoly by driving out [its] competitors," Glave wrote. The worst of his experiences came when state soldiers conducted a raid on a village after two of their number had been killed by locals. The soldiers brought back twenty-one heads, some of women and children, to a Captain Leon Rom. He used the skulls to decorate his flower beds. A similar scene is depicted by writer Joseph Conrad in his novel *Heart of Darkness*. "They talk of philanthropy and civilisation," wrote Glave of the Belgian administrators and officials he encountered. "Where it is I do not know."

As the rubber companies became more rapacious and their methods more brutal, a gathering chorus of condemnation found its voice. The earliest rumblings about Léopold's regime came from the trading companies that were being squeezed out of the lucrative Congo market by Léopold's agents. Some of the loudest protests came from the Nieuwe Afrikaansche Handels Vennootschap, or the New Africa Trading Company (NAHV), a Rotterdam-based firm that had established trade links at the mouth of the Congo in 1857. It dealt in vegetable oil, coffee, cotton, ivory and rubber, making it a direct competitor to Léopold. Before the 1885 Berlin Conference had even started, NAHV lodged a protest against agents of the International African Association, who were trading in ivory when their cause was supposed to be philanthropic. The struggle between Léopold's agents and the Dutch company intensified when they confiscated shipments of ivory and guns belonging to NAHV and prevented its Congo representative from travelling to certain areas. NAHV complained to the

Dutch government, which in turn complained to Léopold, who made all the right diplomatic noises but continued to tighten his grip on the ground. Eventually NAHV was forced to abandon the region, shifting its business to neighbouring French and Portuguese territories. But before the company gave up the fight completely, it joined forces with a visiting American missionary, who launched the first major attack on Léopold's human rights record.

George Washington Williams, a black American author and Baptist minister, had travelled to Africa to research a book and to explore the feasibility of bringing black Americans to work in the Congo. What he saw there so repelled him that he felt forced to write about it. His *Open Letter to His Serene Majesty Léopold II, King of the Belgians and Sovereign of the Independent State of the Congo* exposed the hypocrisy of Léopold's rule in the region. The letter detailed how Stanley had used trickery to persuade the local chiefs to sign land treaties, and it revealed the death and destruction caused by state forces. It ridiculed the idea that Léopold had provided any public services in the Congo. But Williams's most potent criticism was that not only was the king not fighting to eradicate slavery, he had teamed up with Arab slavers and was buying slaves to serve in his army. The letter was published as a pamphlet in 1890 and widely distributed in Europe and the United States, probably paid for by NAHV. It was picked up and printed by various newspapers, including the *New York Herald*, the newspaper that had first sent Stanley to Africa in search of Livingstone.

Léopold's reaction to the criticism set the pattern for how he would deal with future attacks. Through sympathetic journalists and newspapers, the king attempted to discredit Williams, who had wrongly claimed to be a colonel. This gave the king the lever he needed. The Congo Free State administration issued a rebuttal, which again was printed in sympathetic newspapers. Stanley was quoted as saying that Williams's pamphlet was an attempt at blackmail. Eventually the minor storm subsided, but not before attracting the attention of opposition politicians in Belgium and Britain, who began to pay closer attention to events in the Congo. Léopold's agents came under international scrutiny again when one of them—a Major Lothaire—summarily tried and executed an Irish trader named Charles Stokes for dealing in ivory. Stokes's hanging caused both the British and the German governments to protest (Stokes was a British citizen with a base in German East Africa), which caught the attention of the newspapers and again brought scrutiny to the Congo.

At about the same time, Edward Wilhelm Sjoblom, a Swedish missionary with the American Baptist Missionary Union, published a denunciation of the Congo regime in the Swedish press and wrote to Sir Charles Dilke, an outspoken advocate of human rights. Sjoblom's revelations, later published in 1907 in a book called *In the Shade of the Palms*, indicated that the cruelties Williams had written about had intensified. Sjoblom recalled an incident that had taken place in February 1895, when his sermon was interrupted by a soldier who seized an old man and accused him of not collecting enough rubber. Sjoblom asked the soldier to wait until the service was over, but the soldier dragged the old man to one side and shot him, then ordered a young boy to cut off the old man's hand.

Dilke began asking questions in the British House of Commons, putting pressure on the British government to raise the matter with the Belgian government and Léopold. The Aborigines' Protection Society, of which Dilke was a member, also stepped up its campaign in Britain. The society had been established in 1838 to stop the extermination of native peoples after the British had wiped out the inhabitants of Tasmania. Léopold himself was briefly a member, before the events in the Congo were made public.

The furor caused by the Stokes hanging and Sjoblom's revelations did not die down as quickly as the storm in 1890, and Léopold was forced to act. He established a Commission for the Protection of the Natives in the Congo and appointed a number of missionaries as commissioners. None of them were posted in prime rubber areas, and at their first meeting they were instructed by the Catholic bishop in the Congo that on no account were they to look at the methods used to collect rubber and ivory, nor at how the state and private companies obtained recruits. At a stroke, the commission was rendered useless. But the wider public had already lost interest. Once again, Léopold had managed to assuage his critics without changing operations on the ground.

Throughout Léopold's rule in the Congo, there were several hundred Catholic missionaries operating in the area as well as an equal number of Protestants. The Catholic missionaries and those who were Belgian were largely silent about the cruelty they witnessed: the Catholics because the church supported Léopold, the Belgians because they knew that at some point they would have to return home and their careers would be blighted by censure of the king. What public criticism there was came from foreign Protestant missionaries such as Williams and Sjoblom. But even they were taking a risk. The missionaries were largely dependent on the state for transport and supplies. The Congo Free State agents could and did put pressure on them to be quiet, including starving them by preventing the transport of supplies on state steamboats and forbidding the Africans from selling them food.

Some of those who were silent worked secretly to end the regime by supplying information to its detractors. The Congo Reform Association, set up in 1904 by Edmund Dene Morel, a Liverpool shipping clerk, profited from these well-placed sources. Morel's suspicion about the Congo was sparked when he discovered that the official cargo lists of the Congo ships did not tally with the actual cargoes. He realized that someone was skimming millions from the rubber profits. More importantly, he saw that no real trade was being conducted by the king and the rubber companies. Ships that brought in rubber were loaded with guns and ammunition for their return voyage, not with valuable goods to trade with the Africans. Morel realized that slavery could be the only base on which the rubber fortunes were being built. He raised the issue with his bosses, but they preferred not to investigate if it meant the end of their lucrative Congo business. Morel quit in frustration in 1901 and began a campaign, publishing a newsletter and making public appearances wherever he could find an audience. His lobbying attracted the support of Mark Twain in the United States and Sir Arthur Conan Doyle in Britain and was eventually instrumental in forcing Léopold to hand the Congo over to Belgium. But that would take many years.

Léopold did not sit back and let the accusations go unanswered. He set up a Press Bureau in 1904 that bribed influential journalists and politicians and churned out rebuttals to unfavourable coverage. One of his agents even tried to bribe Morel. When Captain Guy Burrows, a British officer, tried to publish a book, called *The Curse of Central Africa*, about atrocities he had witnessed in the Congo, the Congo Free State successfully sued him for libel and the book was suppressed. When the British government voiced objections to Léopold's behaviour, the king cited abuses by the British in Sierra Leone. None of the major powers that had colonies were eager to take Léopold on because they all had misdeeds in their past or present. France had followed Léopold's example by setting up concession companies that used forced labour to extract rubber in the neighbouring colony of Congo-Brazzaville. Germany was still backing Léopold for fear he would lose his colony to France. The United States kept quiet because it was keen to avoid criticism of its treatment of blacks. On a personal level, the king was never swayed by the stories of barbarism emanating from his African colony. His arrogance and sense of divine mission left him devoid of compassion for the Africans.

Helping Léopold to undermine his critics was Stanley. Although he was no longer in Léopold's employ, Stanley had his reputation to consider as well as his successful career as an author and lecturer. He did not want criticisms of Léopold to reflect on him. As late as 1898, he continued to promote the myth that Léopold was waging a philanthropic crusade in central Africa. "Who can doubt that God chose the King for His instrument to redeem this vast slave park whence Dongolawi and Arab, Bakongo and Portuguese half-caste slave traders culled their victims for the slave market," Stanley wrote in an introduction to Guy Burrows's *Land of the Pigmies*. "King Léopold found the Congo region 'stained by wasteful deformities, tears, and hearts' blood of myriads,' cursed by cannibalism, savagery and despair; and he has been trying with a patience, which I can never sufficiently admire, to relieve it of its horrors, rescue it from its oppressors and save it from perdition." Before he died in 1904, Stanley was elected to the British parliament and received a knighthood. Although he was thought to have private misgivings about what Léopold was doing in the Congo, he never voiced them publicly.

Just as the king had worked to discredit Williams, he had his agents attack Morel, accusing the former shipping clerk of working for Liverpool merchants who were simply jealous of the rise in importance of Antwerp shipping companies in the Congo trade. Léopold masterminded a campaign of innuendo and vilification that was backed by his financial supporters and the Roman Catholic Church. More than a decade after human rights abuses in the Congo had first been exposed, the Church still stood behind Léopold and could be counted on to publicly condemn criticism of the king. Protests by the British government were dismissed by Léopold's defenders as sniping from a country that coveted the Congo. This struck a chord with Europeans, especially in the aftermath of the Boer War.

The Belgian public paid no attention to the complaints against Léopold until Belgian professor Félicien Cattier published a report on the Congo in 1905. Here was one of their own confirming that massive and systematic human rights abuses were taking place in the Congo. The report also revealed for the first time the scale of the profits being made by the king and the rubber companies. There is no doubt that rubber transformed Léopold's finances. The Congo had become a tremendous cash cow that he and his friends milked furiously. A commission of inquiry estimated that Léopold's revenues between 1896 and 1905 from the Domaine de la Couronne alone were 70 million Belgian francs.

But even as the Cattier report was published, the rubber trade was dying. Exports had gone from 156,339 kilograms in 1892, the year the rubber companies were founded, to a peak of 6 million kilograms in 1901, after which they started to slide steadily downward. As the rubber harvest declined, agents became desperate and goaded their men on to greater savagery in order to force the Africans to produce. One village headman told a missionary that his people were willing to work but they could not collect rubber because there was none to be had: "If we must either be massacred or bring rubber, well, let them finish us off, then we suppose they will be satisfied." Villagers fled or tried to fight back. In the first six months of 1905, 142 ABIR sentries were either killed or gravely injured.

In this atmosphere of mounting crisis in the rubber areas, Léopold agreed that the Congo Free State should take control of the rubber concessions. The king thought that there was still rubber to be had, and there was one last frenzy of violence when state troops tried to force those Africans left in the area to produce rubber. But in the end they had to admit defeat and send word to the king that nothing could reverse the decline in production. The ABIR and the Société Anversoise had just about completely denuded the territories they had controlled.

The rising tide of international criticism finally forced Léopold to relinquish his colony to Belgium in 1908. He died the following year. Much of what Léopold did in the Congo will never be known because he ordered the Congo Free State's archives to be destroyed before he handed his colony over. Because of his fraudulent bookkeeping, an accurate accounting is impossible. It is a matter of record, however, that when Belgium took over the colony, it inherited debts worth 40 million Belgian francs but also properties in Europe belonging to the Congo Free State worth 60 million francs. The money made by the rubber companies that did not go to Léopold went into private bank accounts in Europe or was invested abroad. Rubber plantations in southeast Asia, diamond mines in Angola, coal mines in Rhodesia, and railways in China were all built with the blood money of the Congo.

Glave, the young Englishman who had served Léopold, never returned to England from his final trip to the Congo. He died of a fever in Matadi in 1895, aged thirty-three, while awaiting the departure of the steamship that was to take him home. He left instructions that his journals be sent to the *Century Illustrated Monthly Magazine* in London, which published them over the following two years. In a letter to the editor of that magazine, written two weeks before his death, Glave talked of his feelings of grief at seeing a group of young children who had been made orphans by what he called "the inhuman policies" of the Congo Free State. They were naked, and many suffered from ulcers that went untreated despite the presence of a doctor on board the boat. Glave died in the mistaken belief that Léopold was not aware of the atrocities that were perpetrated in his name and for his profit. "The whole world seems to think that the Congo Free State is a civilizing influence and that philanthropy and love of justice are prompting every effort of the administration," he wrote. "It is his [Léopold's] duty to learn the true state of things in the dominion of which he is sovereign." Of all the tales of commercial wrongdoing in this book, that of the wily and duplicitous Léopold and his rapacious circle of advisers, businessmen and bankers set a standard of horror that no other company has ever matched.

CHAPTER THREE

SIR PERCY AND
THE DIAMOND KING

IN JANUARY 1954, A SMALL PRIVATE PLANE ARRIVED AT THE AIRPORT in Cape Town carrying a shadowy figure whose very presence in South Africa was meant to be a secret. Sir Percy Sillitoe, recently retired head of the British secret service, MI5, had journeyed from his home in Eastbourne on the south coast of England at the personal request of diamond magnate Sir Ernest Oppenheimer. So pressing was the matter Sir Ernest wanted to discuss with the former spymaster that he had sent his own aircraft to fetch him. And no sooner had Sir Percy set foot on South African soil than he was whisked away to Muizenberg, the Oppenheimer summer home, where his host was anxiously waiting to meet him.

The summons from Sir Ernest had come after Sir Percy responded to a newspaper advertisement in *The Times* placed by the De Beers Group of companies for a new chief of security in southern Africa. The ex-spymaster was vastly overqualified to head a corporate security group. He had spent the early part of his career in the colonial police forces of North and South Rhodesia before returning to Britain to head various municipal forces, ultimately becoming director general of MI5 at the start of the Cold War. But in that first phone call inviting him to South Africa, Sir Ernest hinted at much broader responsibilities requiring someone with Sir Percy's communist-fighting skills.

If truth be told, Sir Percy did not need much convincing to at least investigate the scope of the new job. After his active career, he was finding retirement rather dull. A man could only do so many newspaper crosswords before he went mad with boredom. So when the invitation came, Sir Percy packed his bag, kissed his wife, Dollie, goodbye and left for Africa at the first possible opportunity. After being away from the continent for half a century, he was happy to return to its romance and nostalgia, not to mention the promise of excitement that the new job offered.

Sir Percy was no altar boy when he began his work for Sir Ernest. His time in colonial and municipal policing and then in Britain's secret service had seen to that. But the methods he ultimately used to crack down on diamond smuggling in the West African country Sierra Leone made his previous dealings with criminals and communist spies appear clean and simple by comparison. However, that is getting ahead of the story, which must start with why Sir Ernest so desperately wanted to speak to Sir Percy in the first place.

At the time of their meeting in early 1954, Sir Ernest Oppenheimer stood at the very pinnacle of the diamond world. All around him he could see the companies he had conquered and knit into a vast empire of gold and diamonds known as Anglo American/De Beers. The diamond king had the grooming and appearance of an Edwardian gentleman. There was something about his smoothed-back hair, neatly trimmed moustache and well-tailored suit that placed Sir Ernest permanently in the late 1920s and early 1930s—the period of his greatest corporate triumphs. Friends described him as charming but shy, and said that memories of his impoverished childhood stayed with him and affected his behaviour throughout his life. But that is only part of the story, for in order to win and then retain control of De Beers—and through it, the diamond world—Sir Ernest also had to be ruthless and shrewd.

He had started life in Friedberg, Germany, in 1880 as the eighth child (and fifth son) of a German cigar merchant and his wife. Encouraged by his father to leave Germany for a better future elsewhere, Ernest followed his older brother Louis to London in 1896. There, Louis helped him get a job as a £1-a-week diamond sorter at the dealer Anton Dunkelsbuhler. Six years later, Ernest went with the company to South Africa, where he took over the office in Kimberley, the heart of the diamond industry. Less than three decades later, Sir Ernest became chairman of De Beers, having founded the mining house Anglo American Corporation and picked up a knighthood along the way. *Spero optima*, "I hope for the best," was the motto Sir Ernest adopted when he was knighted in 1921 for taking a leading role in recruiting combatants and labourers on behalf of Britain during the First World War. He was optimistic by nature. But even as he celebrated the achievements of almost six decades in the diamond trade, he knew that control of his kingdom was slipping from his grasp.

Through the years he had survived many challenges to his reign as the king of diamonds. There had been numerous aspirants to his throne. But the daring and foolhardy who thought they could unseat him had been beaten back long ago, and he was now in the process of handing the crown to his son Harry. The more recent challenges to his control came from competitors who were making new diamond discoveries. He was finding it increasingly difficult to uphold the corporate ethos of De Beers founder Cecil Rhodes, who had made it a policy to acquire, by fair means or foul, all important sources of diamonds and to arrange, as far as possible, for the entire diamond production of the world to be marketed through one channel.

Rhodes had lived in simpler times, when the major source of diamonds had been concentrated in one area of South Africa that could be encircled by a barbed wire fence and patrolled by sentries. Oppenheimer had to deal with a series of new discoveries sprinkled across sub-Saharan Africa. The Congo, Angola, Ghana, Guinea, Liberia, Sierra Leone, the Ivory Coast, Southwest Africa and Tanganyika—one by one, these new sources had come on stream, and one by one, Oppenheimer had had to persuade or force the men who controlled them to enter the De Beers fold. The men who controlled the company also controlled the diamond cartel through which sales were regulated. First

Rhodes and then Sir Ernest persuaded producers that it was only by act-ing together to control supply that they could maintain an attractive price for diamonds.

But Sierra Leone was different. It had been blessed with some of the highest-quality gems in the world. Fully 50 per cent of the diamonds recovered there were gem quality, the rest being lower-grade stones that were good only for industrial use. As far back as 1935, Sir Ernest had been warned by one of his geological engineers that Sierra Leone represented a threat to his empire because of the sheer volume of stones it was capa-ble of producing. Sir Ernest had thought he had solved the problem when he bought shares in Sierra Leone Selection Trust, the company with the diamond monopoly in the country, and persuaded its American owner, Chester Beatty, to market the company's production through the De Beers-controlled diamond cartel. But Sir Ernest had not counted on smugglers.

Sierra Leone had kimberlite pipes, but many of these had been erod-ed by water, spreading the diamonds over a vast area and leaving stones just below the surface of the soil. Illegal mining of these alluvial diamonds flourished because anyone with a pick and shovel could seek fortune in the diamond fields with very little risk. As a result, high-quality stones were pouring out of Sierra Leone onto the world market, undermining the artificial price set by the producer cartel and bringing into question the cartel's usefulness. Estimates of the value of the smuggled stones var-ied widely as no one really knew for sure how many were slipping through. It was thought that roughly £12 million sterling worth of dia-monds were being smuggled out of Sierra Leone each year. Smuggling was a problem at other mines in southern Africa, but not on this scale.

Neither the colonial government nor the diamond companies in Sierra Leone had been able to put an end to the practice. Already in tran-sition to independence, the colonial authorities lacked the will and the means to end the illegal trade, and Sierra Leone Selection Trust lacked the power. When the company had initially won its diamond monopoly in 1935, the colonial government had set up what was called the Diamond

Mines Protection Force. While this was a government body, it was paid for by the company. It consisted of one commissioner, two non-commissioned officers and thirty-nine supernumerary court messengers, a special unit of the colonial police force. With the diamond fields covering an estimated 11,500 square kilometres of the country, a force this size was clearly inadequate. Pre-independence politics made it even more so.

Siaka Stevens, minister of mines in Sierra Leone at the time, said that police could only act effectively if they had the support of the general public—and they didn't. The nationalist movement had persuaded many people that the diamond monopoly only allowed white foreigners to steal the resources of black Africans without adequate recompense. Stealing from the company was seen as a way of evening the balance. As well, villagers living near the diamond fields were often quietly supportive of illicit mining because they made money by renting shacks and selling food to the miners and smugglers. The local chiefs were agitating to relieve Sierra Leone Selection Trust of its monopoly in order to stem the social upheaval and criminal aspects of the diamond rush. They were growing tired of dealing with the fallout of illicit mining and smuggling. One prominent chief told the Sierra Leone legislature that there had been forty-five cases of murder in his area alone. One man had been disembowelled by unknown assailants who were after a diamond that he had swallowed. The chiefs thought that individual licences should be made available to miners, which would effectively legalize illegal mining in certain areas.

The lack of adequate police support and rising public tension put extra pressure on Sierra Leone Selection Trust to find a solution to the security problem if it did not want to lose its monopoly. But the security situation was about to get worse before it got better. The company was forced to abruptly terminate the Supernumerary Court Messenger Force when it was discovered that its members were stealing from the company. Management had noticed a steady fall in the percentage of large diamonds in output and had investigated reports that large packets of the type of stones it was missing were finding their way onto the world market. The only place where these larger stones could readily be stolen was in the company's own sorting and concentrating plants, which were under the supervision of the court messengers. In 1952, they were let go with a month's notice and the company set up its own security force, which consisted of ninety-three security guards and twenty-four temporary patrolmen. This was still insufficient to police the diamond areas, but at least the sorting plants could be protected.

Aside from not having enough men and little police support, the company security force was hampered by the fact that its members were not allowed to carry arms and lacked the power of search and arrest. Company managers argued long and hard with Colonial Office officials in London to change these rules, but the officials were reluctant to allow what they thought would be the creation of a private police force at a sensitive time in Sierra Leonean politics. Company officers tried to make up for their lack of power by mounting joint patrols with the police. But this too proved unsatisfactory. The police were stretched too thin to be present in areas where the company needed them most, or they were simply unwilling to help. Smugglers and illicit miners realized they could run with impunity from the unarmed company security force. And even if the company men did manage to catch a thief, the penalties for illicit diamond mining were so weak as to not be a deterrent. Illicit mining was only a misdemeanour; it did not become a felony until 1956.

In this atmosphere of weak or non-existent policing and inadequate law, the smugglers flourished. Sir Ernest's son Harry, whose business was to know as much about the diamond industry as possible, told his father that 10 to 20 per cent of all diamonds reaching the world's cutting centres were smuggled goods, many of them from Sierra Leone. Because these stones were not passing through any of the De Beers Group of companies, they represented money lost from the group's coffers. That was bad enough. Worse was the long-term threat they posed to the cartel. If diamond cutters and dealers who currently bought from the cartel opted for the cheaper smuggled stones (they were selling in Europe for 20 to 30 per cent less), the cartel would eventually collapse. Diamond producers would return to the old days of competition, undercutting each other on the world market, and diamonds—which were not all that rare—would no longer be a luxury good. Sir Ernest could not let that happen. He was annoyed that Sierra Leone Selection Trust could not handle the situation themselves, and he decided he had no choice but to step in.

In the past, Sir Ernest had used various means—persuasion, threats, appeals to greed, coercion—to maintain his monopoly. But the smugglers and miners in Sierra Leone were immune to such tactics. They cared not a whit about staying in his good graces, nor did they care what their smuggling was doing to his empire. Their interests were short-term and strictly monetary in nature—which meant Sir Ernest had to try a different approach.

A great fan of thrillers and spy novels, Oppenheimer lit on the idea of hiring a professional spymaster. In the wake of the Second World War, there were plenty of men around with espionage skills honed while fighting the Nazis. Sir William Stephenson, otherwise known as Intrepid, was first approached for the job, but he turned it down. He said he had spent enough time working underground during the Second World War while running a spy agency for Britain out of New York. He had no appetite for tackling the smugglers, whom he described as "an international murder gang." So Sir Ernest advertised in the *Times* of London in 1953 and was delighted when Sir Percy answered the ad.

The man who strode across the room to meet Sir Ernest at Muizenberg was tall and rangy, with a bearing that hinted at his past as a trooper in the employ of the British South Africa Company Police, the force Cecil Rhodes had initially set up, and later with the Northern Rhodesia Police. When news of Sir Percy's January visit to Cape Town leaked out through the newspapers the next month, it suited the British journalists to portray Sir Percy's contact with De Beers as the whimsy of an aging spymaster. But it was more than that. Sir Percy was no stranger to Africa or to diamond smuggling. His roots were deeply embedded in African soil. He spoke several African dialects and had an intimate knowledge of the people and the land from his years of solitary patrol in what was then Southern and Northern Rhodesia and Tanganyika.

A photo of Sir Percy from the 1950s shows an open-faced man in an unbuttoned suit, wearing the type of awkward grin usually produced at the prodding of a photographer. He may well have been grinning with happiness, so pleased was he to have finally left behind MI5, which he hated, and the doldrums of retirement, which he hated even more. He had taken over as head of the secret service just after the war and quickly found that the intense office politics did not suit him. He had wanted to be head of the Metropolitan Police in London, a job he had spent his entire career working toward. But when that job went to another man, he had been given MI5 in compensation. On more than one occasion, he arrived home after work, threw his bowler hat on the chair, and shouted at the long-suffering Dollie, "I can't work with those bastards!"

It wasn't just that the secret service was going through a rough patch when Sir Percy took it over, although that undoubtedly had a bearing on how he regarded the job. It could not have been easy to head a group that was found to be riddled with communist moles happily trading Cold War secrets under your nose. But the real reason Sir Percy hated going into his office on Curzon Street in the West End of London was that it was staffed by Oxbridge intellectuals who flaunted their disdain for him because he hadn't been born into England's elite. Sir Percy's mother was middle class, and his no-account father had ended up in debtor's prison. A talent for singing had won Percy a place at Saint Paul's Cathedral Choir School, an education his mother could not otherwise have afforded, and he had worked his way up through the ranks of the police services. Some of Sir Percy's staff at MI5 took to conversing in Latin in front of him to make him feel his comparative lack of education. After suffering this abuse with growing anger, he finally brought it to a halt by threatening to fire the next person who spoke Latin—or any other foreign language—in his presence.

Still, such insubordination rankled. Little wonder that during his years at the secret service he appeared dour, insecure, solitary and given to fits of paranoia and depression. He retired in 1953 and decided for lack of something better to do to buy a candy shop in Eastbourne. His involvement lasted about a week before he realized he'd made a mistake and offered the business to his son. The possibility of a job with De Beers was attractive on many levels, but mostly because it rescued him from boredom and brought him closer to the police work he had once loved.

Sir Ernest outlined the scope of the smuggling problem for Sir Percy at that first meeting. While it was impossible to reduce diamond thefts to zero given the portability and availability of the gems, the producers' goal was to reduce the overall total by half. Sir Percy was to survey all the major mines in southern Africa and come up with a plan and a timetable to meet the producers' target. Sir Ernest was willing to give Sir Percy whatever he needed to do the job. Money was no object. Sir Percy also had carte blanche when it came to how he did the job. What mattered was success. Sir Ernest had one stipulation: Sir Percy was to report to him and no one else.

Sir Percy spent some time on that first trip with Sir Ernest, who was only too happy to tell him about the diamond world. He found the senior Oppenheimer an affable host, and the two eventually grew to become friends. But there was one incident during those early days that troubled Sir Percy enough for him to mention it later to his family. One day, when he and Sir Ernest were at the Oppenheimer home discussing the problem of smuggling, the diamond magnate asked Sir Percy to come with him to the basement. A cage similar to a prison cell had been built against one wall. Inside was an old kitchen table and two chairs. When they entered, Sir Ernest locked the door behind them. He then went to the wall, where a safe had been installed, opened the lock, and took out what he told Sir Percy was the world's largest diamond. He set it on the table. Look into it, he instructed the ex-spymaster, who later told his family it was like gazing into a crystal ball. Sir Percy looked for a while and then sat back. But his host was mesmerized. Sir Ernest seemed lost in the glittering depths of the colossal gem. It was then that Sir Percy realized that while diamonds were just a valuable commodity to him, they were much more to

Sir Ernest. This glimpse at his new employer's obsession left him feeling vaguely uneasy.

Sir Percy began his work in March 1954 with a tour of all the major diamond centres in Africa. He needed to get an idea of what he was dealing with. In the space of six weeks, he visited Angola, Ghana, Sierra Leone, the Belgian Congo, Tanganyika, Northern and Southern Rhodesia, and South Africa. He saw that the diamond smuggling chain could be broken down into three distinct parts: the first was at the mines, where diamonds were stolen by employees or illicit miners; the second saw the rough stones sold to middlemen, who moved them out of the source country; and the third was the international diamond smuggling routes that led through Liberia and Lebanon to Europe and around the world. The most worrisome of these routes appeared to end behind what was then called the Iron Curtain, somewhere in the Soviet bloc.

Starting with the mines, Sir Percy found that security arrangements differed widely. He approved of the measures used by De Beers in Kimberley, where the African workers were confined to compounds for the period of time that they worked at the mine. This tactic had been introduced by Cecil Rhodes. The workers were not allowed to leave the mine until their employment was finished, and they were not told in advance the exact day they would be released. When that day came, they were subjected to a strict examination, often an x-ray, to determine whether they had concealed any diamonds on their person. While x-rays were helpful, they had their drawbacks. At one mine, the supervisors had to stop using them when workers began to sicken and die from overexposure to radiation.

At another mine, some diamonds were painted with radioactive paint and then tracked through the production process with the use of Geiger counters. The idea was to see whether the parcels they were in had been tampered with, but again this exposed workers to dangerous radiation. From talking to the mine supervisors, Sir Percy discovered that human ingenuity knew no bounds when vast wealth was at stake. New methods of smuggling were invented every day. In mines where x-rays were not in use, gems were secreted about the body—stuck between toes or fingers, in navels or ears, swallowed, or even placed in a wound that was then allowed to heal over the stone. Sometimes animals were used as unwitting carriers. Pigeons were popular, but snakes and lizards could also be induced to swallow gems. The animals were then put outside the security fence in the hope they could be found afterward. Then there were thieves who dispensed with carriers altogether. One employee wrapped diamonds in lead shot and fired them over the security fence, ostensibly shooting game. Another fired the stones themselves. As fast as security forces cracked down on one method, another was invented. "It is alarming how easily fabulous riches can be hidden when those riches happen to be in the form of 'bright pebbles' of the diamond-bearing soil of Africa," Sir Percy declared in his 1955 memoir, *Cloak without Dagger*.

Despite the diversity of smuggling techniques, Sir Percy found ways to tighten security. One of his main suggestions was to put the European workers through the same type of security searches that the Africans underwent. The assumption until then had been that the Africans were doing the smuggling, and as a result Europeans were not subjected to the same strict measures. "There seems to me to be little doubt that a few Europeans are themselves guilty of theft and unworthy of the confidence placed in them by their employers," Sir Percy concluded.

Simple measures such as these were successful at the enclosed mines—how successful remained a closely guarded corporate secret. However, the same tactics could not be used in Sierra Leone, where the diamond fields, spread over thousands of square kilometres, could be neither fenced nor adequately guarded. The number of illicit miners in the diamond-rich Kono area alone was estimated to be about five thousand in 1952, rising to thirty thousand in 1954, the year Sir Percy was hired. It was to peak at about seventy-five thousand in 1956. Sir Percy could not hope to control that many thieves and miners, so instead he turned his attention to the next link in the chain: the smugglers.

There were two main smuggling routes out of Sierra Leone: one through the capital, Freetown, where stones could be taken on board a plane or boat destined for the Middle East or Europe, and the other through dense forest to the neighbouring country of Liberia, where dealers in Monrovia, the capital, were eager to purchase illicit stones. The diggers themselves rarely, if ever, undertook the smuggling themselves. Rather, it was middlemen who bought stones from the diggers at low prices and then made their money by reselling them in Freetown, Monrovia or beyond. Regular traffic between the diamond areas and Freetown facilitated the smuggling. But when the police began searching the luggage of travellers leaving the country, Freetown became a less desirable route and the smugglers turned increasingly to Monrovia, which offered the added attraction of payment in us dollars instead of British sterling, which was still under currency restrictions in the post-war world. As well, the Liberian government actively encouraged smuggling, and its police were prepared to turn a blind eye as long as they were adequately compensated.

Many of the middlemen were of Lebanese descent; their ancestors had come to West Africa as itinerant traders and then stayed. They were uniquely placed to smuggle diamonds because, unlike African traders, the Lebanese had the overseas contacts necessary to sell the stones and to handle the foreign exchange payments, and they could afford to travel abroad to meet those contacts. Many also had the added advantage of carrying British passports. This meant that they could not be deported if suspected of smuggling, a solution that the British officials running the colony had considered and dismissed. Those Lebanese without British passports were often permanent residents in Sierra Leone, which meant they also could not be deported, unless convicted in a court of law.

With these middlemen involved, it was natural that one of the key smuggling routes passed through Beirut. From there, the stones moved to diamond centres in Western Europe and North America. Western governments also believed that gems from Beirut were finding their way to the Soviet Union and its satellites. This was particularly disturbing because industrial diamonds were crucial to manufacturing arms: only they could cut, grind, bore and extrude wire made of increasingly tough material.

With the Cold War at its height, the Americans and the Soviets were racing to develop a portable hydrogen bomb. Both sides had already tested prototypes—the United States in November 1952, the Soviets in August 1953. There was talk of a third and final world war. us consumption of industrial diamonds had risen tenfold during the Second World War and was still on that upward trajectory in the early 1950s. The Americans assumed that a similar demand existed in the Soviet Union and strove to deprive the Soviets of diamonds from both legitimate and illegitimate sources. While many of the diamonds being smuggled out of Sierra Leone and elsewhere in Africa were of gem quality, smugglers were also discovered carrying industrial diamonds. At talks in Paris in 1950, the United States told its allies that it had learned there was a connection between the diamond dies being imported by the Soviet Union and the Soviet atomic energy program.

The possibility that the communists were involved in diamond smuggling also resonated with industrialists in Africa, who were casting around for the masterminds behind the illicit trade. In addition to using industrial diamonds to build arms, the Soviets could also be using diamonds to support various independence movements in Africa. Sir Ernest and his fellow industrialists feared the emergence of Soviet-backed communist governments, whose first move once in power could well be to nationalize key industries such as mining and manufacturing. Thus, diamond smuggling represented a double threat to Sir Ernest and De Beers: it undercut corporate profits and the stability of the monopoly, and it also put in peril the capitalist structure that made them rich.

Sir Percy was aware of both the American intelligence and the fears of African industrialists when he took the job. If the Soviets really were involved, who better to head the anti-smuggling operation than someone whose entire career at MI5 had been consumed with the fight against communist spies? Sir Percy had left the British secret service with an abiding hatred of the communists. If senior civil servants had not quashed the idea, he would have spent his retirement touring universities and colleges, preaching against the evils of communism. He had also planned to write a book on how the Western response to communism could be strengthened. That too had been halted by senior civil servants, who did not want the ex-spymaster inadvertently providing the Soviets with a glimpse into Western thinking. Sir Percy was left spoiling for a fight with his former adversaries. Although he was never explicit about the Soviet involvement in diamond smuggling, always describing his chief targets in general terms such as "the big shots of the international smuggling racket," the men who worked for him during his diamond security days were in no doubt about whom they were ultimately fighting. John Collard, a lawyer who followed Sir Percy from MI5 to Africa, once showed author Ian Fleming a map of smuggling routes out of Africa. One of the major lines terminated behind the Iron Curtain. Fleming, the creator of James Bond, wrote a rare non-fiction book called *The Diamond Smugglers* based on information Collard gave him.

The Soviets did have some diamonds from domestic production, although this fact was not widely known at the time. Production had begun in the 1940s but was not nearly enough to meet the massive demands of Soviet industry, which mirrored those in the United States. US efforts to deprive the Soviets of diamonds and diamond tools were having an impact, and the government in Moscow was growing increasingly desperate to procure industrial stones. The *New York Times* ran an item in September 1957 that quoted unnamed sources who insisted that US$30 million worth of diamonds were being smuggled from Africa to the Soviet Union every year. This might explain the lengths to which Sir Percy was prepared to go to stop the smuggling.

By July 1954, Sir Percy had decided that what he needed was a quasi-private army. He called in at the Foreign Office in London to argue for the creation of a new government police force that would be funded by Sierra Leone Selection Trust but that would operate as a government body, with all the powers that entailed. Its members would be armed, and its mission would be to track down and stop those who were smuggling the stolen gems out of the country. In effect, it would be a re-creation of the Diamond Mines Protection Force of the 1930s. But Sir Percy's idea was thrown out by officials who, ignoring the historical precedent, worried that such a force would place the Sierra Leonean government under obligation to the diamond monopoly. British colonial officials were not comfortable approving a public-private initiative when they were just about to depart. Corporate funding of new police posts was acceptable, but financing an entire police force was not.

The official British response to Sir Percy was slightly schizophrenic. At the lower levels, officials had their eye on the fragile political situation in Sierra Leone and did not want to jeopardize the colony's move to independence. Yet officials at the upper levels gave Sir Percy special treatment. He was provided with secret information that others were not, invited to government meetings on diamond smuggling and granted access to diplomatic telegraph facilities when he was travelling in Africa. While his role as the former head of MI5 would account for some of these privileges, the British government had two reasons to want Sir Percy to succeed. The first was strictly monetary. For many years, De Beers had used London as the centre of its international operations. Rough diamonds from all over the world were brought to Britain and then sold through the Central Selling Organization to dealers and cutters abroad. This trade was sizable and represented a significant boost to the value of sterling. Britain was loath to lose it to another country, which Sir Ernest sometimes hinted might happen. If helping Sir Percy would keep Sir Ernest on side, then this was a small price for the British government to pay. The second reason was that the British were under tremendous pressure from the Americans to prevent diamonds from making their way behind the Iron Curtain. With anti-communist hysteria being whipped up in the United States by people like Senator Joseph McCarthy, American diplomats were asking their allies to take a hard line with the Soviets.

In a draft chapter from the book Sir Percy had hoped to publish on combatting communism, a copy of which survives at the Public Records Office outside London, he outlines his approach. "To meet this attack, there are two main tasks to be performed at one and the same time," he writes. "On one side, we must identify the enemy; find out who he is, where he is and how he works: pursue and defeat him. On the other side, we must look at the enemy's targets and take every step we can to obstruct his aims. Carried out simultaneously, these tasks are complementary and support each other step by step." Substitute the words "diamond smuggler" for "enemy," and the same phrase could be used to describe Sir Percy's new plan.

He decided to set up his own private spy service. Known as the International Diamond Security Organization (IDSO), it was a smaller, private-sector version of the spy service he had once run for Britain. Sir Percy established offices in London, Johannesburg, Freetown and Antwerp, with headquarters in his hometown of Eastbourne. "To put an international gang of crooks out of action, an international security organisation is essential," he wrote in his memoirs. At least financing wasn't a problem, which must have been a welcome change for him seeing as he had always operated under budget constraints at MI5 and, before that, as a municipal chief constable. He told a group of senior civil servants in London, just after taking the job, that as far as his employer was concerned, money was no object. Sir Ernest cared only that Sir Percy stem what he described as "a tidal wave" of illicit diamonds. Sir Percy did not share with the assembled group of officials the methods he planned to employ.

At the top of the IDSO were a handful of former MI5 men who had worked with Sir Percy in the past. Trust was always a big concern with the former spymaster, and there were only a few people who had earned his. One of them was Collard, the lawyer from MI5. Collard described to author Ian Fleming how he was enlisted by Sir Percy to fight diamond smuggling: "One day in early '54 my old chief—he'd just retired—invited me to lunch at his club and asked me if I'd leave Military Intelligence and join a team to get after the diamond smugglers. We were to be paid by De Beers—big salaries and all expenses. I was tired of routine and, anyway, the late 30s and early 40s are a good time for a man to change his job." Collard and the other MI5 men were to help develop overall strategy. IDSO representatives visited the major diamond centres of the world, including

Beirut, to find out where the smuggled diamonds were heading. They worked with local police forces, including those in Sierra Leone, and with security guards from De Beers and the other diamond companies. Relations between the IDSO and corporate security teams were often tense. The corporate employees saw the very existence of Sir Percy's group as a comment on their own effectiveness. Managers at Sierra Leone Selection Trust also hindered co-operation. They were miffed that Sir Ernest had not only not consulted them, but indeed had not even told them that Sir Percy had been hired until months after the fact.

The national police agencies of African countries affected by diamond smuggling were also ambivalent about the IDSO, although they were happy to avail themselves of the information gathered by Sir Percy's agents. Their intelligence was compiled in a central registry in Johannesburg, where it was available to any interested police force. At the same time, however, the police recognized that the IDSO was a commercial entity whose loyalties might not always coincide with those of government. Delegates at a meeting of police officials held in Accra in 1955 discussed but then discarded the idea of using the IDSO registry as their central point of information on international diamond smuggling. This rejection at the official level helped undermine the IDSO's long-term survival.

Not too far below Collard and the ex-MI5 types were rougher characters prepared to do the dirty work of the organization. Sir Percy had used men of less than sterling character throughout his years in policing. He had never been reluctant to employ whatever tactics and people a job demanded. When he was confronted with continued communist agitation during his time as chief constable in Glasgow, he set up a group of informants known as the C Division Specials, who included pimps, prostitutes, thieves and other denizens of the underworld. The information they supplied kept the Glasgow police one step ahead of the agitators. In another example of his flexible approach, Sir Percy brought to an end a particularly violent outbreak of gang warfare in Glasgow by having some of the key gangsters committed to a mental institution. They were released with the threat that if they continued their gangland wars they would be sent back to the institution permanently. These techniques, while unconventional and quite possibly illegal, worked.

The IDSO hired scores of operatives to identify the smugglers and discover their methods. One such operative was J.H. du Plessis, a former South African policeman. In describing his work in his book *Diamonds Are Dangerous*, du Plessis painted himself as a noble warrior in the global contest between good and evil. He said his undercover activities exposed "diamond-smuggling networks with globe-encompassing tentacles which embrace some of the world's most dangerous criminals and succor murderous political intrigues stemming from behind the Iron Curtain." In reality, his job was to make friends with petty thieves and small-time smugglers to pick up information about them and the people they dealt with. He did this by hanging out in the bars frequented by smugglers, buying drinks and offering cash for their illicit goods.

Buying smuggled diamonds in large quantities was a new strategy— police forces had never had the necessary funds to buy diamonds from smugglers. The IDSO not only set about making purchases, it also promised those who helped it recover stones a payment equal to one-third their value. Paying informants for information on smuggling had been done before in Sierra Leone and elsewhere in Africa, but never on this scale. Sierra Leone Selection Trust paid 15 per cent of the value of returned stolen gems. Sir Percy and the IDSO had an estimated US$5 million to be used for payments to smugglers and informants.

Though Sir Percy's men co-operated with police at times, they often kept information on smugglers and dealers secret until those contacts had been exploited to the furthest extent possible. The Sierra Leonean police were not happy to learn that IDSO operatives were offering to buy stones from illicit diamond miners. They found out about the arrangement when two men, one of whom was a Lebanese gangster called Dip Mansour, were arrested while taking diamonds to an IDSO operative. Mansour had thirty-two gems and an unlicensed revolver in his possession, and the other man, Sidi Bey, had four hundred industrial diamonds. The

Lebanese diamond community was outraged that the IDSO was buying stones that would ordinarily pass through the hands of Lebanese middlemen, and they suspected the operative had tipped off the police. But judging from Police Chief Bill Syer's reaction, the operative had clearly not informed him and his officers of his activities. Syer had called the local IDSO representative, Jack McLintic, to his office and expressed his displeasure at not being given a heads-up on what the local operatives were doing. He was the one who had to deal with the unrest in the Lebanese community caused by IDSO activities.

IDSO money allowed operatives to live a lifestyle that they could otherwise not afford. Du Plessis was stationed in Lusaka, Northern Rhodesia (now Zambia), where he hung out at the racetrack, drank Scotch and bet on horses in order to fit in with the smugglers. His first purchase was from three Africans who had come across the border from Katanga in what was then the Belgian Congo. They sold him 1,000 carats of industrial diamonds and 350 carats in gems. Pleased with himself, he flew to Johannesburg to turn in his haul, but there he was told by his employers that this constituted a small package and that he should be looking for larger deals. He went back and spent the next year in places like Elisabethville (now Lubumbashi) in the Belgian Congo, living in the finest hotels and seeking out the company of illicit diamond dealers. He also broke into the homes and offices of suspected smugglers, wiretapped their phones and roughed up suspects when other methods did not work. But du Plessis looked like a saint compared with Fouad Kamil, a mercenary also known as Flash Fred, who was ready, willing and able to do just about anything for money, up to and including killing people. His recruitment in the fight against diamond smuggling was one the Oppenheimer family would later regret.

Kamil was the son of a Lebanese trader who had moved his family to Liberia to take advantage of import-export opportunities. Kamil stayed on after his father left, working for an import-export business and eventually opening his own store in 1950 at Robertsport near the border with Sierra Leone. In his autobiography, *The Diamond Underworld*, published in 1979, he said he ran an innocent business, catering to hunters and locals, selling food and supplies such as shotguns, hardware, steel traps and materials for turbans and dresses. The Liberian border near Robertsport, however, was also a key transit point for diamond smugglers from Sierra Leone, a fact of which Kamil was undoubtedly aware when he set up his business. While smuggling would not take off in a big way until the mid-1950s, smugglers would have been among his most important customers from the start.

According to Kamil, he was minding his own business, tending his shop in Robertsport, when he was asked for help by a diamond smuggler who needed to pay a bribe to the Liberian officer who had caught him crossing the border. Kamil loaned him the money and did not even take the diamonds as collateral. When the smuggler failed to repay the debt, putting the solvency of the store at risk, Kamil said he suddenly saw what evil men the diamond smugglers were. He declared war on all smugglers and decided to close the border to them by waging a campaign of terror. That, at least, is his version of events. It is far more likely that his change of career came after he realized that relieving smugglers of their diamonds was vastly more profitable than being a humble shopkeeper.

Kamil trawled the bars of Monrovia, rounding up young Europeans, Americans and Africans to make up a mercenary force. Many were drug addicts or alcoholics. "Raymond from Yugoslavia was pushing drugs at the Bamboo [bar], his friend Martin sold drinks there and Benga, a Gambian artist, drew caricatures and drank smoke water [a local brew]," Kamil said of the first three to join him. Former sailors, pimps, army deserters, dropouts and people just looking for adventure would also join Kamil's ragtag army. They were based in Sierra Leone near the border on a hill overlooking the main path taken by diamond smugglers through the forest. There were no towns, villages or roads in the immediate vicinity. With their machetes, Kamil's men cut trails through the thick vegetation between the camp and the smugglers' path, being careful to leave about two metres of bush between the end of their trail and the path. This green buffer zone allowed them to stand close to the path without being seen and gave them the advantage of surprise in an ambush.

The first attack was on a group of five Europeans, each wearing a belt stuffed with diamonds. Kamil sold the diamonds in Monrovia and used the money to buy side arms, ammunition, dynamite and two tommy guns. "We used some of the dynamite to make mines, which we laid between the camp and the smugglers' trail in case of surprise attack," he said. "The rest we kept for use as crude hand grenades." More attacks brought in more diamonds, and Kamil was able to attract more recruits and buy ammunition and dynamite. "We opened up more secret trails, laid more minefields, made more hand grenades." It was turning into a lucrative operation. But Kamil's activities were gaining him powerful enemies, including the diamond producers, who did not like to see their precious stones benefiting anyone but themselves. While the men who controlled the smuggling operation plotted to kill him, the diamond producers took an alternate route. They decided to do a deal with Kamil and turn his murderous attacks to their advantage.

Kamil first learned of their intentions when he was contacted by a Sierra Leonean police inspector who told him that people in Freetown wanted to talk to him. There, Kamil met Bernard Nealon, the assistant commissioner of the Sierra Leone police, and Charles Ashton, an executive of the Diamond Corporation, a De Beers subsidiary that handled the buying and selling of stones. Sir Percy was not at this meeting, and Kamil leaves it unclear in his memoirs whether the ex-spymaster knew of this first meeting between the mercenary and Oppenheimer's man, Ashton.

Nealon, in his laundered and pressed uniform, suggested that Kamil, who had been living rough in the jungle, might want to take a shower before he met Ashton, whom Nealon described as someone "who will play the most important part in your future." The unkempt highway robber insisted on coming as he was. He was ushered into an air-conditioned office—a luxury in the steaming heat of Sierra Leone in the 1950s—and invited to sit in a soft leather chair. He had already been primed by intermediaries who had told him that he had powerful supporters on the international level and that he would make a fortune if he played his cards right. Ashton played to Kamil's vanity by holding up a recent newspaper with the front-page headline "Kamil Strikes Again." "How do you do it?" Ashton asked. "You must tell me all about it some day. But first we must make you comfortable. Have you had lunch?" When the highwayman said no, a three-course meal was brought in for him. Kamil was impressed.

Over lunch, the young executive told Kamil why he had been invited to Freetown. "We are supposed to be in control of the diamond industry in this country," said Ashton. "We spend a great deal of money to help develop Sierra Leone. But our efforts are being hampered, as you know, by parasites from across the [Liberian] border, who corrupt our miners and filch our profits. We've even gone to the length of opening up buying offices to buy back the diamonds which have been stolen from our concessions and so discourage the illicit diamond trade. But nothing seemed to be effective until you, Mr. Kamil, moved to the border. I can tell you, your actions have been carefully observed. From our point of view you have sorted out at least some of our problems. And so it was decided to invite you here and see if we could . . . How shall I put it? . . . Shall we say co-operate to our mutual advantage?"

As Kamil would sum it up later, his men were going to do the diamond company's dirty work "since we were more efficient in stopping the diamond smuggling than they were or the colonial police were. We were going to be paid to do what I had set out to do on my own." That was true up to a point. The difference was that the diamond producers wanted Kamil to turn over to them whatever gems he recovered from the smugglers instead of selling them in Monrovia as he had been doing. In return, they would pay him one-third of the value of his loot. What the diamond producers wanted was to ensure that smuggled diamonds were not leaking onto the world market, undermining the Diamond Corporation's price. The fact that Kamil was killing people, however, did not even enter the discussion, at least not according to Kamil's recollections. While Kamil might have been able to make more money selling the stones himself, there was less risk in the new arrangement. He would have one less enemy to worry about and would enjoy unofficial police protection in Sierra Leone. "My private army would be considered as part of the security force," said

Kamil, adding that it was the diamond company's security efforts he was joining, not those of the Sierra Leonean police. Kamil became part of Sir Percy's greater effort in late 1955 or early 1956—Kamil is vague on the date. When his activities came to light many years later, De Beers put out a press statement saying that he had never been employed by either De Beers or Anglo American. This is undoubtedly true, but the statement does not cover the possibility that he was working for one of the parent company's numerous subsidiaries, such as the Diamond Corporation, or for the IDSO. De Beers later made some payments to Kamil that were never adequately explained.

Just what did Kamil's part in the efforts against diamond smuggling involve? One report described a particularly bloody ambush that took place when a caravan of about twelve smugglers came into a clearing near the border and prepared to cross the Mano River into Liberia. Until the advent of Kamil, smugglers travelled in smaller groups. Now, however, they were banding together for safety. Catching them meant a greater haul for the mercenaries. The group in question wandered unknowingly onto a minefield that Kamil and his men had laid. The mines detonated and the smugglers dashed about in panic, only to be mowed down by the mercenaries' hunting rifles. Those who survived the initial onslaught were only too happy to hand over their diamonds. It is difficult to say how many of Kamil's victims lie mouldering in unmarked graves in the border area. Several hundred would be a conservative guess. More than a thousand would be more likely, given the extent of smuggling by both Lebanese and Africans across the border in this period. Kamil has never given a body count, and the men he employed slunk back to the bars and drug dens they came from when the IDSO was disbanded in 1957.

A series of events beginning in 1954 eventually changed the course of Sir Percy's employment by Sir Ernest. The first was the Soviet discovery of a major source of diamonds in Siberia. It turned out to be the first of many such discoveries. Though inhospitable weather and terrain meant it would take several years to begin large-scale mining, the Soviets were now finally assured of an adequate supply of stones. An article in the *New York Times* in August 1956 predicted that full-scale production in the Siberian fields would be achieved by 1958. That meant there was less incentive for the communists to smuggle stones.

The second important event happened in 1955 when General Electric Company in the United States announced the start of production of synthetic diamonds. The real thing would no longer be the only option for industry. And it was assumed that if an American company could produce synthetic diamonds, so could the Soviets. The third event also took place in 1955: the Soviets exploded their second hydrogen bomb, putting them on par with, if not slightly ahead of, the United States. The race to build a workable bomb was now over, and one of the key reasons for the US diamond embargo against the Soviets no longer existed.

The fourth event occurred when Selection Trust was forced to give up its monopoly, pressured by both the British government and the increasing number of Africans in positions of power in Sierra Leone. The company tried to sell its rights back to the colonial government for £10 million but was told rather curtly that that was not on. In the end, the company received something in the neighbourhood of £1.5 million and was able to keep the choicest diamond areas for itself. As these areas were much smaller than the original monopoly, it was easier for the company to control diamond smuggling.

The Sierra Leone government began issuing individual mining licences in 1956. Local diggers, some of whom had worked for smugglers in the past, could now mine legally. De Beers set up buying offices in the diamond fields, which meant that local miners could now sell their stones close to home and did not have to make the trek across the border to Liberia. Though these changes put pressure on smuggling, they did not eliminate it completely.

Sir Percy acknowledged the significance of the new state of affairs, and was quoted by Anthony Hocking in *Oppenheimer and Son*: "The natives, who only a few months ago were digging these stones illegally, can now do so legally under licence and get a fair price for them instead of being exploited. The revenue of the Sierra Leone government must go up enormously because diamonds which may be worth four million pounds a year are now declared to them. The Diamond Corporation and De Beers will benefit because we have a buyer in the country and can get these stones for the legitimate markets of the world."

The final and most important event in the diamond industry as far as Sir Percy was concerned occurred in November 1957 when Sir Ernest died. As his health had worsened in the months leading up to his death, he had gradually handed over control of his diamond empire to his son Harry. Once firmly ensconced in the position, Harry wasted no time in summoning Sir Percy.

"We don't need you any more," Harry told the surprised and disconcerted ex-spymaster. Sir Percy told his family that he felt as if the junior Oppenheimer could not get rid of him fast enough. The IDSO offices were closed, and the hundred or so people on the payroll were sent packing. Harry gave responsibility for diamond security and anti-smuggling initiatives back to the in-house De Beers security team. There was nothing left for Sir Percy to do but return to England. He was a man accustomed to finishing what he had started. The family motto, *Selito teneto si leto*, meant "see it through." His abrupt dismissal left a sour taste in his mouth.

But it was not the last Harry was to hear of the operatives who had worked for the IDSO. Just as Machiavelli had warned in *The Prince*, mercenaries such as Kamil have a tendency to plunder their employers when no other likely targets are available. Kamil claimed that he was re-employed for a time by De Beers security in the 1960s, although the company denied this. He also said he was asked to gather information by acting as a buyer of smuggled gems and was rewarded handsomely when he recovered them. After his employment ended, however, he felt he was still owed money. He started sending a series of threatening letters to the Oppenheimers, and when that produced no response, he hijacked an airplane on which he believed Harry's son-in-law, Gordon Waddell, was travelling. Waddell was not on the aircraft, and Kamil was eventually caught and imprisoned.

A series of subsequent events, however, lent credence to his claim that he had a connection to De Beers. The first was his release from prison in

Malawi after serving only twenty-two months of an eleven-year sentence. Rumours began to swirl that De Beers had paid the Malawi government to let him go. Kamil, with four accomplices, then tried to blackmail the company for £1 million, which was what he said he was still owed. Though Kamil escaped prosecution, his four accomplices were caught and tried in London. At the trial, four senior managers from Anglo American and its sister company De Beers gave evasive answers about the exact nature of the relationship between the companies and Kamil. And their testimonies were contradictory.

Sidney Spiro, a director of Anglo American, said he had no knowledge of any relationship that Kamil might have had with the diamond empire. He was also unaware of Hocking's *Oppenheimer and Son*, which had described Kamil's hiring by men working for Sir Percy. Hocking had been given access to the Oppenheimer archives for his book research. Colonel Floris Van Zijl, security advisor to Anglo American and De Beers, then took the stand and confirmed that Kamil had been an informant for the company in the 1970s and had been handsomely paid for his efforts. Van Zijl said he had made a subsequent payment of £50,000 to Kamil in Cyprus in 1974 because the former mercenary had threatened to blow up company buildings and assassinate the chairman and members of his family. When questioned by the judge, who appeared skeptical, Van Zijl said the company had made the payment only because it was frightened of Kamil. Taken at face value, this was exceedingly odd behaviour for a company, given that it would confront many such extortion attempts and could not possibly hope to pay them all off.

Whatever the relationship was between Kamil, the diamond companies and Sir Percy's security operation, the benefits it had provided for Anglo American/De Beers were short-lived. Once Kamil left the scene, the illegal transborder shipments picked up again. To this day, smuggling remains a problem on the border between Sierra Leone and Liberia because it still represents an easy route to riches for impoverished people. The use of armed force never changed that reality.

As for Sir Percy, the IDSO, which he referred to as his last great campaign, was neither great nor his last. Back in England he found work
advising other companies on security. In his last major project, he helped
Wells Fargo set up an armoured car service in Britain called Security
Express Ltd.

The Oppenheimers remain at the pinnacle of the diamond world.
Nicholas Oppenheimer now controls his grandfather's empire and has
found a new tactic for stemming the flow of illegal gems. In the late 1990s,
a campaign by several non-governmental organizations, including Global
Witness in London and Partnership Africa Canada in Ottawa, publicized
the fact that smuggled diamonds were funding rebel groups in Africa. The
negative publicity surrounding these so-called blood diamonds threatened to cast a pall over the entire diamond market. De Beers reacted by
branding its diamonds to show that they had been legally mined and had
never passed through rebel hands. It is still too soon to say whether this
move will solve the problem that ultimately proved too difficult for Sir
Percy Sillitoe to crack.

CHAPTER FOUR

UNION MINIÈRE IN KATANGA

IN THE LIVES OF THE DOOMED THERE IS ALWAYS A DEFINING MOMENT. For Union Minière du Haut-Katanga, it was July 12, 1960. Decisions made on that day would embroil the copper producer in a sordid civil war and irrevocably alter its future in the heart of Africa.

The day at Union Minière's head office in Brussels began with the arrival of a telegram from the company's African headquarters in the Congolese province of Katanga. The Congo was in chaos, and the men who controlled Union Minière were anxiously awaiting news. Their fortunes depended on the copper-cobalt empire they had been building for over half a century in that country. Now that empire was threatened. An army revolt had erupted within days of the former Belgian colony's independence ceremonies on July 1, 1960, plunging the country into turmoil and sending Europeans, including some Union Minière staff, fleeing for their lives. Dire news dispatches from the Congo talked of rape, murder, plunder and spreading anarchy.

The telegram that arrived July 12, sent by Aimé Marthoz, one of the company's most senior people, contained more disturbing news: "GOVERNMENT OF KATANGA HAS DECLARED INDEPENDENCE ON RADIO COLLÈGE MONDAY [JULY 11] AT 8 PM. WE NEED TO HELP THE NEW STATE BY EVERY MEANS POSSIBLE." Marthoz went on to outline how the company could help politically, by pressing the Belgian government to recognize Katanga immediately, and financially, by advancing money to the

Katangan government to fill its depleted coffers. "YOU MUST USE EVERY MEANS TO REALIZE THE PROGRAM MENTIONED ABOVE," he wrote. And he ended his telegram with the terse command "INFORM THE GOVERNOR."

The governor was Paul Gillet, who headed both Union Minière and its parent company, the Société Générale de Belgique. The latter was a powerful financial and industrial conglomerate that was older than Belgium itself and that had connections with the royal household. As governor, Gillet carried great weight and prestige in Belgium, a country Karl Marx had once described as "a paradise for capitalists." Gillet's first course of action was to telephone King Baudoin and ask him to use his influence to ensure that the Belgian government did nothing to interfere with Katanga's secession. That done, Gillet convened a meeting of the Société Générale's board of directors, known as the Conseil d'Administration, which included eight members who also sat on the Conseil d'Administration of Union Minière.

The men gathered under the glittering chandeliers of Société Générale's panelled boardroom that night shared the same world view. Staunchly Catholic and violently anti-communist, they had grown fabulously wealthy through the colonial system that Belgium had imposed on the Congo. They were fiercely proud of the empire they had hacked out of the African bush. Through Union Minière, they ruled Katanga. Their reach extended into every corner of daily life. Births, marriages, health care, education, training, housing, even hobbies were all fashioned and co-ordinated by them with one aim in mind: to ensure the continuous and ever-increasing production of copper. And their system worked. Since the first copper ingots had been smelted in 1911 by Europeans in Katanga, production had grown by leaps and bounds. By 1960, Union Minière was the third largest producer of copper in the world and the largest producer of cobalt. They were looking forward to another banner year.

The board members were damned if they would lose it all just because Congolese prime minister Patrice Lumumba, whom they believed to be both anti-clerical and communist, could not control his new country. The only way they saw of protecting their copper kingdom was to do as Marthoz suggested and back Lumumba's secessionist rival, Moise Tshombe, the self-appointed president of independent Katanga. The Conseil, whose deliberations were kept secret, voted unanimously to give Tshombe as much political and financial leverage as they could muster. A first payment of 1.25 billion Belgian francs was to be dispatched immediately, with the promise of much more to come.

Louis Wallef, one of the eight members who served on both boards, telegraphed the Conseil's decision to Marthoz on July 14: "FOLLOWING OFFICIAL CONTACTS, WE CERTIFY AGREEMENT IN PRINCIPLE WITH RECOGNIZING INDEPENDENCE." He instructed Marthoz to organize a government, an army, a currency and a constitution for the new state. The gods of Union Minière had spoken.

That same day, the United Nations Security Council met in New York and agreed to send peacekeeping troops to the Congo. The stage was set for a confrontation between the copper company and the international force. Unlike the British South Africa Company and the rubber giants of the Congo, which were driven to their excesses by the ego and overwhelming ambition of single individuals—Cecil Rhodes and King Léopold, respectively—Union Minière demonstrated that even enterprises led by a collegial group could resort to armed force. There was no one man to blame for the company's actions. Collectively, these men were unable to recognize that their world had changed forever, and they thought that violence would preserve the status quo.

To understand how Union Minière came to dominate and then betray the Congo, it is necessary to take a step back to the early twentieth century, when the Belgian government reluctantly took over King Léopold II's profitable personal colony, the Congo Free State, in 1908. The new rulers of the colony—in reality a triumvirate of state, church and industry— were determined to eliminate the worst excesses of Léopold, whose rape of the Congo for its ivory and rubber resources had become an international scandal. They attempted to build a different, more stable society, with primary education, health care and housing for those living in the industrial centres. The people of the Congo, whose numbers would grow to about 14 million by 1960, were undoubtedly better off under direct Belgian rule than they had been under the king. But the prime benefici- aries of the new colonial order were the giant industrial trusts set up by Léopold in 1906 just before he lost his grip on the colony. Chief among these trusts was Union Minière du Haut-Katanga.

Europeans had known there was copper in Katanga ever since the Portuguese explorer Francesco Jose Maria de Lacerdas mentioned in a 1798 report seeing natives smelting ingots. But it wasn't until 1892 that Léopold sent a geologist, Jules Cornet, to investigate. Cornet confirmed that Katanga was a treasure trove—"a geological scandal," as he put it. Léopold asked him to keep quiet until the borders of the Congo Free State were officially fixed. Once Léopold had consolidated his hold, he began setting up a series of resource and holding companies backed by friendly financiers, much as he had done to exploit the Congo's rubber and ivory resources. Through the Compagnie du Congo pour le Commerce et l'Industrie, the Compagnie du Katanga and the Comité Special du Katanga, Léopold and his backers had complete control of the province. But they needed investment to generate profits.

During the summer of 1906, Léopold held a series of meetings aboard his yacht, *Albertine*, with key advisers, including Jean Jadot, then head of the powerful financial and industrial conglomerate Société Générale de Belgique. Out of these discussions came the decision to cre- ate three new companies to further develop the production potential of the Congo: Société Internationale Forestière et Minière du Congo to mine diamonds in the Kasai region, Compagnie du Chemin de Fer du Bas-Congo au Katanga to build an internal rail system across the country, and Union Minière du Haut-Katanga to mine copper in a concession the size of Belgium and Luxembourg combined. By 1928, Société Générale was the controlling shareholder of all three of these companies.

John Gunther, an American writer who travelled extensively in Africa, described Société Générale in the 1950s as the kind of colossus that might be envisaged if the House of Morgan, Anaconda Copper, the

Mutual Life Insurance Company of New York, the Pennsylvania Railroad and various companies producing agricultural products were lumped together, with the US government as a heavy partner. Through various subsidiaries, Société Générale also had interests in cotton, sugar, pharmaceutical products, automobiles, beer, railroads, insurance, diamonds, cattle, shipping, cold storage and the Belgian airline Sabena. By 1960, the financial conglomerate controlled, directly or indirectly, fully 70 per cent of the Congolese economy. Union Minière was the jewel in this gem-laden crown. Its copper and cobalt holdings were so extensive and its profits so vast that it was paying between 45 and 50 per cent of all of the Congo's taxes.

Among Union Minière's early copper pioneers were two men who would one day help run the company: Jules Cousin and Edgar Sengier. Cousin came from a farming dynasty in the Ardennes connected to that of Jean Jadot, head of Société Générale. He had first approached Union Minière for a job in 1909 but was told he had to do several things before they would consider him for a job: get training in electrical engineering, geology, metallurgy and chemistry, and learn English. The Katangan operations were being run at the time by American and British engineers. A British company, Tanganyika Concessions Ltd. (TANKS), owned shares in Union Minière and supplied managers in the early days. To work for them, Cousin would have to speak their language. He returned just over a year later, fluent in English and with the requisite diplomas. Union Minière promptly sent him off to Elisabethville, the capital of Katanga, where he arrived in early 1911, one of the first Belgian engineers in the area. Until then, this remote corner of the Congo had not appealed to young Belgians looking for adventure.

Cousin was not warmly received by his American boss, who gave him a tent to sleep in and told him to count bricks. Bored with the tedious task, Cousin asked to be given a job as a workman. He was tending the furnace the day the first copper ingots were smelted. From that lowly start, he worked his way up, gradually moving closer to the centre of power in the company, which became more of a Belgian-run entity as the years passed and the Americans and British either left or were forced out.

When Sengier joined the company in 1911, he was already thirty years old and a seasoned engineer with experience building a railroad in China. He and Cousin worked as a team in the 1920s, rescuing Union Minière from crisis when copper prices collapsed as stocks from the first World War were liquidated and copper mines all over the world shut down. Instead of closing operations and putting nine hundred Europeans and twelve thousand Africans out of work, Sengier and Cousin came up with an audacious plan to modernize operations and double output. Union Minière's copper production increased from 18,962 tonnes in 1920 to 43,362 tonnes in 1922. They weathered the copper crisis and earned the company's undying respect.

Their efforts during the Second World War provide further insight into their business acumen. Sengier and Cousin ensured that the war years were profitable ones for Union Minière, which not only churned out copper and cobalt for the Allied war effort—the company shipped 800,000 tonnes of copper to Great Britain between 1940 and 1944 and provided the cobalt for the US bombs used at Hiroshima and Nagasaki— but also supplied the United States with uranium.

Uranium had been discovered in the company concession in 1913 when a prospector working for Union Minière followed up stories about Africans coating themselves in luminescent mud. Pitchblende, the mineral form of uranium oxide, was found in significant quantities at Shinkolobwe, near where the town of Jadotville later grew, 100 kilometres northwest of Elisabethville. What set this pitchblende apart from ore already being mined in Canada and the United States was its high uranium content, averaging between 60 and 65 per cent compared to the 0.2 to 0.3 per cent of the North American ore. The richness of the Katanga ore allowed Union Minière to extract more radium per tonne of uranium than its competitors. Radium was used to make luminous dials, gauges and instruments, and the company cornered the world market until a slump in prices caused the mine to close in 1937.

Union Minière was left wondering what to do with its 6,000-tonne supply of pitchblende.

Sengier became aware of the potential value of his stockpile in May 1939, when he was contacted by French and British teams working on the nuclear bomb. When the Germans occupied Belgium, he arranged for 1,200 tonnes of pitchblende to be sent to the United States for safekeeping. This prescient move meant that when he was asked by US officials three years later to supply material for the Manhattan Project, he was able to deliver within days. Union Minière supplied 4,000 tonnes of uranium to the United States between 1942 and 1944. And while the first shipment was sold at a reduced price, Union Minière drove a hard bargain for later deliveries, which included the addition of a 6 per cent export tax for the Congo. By 1945, the company was sitting on a cash mountain of 2.6 billion francs, compared with 400 million francs in 1939.

The Belgian government also benefited from Sengier's and Cousin's shrewdness. The dollars and sterling received for the uranium and copper shipments meant that the government in exile did not have to borrow foreign exchange from the Allies during the war. This allowed the Belgian economy to recover more quickly than its physically devastated and debt-ridden neighbours. Sengier and Cousin were recognized for the service they had rendered to Belgium, Britain and the United States. Both were decorated by US president Harry Truman. Within Union Minière they became legends.

In 1956, Union Minière du Haut-Katanga published a book to celebrate its fiftieth anniversary. Bound in green leather with gold lettering, it documents the key stages in the company's history. There is a picture of the pipe-smoking geologist Jules Cornet, who first mapped out the extent of the copper reserves. And there is a photo of Jules Cousin and Edgar Sengier, who look like half of a barbershop quartet, their hair slicked back and their moustaches gleaming. Sengier is scowling at the photographer as if he had more important things to do, while Cousin stands behind him, chest puffed out, looking young and proud. Despite their achievements, neither Sengier nor Cousin was a boastful man. They both studiously avoided the limelight. Cousin once told a friend that to live happily, one should live quietly. He was talking about not wanting publicity for his charitable donations, but the sentiment held true for his business life as well. Sengier once told a writer preparing an article on him that it was fine if the writer wanted to write a profile—as long as Sengier himself was kept out of it.

When Cousin and Sengier had first joined Union Minière, the company had been having trouble finding workers. The area where copper was found in abundance—a belt about 320 kilometres long and between 24 and 95 kilometres wide—was on a high plateau where the climate, while perfect for European habitation, was too cold for Africans, who were more accustomed to the hot and humid flatlands found in much of the rest of the country. When forced labour proved unsuccessful in the 1920s, they suggested what was then considered to be a revolutionary idea in Africa: improve living conditions for the workers. Union Minière spent an estimated US$150 million reorganizing its camps, inviting workers to bring their families (most work camps until then were restricted to male employees) and building hospitals and schools. Mothers were paid to keep their children in good health, and the company even helped arrange marriages and paid dowries. It also determined which hobbies its employees should pursue, such as soccer. All of this was done to keep the workers happy and the mines and installations fully staffed. Union Minière's objective was summed up by its motto, adopted in 1927: "Good health, good spirits and high productivity." A saying among the Katangan workers at the time gave a slightly different view of the situation: "On naît dans un berceau de l'UM. On est enterré dans un linceul de l'UM"—"We are born in a Union Minière cradle and we die in a Union Minière shroud."

Union Minière's labour shortage led to its adoption of race policies that appeared progressive to neighbouring colonial administrations. In Katanga, Africans operated shovels, cranes and bulldozers and crewed trains, all of which was unheard of in neighbouring Northern Rhodesia. This image of equality was misleading, however, for it covered only the lower-level positions. Africans were still barred from advancing beyond a certain point in the hierarchy of Union Minière. There were no Africans in management.

Sengier and Cousin did not devote all their time to improving the company's labour relations. Under their guidance, Union Minière took on an ambitious hydroelectric program that saw the construction of four major dams, all named after early European explorers in the region. The Franqui and Bia dams opened on the Lufira River in 1930 and 1945 respectively. The Delcommune and Le Marinel dams opened on the Lualaba river in 1952 and 1956. The last two were enormous. Behind the Delcommune stretched a 20,000-hectare artificial lake. Le Marinel, the most modern of the four dams, produced more power than the other three combined. The hydroelectric program cost an estimated 6 billion Belgian francs to build, and it produced between 2,012 and 2,778 million kilowatt hours of electricity—enough to electrify all the railroads in the area, light all the major towns, power all the mines and installations, and still have some left over to export to Northern Rhodesia. Their network of electrified train lines was larger than the Paris Métro system.

People visiting Elisabethville prior to the Congo crisis marvelled at its avenues lined with flowering jacaranda trees, at its neat housing in the European quarter, at its shops and boutiques along the main boulevard and—wonder of wonders in Africa at that time—at the lights that illuminated its streets at night. Visitors could find restaurants serving fresh lobster, swim or play golf at the local club or dance their cares away at one of the many night spots. All this had been wrought by Union Minière, whose smokestack at the Lubumbashi copper smelter dominated the Elisabethville horizon. At 150 metres, it was the third highest in the world.

The company men felt both proud of and proprietorial toward Katanga. In their eyes, they had created something from nothing. Copper and cobalt production from their main mines, located at Kipushi, Jadotville and Kolwezi, was booming. Reserves at Kolwezi alone were so great that Union Minière calculated it could continue producing copper at its current rate for one hundred years and there would still be copper left in the ground. Was it any wonder then that as late as January 1959, the company managers were still preparing for a future unchanged from the past? In an interview for the Congolese newspaper *L'Essor du Congo* that month Cousin said, "I am extremely confident about the future and I want to share my confidence with everyone. When people ask me about the future I tell them to continue investing in the Congo, as I myself am doing."

But as British prime minister Harold Macmillan so eloquently put it, a wind of change was blowing through Africa. The age of decolonization had arrived. It had started in Asia, with Indonesia attaining independence in 1945, the Philippines in 1946, and India in 1947. It then moved on to Africa, with independence for Libya in 1951, Sudan, Morocco and Tunisia in 1956, and Ghana in 1957. Anti-colonialist movements across sub-Saharan Africa were finding their voice. The Second World War played an important part, both symbolically and practically, in the rise of African nationalism. When both Belgium and France were occupied by the Germans, and Britain was forced to fight for its life, the image of the invincible colonial master was irreparably damaged. The war altered life in the colonies by stripping colonial administrations of Europeans for the war effort and placing demands on Africans for both human and natural resources. It was not just the copper and cobalt of Katanga that were much in demand but also the agricultural products of all the colonies. When the war ended, there was a general feeling among Africans that reciprocal action was required to acknowledge their contribution, action in the form of more rights and responsibilities for the colonized.

The war also changed the balance of global power. The former imperial powers had been weakened by their war efforts. Power was now in the hands of the United States and the Soviet Union, neither of which had a stake in continuing the imperial system. The two began courting prospective post-colonial successors in Africa, further undermining the colonial system. The creation of the United Nations, whose charter made reference to the equal rights and self-determination of peoples, was another blow to prevailing attitudes. Within the UN, the Afro-Asian group gained a public forum for their anti-colonialist demands.

Some imperial powers were quicker than others to take those demands to heart. Belgium was not among them. Though there were voices questioning colonial policy within the country, they did not carry the necessary weight to effect change. Belgian professor A.A.J. Van Bilsen wrote an article in 1956 recommending that the Congo be given its independence within thirty years. He was widely ridiculed and publicly attacked by a government minister. Having been initially hesitant to take over the Congo, the Belgian political and financial elite had grown attached to their profitable colony. The Congo's resources fed Belgian mills and factories. Its administration provided a training ground for ambitious officials. Its industries offered lucrative postings where officials could live in a style that was far beyond their means at home. The Congo was a dependable source of government revenue.

An unofficial estimate circulated at the time indicated that Belgium would lose substantial amounts of money if there were a complete break with the colony. There would be the cost of reintegrating the ten thousand colonial administrators into the Belgian government service. Pension payments would have to be made to retired administrators out of Belgian revenues, rather than those raised in the Congo. Payments on the Congo public debt, guaranteed by Belgium, would also have to be made by Belgian taxpayers instead of being raised in the colony. Belgium would lose its Congo exports, which made up 4.5 per cent of its total exports, and would suffer a drop of 30 per cent in the overseas operations of its transport and insurance firms. The financial incentives for maintaining a tight grip on the Congo were so great that Belgians initially preferred to ignore the changes taking place elsewhere in Africa and to go on believing that the Congo was a happy, peaceful colony.

But a series of events at the end of the 1950s shattered their reverie. The first was the end of the brutal war of independence in Algeria. Despite superior arms and numbers, France was defeated by the Algerians and was criticized in the United Nations for its policies—a message not lost on other Africans desiring independence.

Newly elected French president Charles de Gaulle then stunned other colonial powers when he announced during a visit to the French colony Congo-Brazzaville in August 1958 that French colonies could determine their own future. "Whoever wants independence can have it as soon as possible," he declared, acknowledging France's debt to the Africans who had rallied to its cause during the war. "France will not prevent it." With Brazzaville just across the river from the Congolese capital, Léopoldville, the momentous news spread quickly through the Belgian colony.

Belgium inadvertently lent a hand to aspiring Congolese nationalists when it held the World's Fair in 1958 and set up a Congolese human exhibit. King Léopold had done something similar in 1897, but times had changed and the use of fellow citizens in such a manner gave rise to resentment among the Congolese and fed the push for independence. The fair was also the first time that the Congolese had been allowed to come to Belgium in any significant numbers. Aside from showing them that Belgium was a country like any other, the trip allowed them to talk among themselves about the future of their country, something they could not do in the Congo because of its vast size and the oppressive colonial government. Thomas Kanza, a Congolese man who attended the fair as a tourist and later became a diplomat, noted that a type of "mental decolonization" had taken place there which made it hard for the Congolese to continue to accept the colonial yoke.

In December 1958 came another crucial event: the meeting of the All-African Peoples Conference in Accra, hosted by Kwame Nkrumah, head of newly independent Ghana. Nkrumah encouraged the three-man Congolese delegation, which included Patrice Lumumba, the future prime minister of the Congo, to fight for independence. After the meeting, Lumumba returned to the Congo and announced that independence was not to be regarded as a gift from Belgium but rather as a fundamental right of the Congolese people.

By the end of 1958, anti-colonialist pressure was building within the Congo. During that year, a number of political parties had grown in popularity. One of the oldest was the Alliance de Bakongo, or ABAKO, which had been calling for Belgium to hand over power since 1956. Its leader, Joseph Kasavubu, was widely seen as the father of the Congolese independence movement. But the party was limited by its concentrated tribal base in the western Congo and by its goal of reuniting the areas inhabited by the Kongo tribe, which were located in French, Belgian and Portuguese colonies.

The Mouvement National Congolais (MNC), created in October 1958 and led by Patrice Lumumba, differed from the other parties in that it sought support across tribal boundaries and presented a national program for the Congo. Lumumba, who was thirty-five years old in 1960, came from Stanleyville (now Kisangani) in the Congo interior, where he had been politically active for a number of years within the tight constraints imposed by the Belgian colonial authorities. Though political parties had been banned, the Congolese got around that by forming associations through which they gathered and discussed the problems facing their country. Lumumba was the chair of at least seven associations. Though he had only a primary education, he was an eloquent speaker and was quickly building a political base that cut across tribal lines. Identified early on by the authorities as a potential threat to their power, Lumumba was arrested and convicted of embezzling Post Office funds, a charge his supporters believed had been trumped up by the Belgians. On his release, he took a job as sales manager of a brewery in Léopoldville and used the opportunity to promote his own political ideas along with the brewery's Polar beer. It was in his role as leader of the Mouvement National Congolais that he attended Nkrumah's All-African Peoples Conference in Accra in December.

Despite the growing political agitation by various political parties within the colony, Belgian authorities were not yet ready to let go. It took a series of bloody riots in Léopoldville in January 1959 to force their hand. The riots began when a meeting of ABAKO was banned at the last minute by the Belgian mayor of Léopoldville, who feared political unrest. More than fifty people were killed and two hundred injured. The Belgian authorities panicked. Within days, King Baudoin promised that Belgium would lead the Congolese, without delays but also without precipitate haste, to "independence, prosperity and peace." An electoral timetable was hastily set out, scheduling elections in the Congo's six provinces in December 1959. National elections were to be held sometime afterward, the date still to be determined.

Although Europeans were not allowed to vote in the December elections, they tried to ensure that the outcome would be favourable to Belgian interests. Throughout 1959, other political parties were created, including the Parti Solidaire Africain (PSA), led by Antoine Gizenga, and the Parti National du Progrès (PNP). This last party, led by Paul Bolya, a medical assistant from Léopoldville, was so heavily backed by the colonial establishment that the Congolese took to calling it "Le Parti des Nègres Payés" ("the party for paid blacks").

In Katanga, there were two parties, both concerned mainly with provincial matters rather than national politics, and both tribally based. The Confédération des Associations du Katanga, or CONAKAT, was led by Moise Tshombe. It supported the continued Belgian presence in Katanga. The Association des Baluba du Katanga, or BALUBAKAT, headed by Jason Sendwe, was an offshoot of Tshombe's party. The two had split when CONAKAT had begun promoting xenophobic policies that called for the expulsion of Balubas, who had been brought to Katanga from the Kasai to work for Union Minière. As these Balubas were part of the same tribe that supported Sendwe in northern Katanga, Sendwe felt obliged to defend their interests.

Union Minière initially chose to fund both Tshombe's CONAKAT and Sendwe's BALUBAKAT until it became clear which of the two would better serve the company's interests. Sendwe's group lost Union Minière's support when it began to take an anti-European stance. It published a list of fifty Belgians who would have to leave or be liquidated after independence. European support swung decisively behind Tshombe.

If Lumumba was seen as the enemy of the colonial establishment, Tshombe was seen as its saviour. Educated by American Methodist missionaries, he was the son of a prominent businessman from the Lunda tribe in South Katanga. He spoke excellent French, got along well with Europeans and assured everyone at every opportunity that he was anti-communist. Such credentials were important if he hoped to attract Western backing during this Cold War era. Tshombe is often described as a successful businessman. He was, in fact, a failure. His father owned a string of shops, a hotel, a fleet of trucks and several cotton plantations, and had set his eldest son up in business. The son went bankrupt three times and had to be bailed out. When his father died in 1951, Tshombe took charge of the empire. But the businesses began to falter under his uncertain stewardship, and he decided to hand their management over to one of his seven brothers (his father had twelve children in all) and leave the world of business for that of politics. Here he found his métier. He had good tribal connections through his wife, the daughter of an impor-tant local chieftain, which gave him a ready-made political base among the Lunda tribe, which dominated South Katanga. From the beginning, CONAKAT received behind-the-scenes help not only from Union Minière, but also from other important European organizations, including one representing settlers. Katanga, with 32,000 Europeans out of a total pop-ulation of 1.6 million, was the only part of the Congo where there was a significant settler population. They wanted to ensure that their interests would be protected.

Even with such powerful backers, the CONAKAT party did not win the 1959 provincial election outright, securing only 11 per cent of the vote. But by some creative counting—Tshombe had trained as an accountant—CONAKAT leaders claimed that seats won by members of tribes who paid allegiance to the Lunda tribe should be included in their total. By their count, hotly contested by Sendwe, they had won 427 out of 484 seats and therefore the right to govern. Because the result was unclear, an amend-ment of the law governing elections was needed before Tshombe could assume the Katangan leadership. The Belgian parliament happily com-plied, cementing Tshombe's reputation as a Belgian puppet. Tshombe also had to promise that his government would include representatives of the Baluba of North Katanga. But he did not keep his word.

In January 1960, with the provincial elections over, the Belgian government hastily convened a round table in Brussels, where the colonized and the colonizers were to work out the political aspects of independence. Economic and financial matters would be left for a second round table in May. It was clear even at this late date that many senior members of the colonial elite expected to remain in control of the colony's affairs, with political independence only a pretence. Paul-Henri Spaak, Belgian foreign minister in the latter part of the Congo crisis, wrote bitterly in his memoirs of unidentified Belgians "too clever by half, who thought they would be able to hang on to all their possessions, while at the same time pretending they were giving them up." These calculating individuals, as he called them, combined with some idealists and weaklings, helped to make Congolese independence a mess from the very start.

Lumumba had to be let out of prison in the Congo to attend the first round table. He had been arrested in October for provoking violence and sentenced to six months in prison. Belgian authorities were compelled to include him in the meeting after several prominent Congolese threatened to boycott the conference if Lumumba were not present. Accompanying him was his secretary, Joseph Désiré Mobutu, a former soldier who had become a journalist. Mobutu—now better known as Mobutu Sese Seko—would later play a decisive role in the fate of Lumumba and that of the Congo itself.

The round table delegates represented all the major parties and groups in the Congo, and most would later hold high office in the country. In their haste to get rid of the Belgians, they insisted on an accelerated timetable for independence. By the time the conference broke up at the end of February, they had agreed to hold national elections in May and had set the date for sovereignty: June 30, 1960. They had four months to get ready. It was an impossible task.

One of the biggest challenges facing the Congolese was their lack of an educated class who could run the business of government or hold political office. Belgian attitudes toward the Congolese had changed very little since a government report, *The Annual Report of the Belgian*

Congo for 1915, had declared that "blacks are big children" who could not be relied on because of "their caprices." The Congolese were denied access to higher education until the 1950s, when universities were finally established in Léopoldville (1954) and Elisabethville (1956). By 1960, the two institutions had turned out only twenty-two graduates. If the four students who had attended university in Belgium were added, the total number of university graduates in the Congo at the time of independence was twenty-six. There were no Congolese doctors, dentists, judges, engineers or secondary-school teachers. Ian Scott, the British consul general before independence and later ambassador, praised the type of technical training provided by companies like Union Minière but voiced surprise that law studies had not even been allowed in the colony until 1958 because the Belgians had feared that law school would be a training ground for future politicians. This handicapped the new country from the start.

Thousands of Africans worked in the colonial administration, but they were almost entirely restricted to the lower levels. There were two exceptions, who reached the second highest administrative rank at independence, but they had been appointed late in 1959 and held non-essential posts: deputy commissioner general for information and deputy commissioner general for youth. Unlike in some colonies run by the British, there was no black elite waiting in the wings to take over when the colonizers left. The army, known at independence as the Force Publique, was led entirely by European officers. Neither the colony nor companies like Union Minière had prepared for the day when the Congolese would assume control of their own affairs.

After the round table, potential administrators—those who had some degree of education—were hurriedly sent to Belgium for crash courses. Within the Congo, a college of six commissioners was set up in March and given nominal control over key departments to give them some experience of governing. They were like a cabinet-in-waiting, training to take over the responsibilities that still rested with the Belgian governor general. This was a frantic time for the Congolese politicians. Not only were they expected to learn in four months how to run a country, but they were also trying to organize national campaigns for the election that was now only two months away.

Lumumba's MNC initially received backing from a diverse range of groups, among them Belgian industrialists and the Belgian Communist Party. It was only when Lumumba began to outline his program in detail that the Léopoldville establishment became alarmed. Though no political party advocated severing completely the economic and financial links between the Congo and Belgium, Lumumba announced that he was opposed to colonialism in any form. He did not mention nationalization, but he did say that the resources of the Congo should benefit the Congolese. As far as the men of Union Minière were concerned, the copper riches of Katanga were theirs and theirs alone. They were fearful of Lumumba's intentions, and they relayed their suspicions to the company's directors in Brussels through a series of dispatches. One note, dated January 26, 1960, said, "[Lumumba's] whole being exhibits falsehood; he speaks mediocre French and even when he says reasonable things, one wonders if he believes what he says. Lumumba resembles Ho Chi Min . . . he will give us lots of worries in the months to come."

Another note prepared for the directors, dated February 17, 1960, said that while Lumumba was undoubtedly the best politician in the Congo, he wanted to create a dictatorship and play the role of the great African leader. "He is supported by Moscow," the note said. Herman Robiliart, one of the eight who sat on the conseils d'administration of both the Société Générale and Union Minière, wrote Cousin on March 23, 1960, about Lumumba's supposed communist tendencies: "No doubt on July 1, he [and one of his colleagues] will open wide the doors of the Congo to their friends in the East." Robiliart went on to say that he planned to bring this to the attention of the Belgian government and to tell the ministers that Union Minière was uneasy about allowing Lumumba to hold any position of power. Cousin wrote to Marthoz the following month, saying that Lumumba, as the head of the Congo, would create a dictatorship with the communists pulling the strings.

By the time the national election was held in May, colonial authorities were telling visiting journalists that Lumumba was a dangerous radical with dictatorial ambitions who was being funded by the Soviets. In the
midst of the Cold War, these were extremely serious charges. But there
was nothing to back them up. Lumumba was supported by the Belgian
Communist Party, but his circle was broad and he had also received support from the industrialists in the early stages of his campaign, a fact they
conveniently chose to forget.

Elections took place from May 11 to 25. When the results came in,
Lumumba's MNC had won 35 of 137 seats in the new assembly, more than
any other party and enough to form a coalition government. Lumumba
would become the Congo's first prime minister. Kasavubu, head of ABAKO,
would hold the honorary position of president. There was a ferocious fight
among the politicians over who would hold other key positions.

When Independence Day rolled around just over a month later,
Lumumba was fatigued by the constant infighting in his government and
felt overwhelmed by the task of leadership. He had been working cease-
lessly since the first round table had ended in February. British consul
general Ian Scott said that Lumumba had been averaging two to three
hours of sleep a night during those months. In this state, it did not take
much to enrage him. The Belgians managed to do just that at the official
ceremony to mark the Congo's transition from a colony into a country.

Protocol demanded that Lumumba, as prime minister, be given an
advance copy of the speech that King Baudoin intended to give at the ceremony. Somehow this was overlooked, and Lumumba first heard the
king's comments as they were being delivered at the Palais de la Nation in
Léopoldville in front of a crowd of Congolese and foreign dignitaries.
Condescending to the point of insult, Baudoin told the Congolese they
had been left great gifts by the Belgians—railways, roads, waterways and
air routes—that they should take care in preserving. He advised against
making any hasty reforms. "Do not be afraid to turn to us," he told them
magnanimously. "We are ready to remain at hand and help you with
advice, and in training the technicians and officials you will need." With

every word spoken, he underlined the paternalistic Belgian point of view that they had brought civilization to the Congo and that its people should be supremely grateful.

When it was Lumumba's turn to address the gathering, he gave an angry reply to the king. He recalled eighty years of insults, contempt and blows delivered simply because someone was black. "We shall never forget that a black was called *tu*, not because he was a friend but because only whites were given the honour of being called *vous*." He talked of Congolese lands despoiled by the Belgians, of magnificent houses for whites and crumbling straw huts for blacks, of the tremendous suffering of the oppressed people. Lumumba said that he planned to build a different society, one where rights were respected and discrimination outlawed.

The Belgians in the audience were deeply shocked by Lumumba's hostile words. King Baudoin was so offended, he had to be persuaded to remain in his seat. Even those members of the colonial elite who might have given the new prime minister grudging support changed their minds on hearing his bitter comments. He was not, they felt, displaying the proper degree of gratitude for their gift of independence. His public display of rancour in the presence of the king ensured that when the African members of the colonial army mutinied within days of independence, Lumumba was given no Belgian support.

The army revolted for the same reason that industrial workers went on strike several days later: independence had not fulfilled their expectations, which had become unrealistically high. The Congolese believed their lives would immediately improve with the end of colonial rule. But the only instant beneficiaries were the politicians, who moved into the luxurious homes abandoned by the Belgians, drove around in enormous American automobiles and awarded themselves massive salaries. July 1 had dawned and Belgian flags still flew in the streets. Belgian officials still sat at the same desks they had occupied during colonial rule. And the vast majority of the Congolese felt cheated.

Belgian general Emile Janssens, who had remained commander-in-chief of the army, lit the fuse for revolt when he refused to "Africanize" the army by elevating Congolese soldiers into positions of command. For the benefit of his troops he wrote "Before independence = After independence" on a blackboard. On July 5, the rank and file responded with violence. They attacked and raped the wives of Belgian officers, sacked their barracks and then went on a general rampage. A mass exodus of Europeans ensued; thirty-five thousand of them fled to Belgium in July alone. Lumumba fired Janssens on July 6 and replaced him with Victor Lundula. He named his former secretary, Mobutu, army chief of staff. Mobutu toured the army bases, trying to pacify the restive troops. But while ostensibly working for Lumumba, he was moving to consolidate his own grip on power.

Lumumba reversed Janssens's order and said that Congolese would be appointed officers in the renamed Armée Nationale Congolaise. These moves brought relative calm everywhere but Katanga, where the Belgian officer corps refused to consider Africanization. The soldiers there responded by revolting against their Belgian officers.

After consulting King Baudoin and the board of Société Générale— but not the new government of the Congo—Belgium decided to intervene. It ordered its 3,800 troops across the country to go out and protect European lives and investments. On July 10, more Belgian troops arrived in Elisabethville, bringing their total to 10,000. A Belgian parliamentary commission investigating these events forty years later would conclude, "From the beginning, the Belgian government had little respect for the sovereignty of the Congo." Lumumba assumed that a Belgian coup was taking place.

Events were now moving too quickly for the prime minister to respond coherently. As he and Kasavubu attempted to negotiate with Belgium, Belgian troops attacked the port of Matadi, claiming they were only trying to protect Europeans living there. But before that incursion could be dealt with, Lumumba received the most grievous blow yet. On July 11, Tshombe, the European-backed leader of the province of Katanga, declared independence.

The pronouncement did not come as a complete surprise to those familiar with the Katangan political scene. Jules Cousin told a colleague on December 24, 1959, six months before Congolese independence, that he had been approached earlier that day by members of Tshombe's party who wanted to know whether Union Minière would support a declaration of Katangan independence. Cousin told his colleague that he had refused, and the declaration was not made at that time. As Independence Day had drawn closer and Cousin had become increasingly alarmed by Lumumba's nationalist talk, he begged company executives in Brussels to intervene with the Belgian government to ensure that the provinces had more power. However, when the violence began in July, the men at the top of the company decided that an independent Katanga would be best for them, especially as Tshombe promised them what every company craves: peace and stability. There was also local support within Katanga from white settlers and indigenous Katangans who resented the fact that though they represented 12 per cent of the Congo's population, they supplied 50 per cent of the country's total revenues.

Thus on July 12, 1960, the Board of Directors of Union Minière decided not only to immediately send Tshombe 1.25 billion Belgian francs, but to divert to Katanga all taxes, licence fees and export duties that would normally be paid to the national government in Léopoldville.

Northern Rhodesia, which paid the Congo an export royalty amounting to £80,000 a year on electricity bought from Union Minière, also decided to pay this money directly to the Tshombe regime after its secession. It was no secret that Sir Roy Welensky, who as head of the Central African Federation–controlled Northern Rhodesia, supported Tshombe. It is equally true that had Welensky refused to send the money to Elisabethville, Tshombe could have switched off the current that the Rhodesians needed to run their copper mines.

These enormous sums gave Tshombe the means to establish his government, including all the administrative bodies that were required, such as a national bank. At the same time, the federal government's lifeblood was cut off. Without Katanga's revenues, Lumumba could not provide services to the wider populace or even pay his own army, which fell into complete disorder with the departure of its Belgian officers. Tribes and individuals were settling old scores and fighting new ones without fear of military intervention. In some cases, soldiers joined rebellious groups in the generalized looting and fighting. Central authority from Léopoldville collapsed. It was not just European lives that were threatened, but also those of the Congolese.

Lumumba and Kasavubu attempted to fly to Elisabethville on July 12 to reason with Tshombe, but their plane was turned back at the prompting of Belgian advisers. The Belgians moved quickly to provide Tshombe with advice, setting up a team headed by Count Harold d'Aspremont Lynden, former assistant private secretary to the Belgian prime minister. They wanted to ensure that the new Katangan government had every chance at survival. The team became the centre of power in the province. Its dual aim was to support Tshombe and to ensure that Union Minière, the economic engine of Katanga, kept firing on all cylinders. Even in the early days of the chaos, the radio in Katanga carried appeals every half hour urging workers to return to their jobs. Lumumba suspected that Union Minière was attempting to carve a state of its own out of his new Congo. On July 12, he and Kasavubu asked the United Nations for military assistance to fight what they called "foreign aggression."

The United Nations was led at that time by Dag Hammarskjöld, a Swedish political economist known for his integrity and impartiality. He felt that the Congo should remain intact, and thought that the way to end Tshombe's secession would be to sever Belgium's support for Katanga. However, as secretary general of the United Nations, he had to navigate the conflicting desires of its members. Not only was there no unanimity on whether the United Nations should intervene, but those who did support intervention couldn't agree on whether force should be used. Lumumba wanted UN troops to go to Katanga first, end the province's secession by force and then expel the Belgian troops. But Hammarskjöld believed that the most relevant task for the UN soldiers was to deal with the international aspect of the Congo crisis, which for him meant removing the Belgian troops from all of the Congo. He did not want the UN to become embroiled in what he saw as the internal politics of the country, and he refused Lumumba's request that UN troops forcibly retake Katanga.

The Belgian government was also split over how to treat the Katangan secession. United in the need to get rid of Lumumba, the ministers were divided on the means of achieving this end. Their discord led to a confused Belgian policy from the beginning. D'Aspremont Lynden tended to side with Union Minière in favouring giving as much aid as possible to the secessionist regime. Foreign Minister Pierre Wigny was a great deal more conscious of Belgium's foreign commitments and of the need to respect the wishes of its NATO allies and of the United Nations. He told the United States, Britain, France, Germany and the Netherlands on July 11 that Belgium was opposed to Tshombe's action.

The Afro-Asian countries at the United Nations were highly sensitive to the neo-colonial aspects of Katangan independence. With many former colonies among them, this group felt that it was essential that the Congo survive, sovereign and intact. They wanted the secession ended, but they did not insist on force.

The Soviet Union wanted Katangan independence brought to an immediate end with armed intervention. It saw Belgium's continued presence in the Congo as an attempt by the West to hold on to whatever it could in the newly independent country.

The key factor for US policy makers was Lumumba's reputation as a communist. President Dwight Eisenhower was in his last year of office, and anti-communist feeling gripped the country. On July 1, the Soviets shot down a US RB-47 reconnaissance plane overflying Soviet territory, and tensions were building over Cuba, where Fidel Castro was nationalizing US enterprises. CIA director Allen Dulles declared that Lumumba was another Castro. Aside from the broader issue of Lumumba's political leanings, the United States had a specific fear: it did not want the Congo's uranium, a strategic resource, to fall into Soviet hands. The United States had not forgotten its distaste for colonialism, but that distaste was now tempered by Cold War realities.

On July 14, the UN Security Council passed a resolution in which it agreed to send UN troops to the Congo and demanded that the Belgian troops leave. While the terms of the resolution seemed clear—the UN troops were expected to keep the peace—its implementation was not. UN officials on the ground, and Hammarskjöld himself, were continually pressured by UN members to pursue their divergent aims.

The first contingent of UN troops, supplied by Ghana and Tunisia, arrived in the Congo the following day. When they did not immediately march on Elisabethville, Lumumba was incensed. He let the UN officials know that if the international force did not do as he wished, he would ask the Soviet Union for assistance. On July 20, he followed through on his threat. The Security Council passed a second resolution two days later, repeating its demand that the Belgian troops leave the Congo and warning all its members—including the Soviet Union—not to do anything to inflame the situation.

Seeking international support, Lumumba set off on a whirlwind trip that took him to New York, Washington, Ottawa, London and several African capitals. Eisenhower refused to meet with him. In his eyes, Lumumba had shown his colours by appealing to the Soviet Union. The Congolese prime minister did not help his cause in Washington. State Department officials reported finding evidence of hemp smoking in his lodgings, which persuaded the president that his guest was not only a communist, but a drug addict as well. The Eisenhower administration took a hard line on Lumumba and a softer line on Tshombe.

By the end of July, there were just over eight thousand UN troops in the Congo, most supplied by African nations. The mission, the most ambitious of its kind at that time, was to cost the United Nations dearly in terms of people, money and reputation. Although Belgian troops in much of the Congo began to leave, those in Katanga remained. Commandant Guy Weber, a serving Belgian officer, had became Tshombe's military adviser and was put in charge of national army troops loyal to Tshombe, the existing Katangan gendarmerie and the Belgian troops. He used his combined force to quickly suppress uprisings and to disarm hostile Congolese army troops, restoring order in southern Katanga within days.

In North Katanga, however, the situation was volatile. Sendwe's Baluba supporters rebelled against the Tshombe regime. With Union Minière money, the Katangan government was able to buy arms and equipment, including a fleet of jet fighters, giving them air superiority. Tshombe also hired mercenaries from Algeria, France, South Africa, Britain and Northern Rhodesia to fight alongside the Katangan gendarmerie. The lowliest recruits were paid US$500 per month, with extra money for dangerous assignments. Pilots, considered the most valuable assets, were paid $1,000 per mission, while officers with combat experience could command up to $2,800 a month. At the peak of the fighting, about five hundred mercenaries were employed by Tshombe. Collectively, they became known as *les affreux*, "the terrible ones," first because of their unruly look after months in the bush, but later for their actions. A British newspaper carried pictures later in the war of mercenaries torturing and killing their victims, then using them for target practice.

Tshombe insisted that the mercenaries were there to help "pacify" the Baluba, but Rajeshwar Dayal, head of the UN mission in the Congo, saw it somewhat differently: "They followed the traditional Belgian pattern of pacification, by setting torch to thatched villages and shooting indiscriminately at the fleeing inhabitants, all of whom were of the Baluba tribe," he wrote in *Mission for Hammarskjöld*. "The units then fanned out, spreading fire and terror in the countryside, and villages began emptying themselves into the surrounding bush to escape the advancing scourge." One of Tshombe's mercenaries described the battles as mutual carnage. "Our units lose few men but we no longer count the loyal villagers assassinated by the rebel raids," the unnamed soldier told journalist Pierre Davister. "As for the rebels, sure, we make them pay a terrible price for it." Dayal called what was happening "virtual genocide," with an estimated seventy thousand Baluba killed in the first six months of the war. In North Katanga, as elsewhere, he said, the Congo was experiencing an "orgy of violence."

Union Minière did not sit on the sidelines as the battle for Katangan secession continued. On the ground in Katanga, the company supplied the financial resources to keep the secessionist regime going. In Europe, its executives were busy lobbying various governments to back Tshombe and recognize Katanga. The record of a visit by Sir Charles Waterhouse, chairman of Tanganyika Concessions (TANKS), to the British Foreign and Colonial Office in late July provides an indication of how Union Minière bosses operated. TANKS was still a major shareholder in the copper company—its stake was worth about £180 million—and Waterhouse had been asked by the men who ran Union Minière to intercede with the British government on their behalf. Waterhouse told John Profumo, then the British minister of state for war, that he was just back from Brussels, where he had met with Edgar Sengier, Edgar Van der Straeten and Herman Robiliart, whom he described as the triumvirate who ruled Union Minière. They had told him that in the weeks preceding independence they had been unable to exercise their customary influence over the Belgian government but that they had now recovered full access to ministers in favour of recognizing Tshombe's government. The Union Minière trio wanted Waterhouse to persuade the British government to look more favourably on Katanga and to at least give Tshombe what Waterhouse called "sub rosa" or unofficial encouragement.

Profumo explained that Britain could not break with its allies, not to mention with the United Nations, and recognize the government of Katanga. What Britain would do, though, was to tell Hammarskjöld to keep UN troops out of Katanga for the time being because Belgian troops were maintaining order there. Waterhouse went to some lengths to paint a bright picture of the Tshombe regime and suggested it might soon spread its influence to the neighbouring provinces of Kivu and the diamond-rich area of Kasai. He snorted with derision when Profumo pointed out that the governments of those two provinces had been legitimately elected and held majorities. According to the record, "Captain Waterhouse manifested a humorous contempt for arguments based on the suffrage and implied that the Union Minière had a short way with difficulties of this sort. After all, Tshombe himself was a man of no personality and slender capabilities, but there he was, firmly in the saddle, if the UN did not unseat him. And there was no reason why the system which had brought him in in the Katanga should not be extended over much wider areas where there might not be copper but were at least diamonds."

Profumo suggested that this was not the time for Britain to take any active measure out of step with its allies. "Captain Waterhouse agreed with this on the whole," the record states, "but his attitude at this stage suggested that he felt he had not got his way and there was little else to be said." The TANKS chairman was told to advise the leaders of Union Minière to use their influence with the Belgian government to make it easier for UN troops to peacefully enter Katanga. Division of the Congo would prove disastrous to the company in the end. "Captain Waterhouse said the Belgians would never consent to this," the record says. "It was a question of pride. The Congo touched the very depths of their souls. The burglar had run off with the key and they wanted to save anything that remained in the house before he could get his hands on it."

Belgian foreign minister Pierre Wigny was irked that Union Minière had presumed to mount its own diplomatic efforts, undermining Belgium's official foreign policy. "It's very dangerous to let businessmen get involved in policy," he wrote. Both Wigny and his successor in the job, Paul-Henri Spaak, felt continually undermined by Union Minière's decision to pursue its own policy in Katanga and abroad.

Emboldened by the lack of UN action against Katanga, the provincial leader of South Kasai, Albert Kalonji, declared independence on August 8, 1960. Forminière, the diamond-mining company controlled by Société Générale, was implicated in the secession. The next day, the Security Council passed yet another resolution calling on Belgium to withdraw its troops from the country. Lumumba, who had returned from his tour abroad empty-handed, decided to challenge Kalonji. The Armée Nationale Congolaise successfully retook South Kasai in mid-August, but the battle resulted in the massacre of two hundred Baluba civilians by the unruly national troops. Lumumba was held personally responsible even though the troops had been under the command of his former aide Mobutu.

By this point, Mobutu was one of many rivals who were manoeuvring behind the scenes to replace Lumumba, supported financially by Western governments such as Belgium, France and the United States. The army leader had been identified early on by the CIA as an ambitious young man who might work well with the United States. It now decided to back him financially and politically. Mobutu stayed in the background when Kasavubu and Lumumba began to fight publicly over Lumumba's handling of the crisis. On September 5, 1960, they announced in separate radio broadcasts that they had fired each other. On September 14, Mobutu pounced, announcing that he had taken over the Congo. He promised that it was only a temporary measure to stop the infighting between the politicians in Léopoldville. A month later he put Lumumba under house arrest. Kasavubu was allowed to continue as president, and a College of Commissioners was set up to run the government. The commissioners were young Congolese who had studied abroad. None of them was considered a political rival by Mobutu or Kasavubu.

The United Nations refused to recognize Mobutu's new government and continued to act as though Lumumba was still in power. Meanwhile, UN troops were being drawn inexorably into the Congo's internal fighting. In October 1960, UN soldiers stopped two incursions by the Katangan gendarmerie into neighbouring Kasai. In November, several UN soldiers were killed defending the Ghanaian embassy in Léopoldville against the national army. In December, there was further fighting between UN troops and the army. UN head of mission Rajeshwar Dayal compared the army to "a rogue elephant, rampaging wildly over the countryside, unresponsive to the command of its officers and resisting the efforts of the UN to calm it." Tshombe had allowed a small contingent of UN troops into his province in August, but they remained vastly outnumbered and thus unable to take on the Katangan forces.

Throughout 1960, Union Minière continued to give as much support as possible to Tshombe. When the company issued a new protocol list at the end of that year, it referred to Tshombe as "His Excellency the President of the State of Katanga." The company was encouraged in its course by its corporate results: 1960 turned out to be a record year for copper production, which reached 300,675 tonnes. Morale among employees was also good and was expected to improve once all those who were planning to return to Belgium had left. Just 130 of the 1,700 European staff had already opted to leave, and only 30 more would follow. Company leaders believed they had survived the worst.

But what looked like disaster averted merely turned out to be disaster delayed. During the following year, three events would destroy Union Minière's careful plans and threaten the existence of the company. Most important was the death of Lumumba. After being jailed near Léopoldville by Mobutu, Lumumba was delivered into the hands of his enemies in Katanga with the blessing of the Belgian authorities in Brussels. He was assassinated on January 17, 1961, by members of Tshombe's regime while senior Belgian officers looked on. The United Nations set up a commission to investigate Lumumba's death, but witnesses were uncooperative and gave conflicting accounts. Jules Cousin of Union Minière simply refused to participate. Forty years later, a Belgian parliamentary commission investigating Lumumba's death determined that the execution had been carried out on the order of the Katangan authorities but with the active encouragement of the Belgian government, which the commission held morally responsible; Union Minière was indirectly implicated. It was difficult to separate public and private interests in Katanga because the technical mission headed by d'Aspremont Lynden and its replacement, known as the Bureau Conseil, used money and other amenities provided by Union Minière to carry out their business.

Tshombe tried to cover up the circumstances surrounding Lumumba's murder by fabricating a tale about Lumumba's having been killed by angry villagers. Suspicions, however, surfaced immediately that both Tshombe and Union Minière were deeply involved. There were rumours, later discounted, that the body had been hidden in a Union Minière freezer and then disposed of using vats of sulphuric acid supplied by the copper company. The loose barroom talk of one of the Belgians who had been at the scene of the murder led to stories that Tshombe had ordered Lumumba's execution after a drunken meeting with his cabinet.

The scandal led the Western powers to reconsider their support of Tshombe. "The man who had been presented as, above all, an upholder of law and order, now looked uncomfortably like a murderer," said Conor Cruise O'Brien, who helped lead the UN mission after Dayal left. "His admirers pointed out—quite rightly—that he was not the only murderer in the Congo, but even this did not altogether recommend him to the wider public in the West."

The longer-term consequences of disposing of Lumumba were far more serious. Had either Tshombe or Union Minière thought it through, they would have seen that the end of Lumumba would only lead to the end of the secessionist regime. As long as Lumumba survived, the Western powers thought they needed Tshombe as a bulwark against communism in the Congo. With Lumumba gone, the rationale for supporting Tshombe disappeared as well. Governments that had once argued that Tshombe's survival was necessary in order to prevent the Soviets from gaining a foothold in Africa began to say that the continued existence of an independent Katanga was helping the Soviet cause because it weakened the Congo as a country.

A change of government in the United States also caused the ground to shift under Tshombe and Union Minière. When John F. Kennedy came to power on January 20, 1961, the Congolese government, still led by the College of Commissioners, controlled only two of six provinces. Kennedy was alarmed by the continuing deterioration of the former Belgian colony. Like his predecessor, he saw the Congo in Cold War terms. But unlike Eisenhower, he felt that the United States should try to align itself with the rising tide of black nationalism in Africa. A change in US policy was widely anticipated once Kennedy took office. There were some who felt that Lumumba had been killed three days before Kennedy took over because the murderers wanted to avoid any preventive action on the part of the United States. In February 1960, the Kennedy administration announced its new plan: the UN mandate would be strengthened. Belgian and other outside influence in the Congo would be severely curtailed. And Mobutu would have to hand power back to the civilians, which he did.

The UN Security Council passed a fourth resolution on February 21, 1961, calling for the remaining Belgian troops to withdraw and for all Belgian political advisers to leave. The resolution also included the proviso that UN troops could use force as a last resort, opening the door to offensive action.

Neither Tshombe nor Union Minière was pleased at this turn of events. The estimated three hundred Belgian officers in the Katangan gendarmerie offered the company a measure of security for its mines and installations that it could not get elsewhere. Union Minière did not trust the African members of the Katangan gendarmerie, and the mercenaries were too few in number to offer blanket protection.

The third decisive event of the year occurred when the Eyskens-Lilar government in Belgium, which had proven so supportive of Tshombe, was replaced by the more moderate Lefèvre-Spaak government. Spaak, who became foreign minister on April 25, 1961, had opposed the Katanga secession from the start. The change of government also meant that d'Aspremont Lynden, one of Tshombe's strongest advocates, was no longer in cabinet. Official Belgian policy on the Congo began to shift closer to that of the Kennedy administration. Now that Lumumba was gone, it was time to reunite the Congo. The pressure was on for Tshombe to end the Katanga secession.

Had Tshombe chosen to compromise at this point, the story of the Congo and Union Minière might have had a different ending. But he still believed he had the upper hand. He had an army to protect his territory, and he had the funds—courtesy of Union Minière—to pay his troops. Instead of making conciliatory gestures, he launched a new mercenary recruitment drive in Belgium. That this directly contravened Belgian law was ignored by Belgian authorities. There were still elements within the government and most certainly in financial circles that supported him. The Belgian security police and the ministry of national defence even helped Tshombe contact potential recruits.

The US and Belgian governments began lobbying Union Minière directly to restore tax payments and other revenues to the national government in Léopoldville. Tshombe got wind of these talks and let the company know that it would suffer if it negotiated with either the Congolese national government or the United Nations. He and his ministers began talking about a scorched earth policy, where they would destroy all Union Minière facilities if they did not receive the copper giant's massive revenues. "I know that the Union Minière has abandoned me and now deals with the central government," Tshombé told a French reporter for *Le Monde*. "This company will pay dearly for its treason. We are all set to blow up every Union Minière installation in Elisabethville, Kolwezi and Jadotville."

Union Minière had entered corporate hell. It had thrown in its lot with Tshombe, who now seemed destined to lose the battle for independence. In Katanga, the company was being treated as the enemy by the United Nations and being held hostage by Tshombe. A conference of Congolese politicians in July 1961, organized in part by the UN, produced a new prime minister, Cyrille Adoula. Adoula informed Union Minière that it was liable for double the amount of money that had been owed to the central government but that had instead been paid to Tshombe.

In August 1961, UN commanders began to expel all foreign military personnel from Katanga. With the element of surprise on their side, they quickly rounded up and deported eighty-one of an estimated five hundred foreign mercenaries. There were howls of protest from Belgium, Britain and Rhodesia, whose diplomats persuaded the UN to stop by promising that they themselves would be responsible for ejecting the rest. These promises were not kept, and some of the mercenaries who had been deported slipped back into Katanga. The United Nations decided to mount a second roundup in September. But this time, the Katangan gendarmerie, which outnumbered the UN force by 9,500 troops, was ready and waiting. There were fierce clashes in Elisabethville, with casualties on both sides. Union Minière facilities were targeted by UN forces after units of the gendarmerie holed up in the company's headquarters and hospital.

The company denied it was giving refuge to Tshombe's forces and decried the destruction. It said it could not be held responsible for employees who, acting in their own personal capacity, fired on the UN.

The renewed hostilities between the UN and Katangan forces prompted an explosion of outrage from Tshombe's remaining supporters in the West. Funds from Union Minière and Société Générale were used to finance a major publicity campaign in Britain, Belgium and Rhodesia. The British government, mindful of TANKS's interest in Union Minière, weighed in with a protest, saying it was deeply disturbed by what was going on in Katanga, specifically mentioning the UN attacks on industrial installations. The British asked for a ceasefire.

Hammarskjöld agreed to travel to Northern Rhodesia to negotiate with Tshombe, but he was killed when his plane crashed just short of Ndola in Northern Rhodesia. The cause of the crash was never determined, but suspicions fell on Tshombe and Union Minière. Following Hammarskjöld's death, Tshombe and the United Nations agreed to a ceasefire. It did not hold for long.

Meanwhile in New York, a public relations office set up by Tshombe was churning out negative reports about the UN, emphasizing the loss of life of civilians. The stories struck a chord with elements of the American public and politicians who believed Tshombe to be an ardent anti-communist, unfairly targeted by their government. This raised the ire of the anti-Tshombe group in the Kennedy administration. Carl T. Rowan, the deputy assistant secretary of state for public affairs at the US State Department, accused Union Minière of supporting Tshombe's propaganda initiative, pointing out that the money the company paid him represented 80 per cent of all Katangan revenues. "Mr. Tshombe's most vocal support arises not so much from the fact that he is anti-Communist as the fact that he is pro-Union Minière," Rowan said. The US administration publicly disowned Rowan's comments, although President Kennedy himself would later make similar charges.

In December 1961, Jules Cousin broke what had been a lifelong rule and spoke out about what was happening in Katanga. What prompted his angry outburst was the fighting that had taken place near the Katangan mission school he had set up in memory of his wife after her death in 1944. The school trained young Congolese women in housework, sports and what were described as the feminine arts. None of the girls had been injured in the gunfire, but two workmen bringing wood to the school had been wounded. Cousin, who had not said a word about the seventy thousand Baluba killed earlier by Tshombe's forces, now sent a telegram to President Kennedy deploring the killing and wounding of innocent people by the UN forces. "I wish to register a most indignant protest against these veritable murders by the hired killers of the United Nations, which is financed primarily by the United States of America," he wrote in the telegram dated December 15. "As a symbol of this protest, I am returning to President Kennedy the Freedom Medal that was conferred on me in 1946." Whatever attachment Cousin had felt for the Americans while shipping uranium to them during the war had evaporated. In his mind, they were complicit in the destruction of the world he had helped create in Katanga.

Although 1961 had been a year of turmoil and increased political and military pressure for Union Minière, its corporate results were excellent. Copper production had reached 293,509 tonnes, down only slightly from the 1960 record, and cobalt production had increased to 8,326 tonnes. The company had even held what it called an international fair in July to mark the fiftieth anniversary of the founding of Elisabethville. Companies from Belgium, Portugal, South Africa, the Rhodesias and Switzerland participated, and both Mobutu and Tshombe made an appearance. Although the two politicians were on opposing sides of the civil war—Mobutu fighting for a unified Congo while Tshombe battled for independence— they set aside their differences long enough to celebrate with Union Minière. But the company's spirit of invincibility would prove to be short- lived as the war continued throughout the following year and Tshombe's regime limped toward its demise.

UN secretary general U Thant (who succeeded Hammarskjöld) and the Kennedy administration were growing increasingly frustrated with

Tshombe's prevarication. The Katangan leader had no incentive to stick to any of the peace agreements he signed and then repudiated as long as he knew Union Minière money was coming in. Kennedy and U Thant recognized that the Katangan secession would not end as long as the copper giant continued to pay its taxes and fees to Elisabethville. Kennedy stepped up pressure on the company and on the Belgian government to stop the flow of funds, but Union Minière refused out of fear of Tshombe. U Thant offered the company UN protection for its installations, but the company still felt unable to change its position. On July 23, Kennedy held a news conference in Washington at which he blamed Union Minière for weakening the national government in the Congo. He warned of the chaos to come if the company continued. At another press conference on August 30, the president linked support for secession with Communism. Unless Congolese union was achieved, Kennedy said, "you are liable to find a very critical situation in the rest of the Congo, which would be very dangerous to the free world." Union Minière had gone from being the champion of capitalism to the lackey of communism.

Two days after Kennedy's verbal attack, an unnamed Union Minière official attempted to justify the company's lack of action to the *New York Times*. "We do not run this country," he said. "We are like hostages here. If the blacks do not like what we do and where we pay our taxes, then they have an army and they have all the guns. Then what good will all your United Nations and United States be worth?" The official went on to point out that the company's installations were spread throughout Katanga, with some in areas the UN had yet to penetrate and where the Katangan gendarmerie remained in control. "Can the United Nations guarantee us control here? Can they guarantee that they can stop the Katangese from shooting those who tried to go to work? Can they guarantee that the railroad which goes through the bush to Angola and Rhodesia won't be sabotaged and can they guarantee they can protect the lives of our white officials?"

The United Nations upped the ante by adopting a peace proposal in mid-1962 that threatened Katanga with economic sanctions targeting copper and cobalt if it did not comply. Congolese prime minister Cyrille Adoula and Tshombe both accepted the peace plan but then dragged their feet in implementing it.

December 1962 started on a hopeful note. Tshombe indicated to the UN that he was ready to allow Union Minière to send some of its money to the national government. The Belgian government pressed Union Minière to take the initiative and send representatives to Léopoldville to begin negotiations on the transfer of foreign exchange. The company hesitated. While it had jumped too quickly to support Tshombé when he first declared independence, it now waited too long to abandon him for fear of retribution. This proved fatal to the deal. Tshombe decided that he and not Union Minière would send representatives to Léopoldville. The agreement fell apart. Just before Christmas, the Katangan gendarmerie attacked a number of UN positions and shot down a UN helicopter. Tshombe ordered a ceasefire, but his forces ignored him.

The UN commander sought and received permission from New York to counterattack, and this time the United Nations had the upper hand. Kennedy's administration had increased its military support, most notably with aircraft, and UN troops had grown to almost twenty thousand. They now outnumbered the Katangan gendarmerie and were able to take Elisabethville in a matter of days. Tshombe avoided capture by riding, bandaged as a casualty, in an ambulance driven by a Belgian adviser. He moved his government to the Union Minière town of Jadotville, 100 kilometres northwest. UN troops went after him.

In a radio broadcast, Tshombe ordered Katangans to fight the UN to the death and to use poisoned arrows and spears if they had nothing else. The UN responded with its own radio appeal, telling Katangans that they were fighting only for foreign interests and for a company whose goal was to make as much money as possible from the province's resources. Tshombe began to implement his scorched-earth policy, ordering his mercenaries to destroy everything in the path of the UN troops. They began by blowing up a major road and railway bridge across the Lufira River on January 1, 1963. Then they mined but did not blow up the major

Union Minière installations in Jadotville and Kolwezi as well as the massive Delcommune and Le Marinel hydroelectric dams. The company's worst nightmares were coming true.

When Jadotville fell on January 2, the Tshombe government fled to Kolwezi, farther to the northwest. There, Jean-Jacques Saquet, a Union Minière manager, was a witness to the regime's final, desperate days. The only radio transmitter in town was located in the company's office, and Tshombe and his government used it to communicate with the outside world. Saquet also used it to keep his superiors informed as bridges and power lines were blown up, installations occupied and dams seized and mined. The potential for destruction was enormous. If the Delcommune dam were blown, an estimated 100,000 people living downstream in the Lualaba valley would be killed. Saquet's terse radio messages conveyed the mounting panic in Kolwezi as UN forces closed in. The Union Minière leaders held their collective breath as they waited to hear whether their industrial empire had been reduced to rubble. They pleaded with Tshombe to call off the destruction and assured him they were doing all they could to persuade the United Nations to call off its troops. But Tshombe refused to give them any assurances as long as the UN offensive continued.

Then, on January 14, 1963, it was all over. Cornered in Kolwezi, Tshombe announced that the Katangan secession had ended. In return for amnesty for himself and his ministers, he would negotiate Katanga's reintegration in the Congo. The next day, Union Minière signed an agreement with the Léopoldville government to transfer foreign exchange from Katanga to the national bank in the capital. By January 21, UN forces had subdued the last holdouts among Tshombe's unruly troops. Many of the mercenaries slipped into the bush and made their way across the border.

The Congo never recovered from its violent birth as a nation. Several stabs were made at "democratic" government in the early 1960s, including by Tshombe, who went into exile after his long fight with the UN and returned to become prime minister of the country for fifteen months. In

1965, Mobutu, who had been waiting in the wings while various administrations tried and failed to govern the country, took control in a second military coup. The dictatorship he imposed lasted until 1997, when he fled the country as it was being consumed by revolution. He died four months later in Morocco of prostate cancer. Today the Congo remains destabilized. A war in 1998 saw rival groups backed by the governments of Angola, Uganda, Rwanda and Zimbabwe fight for control of the rich mineral resources of the country. Though a peace deal has been signed, it is too soon to say whether it will hold.

As for Union Minière, the company at first appeared to have enjoyed a lucky escape. The damages it suffered fell far short of Tshombe's threatened destruction, partly thanks to the handsome payments it offered the mercenaries for inflicting only superficial damage. Although all of the installations had been shut down during the final days of the war, they quickly reopened at the end of the conflict and there was no interruption in mineral shipments to customers. Union Minière shipped 296,236 tonnes of copper in 1962, compared with 293,509 the previous year, and 9,683 tonnes of cobalt, up from 8,326.

The ultimate consequences of Union Minière's meddling in Congolese politics came later. Once Mobutu was firmly ensconced in Léopoldville, he imposed an avalanche of new taxes on the company. By May 1966, Union Minière's tax burden amounted to 50 per cent of the value of copper shipments leaving the country. In June 1966, Mobutu appropriated all concessions in the Congo, including those of Union Minière. Companies were invited to reapply for their concessions at exorbitant prices. Union Minière was still hoping to negotiate a reasonable price when Mobutu delivered the *coup de grâce* on January 1, 1967. He nationalized the company and replaced it with a new state-owned body. Union Minière threatened to sue anyone who purchased Katangan copper or other minerals from its former holdings, which forced Mobutu to negotiate compensation for the expropriation, valued at 7.5 billion Belgian francs. That payment, along with the money it had made from Katanga over the years, allowed Union Minière to branch out around the world.

Subsidiaries sprang up in Canada, Australia, Brazil, Mexico, Iran, Spain and the United States. The company continues to operate globally under the new name Umicore SA. Its promotional material outlines its activities in places as far-flung as Bulgaria and Japan. But there is no mention of the Congo. It may be some small consolation to the company that continued unrest in that country has scuppered attempts made by corporate rivals to revive its aging installations.

Unlike the divine beings they emulated, the men at the top of Union Minière proved fallible. They exacerbated the crisis in the Congo and involved themselves in a squalid world of tribal warfare, mercenaries and corruption. Far from controlling events, the company quickly became a hostage to fortune. It chose to put its massive financial resources at the disposal of a weak and prevaricating leader and then watched helplessly as he used those funds to wage a genocide in Katanga and a war with the United Nations that would cripple the Congo. Tens of thousands of people died and the company's reputation lay in tatters. The copper kings became international pariahs, condemned publicly by the president of the United States and the secretary general of the United Nations. They had misread the geopolitical situation and backed the wrong side, erroneously presuming they could prevail against all the governments and international organizations ranged against them. And in the end, the very shareholders' interests that the company had been trying to protect were irretrievably damaged. The enemies they had made had long memories and the power to exact retribution. Union Minière was consigned to corporate oblivion in the Congo. Its great copper empire, founded on the riches of Katanga, is no more.

CHAPTER FIVE

LONRHO IN MOZAMBIQUE

IN JANUARY 1983, MOZAMBICAN PRESIDENT SAMORA MACHEL INVITED the devil to dinner. He had no choice. His country lay in ruins, battered by two decades of almost constant conflict. It was time to re-examine his options.

The future had looked so promising in 1975 after his guerrilla force, the Front for the Liberation of Mozambique (FRELIMO, Frente de Libertação de Moçambique), had wrested independence from the Portuguese. Machel eagerly put in motion the radical socialist agenda that movement leaders had envisioned during their years in the bush. He instituted sweeping nationalization of businesses and property, and he set up state farms and villages where peasants were resettled. He built health clinics and schools and told his people that the legacies of colonialism—illiteracy, disease, poverty and economic dependence—would be erased within three years.

But the white regimes in neighbouring Southern Rhodesia and South Africa were determined that Machel would not succeed. His government of black, godless communists threatened the continued survival of their white, Christian, capitalist authority. It angered them that Machel gave refuge to rebels who challenged their regimes. In 1977, Southern Rhodesia helped create the Mozambique National Resistance (RENAMO, Resistëncia Nacional Moçambicana), a rebel group that targeted civilians and military alike. RENAMO fighters attacked Mozambican schools and clinics—the most obvious symbols of socialist success—burned buses and all their occupants and conducted brutal executions. When white-ruled Southern Rhodesia became black-ruled Zimbabwe in 1980, South Africa took up the RENAMO cause.

By 1983, the Mozambican president was desperate for outside help. Industry had ground to a halt because of the ongoing civil war. His socialist farm system was a failure, and what little agricultural capacity remained was withering in the midst of a punishing drought. Faced with this grim reality, the FRELIMO leader began to think the unthinkable: socialist Mozambique needed to integrate into the capitalist economy it had previously spurned. He would have to throw his energy into courting foreign investors.

The problem was that capitalists willing to invest in the southern African country were not lying thick on the ground. Mozambique's government remained officially socialist, which did not recommend it to Western businesspeople, who tended to view the world through a Cold War lens. Although Machel had been received by British prime minister Margaret Thatcher and later by US president Ronald Reagan, his change of heart was still too fresh to be seen as convincing proof that he had seen the error of his socialist ways. In addition, the wind of change that had blown through sub-Saharan Africa in the 1960s, bringing independence and then turmoil in its wake, had generally turned off Western investors.

There was one businessman, however, who was bucking the general trend. Roland Walter Rowland was making a name for himself in Africa as a friend of black leaders. Better still, he already had an investment in Mozambique: a pipeline stretching 300 kilometres from the port of Beira on the Indian Ocean to Umtali, just across the border in Zimbabwe. It ran along the same route as the railway built by Cecil Rhodes in 1897. Rowland had held on to this asset through years of uncertainty and war and had recently refurbished it at a cost of us$20 million. The Machel government had done Rowland a favour by not expropriating the pipeline during its nationalization program. Unlike other assets, the pipeline was not seen as a colonial cash grab. "It was not on the table," said a former minister. "We had nothing against it." Machel decided that Rowland, whom he had yet to meet personally, represented Mozambique's best hope of attracting desperately needed investment.

At the time, Rowland, known more familiarly as "Tiny," stood at the top of a huge conglomerate called Lonrho PLC, which had more than eight hundred companies operating in eighty countries all over the world. These companies engaged in a bewildering range of activities: gold, platinum, copper and coal mining, sugar and tea plantations, brewing and whisky distilling, distribution of agricultural equipment and cars, engineering and steel production, printing and publishing, hotel management, and the manufacture of furniture and refrigeration equipment, to name but a few. Rowland was famous for arriving in a country in his private jet and driving straight from the tarmac to the presidential palace to negotiate business deals that would further expand his empire. He established a reputation as someone who believed in the future of Africa, and he had the ear of its new black leaders. It helped that he was generous with his money. Student fees were paid, medical bills covered, hotel and travel expenses taken care of and outright "donations" made to causes of a leader's own choosing. A lucky few were even loaned the corporate jet.

Machel and his advisers knew Rowland had his detractors. He was accused in an official inquiry of running his public company as a personal fiefdom, refusing to consult with his board of directors, dispensing corporate money to political leaders with abandon and engaging in fraud. In the wake of that inquiry, British prime minister Edward Heath called Rowland "the unacceptable face of capitalism." But what was unacceptable in Britain did not look as bad in Africa, especially when those doing the looking hoped to be recipients of Rowland's largesse.

Members of Machel's government voiced concerns about doing business with Tiny Rowland when the idea was first proposed. "Some people thought that to deal with Lonrho was to deal with the devil," recalled one minister twenty years later. "They said that Tiny Rowland was behind various *coups d'état* in Africa." Rowland had indeed fuelled conflict in the troubled continent by funding groups involved in civil wars. Like Rhodes, King Léopold, Oppenheimer and the men of Union Minière, he thought the end justified the means, even if those means resulted in the loss of human life. He demonstrated that dubious business practices could still be employed in the late twentieth century without fear of retribution.

The complaints Machel's ministers raised were not strong enough to deter the Mozambican leader from his course. He instructed an adviser to contact Rowland and invite him to dinner. That adviser was Alves Gomes, a former journalist and confidant of Machel's who would later work for Rowland as chairman of Lonrho's southern Africa operations. I met Gomes in Maputo in 2002, first at his office in a travel agency and later at the bar of an upmarket hotel favoured by government officials and visiting diplomats. At the time of my visit, Mozambique was still recovering from the punishing floods of 2000, which had submerged vast tracts of farmland and had led to images flashed around the world of babies being born in trees and helpless civilians being plucked from muddy waters by South African soldiers in helicopters. The deluge had struck just as Mozambique was hitting its economic stride, registering growth rates that were the envy of the developing world. Though the waters had now receded, the tourists who were normally drawn to the white, palm-fringed beaches on the Indian Ocean had not yet returned in force. Gomes and I were alone at the bar that night.

Gomes is a lean, gregarious man who speaks with great passion about Mozambique's past. He worked for Lonrho when it was the reigning power in this part of the world, with vast cotton plantations, the pipeline, car dealerships, hotels and mines. The company is now a shadow of its former self, most of its Mozambican assets either sold or closed. Having worked intimately with both Machel and Rowland, Gomes could speak knowledgeably about their motivations and their weaknesses. According to him, Rowland's weakness was vanity. Profits were important, but personal prestige was paramount. "Tiny liked to impress people," said Gomes. "He came in his nice suit and silk shirt." It helped that Rowland was a handsome man, with the smooth looks of a matinee idol.

As part of the team assigned to the courtship of the British businessman, Gomes decided they should target Rowland's sense of importance.

When Rowland arrived in Mozambique, they took him to see the governor of the central bank, to the minister of finance, and then to Marcelino dos Santos, a key FRELIMO official and a violent opponent of capitalism. "Marcelino told him that we were in a desperate situation.'We have a big drought. We wish you could help us,'" recalled Gomes. "Here was the strongman of FRELIMO begging for help." He laughed at the memory, portraying the meeting with dos Santos as all part of the scene they were setting to entice Rowland to invest.

With Rowland sufficiently primed by his meetings, the Machel team executed their *coup de grâce*. They escorted their visitor to a state dinner in an ornate colonial mansion that had been built by the Portuguese. The dining room boasted an immense marble table that weighed three and a half tonnes. The president and all the party notables turned out to welcome the visitor. "So this is the monster," Machel said when introduced to Tiny Rowland."I'm told you take over governments and countries." Rowland was clearly flattered by this description of his powers. Making a gesture in return, he told the Mozambicans he was going to help them by flying in US$4 million worth of seeds for special drought-resistant maize that was being grown on his plantations in Kenya. He would do this using a fleet of 707 aircraft owned by a Lonrho subsidiary for transport, even though Kenya currently had an export ban on such seeds."He did it for free. He never charged a penny," said Gomes."And he was doing it out of vanity."

Machel reciprocated by promising Rowland the use of state-owned land for farms. He wanted Lonrho to help reactivate food production in Mozambique. Rowland agreed to make the necessary investment. When the deal was settled, the Machel team congratulated themselves on their successful strategy. They had caught their prey. Now he would be working for them. "We played it very well," said Gomes. "And it was advantageous to both sides."

But in all their careful study of Tiny Rowland, the Mozambicans had missed one crucial piece of information that would have changed everything had it been unearthed. Rowland had already done business with their sworn enemy, the rebel group RENAMO. He had entered into a secret

deal with rebel leaders in 1982 under which they received payments of
US$500,000 a month for leaving the pumping stations on his pipeline
alone. These protection payments were so secret that even some in the
higher echelons of the rebel movement did not know about them.
Certainly the FRELIMO members on Machel's team were unaware of
Rowland's involvement with the rebels. Years later, when the news finally
broke, they still refused to believe they had been duped.

But Rowland often played both sides in a conflict, sometimes switch-
ing from one to the other, sometimes engaged with both at the same time.
In Angola, he supported the rebel movement while negotiating with the
government for mineral exploration rights. In Sudan, he did a deal with
the government and then provided support for rebels in the south. In
Rhodesia, he backed rebel leader Joshua Nkomo but slipped money to
rival leader Robert Mugabe in the days leading up to independence. And
throughout the years of international sanctions against the illegal white
government in Rhodesia and the apartheid government in South Africa,
he maintained profitable businesses in both countries while publicly pro-
claiming his abhorrence of their policies. The Mozambicans' belief that
Tiny Rowland would play straight with them says much about his personal charm but not much about their analysis.

There was one other factor guiding Rowland's conduct that the
Mozambicans did know about but whose import they may have missed:
Tiny Rowland loved the oil pipeline that stretched from Beira to Umtali.
"It was his pearl," acknowledged Gomes. Lonrho had grown into a huge
conglomerate mainly by acquiring existing businesses, with a few key
exceptions. The pipeline was one of them. To understand why Rowland
acted as he did in Mozambique, including paying money to RENAMO, it is
necessary to understand his emotional attachment to the asset he had
struggled to bring to fruition. And for that, it is necessary to look at
Rowland's early roots and the route he took to become a big man in Africa.

Roland Walter Rowland was born Roland Walter Fuhrhop on November 27,
1917, to a German father and Dutch mother interned in an enemy alien

camp in Belgaum, India, during the First World War. His father had run a successful import-export business in India until the outbreak of war. It was during that time that Rowland got his nickname. A curious tot, he liked to roam, and his Indian nanny was forever saying that she could not find "the tiny one." The name stuck, even after he achieved his full height of six foot two.

After the war, the family moved to Hamburg, Germany, where Rowland's father established another trading business, which prospered. While still in Germany, the young Rowland, along with many other boys his age, joined the Hitler Youth. Some subsequent accounts suggest he maintained pro-Nazi sympathies throughout his young adulthood. But many of these stories must be treated carefully, as there has been much disinformation spread about Rowland over the years by corporate rivals. In 1934, he was sent to a public school in England called Churcher's College, where some of his peers saw him as an arrogant young man who didn't bother to hide his support for Hitler. He quit school a year later to join a shipping firm in England owned by a relative of his mother's. In 1939, he changed his name by deed poll to Roland Walter Rowland. Some years later, he would tell an associate that his father's Dutch wife was not his real mother. The woman who bore him, according to Tiny, was the sister of Sir John Rowland, a British civil servant in India.

When the Second World War broke out, Rowland was conscripted into the British army. His brother, who had remained in Germany, joined the Wehrmacht. British army reports from that period indicate that Private Rowland was not trusted around sensitive material, that he socialized openly with Nazi sympathizers and that he was eventually drummed out of the army and interned on the Isle of Man when he was caught listening to a radio broadcast by Lord Haw-Haw—William Joyce, the propagandist for Germany. Those close to Tiny said he had ended up in the internment camp after he went to his superior officer and told him he would fight anyone but the Germans because his brother was in the German army. His parents, who had moved to Britain by this time, were also interned by the British.

With such a past, it might appear puzzling that Rowland was later able to establish himself in business in Britain and to attract members of the elite to serve on the Lonrho Board of directors. However, despite conventional wisdom that Britain stood united in its disgust of Hitler, a good number among the Conservative establishment were pro-Nazi up to and even during the war. For them, the enemy was Stalin rather than Hitler. Rowland appeared to support publicly what they believed privately.

But while Rowland was not ostracized on those grounds, he was held at arm's length, partly because he hadn't been born and bred in Britain. Even in later years, when he headed a huge conglomerate, Rowland refused to conform to the British establishment's unwritten rules. He belonged to no club, had no entry in any Who's Who and made no effort to appear at events frequented by high society. Some thought he was making a virtue out of necessity for he knew he would never fit in. Others say he was bored by anything other than business and thought going to parties and frequenting clubs was a waste of time.

In 1948, at the age of thirty, Rowland left England for Africa. He went to Southern Rhodesia, a magnet at the time for ex-servicemen looking to reinvent themselves after the war. A thousand immigrants a month were arriving from Britain, drawn by the lure of land and a white society free of most of the constraints of stuffy, hierarchical Britain. At first, Rowland stayed in a hotel on Cecil Square in Salisbury (now Harare), near where the Pioneer Column created by Cecil Rhodes made their first settlement after invading Mashonaland. He soon bought a working farm in Gatooma called Shepton Estates. He later bought a villa in Salisbury called High Noon but kept the farm and used its name for his holding company, Shepton Estates (Private) Ltd. He tried his hand at distributing Mercedes automobiles and dabbled in mining, buying a chrome mine, which failed, and then a gold mine, which also failed but which he made money on by taking it public before it collapsed.

It was during this period that he laid the groundwork for the pipeline that would bring oil from the port of Beira on the Indian Ocean to landlocked Southern Rhodesia. Rowland started thinking about the project after reading in *Reader's Digest* about pipelines in Russia and the Middle East. He set up Associated Overseas Pipelines of Rhodesia Inc. in 1957 and embarked on the long process of acquiring the necessary permits. He needed the permission of four governments: Southern Rhodesia; the Central African Federation, set up by the British in 1953 to tie together the colonies of Northern Rhodesia (now Zambia), Southern Rhodesia (now Zimbabwe) and Nyasaland (now Malawi); Mozambique, which was still a Portuguese colony; and Portugal, then ruled by dictator António de Oliveira Salazar.

Rowland began shuttling back and forth between Salisbury and Lisbon to lobby the Portuguese government. In the space of three years, he flew to Lisbon sixty-eight times. Side trips were made to Mozambique to get the Portuguese governor on side. Rowland gained access to the colonial ruler through the intercession of the bishop of Beira and his counterpart in the capital city of Lourenço Marques (now called Maputo). Both bishops had received donations from Rowland for their favourite charities. He had to promise the Portuguese governor that he would compensate the railway company that already transported oil to Southern Rhodesia, and he had to take on a Portuguese partner, the Companhia da Moçambique, a royal chartered company that held sovereign rights over the territory in Mozambique through which the proposed pipeline would run. The Portuguese were still considering Rowland's proposal when he entered into an entirely separate set of negotiations on a business deal that would dramatically change the course of his career.

Years earlier, Rowland had landed a consulting job with the mining company Rio Tinto, which would later become Rio Tinto-Zinc, and it was through this job that he made contact with the London and Rhodesia Property Company Ltd., otherwise known as Lonrho. That company, founded in 1909, had ranches, plantations and gold mines in Rhodesia. Its major shareholders included firms associated with Harry Oppenheimer of De Beers and Anglo American; Lord Robins of the British South Africa Company, and Harley Drayton, head of 117 Old Broad Street Group in London, which invested money on behalf of the Church of England and the Crown. London and Rhodesia was the biggest firm in Rhodesia the year the war ended, but by the time Rowland came on the scene, its agricultural plantations were struggling as a result of a severe drought.

In 1959 Rowland approached Lonrho management about selling its Cam and Motor Gold Mining Co. Ltd. in Southern Rhodesia. Though Rowland was acting on behalf of Rio Tinto, he did not tell Lonrho who the ultimate buyer was until after the sale was complete. Lonrho's price might have been much higher if the company had known Rio Tinto was behind the deal. Unsubstantiated rumours alleged that Rowland had bribed the selling agents to seal the deal. But far from antagonizing Lonrho's leaders, Rowland's clever negotiating tactics secured him favourable attention. Drayton sent his personal assistant, Angus Ogilvy, a Scottish aristocrat married to Princess Alexandra, a cousin of Queen Elizabeth's, to feel out Rowland on a possible role at Lonrho. The approach was made in April 1961, and the deal was done in time to be put to shareholders at a general meeting on August 29, 1961. Tiny Rowland was to be joint managing director of Lonrho, along with the company's chairman, Alan Ball. The deal gave Rowland 1.5 million Lonrho shares, or 48 per cent of the company. In return, he turned over his interests in Norton Development Company Ltd., which distributed Mercedes cars; his stake in two gold mines held through Kanyemba Gold Mine and Mashaba Gold Mines Ltd.; and Associated Overseas Pipelines of Rhodesia Inc.

Harry Oppenheimer had been opposed to the arrangement. "We are very doubtful of the value of the pipeline," he wrote a colleague. "But [we] do agree that Rowland will probably put new life into the company." Alan Ball and others weighed in on the side of Rowland. Ball told people that the two main attractions for him were Rowland's energy and ability, and the potential of the pipeline to make money.

After the deal closed, consulting engineers hired by Lonrho discovered that the reserves in one of the mines, Kanyemba, were not as great as Rowland had claimed. The Mashaba mine registered a loss instead of the promised profit, and within six months it was clear that both gold mines were failures. Profits at Norton also fell short of Rowland's forecast.

That left the pipeline as the only real asset that he had brought to the table. Fortunately, the Portuguese government came through with its pipeline permission in December 1961. One last approval was required: that of the Rhodesians.

Salazar proved to be an easier nut to crack than the men running Southern Rhodesia. They wanted a pipeline to supply their landlocked country with oil, but they wanted to own it themselves, and they had already hired a Texan company to develop plans. The Rhodesian elite were suspicious of Rowland. There were rumours about his shady business practices. On the plus side, Rowland had the powerful backing of Sir Roy Welensky, prime minister of the Central African Federation, who called him "the best thing to happen to Africa since Cecil Rhodes." His support helped Rowland secure the approval of the Rhodesians in 1962.

It had been a five-year struggle to get the pipeline off the ground. A new company called Companhia do Pipeline Moçambique-Rodesia (CPMR) was created to build and operate it. Rowland's Portuguese partners owned 51 per cent of the company on the Mozambican side, and Lonrho held 49 per cent. The reverse ownership structure existed on the Rhodesian side of the border. Over the next two years, construction workers toiled in difficult conditions to lay the 300-kilometre line through marshes and mountain passes. A group of major oil companies, including Royal Dutch/Shell, British Petroleum, Caltex, Mobil and Total, built a refinery at the pipeline terminus in Rhodesia in anticipation of the line's completion.

In February 1965, the spigots were turned on and the first oil started through. Rowland was well pleased with himself for overcoming all the obstacles in his way, and he looked forward to having what he hoped would be a ceaseless money-making machine at his disposal. But this was not to be. Within the year, the pipeline was shut down. It would remain that way for almost fifteen years.

The situation had deteriorated in Mozambique, where the Portuguese were holding fast to their African possession. In response to the war of liberation that FRELIMO launched, the Portuguese implemented a scorched-earth policy and thousands of civilians were murdered. However, it was not these events that forced Lonrho to close its pipeline. The spigots were turned off on the orders of the British government.

The immediate catalyst for this action was the Unilateral Declaration of Independence made on November 11, 1965, by Ian Smith, the white prime minister of Rhodesia. Smith and his small, white ruling elite refused to give in to growing pressure within the British colony for black majority rule. The previous year, black governments had won independence for Northern Rhodesia, which had become Zambia, and for Nyasaland, which had become Malawi. Smith and his supporters were determined that whites would not lose control of Southern Rhodesia.

His declaration, made at a time when thirty-five former colonies in Africa had won their independence and established majority governments, provoked an international outcry. The United Nations Security Council passed a resolution the next day condemning the declaration and calling on all its members not to recognize "this illegal, racist, minority regime in Southern Rhodesia and to refrain from rendering any assistance to this illegal regime." A similar resolution was passed on November 20, stating that the United Kingdom, as the administering power in Rhodesia, looked upon the declaration "as an act of rebellion" and would take unspecified measures. One such measure was to deprive Southern Rhodesia of oil from the Beira pipeline.

Britain played a curious role in the period that followed. It could have crushed the Smith regime with its military might, but it did not, despite repeated calls by the UN Security Council to do all in its power to end the Rhodesian rebellion. And while Britain cracked down on Lonrho immediately, forcing the company to close down an asset Lonrho had not yet paid for, the authorities in London turned a blind eye to the activities of Royal Dutch/Shell and of British Petroleum, which was half-owned by the government. These two companies were shipping oil into Rhodesia by more southern routes. Political opinion in Britain was divided on how to deal with Smith, which partly explains the inconsistent application of

official policy. Still, it gave Rowland a jaundiced view of the British government and its claims of impartial behaviour. He vowed to deal with the
government in the future the way its officials had dealt with him.
Government officials, for their part, quickly realized that Rowland had a
knack for backing them into a corner if they were not careful.

At the time of the pipeline's closure, the CPMR was heavily in debt to
the Industrial Development Corporation of South Africa, which had
funded the pipeline's construction. The CPMR was expected to make loan
payments of £200,000 every six months—even without its pipeline revenues. A solution arrived in April 1966 in the form of the *Joanna V*, a
Greek ship carrying 16,000 tonnes of crude that was owned by a South
African company. It sailed into the port of Beira on April 5 and prepared
to unload. Official Portuguese policy was to allow free transit of goods
through its territories to its neighbours, no matter what those nations'
political stripes. There would be no opposition from the Mozambique
governor nor the Portuguese government to sending the oil through the
pipeline to Rhodesia. Britain, however, had other ideas.

The British government sent a representative, Lord Walston, to
Lisbon to persuade the Portuguese to change their official policy, but to
no avail. Walston then unwisely told Lonrho director Ogilvy that the
British government would pay the company £54,000 a month toward
their loan payments if the company would undertake to keep the pipeline
closed. The Board of Directors accepted the deal on April 7, and payments began the following month. Had Walston only waited a couple of
days, his offer would have been unnecessary. On April 9, the Security
Council passed another resolution. This one imposed a complete oil and
petroleum embargo on Southern Rhodesia, calling on the Portuguese to
refuse any products destined for the country and inviting Britain to
impose these sanctions by force if necessary.

The British government honoured Lord Walston's deal only until the
Joanna V sailed from Beira in August with its cargo still on board. They
then set up a naval blockade of the port to prevent other ships from arriving and gave Lonrho notice that the payments would end in October.

Rowland remonstrated with the government and threatened to sell the pipeline to South African or Southern Rhodesian interests, which would care a great deal less about British or UN sanctions. The government then passed an order-in-council giving it broad powers to prohibit property transfers when sanctions were involved. The sale, which some officials privately believed existed only in the mind of Tiny Rowland, was effectively quashed, and the payments were stopped on schedule.

Rowland let loose a barrage of complaints against the British government. He pointed out that Rhodesia was awash in oil that was being shipped in by Royal Dutch/Shell and British Petroleum through South Africa and the Mozambican port of Lourenço Marques. A letter Rowland wrote to J.R.A. Bottomley, the assistant undersecretary of state in the Commonwealth Office, on May 23, 1967, summed up his attitude. "The position, as I see it, is that HMG [Her Majesty's Government] has effectively throttled CPMR's trade in oil with Southern Rhodesia (its only trade) but is unable or unwilling to do anything about the trade through Lourenço Marques," wrote Rowland. "My representation is that, in fairness, HMG should either apply a closure to the latter trade or free the Beira trade. As the position stands, CPMR is the subject of a discriminatory sanction which is both totally unfair and against which, subject to advice which we are obtaining, it has no remedy but to seek legal redress. Not only is the present situation ruining our business in the short and medium term, but the Lourenço Marques trade is establishing a long-term pattern which will destroy our chance of recovery, even when the Rhodesia situation is finally resolved."

British officials brushed off his protests, claiming that Royal Dutch/Shell and BP had assured them that none of their oil was going to Rhodesia. They suggested that French or, perhaps, Dutch companies in Iraq were sanctions-busting. Those close to Rowland said he was approached by a senior executive of one oil company and offered money to keep quiet. He refused. Vindication finally came in 1978 when a government inquiry found that Royal Dutch/Shell and BP had flouted the sanctions regularly and that government officials had known about it. But by then Rowland was attracting little sympathy in Britain because of revelations about his questionable business tactics.

It was alleged that Rowland had himself circumvented the sanctions imposed on Rhodesia by setting up an offshore company in the Bahamas called Yeoman Investments Ltd. and transferring, through a complicated financial deal, his option rights in Lonrho to the new company. In this way he regained access to money that should have been frozen by sanctions. Two of the directors who agreed to the new package, Ogilvy and Ball, did so because Rowland promised to reward them financially, which he eventually did. Lonrho also managed to get copper from its Rhodesian mine onto world markets by buying a second, derelict mine just across the border in Mozambique and claiming that all the copper came from it. As rumours of these shady dealings swirled through financial circles in London, Warburgs, a prestigious name in the banking world, resigned as merchant bankers to Lonrho, and two of the company's directors left its board. "I have felt for a long time, and these feelings I have not hidden from you or the Board, that Tiny pays little heed to any advice or any views which his co-directors might offer him and that the company is run more as Tiny's private empire than as an important public company," wrote former director Andrew Caldecott in his letter of resignation. Caldecott later testified before an official inquiry that while Rowland had rejuvenated the "sleepy, dozy company [Lonrho] into something dynamic," he was also "a sort of tyrant and part madman to boot." For his part, Rowland referred to his Board of Directors dismissively as "plastic gnomes" or "Christmas tree decorations."

Following the resignations of the directors and the departure of Warburgs, Lonrho's board was restructured. Members of the new group, however, led a boardroom revolt in 1973. Rowland announced that he would not accept any kind of limitation on his personal authority and freedom: he would stay on his own terms or not at all. In the end, it was his challengers who were sent packing. But the revolt did spark an official inquiry into Lonrho's activities.

That inquiry shed light on the so-called special payments Rowland made to black leaders. Rowland had never made a secret of the fact that he regularly doled out gifts, rewards and inducements. He had once shocked a Foreign Office official by saying that he found ministers in Kenya "were much more sensible" than those in Zambia when it came to having a little bit of money invested for them in offshore accounts. When the official told Rowland that the less he said about this to a government official the better, Rowland laughed heartily. Another time, he told a Zambian minister accompanying him on a flight over Africa that there was not a president in the countries they were flying over whom he could not buy.

The inquiry asked Lonrho for a list of "special payments" that had been made overseas since 1961, the year Rowland had joined the company. Lonrho produced a list of 194 items totalling £1.2 million, a substantial amount in 1973. Rowland would ask the company accountant to transfer money to his personal account without saying what it was intended for and would then write a personal cheque to the recipient. He told the inquiry that this gave the gift the personal touch needed to create a bond between the recipient and himself. For accounting purposes, the payments were spread among a number of companies within the conglomerate, making it difficult for anyone but Rowland to determine the total amount spent in this manner. The inquiry report upbraided Lonrho's directors for not being more forceful in questioning where the money went, but concluded that the payments had been made to further Lonrho's business interests outside the UK. Business bribes did not raise eyebrows then the way they do now.

Although clear-cut examples of bribery, fraud and larceny were uncovered by the inquiry, no government sanction was forthcoming. The report was released at a sensitive time in Britain's relations with Africa. The government did not want to harm its relations with the recipients of Rowland's gifts, some of whom now headed African countries. Most of these leaders were indebted to Rowland in more ways than one. He had invested money in their countries when most other Western businesspeople were giving independent Africa a miss, and he had spent time developing personal relationships, giving them gifts to help secure their loyalty and admiration.

After the report came out, Scotland Yard began an investigation, but decided two years later not to press charges. The man who had headed that investigation was subsequently hired by Lonrho. Rumours spread, though they were never substantiated, that Rowland was protected because he had ties to Britain's secret services. Some official files bearing his name at the Public Records Office near London remain closed to the public for national security reasons even though the customary thirty-year deadline for opening them has passed.

The inquiry left Rowland unchastised and unchastened. No one could be under any illusions about how he operated. Directors were to be ignored or circumvented if they disagreed with his plans. "Special payments" were the order of the day. There was no reason to believe that Rowland would change his behaviour after successfully surviving a boardroom revolt and official scrutiny. And he did not.

When Rhodesia finally gained independence in 1980 under Robert Mugabe and international sanctions were lifted, Rowland thought that at long last he could reopen his pipeline and recoup the investment he had made in time and money. The mothballed asset had lain idle for almost a decade and a half, and it was unclear whether the equipment could still function. Engineers began pressure testing the line in September 1980 and found that an 80-kilometre stretch running through the Pungwe marshes had to be replaced. Rowland set about refurbishing it at a cost of US$20 million. But his efforts were soon to be disrupted again. In April 1981, the rebel group RENAMO vowed to destroy the pipeline, and then hit it several times as repairs were being made. This was the period when RENAMO was entering the most brutal phase in its campaign of terror, aided and abetted by South Africa.

The apartheid regime in Pretoria had been watching with alarm as one African country after another gained independence under a black majority government. To counter this threat, Prime Minister P.W. Botha put in place what was known as the "total strategy," which aimed to destabilize neighbouring governments by political, economic and military means. To garner Western support, Botha cast his program in Cold War terms, claiming that South Africa faced "a total Marxist onslaught" within the region.

South Africa's "total strategy" had several aims: to arm and support rebel movements in order to keep neighbouring governments busy dealing with unrest within their borders, giving them less time to oppose the apartheid regime; to attack and destroy infrastructure such as ports, railways and roads in those countries in order to make them more dependent on South African links; and to undermine their economies and governments in order to show the world that black government did not work.

RENAMO, a collection of dissident FRELIMO officers and traditional religious leaders who were angry at their loss of power to Machel, had been created by the Rhodesian secret service in 1976 and was funded and armed by them until 1980, when Rhodesia became Zimbabwe. South Africa stepped in at that point and began teaching RENAMO how to use terror tactics to strike at civilians as well as the military. The rebels derailed trains and shot at passengers as they scrambled for safety. Buses and trucks were targeted the same way. People attacked in their cars were sometimes roasted alive. Crops were razed, shops burned and entire villages put to the torch. Relief convoys carrying food were hit. People suspected of supporting Machel's FRELIMO government were mutilated, their noses, ears, breasts or limbs chopped off. Bodies were thrown down wells to poison the water supply as they rotted.

Rowland could have been in no doubt about the nature of RENAMO when he met with its leader, Afonso Dhlakama, to try to work out a deal that would prove advantageous to them both. Rowland needed to protect his pipeline. The Mozambican army couldn't do it because it had its hands full fighting the rebels. Physical surveillance was impossible because of the length of the line and the difficult terrain it passed through. The only practical alternative for Rowland seemed to be to pay the rebels not to attack it. The rebels were definitely in need of money. In Sierra Leone, Angola and the Congo, rebel groups used illicit diamonds to buy food and weapons. "Mozambique has no diamonds," said a former minister in the Machel government. "It has cashew nuts. It's very difficult to make war with cashew nuts."

In exchange for funds, Dhlakama agreed not to attack the manned pumping stations in order to avoid loss of life and destruction of expensive pumping equipment. But in order to preserve his rebel credentials, Dhlakama would continue to attack the pipeline running between the stations. Details of the arrangement between Lonrho and RENAMO are contained in a British government document that was subsequently confirmed by Rowland. Under the agreement, RENAMO would be paid US$500,000 a month for three months, starting on June 1, 1982. The timing of the first payment was significant: it ensured that RENAMO had money in hand before the pipeline reopened for business on June 19, 1982. Though the initial agreement was to run until the end of August 1982, the deal stipulated that it would continue indefinitely until one or the other party gave one month's notice of termination.

It is not clear how much money was paid under the deal. As the inquiry's report had established earlier, Rowland handled his special payments personally. He preferred not to take others into his confidence on these matters, even his own board members. Gomes, the FRELIMO supporter who joined Lonrho in 1987 as chairman for southern Africa, said he saw no evidence during his time with the company that would have led him to believe Rowland had been paying RENAMO. But Rowland would not have confided such a dangerous secret to anyone with links to the Machel government—the farms he received from Machel would have been repossessed and his influence undermined.

On the RENAMO side, the deal was also kept a close secret. At the same hotel where I met with Gomes in Maputo, I later interviewed Raul Domingos, rebel chief of staff, who had directed guerrilla actions and had overseen the armament and keep of the rebels during the war. When peace arrived, Domingos had entered politics and had since become a political consultant. Domingos said he had had little contact with Rowland himself. Dhlakama preferred to conduct his meetings with Rowland in private. Questioned about the arrangement to protect the pumping stations, Domingos hedged his answer: "If there was anything given, it was not officially given." He did not see any of the money. It may well have been that instead of trickling down to the rebels who were fighting on the ground, the money was salted away in European bank accounts for that day in the future when the war would be over and the former rebel leaders would need something to fall back on. That would have been in keeping with Rowland's modus operandi. Paul Spicer, who was Lonrho director for many years, said in a different context that Rowland understood that guerrilla leaders worried about what would happen to them when peace arrived: "He understood the psychology of the guerrilla leader."

The protection payments represented a huge amount of money, but Lonrho was by now a massive conglomerate. Throughout the late 1960s and the 1970s, the company had experienced a growth spurt, with sales leaping to £2.1 billion in 1981, up from £4 million twenty years earlier. Lonrho had expanded into Kenya and Uganda with coffee plantations, packaging, engineering and newspapers, into Malawi with sugarcane plantations and into Ghana with the acquisition of the rich mine belonging to Ashanti Goldfields Corp. Ltd. It entered Nigeria, buying the largest textile firm in West Africa. At one point, Rowland persuaded the members of the Organization of African Unity, a body set up by black leaders in the 1960s, to co-ordinate their policies and their stand against South Africa, to let Lonrho control oil supplies in the region. The idea collapsed, however, when a group of OAU countries complained about the quasi-diplomatic status that the deal would give Rowland. Ugandan dictator Idi Amin wrote his fellow OAU members claiming that Lonrho was a leading imperialist and Zionist company that sold military weapons, propaganda machinery and petroleum products to racist regimes that used the supplies to fight OAU members.

Despite such setbacks, Rowland had built the company into a huge, sprawling conglomerate with worldwide operations and a strong African base. There were plenty of sources of funds to tap for the RENAMO payments and an equally large number of places where such payments could be hidden.

But the peace Rowland had purchased for his pipeline did not last long. Whether the money stopped or RENAMO unilaterally abrogated the deal is not clear. But in October 1982, rebels backed by South Africa attacked the oil pumping station at Maforga and kidnapped three pipeline workers, their wives and a five-year-old child. Kidnapping was becoming an increasingly popular way for the rebels to raise money. Roman Catholic nuns, an Italian electrical engineer and eight Soviet geologists would all be kidnapped by RENAMO over the next twelve months. In the case of the pipeline workers, Lonrho denied that it paid a ransom; but company insiders said that money must have changed hands in order to secure the release of all seven hostages a month later.

Rowland saw that despite his best efforts, his pipeline remained vulnerable. The day after the attack at Maforga, he met in London with the minister of defence of Mozambique. They agreed that Machel would have to ask Zimbabwe for help. The president travelled to Harare and told Mugabe that Mozambique was not capable of protecting the pipeline. Because Zimbabwe was in desperate need of the oil, Mugabe reluctantly agreed to send his soldiers to defend it.

The appearance of the Zimbabwean troops ushered in another brief period of calm in the corridor. In 1982, the pipeline had shut down for twenty-four days after its mid-year start-up because of rebel activities. In 1983, it was out of commission only a few days and Lonrho claimed in its annual report that oil had been pumped without interruption throughout the year. But in 1984 closures amounted to thirty-two days, and in 1985 another twenty-four days were lost. The pipeline was profitable, but attacks and disruptions were a constant headache.

Much of the economic sabotage on the pipeline and elsewhere was actually conducted by well-armed and well-trained South African commandos, who then allowed RENAMO to take the credit. This was the case in December 1982 when South African commandos destroyed a fuel depot at Beira and caused £15 million worth of damage to the port. A RENAMO spokesman in Lisbon said the attack was a warning to the government of Zimbabwe to withdraw its troops from Mozambique. Machel decided that war in his country would not end unless he negotiated a peace deal directly with the Botha government in South Africa. FRELIMO began low-level negotiations with the South Africans at the end of 1982.

It was at this point that Machel invited Rowland to Maputo, unaware that the business had been financing RENAMO. Rowland took up Machel's

offer of state-owned land and set about establishing agricultural plantations in the country. To do this, he turned to British agricultural expert
John Hewlett.

I reached Hewlett by satellite phone at his new home near Pemba, on
the Indian Ocean coast in the far north of Mozambique. Hewlett said he
had initially come to Africa in 1979 to join a British firm that was growing cotton in Zambia. The firm was then taken over by Lonrho. His first
meeting with his new boss took place in the parking lot of a building in
Lusaka, where he lived and where Lonrho maintained a flat. "I got on with
Tiny Rowland fantastically well," recalled Hewlett. "I was an underling,
but he didn't put on airs. Quite the opposite. He was the most down-to-
earth person you could wish to meet."

Rowland sent Hewlett to Mozambique to set up the promised agricultural investments. Hewlett and agriculture minister João Ferreira went
around the country selecting land for cotton and tomato farms. Rowland
had originally wanted the farms to produce maize cereal to feed
Mozambicans, as a political gesture. But the decision was made to go with
cotton because maize would not be profitable. A tomato farm was set up
near Machel's home village.

The plantations faced immediate problems because Mozambique
was still embroiled in civil war. Though talks with South Africa appeared
to bear fruit in March 1984 with the Nkomati Non-Aggression Pact, in
which South Africa agreed to stop supporting RENAMO and Mozambique
agreed to stop supporting the African National Congress, the South
African military was not monolithic. Elements within the military and
intelligence forces disagreed with the Nkomati pact and continued to
support RENAMO surreptitiously. This was confirmed when the RENAMO
base on Gorongosa Mountain was overrun in August 1985, and captured
documents revealed that South African support had not stopped. Machel
had suspected as much all along because the civil war had not abated in
the wake of the Nkomati Pact. In some places, it had intensified.

The employees working on Lonrho's pipeline and farms were under
tremendous stress because they were targets in the ongoing conflict. One

former Lonrho manager who worked on the farms said he needed a bul-
let-proof vehicle just to get to work. When one of his employees refused
for a month to leave the office building, he had to push the man to go out
and survey operations. The employee was shot at eighteen times that first
day. What kept employees going, said the former manager, was that they
thought they were making a difference in Mozambique. The farms and
the pipeline represented jobs for the people and revenue for the government. "Where I worked," he said, "people had no food, no clothes, and no
roads. In one area people had to walk seventy-three kilometres to the
nearest shop." Lonrho set up shops in 360 villages in the areas where it
operated. "Money always helps," the former manager said, referring to the
salaries Lonrho workers were paid. "But it is not the only motivation."

The civil war intensified in 1985 and 1986. Machel was killed in a plane
crash the exact cause of which has never been determined, although suspicions were rife that the South Africans were behind it. He was replaced by
his deputy, Joaquim Chissano. RENAMO became more predatory as its overt
support from South Africa ended. When Malawi bowed to pressure from
neighbouring countries and stopped allowing RENAMO forces to use its territory for their rear bases, the rebels went home in force and violence increased
in Mozambique. Zimbabwe augmented its troops in the country to ten
thousand, of which about two thousand were assigned to the pipeline.

The Mozambican government hired a British private military company called Defence Systems Ltd. (DSL) to help train its army and to protect strategic assets. Gomes said that one attraction DSL held for the
Mozambicans was that the wife of the head of the company worked as a
secretary for Margaret Thatcher. The government reasoned that this
would give them a direct line to the top. Lonrho decided to hire the
military company for farm security. It later replaced DSL with another
British security firm, Gurkha Security Guards. By one estimate, Lonrho
was spending US$1 million a year on security alone, which accounted for
30 per cent of its operating costs in Mozambique. While the pipeline was
profitable, recouping the original investment within the first two years of
its renewed operation, the farms were too new to be making money. The

cost of security and the attendant difficulties in doing business in a war zone were slowly grinding Lonrho down.

The turning point came in 1990 when RENAMO attacked one of the farms, killing six people. The attack had succeeded despite the fact that the farm was protected by a company militia numbering 1,500, supported by the Gurkha Security Guards. Hewlett said he told Rowland that he saw no point in carrying on. Rowland agreed that a new approach had to be found. He decided to try peace negotiations.

The rebels and FRELIMO had already made tentative contact, and a peace process led by the Sant'Egidio community of the Roman Catholic Church and by the Italian government was just getting off the ground. Rowland decided to support their efforts. Over the course of the next two years, he used his private jet to ferry various leaders to and from negotiations in Africa and Europe. He lavished attention on Dhlakama, once even flying the rebel leader's wife to Rome for a shopping spree. How much money he gave Dhlakama during this period remains unclear. One report alleged that Rowland agreed to give RENAMO between US$6 and US$8 million to sign a peace deal. But whether that money came from Lonrho, the United Nations or the Italian government was not spelled out.

When the terms of a peace deal were announced in Rome in 1992, both Dhlakama and Chissano thanked Rowland personally. Gomes, who had left Lonrho's employ, says his former boss would have done anything for Dhlakama at that moment because the rebel leader had thanked him publicly. How big a role Rowland played in the process, however, is debatable. "The peace was made by the churches and Italy," says Gomes. "It was not done by Tiny. But no one wanted him completely out because he would disrupt the thing." Hewlett says Rowland considered the peace talks a great personal triumph: "He used to say, 'Now we've done Mozambique, the next thing is Sudan.'" But that never happened because just as the Mozambique peace deal was concluded, Lonrho slid into turmoil.

Although the company's operations were diverse, spread both geographically and across business sectors, it had relied on its mining operations to make up for losses in other areas. When the price of precious metals fell precipitously in the early 1990s, Lonrho was hit hard. In the past, Rowland had turned to some unusual sources to solve the company's financial problems. He had sold one-third of the shares in the Metropole Hotel Group to Libyan dictator Mu'ammer Gaddafi for £177.5 million, prompting an uproar and accusations that he did business with terrorists. To solve his latest difficulties, he turned to a rank outsider, German financier Dieter Bock. Rowland made Bock the major shareholder in the company and hoped to act as his mentor. But the financier had other ideas. Bock used his controlling stake to change the company's management structure, divesting many operations to focus on a few core areas. He then trained his sights on the man who had brought him into the company.

Rowland's position was considerably weaker now than it had been in 1973, the last time he had taken on his board. He was no longer the controlling shareholder of the group, nor were his business practices considered completely sound. He had waged a long battle with Egyptian businessman Mohammed Al Fayed for control of the Harrods luxury department store in London, a battle that had cost Lonrho shareholders millions of pounds and that was seen as a personal vendetta. In addition, the mood in London financial circles was firmly against him. Charismatic tycoons who ran their empires single-handedly had fallen out of favour following the mysterious death of publishing magnate Robert Maxwell in 1991. Initially honoured by commentators, Maxwell was vilified when it was discovered that he had been pilfering money from his companies' pension funds to prop up a sagging corporate empire. Hewlett, by then a director on the board of Lonrho, says these revelations sparked a wave of "tycoonitis." Since Lonrho had been controlled for more than three decades by just one man, it seemed an obvious company to examine next. "People got nervous," says Hewlett. "There was a run on the share price."

The end for Rowland came in 1994 when the board decided he would no longer be chief executive, or even a director. He did not leave without a fight. At the first Lonrho annual general meeting following his dismissal, he made a dramatic entrance, sweeping into London's Barbican

Hall surrounded by an entourage. Although journalists were barred from the meeting, I gained access by lingering on the fringes of his circle and passing for one of this group.

For the first time, Rowland took his seat among the shareholders and glared up at his successor on the podium. Bock managed to get through most of the meeting without even mentioning Rowland. But when the period for questions and answers arrived, some shareholders spoke in Rowland's defence. "How can you stab in the back the very man who devoted his life to building up this company?" asked one. "Tiny Rowland is the jewel in the crown of Lonrho," said another. "Judas!" shouted a third at Lonrho chairman Sir John Leahy after a proposal to make Rowland honorary president was defeated. While Rowland retained the affection of these small shareholders, Bock had the large institutional holdings on his side. With drama and pathos, Rowland's career with Lonrho came to an end. Three years later, at the age of eighty, he died of skin cancer.

Tiny Rowland stands out from most of the other business leaders chronicled in this book in that he was not motivated solely by the bottom line. His managers were united in saying that he rarely wanted to know about the details of operations and preferred to focus on the big picture. As the years went on and he grew bored with the business world, the big picture he was interested in was the African political landscape. But even in African politics, his actions did not add up to a considered policy. He backed groups and leaders of every political stripe and even kept his hand in with colonial governments. Sometimes his involvement advanced his business interests, other times there was no obvious gain to be had. After researching his activities in Mozambique and interviewing the men who had either worked with him or had dealt with him on a political level, I was still no clearer on what had drove Tiny Rowland. To learn more, I decided to meet with the two people who had known him best: his widow, Josie Rowland, and Kenneth Kaunda, the former president of Zambia.

Josie Rowland invited me to her sixteenth-century home on the banks of the Thames River outside London to talk about the man she first met in Rhodesia when she was just seven years old and her father was his local manager. Ensconced in comfortable armchairs, with a fire roaring in the grate, we had a view of the expanse of green lawn that rolled down to the water. She chatted about Rowland's early years in Germany, mentioning his membership in the Hitler Youth and his later internment by the British. That experience had shaped his view of the world, she said: "With that background, Tiny had sympathy for people who couldn't get a hearing. He had a strong feeling that if only people could talk, there was a chance they would reach a solution."

She pulled out the family photo albums, which were unusual in that they showed both the public and the private faces of Rowland. Interspersed with images of children's birthday parties and holidays in the sun were photos of him on board his jet in the company of African leaders or speaking at a Lonrho annual meeting. When I remarked on the holiday snaps of her husband playing in a pool with his children or sitting on a sun-drenched terrace eating lunch, Josie Rowland said that holidays were rarer than the pictures might suggest. Her husband could not stand sitting still and always had to be working on something. She laughed as she recalled Rowland's reply when one of his executives asked him if he'd enjoyed a rare business-free excursion to Venice with his family: "If you've seen one museum, you've seen them all." She insisted that money wasn't what had governed his actions—he had made enough of that early on. What he liked about business, and later about African politics, was negotiating and solving problems. Throughout their married life, Rowland travelled extensively. It was the practice of certain hotels to put up a board in the lobby for visiting businesspeople to post their cards, letting others know they were in residence. "Tiny used to tell me he'd like to have a card that just said, 'Any business problems? Call room xxx,'" she said.

I left Josie Rowland that day thinking that I now had a more personal, if sympathetic, portrait of her husband. But there were still questions in my mind about the business tactics that had gotten him into so much hot water with the media and his peers. Perhaps an African leader who had seen Rowland in action might provide some answers.

I was in Lusaka when the opportunity arose to meet former Zambian president Kenneth Kaunda, whose relationship with Rowland had spanned decades. Kaunda was one of the leaders who had benefited from the use of Rowland's private jet. He had approved Lonrho business deals in his country, including the purchase of an amethyst mine, and had gone into business with Rowland himself for a time, marketing amethysts. He had also nationalized some of Lonrho's assets. Rowland's biographers suggested that he relied heavily on Kaunda for advice.

When Kaunda and I met at his residence in Lusaka, he had retired from active political life and was concentrating his efforts on publicizing the dangers of AIDS, a disease exacting a horrible toll in Zambia. The aging politician was reluctant to say much about Rowland, perhaps because he wanted to save that material for his own memoirs, or perhaps because of the strong African taboo against speaking ill of the dead. "I think it is difficult to say what drove Tiny Rowland," said Kaunda. "Some of the things he did were quite helpful." Here he paused while carefully considering his next words. "Others were not." Despite his long relationship with the colourful and contradictory Rowland, the man remained a bit of a mystery for him. "I'm not sure I understood him myself," he said.

Unfortunately for Mozambique, the farms Rowland had started with such fanfare in the 1980s were never a financial success. They went bankrupt and were sold. Lonrho's interest in Tiny's treasured pipeline was also disposed of by the new company management. Even though the pipeline had been profitable, it did not fit with Bock's idea of a new, streamlined conglomerate. On the political side, the peace deal Rowland had been involved with held, and RENAMO was integrated into the political process. If that were the sum of his actions in the country, his record could be viewed positively. But there remains his financial support of RENAMO during the period when it was waging its fiercest battle against Mozambique's government and the civilian population. Rowland's money helped sustain its brutal force. The enormous loss of life that resulted must also be weighed in any overall assessment of his role in the country.

$$\left(\text{CHAPTER SIX} \right)$$

SHELL IN NIGERIA

LOOKING DOWN ON THE NIGER DELTA FROM THE AIR, THE FUNDAMENTAL reason why dissent has been simmering in the oil-producing area for decades becomes clear. Below lies a riverine landscape. Muddy brown rivers snake every which way, and mangrove swamps spread in a knobby emerald carpet to the sea. The delta is one of the world's largest wetlands. It is also the source of great oil wealth. Since the late 1950s, Royal Dutch/Shell and other multinationals have extracted an estimated US$340 billion worth of oil from underneath the giant green sponge of the delta. Their installations mar its undulating curves. Angular clearings surround company sheds, production rigs and equipment. Ruler-straight channels link the installations with the river or mark the route of underwater pipelines. More spectacularly, giant gas flares reaching several storeys high make it perpetual day for the villagers living nearby. While the oil industry has implanted itself in the delta, there is little sign of the wealth it has generated in the impoverished communities. Villagers live much as they have for hundreds of years, in thatch-roofed wooden huts sitting on stilts by the river. Communal latrines empty directly into the water, and there is little electrification. The most common means of transport is still a dugout canoe. People survive by subsistence farming and fishing. Cherished jobs in the oil industry are only for the lucky few.

In the early days of the Nigerian oil industry, colonial authorities passed legislation to ensure that all mineral rights belonged to the central government and that all oil revenues pertaining to the state would flow to them before being disbursed. At independence in 1960, there was a rough formula in place that sent 50 per cent of revenues back to the region from which they were generated. However, as oil production in the delta became the largest source of revenue for the government, a succession of military rulers began reducing that figure, first to 45 per cent in 1970, then to 20 per cent in 1975. The regions' share was cancelled altogether for a time, and when it was reintroduced in 1982, it was a paltry 1.5 per cent—far short of the rate at independence. The delta communities have watched helplessly as the riches from their region have been siphoned off and used to line the pockets of corrupt leaders, to profit foreign share-holders or to provide services elsewhere in Nigeria. The capital, Abuja, with its wide avenues, monumental buildings and reliable infrastructure, was built with oil money. For decades, the delta people have pleaded for some of that wealth to improve their living conditions. For decades, their calls have gone unanswered. On October 30, 1990, their frustration boiled over.

It started, as so many cataclysmic events do, with a seemingly trivial occurrence. The road linking the village of Umuechem to a nearby market had washed out, as it did every rainy season. Even though the state was responsible for the upkeep of the roads, the villagers decided to mount a peaceful protest against Shell. Their logic was simple: unlike the military rulers in far-off Abuja, Shell had representatives right there on the ground, tending a flowstation where pipelines from several oil fields joined together and a giant gas flare burned. Shell Petroleum Development Corp., to give the local subsidiary its full title, was a joint venture between the multinational and the Nigerian state oil company, and it had been pumping 60,000 barrels a day from beneath the villagers' lands for decades. In the past, the oil company had responded to protests in other communities by funding hospitals and building schools. The thinking in Umuechem was that a demonstration might persuade the company to fix the road. In the consensual way that decisions are made in delta villages, a plan emerged for the men to occupy the flowstation in order to get the company's attention. They saw it as the opening gambit in negotiations. Shell treated it as a declaration of war.

There are two versions of what happened that day. Some witnesses said that the several hundred demonstrators who participated in the protest were nothing but peaceful. They sang songs, ate oranges and drank palm wine, the poor man's drink in West Africa. Others reported that the men who chased Shell security guards and staff away from the flowstation facilities were armed with machetes. It is very likely that they were—the machete is a symbol of masculinity in this part of Nigeria, as well as a ubiquitous tool, and it is carried to almost every public gathering, even burials. It would have been in the eye of the beholder whether the machetes were brandished aggressively or carried peacefully.

Shell managers felt it was too dangerous for them to go to Umuechem and negotiate directly with the villagers. They were concerned for the lives of their staff and the safety of their property. So they asked the military government of Rivers State, in which Umuechem is located, to send in the police. And not just any police. Joshua Udofia, the Shell manager who made the request to the state police commissioner, specifically asked for the Mobile Police, known to the locals as the "Kill and Go." Unlike the local police, who are widely regarded as corrupt but weak, the Mobile Police are feared because of their reputation for brutality. They are trained to deal with riots and violent demonstrations. In his urgent message to the commissioner, Udofia wrote that he had reason to believe that the villagers were going to be violent.

The police commissioner first sent a unit of regular police to Umuechem. The demonstrators were infuriated—they wanted to talk to Shell representatives. They chased the police away and shut down the flowstation, figuring that turning off the spigots and preventing the flow of oil would accomplish their goal. But Shell managers still refused to come. Instead, they sent a second letter to state authorities, asking for more police support. That same night, Shell got its wish. The Mobile Police arrived at dusk and unleashed their fury on Umuechem.

The police killed villagers indiscriminately, shooting whomever stood in their path. Homes were looted, then blasted apart with grenades and burned to the ground. An official inquiry into the massacre would later conclude that the Mobile Police had acted like an invading army that had vowed to take the last drop of its enemy's blood. In the end, 495 houses were destroyed and an unofficial estimate put the death toll at 80. The inquiry could not determine exactly how many people had died because many bodies and body parts had been tossed into the Otamiri River. Responsibility for the slaughter was laid at the door of the Mobile Police, and the inquiry recommended that legal action be taken against some officers. Rivers State agreed to pay damages to 1,032 villagers for the loss of lives, homes and worldly goods. But many of the cheques bounced.

Though Shell officials said they were stunned by the Umuechem massacre and that they very much regretted the suffering and loss of life, they felt that all responsibility lay with the police. Shell had only had the best of intentions, they said, when requesting police services because this represented the best chance of a peaceful solution. But critics of the company were quick to point out that the federal force had been called out to quell a similar demonstration in another delta village three years earlier and had killed two people. Shell, they believed, should have foreseen what would happen when they requested the "Kill and Go."

Umuechem was one of ninety-five community disruptions to Shell operations in 1990, but it stood out because of the violence of the police response and because it could be proven that the oil company had explicitly asked that the demonstration be quelled by a police unit notorious for its brutality. Shell hadn't built its own army, hired mercenaries or employed a former spymaster to create the conditions necessary for its operations, but it had relied on the security arm of a repressive regime. The bloodletting at Umuechem had been carried out on the company's behalf.

What is so striking about Shell's professed shock at the incident is that the company was winning kudos around the world at the time for its strategic vision. It had correctly anticipated the oil crisis that had crippled the West in 1973, the prolonged drop in oil prices in the late 1980s and the collapse of communism in 1989. Credit was given to the company's practice of scenario planning, which involved pulling together the company's brightest minds on a regular basis and asking them to peer five, ten, twenty years into the future and work out possible scenarios of how the world would change. Managers were given the information and asked to think through how the company could react to each scenario should the need arise. In this way, the company hoped to stay one step ahead of its competitors. Over the years, Shell's planning department spawned a host of management gurus revered in the international business community for their insight.

Yet despite the application of all this impressive brainpower, Shell was caught completely off guard by the dissent that roiled the Niger Delta in the 1990s as villages began demanding a share in the oil wealth and redress for environmental damage caused by decades of oil production. Even after the tragedy at Umuechem, it took another five years of increasing violence in the delta, namely in nearby Ogoniland, before Shell became fully aware that it had a problem. And that happened only after Nigeria's military rulers executed Ogoni spokesperson Ken Saro-Wiwa and eight of his colleagues in 1995 on murder charges that were widely believed to have been trumped up. Saro-Wiwa had been a thorn in the side of the Nigerian government and the oil companies for his outspoken protests against the environmental damage being done to Ogoni lands. Shell was suddenly in the international spotlight, blamed for not doing enough to prevent the executions and for polluting the Niger Delta. That same year, the company was hit with another wave of bad publicity over its plans to dispose of the oil storage platform Brent Spar by dumping it in the Atlantic Ocean. International boycotts of the company's products sprang up in key consumer markets, and Shell became a byword for corporate wrongdoing. Shell is currently being sued in a US court for complicity in human rights abuses in Nigeria, in particular for the hanging of Saro-Wiwa. If anticipating the 1973 oil crisis was the company's greatest forecasting success, Nigeria was its greatest failure.

To understand why Shell remained blind to the problems in the delta for so long, it is necessary to reach deep into the history of the company in Nigeria and examine the roots of its relations with a succession of military despots. The symbiotic nature of that mutually advantageous relationship was one source of blindness. Another was the character of the company itself. Shell is a global conglomerate, with decentralized management and operations in 140 countries. Like the supertankers it uses to transport its products to the four corners of the world, the oil giant has difficulty changing course even when the map clearly indicates there are reefs ahead.

Shell Transport and Trading Company was started in 1897 by two brothers, Marcus and Sam Samuel, who had inherited a trading concern from their father. The new company began life as a shipping company, transporting kerosene and other oil products around the world. The brothers branched into production, starting in Borneo, to ensure that there would always be a ready supply of oil on hand for its ships. At the beginning of the twentieth century, a series of commercial disasters drove Shell into the arms of its competitor Royal Dutch of the Netherlands. The two companies agreed on a novel arrangement whereby they would merge all their subsidiaries but keep the parent companies separate. Royal Dutch/Shell does not exist as a legal entity. The closest it comes to having a chairman is the head of a body known as the Committee of Managing Directors whose members are the heads of all the various group subsidiaries. Its decision-making process is collegial rather than hierarchical. Like some African societies, it is acephalous, an organization with many heads, which makes interacting with it confusing for outsiders.

Throughout its history, Shell maintained particularly tight links with the British government, putting its tanker fleet at the government's disposal at the start of the First World War; helping to create the Petroleum Board in Britain during the Second World War, an agreement under which the oil companies suspended competition during the conflict; and loaning its film unit to the government during that same war to pump out propaganda and training films. Shell built its headquarters, the first skyscraper in London, almost directly across the Thames River from the seat of government at Westminster. Its executives could look forward to a knighthood or elevation to the House of Lords at the end of their corporate life. It was on the basis of this cozy relationship that British authorities gave Shell an exclusive oil licence for Nigeria at the end of 1938.

Shell's decision to go to the African country was made in the midst of a four-year battle between the company and the left-wing Mexican government of General Lázaro Cárdenas. Fearing that the outcome of the dispute would be the nationalization of Shell properties in Mexico, the company went looking for other sources of production safely within the British Empire. Nigeria was a British colony, and other oil companies had done some prospecting there as early as 1907. But the oil industry in the region didn't really begin until Shell arrived in 1938. The company's original concession was 357,000 square miles, and it had the country to itself until 1955, when Socony-Vacuum Oil Co. (which later became Mobil) was granted an exploration licence for northern Nigeria. In 1951, Shell's concession was reduced to 58,000 square miles and then further lowered to 40,000 square miles in 1957. But the company ensured that it was left with the most promising areas of the Niger Delta. Its first significant oil discovery in commercial quantities was made at Oloibiri in 1956. Umuechem followed shortly afterward, along with a raft of other finds. Oil production officially began in 1957, and the first cargo of Nigerian oil was exported in 1958.

Under pressure from the United States, the colonial authorities decided to open the Nigerian industry to other players following the nationalization of the Suez Canal by Egyptian president Gamal Abdel Nasser in 1956. Tennessee, Gulf, American Overseas, Agip, SAFRAP (later Elf), Philips and Esso all acquired licences in the early 1960s. By that time, Shell was already well established onshore. The latecomers got its leavings, plus newly opened concessions offshore. Initially, this was a huge advantage for Shell. Producing on land is cheaper and easier than producing offshore. Ultimately, however, it left the company with the most exposure to the local communities. The delta people blame Shell for their plight because more often than not Shell is the company operating in the area or it held the concession historically. Its subsidiary produces about half of the total 2 million barrels a day pumped in Nigeria.

In the beginning, the oil companies operated at arm's length from the Nigerian government. But that changed after independence when a series of military rulers sought to tighten their hold on the industry and its burgeoning revenues. That these rulers remained indifferent to the plight of villagers in the delta was largely due to ethnic politics. There are an estimated 250 ethnic groups in the country, but politics are dominated by the three largest. During colonial times, Britain ruled the region through elites drawn from the Yoruba in the southwest, the Hausa-Fulani in the north, and the Igbo in the southeast. When the colonizers left, these groups took over the levers of power. The military men who seized control in 1966 and ruled almost continually until the 1999 elections were mainly from the north and cared little for the smaller minority groups of the delta. In a country of 110 million people where the abiding culture is to look after yourself first, then your family, your village and finally your ethnic group, the 7 million people in the delta are orphans, cut off from wealth and power.

The formation of OPEC (Organization of Petroleum Exporting Countries) in 1960 was a turning point for the oil industry in the developing world because it prompted a wave of nationalization. State expropriation had been a prevailing fear in the oil sector ever since 1909, when the US government seized vast tracts of land where oil companies were operating. The Communists nationalized private holdings in Russia in 1918, a move that directly affected Shell. Persia cancelled the Anglo-Persian Oil Company's concession in 1932. Most governments who nationalized oil companies quickly discovered that they lacked the skills to keep the seized assets operating efficiently. In order to secure ownership of its oil resources and at the same time keep the expertise of the foreign oil companies, Saudi Arabia pioneered the concept of partial state ownership in 1968. It was this model that the Nigerians chose to follow.

In 1971, the same year Nigeria joined OPEC, the military government decreed that all oil companies would now have to operate as joint ventures with the state. Shell acquiesced because the alternative—banishment from the region—was too dire to contemplate. The company entered into a joint venture with the state-owned Nigerian National Petroleum Corporation. Initially, the Nigerian state held 35 per cent of the company. By 1979, its ownership had soared to 80 per cent. It has since dropped to its current level of 55 per cent. Shell, which holds 30 per cent, is the operator of the joint venture. The remaining 15 per cent is held by TotalFinaElf and the Italian firm Agip.

Not content with seizing a sizable chunk of ownership, Nigeria's military rulers began redirecting an increasing share of oil revenues from the delta to Abuja to reward their supporters and feather their own nests. Not just millions but billions of dollars went missing over the next few decades. In 2002, banks in Switzerland, Britain, Luxembourg, Liechtenstein and Jersey agreed to give back to Nigeria US$1 billion in pilfered state funds. The money had been sitting in accounts opened by the late General Sani Abacha, who died of an apparent heart attack in 1998 while still in office. This was only one case and a good indication of why Nigeria routinely tops the index of perceived corruption that is compiled annually by Transparency International.

Having given themselves control over oil revenues and a say in the industry, the military rulers then set about eliminating any existing obstacles to oil production. The Land Use Act of 1978 vested all land within a state with the state governor. Since state governors were appointed by the military rulers, the act essentially gave them control over all the land in Nigeria. They could now expropriate property for oil development or production. And the annual rent that communities had been receiving from oil companies up to that point was rerouted into state coffers. Though the act benefited Shell in the short term, making it much easier for the company to acquire land without having to deal with local chiefs who were often reluctant to allocate communal land to oil production, the longer-term effect was to increase tensions between the oil industry and the communities. The delta people felt doubly robbed, first of their land and then of compensation for its loss. The only way that a community could now get money directly from an oil company was if its land or crops were damaged by oil activities. This encouraged villagers to sabotage pipelines, making it look as though the oil spills were accidents. Not only did they receive reparation payments for the damage, they sometimes even obtained short-term jobs cleaning up the spills.

The military rulers consolidated their grip in 1979 by passing a constitution that gave them the sole power to legislate on matters relating to oil. In any confrontation with villagers, the government and the oil industry already had a huge advantage in that they operated under Nigerian federal laws whereas the villagers continued to conduct their affairs under customary tribal laws. Those who had the knowledge, the willingness and the money to press their case in court found they were dealing with a legal system totally foreign to them. If that weren't enough of a disadvantage to the plaintiffs, the judges dealing with their cases were beholden to the military government for their continued employment.

In 1988, two thousand drums of toxic waste were found dumped in the village of Koko in the Niger Delta. The ensuing protests spurred the government to pass environmental legislation, creating the Federal Environmental Protection Agency (FEPA), which was modelled on the US Environmental Protection Agency. The FEPA had broad powers to enforce environmental controls, but it was hamstrung from the start by interference from the Ministry of Petroleum Resources, with which it was supposed to co-operate, and by the military rulers, who granted waivers to oil companies that could not meet the tighter rules on pollution.

Though Shell could rightly say that it was the Nigerian government that was responsible for all the moves that had tightened the national government's hold on the delta's oil riches—control over oil revenues, widespread powers of land expropriation, first dibs on compensation, sole power to legislate on oil matters, and a system of friendly courts tasked with hearing oil-related cases—the company had benefited from them. When the unequal setup resulted in open confrontation with delta communities in the 1990s, the government helped the companies again by putting its formidable security apparatus at their disposal. Having put themselves in an untenable position in the delta, the oil companies now needed to use armed force in order to stay there.

That force was provided by a variety of federal and state security units, plus supernumerary police, sometimes known as "spy police," who were recruited and trained by the national police force but paid for by Shell and the other oil companies. Though these forces were supposed to be unarmed, Shell received a blast of bad publicity in 1995 when evidence in a court case revealed that the company had put out tenders to buy weapons for its supernumerary force. The state governments in the delta also set up a number of paramilitary task forces with names such as "Operation Salvage," "Operation Flush" and "Operation Storm" to deal with unrest that directly threatened oil production. When Nigerian judge Chukwudifu Oputa conducted an inquiry into human rights abuses in Nigeria during the period of military rule between 1966 and 1999, he singled out government security forces for particular criticism: "The greatest offenders and gross violators of human rights of fellow Nigerians were the military dictatorship and their over-zealous security outfits." Given the passive posture adopted by the oil companies, the military rulers' appetite for oil money and the harsh tools they used to protect its source, the only surprise about the massacre at Umuechem is that there weren't more just like it.

In the summer of 2000, I travelled to the Niger Delta to visit the Shell operation. It had been ten years since Umuechem and five years since the execution of Ken Saro-Wiwa—plenty of time for even the most sluggish of corporations to think through what had gone wrong and start moving to correct it.

Just as Union Minière dominated Katanga, Shell Petroleum Development Corp. dominates the delta. Its offices and installations are spread throughout Port Harcourt, the largest city in the region and the local hub of the oil industry. The company employs five thousand people directly, 97 per cent of them Nigerian, and another ten thousand on contract. Shell sees itself as a company that cares about its people. The drive up to the gate at the main complex, known as the Industrial Area, is dominated by signs advising employees to obey health and safety laws. "Wear that seat belt," warns one. "No seat belt, no entry." Another huge sign could be read on a number of levels: "Don't start that job until you analyze the hazards." If Shell had followed its own advice, would it have come to Nigeria in the first place?

Stepping through the front door of the company's low-level office building is like leaving Nigeria. There are telephones on every desk—and they work. There are computers hooked up to the Internet. The electrical supply does not cut out ten to twenty times a day, as it seems to elsewhere in the country. And some offices even have air conditioning. These are unheard-of luxuries for most other businesses in Nigeria. To work at Shell is to become a member of an elite. Little wonder, then, that when a job becomes available, the company receives a deluge of applications.

Bobo Sofiri Brown is the genial face that SPDC shows visitors who come to Port Harcourt. A former journalist, he is now manager of public affairs, SPDC East. Part of his job is to present the company view, which he does with humour and conviction. Not surprisingly, that view stands in stark contrast to that of Shell's critics. Basically, it boils down to a three-pronged defence of the company's behaviour in Nigeria. I had heard the same set of arguments from Shell officials at their headquarters in London and found it indicative of a corporate mindset that had blinded the company to the gathering storm in the 1990s.

The first part of Shell's three-pronged defence is that it is blamed for everything that happens in the oil patch, regardless of whether the company is actually involved. As Brown put it, "When the Niger Delta is angry, the first port of call is Shell." Such thinking skips lightly over the company's long history in the area and the fact that it once held a monopoly. The second part of the argument is that protestors who disrupt the company's activities are only using the company to send a message to the government. It isn't Shell they are angry with, but their distant rulers in Abuja. "Communities have found a powerful way to express long-held grievances," Brown explained. This factual statement disregards the long and mutually advantageous partnership that has existed between the oil company and the Nigerian government. And even at that, Shell officials seem to be of two minds about it. When explaining why Shell cannot spend more money on environmental projects or infrastructure improvements, the company points to the government, which must approve its budget. But the company disclaims the relationship when it becomes the target of protests. The clear distinction that Shell sees between itself and the Nigerian government is lost on demonstrators in the delta communities. The last part of Shell's defence is that the company is not a government and should not, therefore, be expected to act like a government. The company's responsibilities do not include questioning sovereign governments or providing state services and amenities such as roads, schools, hospitals and clean drinking water. "Oil companies cannot solve the problem in the Niger Delta," stressed Brown. "People are asking for a stake in the national economy."

Respecting the rights of sovereign governments is a tricky area for multinational companies, who rightly complain that questioning the state leaves them open to the accusation that they are setting themselves up as quasi governments in the countries in which they operate. But though Shell states that it does not interfere with the sanctity of Nigeria's laws, it has actively lobbied the government on energy and tax laws and on policies that would directly affect its operations. It isn't that Shell never intervenes, only that it is selective about what it is willing to go to bat over. There is a degree of self-interest in the corporate defence of the sanctity of the state. Oil is pumped in countries controlled by some of the world's most repressive regimes. If oil companies questioned the legitimacy of one government, where would it end? Would Angola be next? Or Saudi Arabia? What about some of the former Soviet republics? When companies use words and phrases like "sovereign governments," "laws" and "legal authorities," they are playing on the images they evoke for Westerners accustomed to their own stable governments, sound laws and accountable authorities. The reality in Nigeria until 1999 was that the government was a military dictatorship that had seized power in a coup. It passed laws to enrich its own members and it abused its authority to enforce its claim on the nation's oil reserves. That Shell was still using the same three-pronged argument ten years after Umuechem seemed to indicate that not much had changed at the company.

Before arriving in Nigeria, I had asked Shell to brief me on the situation in the delta, expecting to spend the day at its offices talking to various officials. But Brown had a surprise in store for me: we were to take a helicopter trip over the delta en route to one of the company's model farms. Over the years, Shell had initiated a number of community development projects in the area, and the farm was one of the company's success stories. But in the manner of all such public relations exercises, the trip revealed much more than the company had intended.

There are several advantages to flying rather than driving in this part of Nigeria, particularly if you work for an oil company. The first is that you are spared the backbone-jarring ride on roads that seem little more than an endless line of potholes, some large enough to swallow a car. The view from a helicopter is reassuring, if a bit misleading. Everything looks green and pleasant from the air, aside from the giant flares that signal the presence of flowstations. Flying also means that there is less risk of being kidnapped, or even confronted with hostile locals—a very real threat. Oil company workers are targets because their capture is a way of extracting money from the company. The helicopter pilot himself had previously been taken hostage when dropping a Shell maintenance crew at a remote location. His story, delivered partly through the intercom during the helicopter ride and later embellished over a beer at the local hotel, provides an interesting perspective on the situation in the delta.

Geza Sarkozy was held for nineteen days, six hours and twenty minutes in a village that had no electricity, no telephones and no roads, and where the river was both the communal toilet and the only way out of town. A Vietnam veteran, he said that given the choice, he would rather endure another tour in a war zone than go through his hostage experience again. Sarkozy and his co-pilot were not harmed by their captors, although they were threatened by the group leader with being the main course on the village menu if Shell or the pilots' employer, Bristow Helicopters, did not come up with the demanded ransom of US$3 million. "He [the leader] looked straight at me and said, 'Here we still eat flesh,'" recalled Sarkozy with a shudder. "And you know, I believed him." The hostages were released after a prolonged negotiation with Shell and the intervention of the governor of Rivers State. They were put in a boat one night and told they were going to be freed. Sarkozy did not really believe it until the boat touched up against a riverbank and he saw a member of the Mobile Police looking down at him."He reached out his hand and I grabbed it and it was the most pleasant sight I have every seen." He had no idea whether the money was paid for his release, although he suspected it must have been. Since his capture, pilots flying for Shell have been told not to set down anywhere unless they can see security on the ground. Kidnappings and violent confrontations were on the increase in the delta that year. People were finding that their peaceful protests were not working, so why not try violence?

When we reached Engema, Sarkozy followed corporate policy and did not set down until he saw the armed security guards on the ground. Four of them ran to greet us, gesturing that it was safe to land. We disembarked and got into a plain-coloured sport utility vehicle that had no company logo on its sides. The door locks were snapped in place before we set off.

Shell used to maintain housing for workers near the spot where we landed so that employees working in the area and further upcountry would not have to make the long, dangerous drive back to Port Harcourt at night on a road plagued by bandits. But the Shell officials who accompanied me that day said they'd had to close the housing facility. Problems had started when the company had begun running technical training programs in the area to teach local youths skills such as welding. The idea was that once finished the training, they would set up their own businesses. Instead, they demanded jobs from the company. When Shell did not comply, the disgruntled youths forced the closure of the housing facility. The training program was only one of many community development projects gone wrong. Shell had spent an increasing amount of money over the years, starting with $330,000 in 1989 and rising to over US$52 million in 2001, to build or fund hospitals, schools, community centres, model farms and the like in the thousand communities in its area of operation. A review commissioned by SPDC of all its community projects between 1992 and 1997 concluded that only 326 out of a total of 895—36 per cent—of the projects had been fully successful. Austin Onuoha, a human rights activist from the delta, described what Shell had been doing as "development dumping": "If a community protests, they go there and dump a hospital." This method of proceeding had only littered the country with projects that were abandoned as soon as the company's engineers left the community. Shell officials acknowledged the problem and vowed to remedy it by talking to communities about their needs before starting a project.

Driving from Engema to the model farm, the Enigbo Resource Centre, we slowed every now and then to pass women who were using the edges of a brief stretch of tarmac to spread melon seeds for drying. At 100 hectares, Enigbo was the largest of the model farms Shell had set up. It employed forty-two locals to tend to the bananas, pineapples, cassava, yams, ginger and rice crops and to teach farming methods. Although there were two gleaming red Massey-Ferguson tractors parked in the shed, farm manager Dennis Minimah said the emphasis in the training offered was on manual labour, which was more pertinent to the impoverished local farmers. One of the programs Minimah spoke about at length encouraged the sowing of oil palms—the crop that had first brought Europeans to the delta area over a century before.

In an interesting parallel with the present, the Europeans who traded in Nigeria's palm oil in the late nineteenth century also relied on armed force. One particular incident bears mention because of what it says about the unchanging nature of the conflict in the area. When the local traders of the village of Brass were forcibly squeezed out of the palm oil trade by the British Royal Niger Company, which had its own private army, they revolted in 1895. They took sixty-seven Europeans hostage from the company post at Akassa and said they would not return them until the villagers were allowed to resume their traditional trade. The firm called in British Royal Navy gunboats, which attacked the Brassmen, killing hundreds, if not thousands. George Goldie Taubman, the head of the Royal Niger Company, told British authorities in London that he had been shocked by the Brassmen's attack. "We always looked on Akassa as being as safe as Picadilly," he said. When the authorities investigated, they found that the company's practices had provoked the rebellion, but nothing was done. The local people were left to their fate. Palm oil has since been replaced by crude oil, but the dynamics remain the same.

As we drove through Enigbo, doors once more securely locked, we passed fields that were lovingly tended and lushly fertile. The whole facility was a showpiece, which is why Shell officials had brought me there in the first place. I could see why the company was proud of what it was doing in this small patch of land in the delta. But I could also empathize with the dissatisfaction of the local inhabitants, who were being instructed to live their lives in the same manner as their forebears while the oil beneath their land was extracted and sold to power the machines of modernity elsewhere.

I left Shell at the end of that day pondering a paradox. To an outsider, it seemed obvious that the great gap between the poverty of the delta people and the wealth of the oil industry would be a source of growing discontent that could threaten the company's operations. Why hadn't Shell's famed scenario planners, with all their brilliance, steered the company away from the looming crisis? When I posed this question to Shell officials, I discovered that the information that would have alerted them to the problem hadn't been passed up the line in a timely fashion, if at all. It had taken two years, for example, before the Nigerian subsidiary had even been aware that the Ogoni had published a bill of rights in 1990 which accused Shell and other oil companies of genocide. According to Emeke Achebe, one of the communications staff in Nigeria at the time, SPDC had found out about the bill of rights only in November 1992, when Ken Saro-Wiwa's group, the Movement for the Survival of the Ogoni People, sent it directly to Phil Watts, Shell managing director in Nigeria from 1991 to 1994, and demanded US$6 billion for damages caused by the company's operations in Ogoniland. The Nigerians on staff had either not known about or had not cared enough to tell their superiors about the Ogoni accusations. Often it is the case that local elites, as the Nigerians within Shell clearly were, seek to preserve the status quo and all their privileges, acting as a conservative break on multinational companies. As well, many if not most of the Nigerians working for Shell were living in Port Harcourt and other cities and had infrequent contact with their former communities. Onuoha, the human rights activist, said that Nigerians with traditional roots and Western education suffer from what he called a split personality: when they get a job at Shell, they transfer their loyalty from the community to the corporation.

Shell's managing directors in Nigeria were even less familiar than their Nigerian staff with what was happening in the villages. The company rotated its managing directors every three years to give them an international perspective. Brian Lavers was managing director of Shell Nigeria from 1987 to 1991. He was replaced by Phil Watts, who was himself replaced by Brian Anderson in 1994. Anderson moved on in 1997 and was replaced by Ron van den Berg. Just as they were becoming acclimatized to the area, they were preparing to move on. Something was definitely lost in terms of local knowledge.

The decentralized structure of the Royal Dutch/Shell Group also played a part in the faulty information exchange. Units within the group had a great deal of independence, which had its positive aspects as far as those working in the unit were concerned. Peter Holmes, who retired as chair of the Committee of Managing Directors in 1993, said that decentralization meant that the heads of local Shell operations could respond to governments on the spot. The negative side, however, was that the units saw themselves as distinct from each other. Shell Canada, for example, made a point of saying it had no operations in Nigeria when the Nigerian unit was under fire. Shell South Africa made the same claim.

But what about the information that was passed on to head office and the scenario planners? Here, several problems arose: the nature of the scenario planners themselves, their delayed focus on Nigeria and the rank the scenario builders occupied within the larger corporate structure.

In 1992, then head of scenario planning at Shell, Joe Jaworski, invited US academic Betty S. Flowers to join the scenario team as editor. Flowers was not your usual scenario team member. She had a degree in psychology and a doctorate in English—her topic was Browning's influence on contemporary poetry—and she had spent a good part of her academic career studying myths. In 2002 she was named director of the Lyndon B. Johnson Library at the University of Texas. Flowers said she was chosen by Shell for her global view and because Jaworski wanted someone who would not be, as she put it, totally "seduced" by the economists on the team. Of the twenty team members, most were economists, "and they wanted to talk about things in terms of GNP [gross national product] and arguments about PPP [purchasing power parity] versus GNP," said Flowers. "They wanted to tell a story that didn't have any kind of implicit moral. Even if the moral appeared to emerge naturally, they wanted to squelch it."

Flowers said the economists recognized that people do things out of fear or out of nationalism, but the underlying assumption that governed their thinking was that all people are motivated by selfish economic self-interest. "They fought over having any values in [the scenarios] whatsoever besides economic self-interest." She argued for a section of the scenario to deal with the human being—how workers saw their lives, what gave them a larger sense of themselves—but was fiercely resisted. The team members thought that economic and military factors were much more important to consider than the views of human beings. Flowers won out in the end, but her battle underscored a problem with the scenario process: the planners were reluctant to consider the type of softer issues—human rights and the environment—that were about to cause Shell giant headaches in Nigeria and around the world.

It is interesting to compare the attitudes Flowers perceived at head office with the work being done by another scenario team working in South Africa around the same time. The white government was still in power there, and it was not clear how the transition to black majority rule would be made. Shell was instrumental in setting up a process to look at that troubled country's future. The results were then shared with the key players in South Africa's political transition, who used the scenarios to make decisions. That team was more successful in dealing with soft issues, in part because its twenty-two members included not just economists, but people with backgrounds in communications, education, social planning, political studies and business.

It wasn't until 1992 that Shell even produced a detailed scenario focusing solely on Nigeria, and it was plagued by gaps in information at the community level. Just because a scenario was produced, it didn't always mean that it had any impact on the key decision makers within the corporation. Despite the scenario planners' string of successes in anticipating major global changes in the late 1970s and 1980s, they did not always have the ear of senior management. This problem was highlighted in 1995 when the company decided to dump the Brent Spar in the Atlantic Ocean. A month before the facility was set to be towed out to sea, a member of the scenario team sent an e-mail to the men in charge, expressing alarm at the possible consequences. He asked them if they had thought through the possibilities and suggested they take more time to consider the plan. In the end, they did not take his advice and suffered from the ensuing public uproar. Greenpeace mounted a series of successful protests to prevent the dumping, and Shell was forced into an embarrassing retreat.

The controversy set off by Brent Spar happened around the same time that Shell's activities in Ogoniland became the focus of international protest. The combination of those two events provoked an international furor loud enough to be heard on the top floor of the Shell Centre in London. For the first time, the men running the corporation had to seriously consider the company's record on human rights and the environment, at the very least in terms of how it was affecting their image. Phil Watts was asked to organize the company's response. "My awareness level on the broader, softer issues went up by a factor of ten to one hundred," Watts told researchers preparing a case study of Shell at Harvard Business School. He now holds the highest post in the Royal Dutch/Shell Group: chair of the Committee of Managing Directors.

The supertanker conglomerate finally began to change course. The most obvious change to outsiders was in its publicity. Ads began to emphasize Shell's regard for the environment, attracting accusations from environmental groups that Shell was treating the issue as a public relations problem. "Shell has merely improved its rhetoric," said Oronto Douglas, a delta activist. "They are more adept in public relations, more careful and humble in their presentation." However, the company had always shown a sensitivity to public opinion, at least in its consumer markets. In the 1920s, when Britain was going through a period of xenophobia, Shell ads emphasized the company's Britishness. One poster showed the figure of Britannia filling a flagon at a fountain, and the caption read, "Shell distributes more petrol refined from crude oils produced within the British Empire than all other petrol distributing companies in Great Britain combined." When the public was caught up in the romance of air travel, Shell ads sported biplanes. When there were doubts about the purity of petrol being sold to consumers, Shell came out with its "You can be sure of Shell" campaign and another that stressed that its products were "Unadulterated." Shell's ads after 1995 followed this trend by focusing on human rights and the environment.

Despite the skepticism of its critics, Shell was also attempting to change on the inside. In 1995, the company hired management consultants McKinsey & Company to complete a company review. While some departments at Shell perished, the scenario team survived, even though planners worried that they too would be shut down because they did not produce anything of physical substance. Their position within the company was actually strengthened by the review process because they now reported to the Committee of Managing Directors, the body that ultimately runs Royal Dutch/Shell. The team altered its makeup with the addition of people with political science and social science backgrounds. And the issues they currently consider range across a broad spectrum, from the purely economic—how much will oil sell for in ten years?—to softer areas—how do you persuade people to join a boring multinational when exciting high-tech jobs are on offer elsewhere? In building national scenarios for countries like Nigeria, they now ensure that managers from the operating company are actively engaged in the process. This way, they believe, local managers are more likely to act on their findings.

In 1996, Watts was made director of environment, planning and external affairs and was charged with looking at the softer end of Shell's business: its values, principles and image. He referred to his job as "reputation management," and set in train initiatives that examined ethics, human rights and political involvement. He began a global review of the company's business principles, involving Shell's own employees to begin with and then turning to a broader cross-section of the public. The principles had first been published back in 1976, when Shell was suffering a crisis of confidence similar to that of 1995. Shell's general manager in Italy had been caught paying £2.5 million in extortion money to Italian political parties. At the same time, rumours—which would later turn out to be true—were circulating that Shell was breaking international sanctions against the white regime in Rhodesia by supplying it with oil.

The 1976 principles contained general statements about the company's responsibilities to employees, customers and society, about the need to act commercially and avoid involvement in politics and about the company's belief in the supremacy of the market economy. A specific section was included because of the Italian scandal. It read, "The offer, payment, or taking of bribes are unacceptable practices."

Watts and his team began to think about updating these principles. Mark Moody-Stuart, head of Shell Transport and Trading at the time and chair of the Committee of Managing Directors from 1998 to 2001, said it was difficult to get employees to talk about human rights in the review process because it had not traditionally been a topic of conversation within the company. Shell's lawyers weren't sure they wanted to say anything about it because it might open the company to litigation and liability risks. And others in the company pointed out that a straightforward declaration on human rights might damage the company's business in countries like China and Saudi Arabia, where any mention of the term "human rights" was considered provocative. Despite these problems, the company managed to find wording for its business principles that satisfied its internal constituency. The 1997 version expanded on the company's commitment to society, adding a section that dealt with its support for fundamental human rights and sustainable development. The section on political affairs included a statement on the company's right to make known its position on matters affecting the community.

Shell's external constituency was a different matter. The company's inward-looking corporate culture meant that communicating with groups outside the oil industry was a struggle. This manifested itself when the community development staff in Nigeria did not think to consult with local villagers before starting a project. But it was symptomatic of a greater reluctance within the corporation to try to engage the world outside the oil industry. It took the events of 1995 to jolt Shell out of this mindset.

Watts said that the consultation he had set up with broader groups as part of the company's policy review was the first time that many Shell people had met face to face with outsiders. Bruce Naughton Wade, an independent British consulting company that oversaw the review process for Shell, wrote a report that shocked some of Shell's executives. The consultant said there was a mismatch between what society expected from Shell and what the company thought it should be doing. "Society's expectations have moved on, whereas Shell has not," said the report. It went on to list perceptions that outsiders had about the company. Among them were that Shell was "Eurocentric, arrogant, focused on the short term, insufficiently interested in renewable sources of energy, adhering to outdated Business Principles, and applying double standards."

That it took a paid consultant to make Shell management understand what outsiders had been telling them all along for free speaks volumes about the insular nature of the company. Years before, the 1990 report of the Judicial Commission of Inquiry into the Umuechem Disturbances had pointed to almost all of the same problems highlighted by Bruce Naughton Wade, with the exception of the company's insufficient interest in renewable sources of energy. The Rivers State report urged Shell to go out and talk to the people in the communities in which it operated because lack of consultation was leading to "confusion, disorder and all that make for disturbances."

After some initial hesitation, Shell decided to look at ways to independently verify whether it was meeting its revised business principles. "We have 300 years' experience with financial accounting, 30 years with environmental accounting, and virtually none with social accounting," Watts told researchers from Harvard Business School. Consultants KPMG verified Shell's report on the environment in Nigeria in 1999, 2000 and 2001. Both KPMG and PricewaterhouseCoopers verified the Royal Dutch/Shell Group's statements on health, safety, the environment and social performance in the 2002 report while noting there were no accepted international environmental and social reporting or verification standards. They said they had based their approach on emerging best practice and principles.

In making these efforts, Shell has won praise—even from some of its critics. It is still too soon, however, to judge whether the global conglomerate has truly altered its course or just its rhetoric. It is also impossible to say what would have happened in Umuechem had Shell's new initiatives been in place. Would a different type of scenario team have been able to assess the situation and issue a warning in time? Would managers more sensitive to human rights have reacted differently? It would be comforting to think that Shell has learned important lessons from Umuechem and that a similar tragedy will never happen. What the company has since done with the people who were in charge during those fateful days in October 1990 and their aftermath is one measure of how Shell still views that event. The record here provides few hopeful signs.

Joshua Udofia, the Shell manager who wrote the letter requesting that the Mobile Police be sent to Umuechem, has since been promoted to the position of deputy managing director of Shell Petroleum Development Corporation in Nigeria. Phil Watts, who was managing director of SPDC from 1991 to 1994, became chairman of the Committee

of Managing Directors of the Royal Dutch/Shell group, the highest position in the conglomerate. Brian Anderson, who took over from Watts as
managing director of SPDC in 1994 and was the senior Shell person on the
spot throughout the trial and execution of Ken Saro-Wiwa and other
Ogoni dissidents, was promoted to head Shell operations in China. And
Jeroen van der Veer, who was area co-ordinator for sub-Saharan Africa for
Royal Dutch from 1990 to 1992, was promoted to president of Royal
Dutch in July 2000.

CHAPTER SEVEN

RANGER OIL IN ANGOLA

The offshore oil industry in Angola exists in a state of splendid isolation. The only reminders of land in this watery world are the mats of vegetation that float down the Congo River from deep within the continent and drift past the oil platforms on their way farther out to sea. Offshore oil never touches Angolan soil. It is pumped from deep beneath the warm waters of the South Atlantic into waiting tankers that carry it to markets all over the world. This almost perfect arrangement is marred only by the oil companies' need to maintain supply depots on land. Tubes and casings must be stockpiled somewhere, as must be the bulk compounds and masses of equipment used in the modern oil industry. Space is also needed for the specialist services companies, and housing must be constructed for workers making the transition between the rig and home. Unfortunately, the only place where such facilities could be established for the oil installations off the coast of Angola was on its shore. It was at one depot, called Soyo, that Ranger Oil (Canada) Ltd. discovered in 1993 that even offshore oil projects can be drawn into the savagery of civil war.

Ranger had first considered starting an operation in Angola twenty years earlier, when the country was still a Portuguese colony. Oil had been discovered onshore in 1955 by Petrofina of Belgium (now part of the huge TotalFinaElf conglomerate) and offshore in 1961 by Cabinda Gulf Oil Co. (now part of ChevronTexaco Corp.), and the prospects looked promising. Intensive discussions with the Portuguese government could have culminated in a licence for Ranger for the entire offshore. But the company was scared off by rumblings of political trouble. In the 1960s, Angolan nationalists, encouraged by similar movements elsewhere in Africa, had risen en masse, only to be brutally suppressed by the colonial regime. Portugal had attacked villages and dropped napalm bombs. Tens of thousands of people died and hundreds of thousands more fled the country. As Angolans began to agitate again for independence in the early 1970s, the threat of renewed violence led Ranger to re-evaluate setting up operations there. It decided to drop out of the negotiations.

Ranger's instincts about the rumblings proved to be correct as Angola descended into turmoil. But what the company had not anticipated were the spectacular oil discoveries of the 1990s that would have made the holder of the offshore licence wealthy beyond all imagining. Unfortunately, that opportunity had come and gone. Somehow Ranger never managed to be in the right place at the right time in Angola.

The company's headquarters in the clean, crisp city of Calgary are half a world away from the torpor of the African tropics. For most of its history, Ranger was run as the personal fiefdom of Jack Pierce, known to all just as Jack. Originally from Montreal, Quebec, Pierce moved west to work as a geophysicist for Sun Oil in Texas and Wyoming. When he decided to go out on his own, Pierce took Ranger Oil of Wyoming north to Canada in 1958, taking over a smaller operation called Maygill Gas and Oil and renaming the new entity Ranger Oil (Canada) Ltd. At a time when most Canadian oil companies were sticking close to home, Pierce went international. Over the life of Ranger, it set up operations in China, Peru, Ecuador, the Gulf of Mexico, Algeria, Australia, Côte D'Ivoire and Namibia. But the big strike, the one that made the company, came in 1974 in the North Sea, when Ranger and British Petroleum discovered the Ninian field. The money Ranger made from Ninian and subsequent North Sea plays allowed the company to finance its other, less successful international ventures.

Jack's friends and colleagues describe him as a "rugged individualist," "old-style wildcatter" and "maverick"—words that in western Canada are meant as the highest compliments. But there is also a sense that he might not have been the easiest man to work for, preferring to run the public company like a private concern, relying on his instincts when consultation would have been the safer route. His individualistic approach did have its advantages. Pierce used his energy and intelligence to drive the company forward into places that more conservative oilmen shunned. But there were also disadvantages. The company's image suffered during his prolonged row with financial analysts who criticized him for his reluctance to disclose negative information. Even within the industry he had had his fights. He once stormed out of the Canadian Association of Petroleum Producers, the main industry group in Calgary, and refused to come back for three or four years. "Jack was a brilliant guy," says former Ranger executive John Newman. "He really thought outside the box. He really was a technically capable guy and he was very, very good at government relations. On the other hand, he sometimes had ideas that were pretty wild. There were dozens of them. My job and the guy who was on my level at finance, our job was to filter out the 99 per cent wild ideas and come along with the one that was brilliant."

Running the company—Pierce was chairman for more than thirty years, as well as president from 1955 to 1985—allowed him to indulge his private passion: flying. He learned to fly at the age of fourteen. During the Second World War, he took time off from his university studies to ferry warplanes for the Royal Air Force, and he maintained a lifelong interest in the military. He equipped his Turner Valley cattle ranch south of Calgary with an airstrip and amassed a fleet of aircraft, including a Gulfstream jet purchased from Lee Iacocca of Chrysler Corp., a Lear jet, a Beaver float plane and a helicopter. While some within the company questioned whether a firm Ranger's size needed so many aircraft, Jack went ahead and bought them anyway. Eccentric, brilliant, passionate and blunt—even in an industry full of characters, Jack Pierce stood out.

As the riches of Ninian began to swell its coffers, Ranger decided to look farther afield. Domestic pressures were also pushing the company in this direction. Ranger, along with other oil companies in western Canada, was hit hard when the federal Liberal government reacted to the oil crises of the 1970s by bringing in the National Energy Program. Using price controls and federal taxes on oil and gas production, the government sought to protect Canadians from high oil prices. Westerners, who produced most of the oil, saw the program as a cash grab by the central provinces, who were the biggest consumers. Bumper stickers were produced inviting "eastern bastards" to "freeze in the dark." The program, which ran until 1984, when it was amended, remains a festering sore in the Alberta oil patch.

It was at the start of this grim period that Ranger Oil's representative in Britain, Gordon Bowman, received a phone call from the London-based agent general for Alberta. At one time, most of the Canadian provinces maintained agents general in London to drum up trade and investment for businesses back home. Alberta's agent general kept abreast of developments in the oil industry because of its prominence in the provincial economy. Bowman had been recruited by Pierce from Philips Petroleum in the United States in 1975 to run Ranger's North Sea operations and keep an eye out for other international opportunities. I contacted him at his retirement home in the Bahamas and asked him to cast his mind back to the late 1970s, when he received the call that would ultimately bring Ranger to Angola. He told me, "He [the agent general] called me and said, 'Would you be interested in looking at some opportunities in Angola?' I said sure, and he put me in touch with Tony Buckingham."

Anthony Leslie Rowland Buckingham was introduced to Bowman as a former member of Britain's elite Special Services who had gone into private business. Bowman described him as a promoter who was "very, very aggressive." Buckingham said he specifically wanted to join forces with a Canadian company because, as he put it, Canadians are "low on the radar screen politically" in Angola. At the time, the Cold War was still raging, pitting the United States and its Western allies against the Soviet Union and its satellites. Angola was in the Soviet camp, and while some US oil companies were pumping oil there despite the geopolitical situation, new ventures had a better chance of winning concessions if they were not flying the Stars and Stripes. Although Canada was a US ally, it was seen by the Angolans as rather nondescript. Canadian companies posed none of the economic and political threats that involvement with a US company entailed. Bowman agreed to meet with Buckingham, and the two set a date for dinner.

The proposition Buckingham put to Bowman was straightforward: he had heard of an opportunity to pick up some offshore concessions in Angola, but he needed to team up with a company that had expertise in exploration and production and could also provide financing. Buckingham would supply the contacts; Ranger would provide the rest. Bowman left that first meeting promising he would look into it and get back to Buckingham. Then, he says, "I did a little research on Angola to see what was going on."

The political situation in Angola had deteriorated significantly since Ranger had last looked at possibilities there. Long after other colonial powers had abandoned their colonies, Portugal doggedly hung on in Africa. An estimated eleven thousand of its soldiers and settlers had died while trying to prevent the independence of Angola and Mozambique. Their deaths became a political issue at home. Then, when the fascist regime of Marcello Caetano was overthrown by the military on April 25, 1974, the new rulers let it be known that the colonial era was over. After five centuries of Portuguese domination, Angola would become an independent country on November 11, 1975.

This decision that should have brought peace, however, only brought more war. In January 1975, the three separate independence movements that had been fighting colonial rule—the Popular Movement for the Liberation of Angola (MPLA, Movimento Popular de Libertação de Angola), the National Union for the Total Independence of Angola (UNITA, União Nacional para a Independência Total de Angola) and the National Front for the Liberation of Angola (FNLA, Frente Naçional de Libertação de Angola)—agreed to unite and form the new government. But they soon reneged on the deal. In July 1975, fighting broke out as they each struggled to win control of the country.

The Marxist-Leninist MPLA, led by Antonio Agostinho Neto, a doctor and poet who had been educated in Portugal, had strong support in the coastal cities, among educated Angolans and those of mixed Portuguese-Angolan descent. Neto had been receiving weapons and diplomatic backing from the Soviet Union since the 1960s. The MPLA quickly secured the capital, Luanda.

UNITA, whose political philosophy had evolved over time from Maoist to capitalist, was led by Jonas Malheiros Savimbi, a charismatic leader who had also been educated in Portugal, as well as in Switzerland. His support base was in the central highlands, home of the Ovimbundu tribe. In the run-up to independence, UNITA won backing from South Africa.

The right-wing FNLA was led by Holden Roberto, the son of a worker at a Baptist mission. Roberto had spent most of his life in exile in the Congo and Zaire. His party's support came from the northern border areas, where Kongo nationalism was firmly entrenched. Congolese dictator Mobutu Sese Seko (born Joseph Désiré Mobutu) supported the FNLA, and in the pre-independence fighting, the group had received covert assistance from the CIA.

As the date neared for the official departure of the colonial power, the situation in Angola grew increasingly precarious. Of the 340,000 Portuguese thought to be in the country in 1974, an estimated 300,000 left before independence. The economic machinery they did not destroy on departure ground to a halt for lack of skilled workers and managers. Total destabilization was achieved when the outside world chose this moment to intervene. South Africa made the first overt move in August 1975, invading from the south. It teamed up with UNITA and the FNLA against the MPLA. South Africa claimed that SWAPO (the South West African People's Organization), the nationalist group fighting South African rule in Namibia, was using southern Angola as a rear base. But South Africa was also fiercely anti-communist and did not want to see the MPLA seizing power in Angola.

The South African invasion prompted the main protagonists in the Cold War to emerge from cover. Cuba, which already had military advisers in the country, decided to send a combat unit to support the MPLA, and the Soviet Union provided heavy weapons. The United States weighed in on the other side, giving assistance to both UNITA and the FNLA. Angola became one of the many proxy battlegrounds of the Cold War.

In the midst of all the bloodshed and upheaval, independence day arrived. Neto's MPLA, which held the capital, Luanda, formed the first government of the People's Republic of Angola. But power did not mean peace. Angola's civil war ground on, punctuated by ceasefires and peace agreements that never held for long. When Mobutu established relations with the MPLA in the late 1970s, the FNLA disintegrated. UNITA retreated to the bush to continue the battle.

A non-resource company would look at such chaos and decide its money would be better invested elsewhere, but such is the global thirst for oil that the petroleum multinationals could not bring themselves to turn away from Angola's oil riches. While the civil war raged, the oil industry adapted by abandoning promising fields onshore to concentrate on offshore finds. The only major exception was the American operation in Cabinda, which was separated from the rest of Angola by the mouth of the Congo River and a small sliver of Zaire (now the Congo).

The oil companies' operations benefited from the quirky logic of oil politics. Needing the revenues generated by oil production, the MPLA was prepared to overlook the fact that oil was being produced by capitalist enterprises headquartered in the United States and Europe. The most startling manifestation of this occurred when the Marxist-Leninist government sent Cuban soldiers to protect American oil installations from UNITA forces who were being funded and trained by the United States. While the oil multinationals regarded themselves as neutral in the conflict, they were not seen to be so by the UNITA rebels. The companies had signed contracts and paid revenues to the MPLA government, which used the funds to purchase weapons and military services. In the eyes of UNITA, that put the oil companies squarely in the government camp and made the oil industry a legitimate target in the war.

Security became a prime concern for any potential investor, especially for a small Canadian company whose government had no military presence in the vicinity. But Buckingham had already reassured Bowman on that score.

"He had a lot of good military connections in Africa and through the Brits," Bowman said. "That was a very essential part of being secure down there."

There are many stories about Tony Buckingham. Most bear the hallmark of myth. He is reputed to be a former member of the Special Boat Squadron, one of the elite special services in Britain's armed forces, and to have worked for a time as a diver in the North Sea oil fields before entering the oil business himself. Buckingham refuses to give interviews unless they're about his current passion, ocean sailing. Instead, he lets his associates speak for him. Michael Grunberg, an accountant based in London who has provided office space and consulting services to Buckingham's various companies in the past, is the key spokesman. Tim Spicer, a former member of Britain's Scots Guard Regiment whom Buckingham recruited to form a private military company called Sandline International, is also an approved source.

The stories Grunberg and Spicer tell make Buckingham sound like a sharp businessman and a jolly pal with a taste for adventure who just happens to count a number of mercenaries among his friends. In his autobiography, *An Unorthodox Soldier*, Spicer says Buckingham is "a solidly built individual, usually sporting a suntan, always with a twinkle in his eye, often chomping on a huge Havana cigar. He has a penchant for matters military and adventures generally and has been described as a pirate, but I would describe him as more of a buccaneer; buccaneers tend to be on the side of the good guys." According to Spicer, Buckingham makes friends easily and is adept at talking to heads of state "and other important players." A lover of fine wines, fast cars and paintings, he is also interested in diving, skiing and hunting. A 1997 photo shows Buckingham posing with friend and business associate Simon Mann, beside the car they drove in the Peking–Paris rally. A stout man with greying hair, Buckingham is smiling broadly as he puffs on a cigar.

But there is another, darker side of Buckingham that his critics hint at but refuse to talk about on the record. Though they complain privately about his business methods, they don't want their objections attributed to them publicly. In fact, mentioning Buckingham's name to anyone who has done business with him is guaranteed to end the interview. "Tony has his own model for operating in Africa," is all one former business partner would say. Another was slightly more explicit about why he did not want to go public: "I don't want the mercenaries mad at me." The impression given is that Buckingham is a strong man with powerful friends—someone not to be crossed. But none of this was known when Bowman met with him to discuss Angola. Buckingham's notoriety would come later, partly as a result of what was to happen in Angola.

After meeting Buckingham, Bowman talked to some people at Chevron, Ranger's partner in the United Kingdom. They put him in touch with Joachim David, managing director of Sociedade Nacional De Combustíveis de Angola, or SONANGOL, the Angolan state oil company. David had been trained by the American oil company Texaco before going home to head SONANGOL. He and Bowman met in London in the early 1980s. They shared similar experiences, in that they had both worked for an American multinational. Bowman says, "I got to know enough to whet the interest for Ranger to go and look at what Tony was looking for down there."

Bowman ran the idea of an operation off the coast of Angola past the Ranger directors in Calgary. There he met unexpected resistance from Pierce: "As soon as he heard I was interested in Africa, he said, 'Wait a minute. They're going to throw you out quicker than you got in there.' He wasn't that enamoured [with] the fact that I was interested in Angola because there was a war going on." But Bowman managed to secure approval to at least go and take a look.

It was a particularly violent time in Angola. The South Africans were helping UNITA mount heavy assaults, providing them with air cover and heavy artillery. As a result, the rebels had gained control of vast areas of the country, right up to the border with Zaire. Bowman had to wait several years for the violence to simmer down before he and Tony Buckingham finally set off for Luanda in 1986.

The two visited SONANGOL in the Angolan capital, as well as several senior government officials, whom Bowman described as unsavoury characters known by Buckingham. They made a second trip that took them to the American operations in Cabinda. Bowman also met with the local managers of Conoco, an American firm that was pulling out because of the political situation. They showed him maps of the Angolan offshore that covered the area Ranger was interested in. A geological analysis indicated that the area had some promise. "We [Ranger] wanted to do something outside of the North Sea, so this was one of the best things that hit the horizon for us," says Bowman. "And besides, I was assured that politically and militarily, we would be protected. We wouldn't have any difficulty."

Though the offshore was growing more popular with large multinational companies, there were still opportunities for a niche player like Ranger. The amazing deepwater discoveries had yet to be made; industry giants would stampede to the area after French company Elf Aquitaine discovered the Girassol field in 1996, estimated to contain up to 3.5 billion barrels of oil. Ranger wanted to find a field that would produce 50 to 200 million barrels of oil—the majors would elbow Ranger out of the way for anything above 200 million, and anything below 50 million would not be worth pursuing. In a perverse way, Angola's civil war was actually proving to be an advantage to the company because it reduced the competition. And that meant lower entry costs. The enormous signature bonuses of US$300 million, which was what Elf Aquitaine would pay the government following the Girassol find, were not yet standard practice.

The technical environment off the Angolan coast also looked promising. Unlike the weather in the North Sea, where Ranger had experience, or the North Atlantic, which was starting to come into play, the conditions in the South Atlantic were relatively benign. In terms of equipment, it would be cheaper to operate there because platforms could be built closer to the water and constructed of lighter steel than those used in areas where monster waves and icebergs were a constant threat. Ranger intended to follow the lead of the other oil companies and keep its links to the mainland to a minimum.

Armed with all this information, Bowman pitched the proposal to the Ranger board once more. "Tony Buckingham wanted to make sure

that Ranger should put this thing together," says Bowman. "I finally convinced the company that we should go down there." Bowman says he won
Pierce over by telling him that David, the general manager of SONANGOL,
had said Ranger would get the specific area that it was after.

Backed by his board, Bowman began serious negotiations with
SONANGOL: "They wanted to have meetings pretty well everywhere—
Paris, London, Lisbon and Calgary—and they wanted to bring all their
friends and relatives. They'd pick the first-class hotels and first-class air-
fares. It was a pretty expensive exercise. And we had to pay for the whole
thing, including Tony's share."

At one point during these drawn-out negotiations, Bowman brought
Buckingham to Calgary to meet Pierce and the other Ranger directors.
He was careful to keep the meetings brief because his instincts told him
that Pierce would not take a shine to Buckingham. The two men were too
much alike—mavericks who liked to run their own show. Stories written
later suggested the two got along famously and became fast friends. But
those close to Pierce say that was a myth. The relationship was strictly
business. Buckingham had something Pierce wanted—an in with the
Angolan government—and Pierce had something to offer in return—a
company with expertise in the offshore oil industry and the ability to raise
money on a stock exchange.

Just as the negotiations between Ranger, SONANGOL and Buckingham
were coming to a head, the political situation began to change for the better in Angola. The Cold War ended with the collapse of the Soviet Union
in 1989, and the superpowers ceased their support of the opposing sides
in the civil war. South Africa turned inward as the apartheid regime
crumbled and the ANC (African National Congress) was legalized. Now
that the United States, the Soviet Union and South Africa were no longer
stoking the violence, hope grew that peace was finally at hand. Fresh fruit
appeared in urban markets for the first time in ages—a sign that the peasants felt sufficiently safe to return to their land and raise crops. Jose
Eduardo dos Santos, who had become president when Neto had died in
1979, changed the constitution to allow what had been a one-party state

to become a multi-party democracy. Peace talks began and would eventually result in a ceasefire to be monitored by the United Nations as well as a set date for upcoming elections.

In 1991, Ranger, SONANGOL and Buckingham reached a deal that awarded Ranger a production sharing agreement on what was known as Block 4 (the coastal waters had been divided into blocks in the 1970s). Ranger would be the operator of the field, and Buckingham would be rewarded for his efforts with a 10 per cent interest in the deal. The 10 per cent was initially paid to Branch Energy Ltd., one of Buckingham's corporate vehicles. Branch later assigned its interest to Heritage Oil and Gas Ltd., which was created and registered in the Bahamas. Heritage held only a financial interest and had no other operations in Angola at the time.

Separate from the production-sharing agreement, Ranger and Buckingham also agreed to set up a corporation in Barbados known as Ranger Oil West Africa Ltd. Ranger would own 51 per cent of this company, and the other 49 per cent would be owned by Heritage Oil and Gas. This jointly owned subsidiary was to provide technical and advisory services to SONANGOL, which was eager to develop Angolan expertise in offshore oil production. Ranger Oil helped set up SONANGOL Pesquisa e Produção, which eventually became an operator in its own right.

Choosing to register in an offshore financial centre such as Barbados was in line with industry practice. Companies use tax havens for both legitimate and illegitimate purposes, depending on the firm involved. Legally, they can be used to avoid registering profits in a higher-tax jurisdiction, thus reducing the company's tax burden. But the veil they draw over a company's operations and ownership means that activities that might attract the attention of legal authorities, regulators, shareholders or the media are hidden. Disclosure requirements are usually weak or nonexistent, and unscrupulous companies, not to mention criminals, take full advantage of this situation. While there have been renewed efforts in the wake of the September 11, 2001, attacks on the United States to force tax havens to meet certain standards of openness in order to make them less attractive to money launderers, terrorists and other criminals, the tax havens and some of the companies that use them are fighting to maintain their secretive status. In Ranger's case, the registration of its subsidiary in Barbados shielded its operations from scrutiny. Ranger Oil West Africa barely rated a mention in the parent company's annual reports and official documents filed with the Alberta Securities Commission during that period.

By mid-1991 the deal was finally ready for signing. Bowman, who had been made Ranger president in 1985, had retired in the meantime, but he was kept on retainer to complete the negotiations. Fred Dyment, a long-time vice-president of finance who had been with Ranger since 1978, succeeded Bowman as president. The two were overseas signing the deal when news came that Jack Pierce had died. Pierce collapsed while herding cattle on his Turner Valley ranch. He had undergone heart bypass surgery several years earlier but was working full-time and had no plans for retirement. After the deal was signed, Bowman bowed out.

I met Fred Dyment at the Calgary Petroleum Club a decade after those events to discuss what had happened next. The Petroleum Club is the heart of the Alberta oil patch. Its nondescript modern facade is in keeping with most of the architecture in the recently built city, but inside there is a surprise. The oil industry has built itself a gentleman's club, western style, with cozy leather armchairs, wood-panelled walls and oil paintings that feature traditional landscapes and a few cowboys. This is where the oilmen—and they are mostly men—get together to socialize, network or just brag, depending on their recent fortunes.

Given pride of place in the foyer is a sculpture of a poker game whose regular members were known as the Choir Boys. Back when the game first started, members would tell their wives they were heading off to choir practice and then hightail it to the club. A figure representing Dyment sits at the table. It's a pretty good likeness—close-cropped hair, then brown but now going grey, trim figure dressed in an open-necked shirt and slacks. He is holding the winning hand in the game. But Dyment is too much of an accountant by training, or perhaps just too honest, not to point out that the cards on the table add up to more than a full deck.

When Dyment was made president of Ranger in 1991, he inherited a mess. Pierce had left no succession plan. "You have to know Jack to know it wasn't his style," Dyment said in a *Globe and Mail* article at the time. "Jack felt he would go on forever." And the way the founder had run the company did not completely accord with the way Dyment wanted it run, as Dyment describes in a 1996 *Globe* article: "Jack was a one-man show, no question. He was a 'my way or the highway' kind of guy and one of the last of the old-style wildcatters. He always said, 'You find hydrocarbons, you make money.' And I always argued with him that it wasn't that simple." In stepping into Pierce's shoes, Dyment had to change the way the company operated internally. And he would have to find a way for the company to live with the decisions that Pierce had made and hadn't always explained.

Before Dyment could even address the organizational issues, Ranger was hit with several blows. Within a month of Pierce's death, Westcoast Energy Inc. of Vancouver surprised the market by selling its 10 per cent holding in the company. Norsk Hydro AS of Norway followed suit, finding a buyer for its 10 per cent share, which had been on the block for some time. Ranger was left with no controlling shareholder. Pierce's estate held the largest block with 5.5 per cent.

To replace Pierce as chairman of the board, Ranger turned to Simon Reisman, former chief negotiator for Canada during the Canada-US Free Trade Agreement talks. Reisman, a straight talker with formidable trade expertise, had been a Ranger director for just over a year and had acted as a consultant to the company before that. Other changes followed, both on the board and in the executive suite. There were a few stalwarts left on the board, including Edward M. Bronfman, from the Toronto branch of the family, who had been a director since 1965, and F. Richard Matthews, who had served two separate stints starting back in 1956. However, most of the men who would have to deal with the consequences of getting into bed with Tony Buckingham were new to their positions of power. And much of their time was taken up with the problems that were facing the company in the wake of the sales by Westcoast Energy and Norsk Hydro and the lack of sustained success by operations outside the North Sea. Angola was only a small part of Ranger business: a full 80 per cent of the company's revenues came from its operations in the North Sea.

Ranger began to take its first steps in Angola, choosing to use the supply depot on the coast at Soyo, which was closest to its offshore concession. Soyo had been set up in 1984 by Bouygues of France and SONANGOL when the offshore fields were beginning to attract interest. The mouth of the Congo River was situated to the north of the site, and the damp wilderness of the estuary lay to the east, west and south of it. Like many such facilities, it was built on a site hacked and bulldozed down to the red earth of Africa. Where once was dense bush, the companies had imposed their own vision of order, constructing utilitarian metal sheds in precise rows. A prefab hotel was erected, complete with air conditioning, a refuge from the intense heat and humidity. A worker sipping a cool beer at the bar could almost believe he was somewhere far from the turmoil of Angola.

Ranger had just completed a seismic survey of its acreage, mapping the underwater layers of the earth, when the uneasy peace that had prevailed in the run-up to the 1992 elections fell apart. UNITA's Savimbi had assumed he would win the vote easily. The MPLA government of dos Santos had been dogged by allegations of corruption, and Savimbi promised a new start. But public opinion began to turn against the UNITA leader when news broke that two of his lieutenants had been brutally executed. Election graffiti in Luanda summed up the unappealing choice being offered to voters: "The MPLA steals, UNITA kills." Savimbi made the situation worse by telling Angolans that their choice in the election was war or peace, implying that if he lost he would renew his attacks on the MPLA. His rhetoric was anti-white and anti-*mestiço* (people with mixed Angolan-Portuguese blood). He told American freelance journalist Karl Maier that if he lost, it would be proof that the elections had been rigged. "If they [the MPLA] provoke me," he said, "this is going to get ugly."

The initial results of the UN-supervised elections that were held on September 29 and 30 pointed to an MPLA victory. Even before the final count was in on October 17, showing that Savimbi had secured only 40.1 per cent of the vote compared with 49.6 per cent for dos Santos, the

UNITA leader had gone back to war. He refused to participate in the run-off vote stipulated under Angolan election rules, and his fighters, who were supposed to have been demobilized prior to the elections under the watchful eyes of a UN force, remained armed and ready to fight. "He just went back into the jungle and pulled out the guns," says Dyment. "There was a number of firefights in Luanda, and each time the government beat him back and drove him out."

Had the United Nations been given the support and the funding it needed, the demobilization process might have been completed and a new war averted. But international attention was drawn elsewhere during this crucial period. The Bosnian war had erupted on April 5, 1992, and Cambodia was organizing its own UN-administered elections after years of turmoil. Angola was overlooked. What followed were three months of fighting between UNITA and the MPLA, during which both sides repeatedly violated the international laws of war. The MPLA conducted a purge of the cities it controlled, torturing and killing thousands of suspected UNITA supporters. And UNITA rampaged through the countryside committing its own atrocities. By January 1993, an estimated ten thousand Angolans had died in the post-election explosion of violence.

Savimbi's rebels found a dependable source of funding to replace the external backing they had lost at the end of the Cold War: the diamond fields of the northeast. They controlled this area for long periods during the conflict. Anyone with a strong back and a shovel can mine the alluvial diamonds in the area; they lie just beneath the topsoil. UNITA sold these diamonds, known as "blood" or "conflict diamonds," with the complicity of the diamond intermediaries and raised hundreds of millions of dollars. With oil revenues on one side and diamond revenues on the other, the two parties settled in for a long war. Though the conflict had not originally been about resources, in this new phase oil and diamonds provided the means and the motivation to keep it going. The winner could count on controlling great wealth.

In January 1993, UNITA forces overran Soyo. "Soyo was an operating base for the oil companies." Dyment says, "It was the Aberdeen of

Angola. . . . [UNITA] took that and destroyed it." Ranger was forced to hurriedly set up a new supply base at Pointe-Noire in Congo-Brazzaville. Accounts differ on how badly the company's operations were disrupted by the UNITA attack. There are also conflicting versions about who owned the material seized by UNITA and who funded its retrieval. What there is no debate about is that Tony Buckingham called in a group of South African mercenaries called Executive Outcomes to take Soyo back.

Executive Outcomes was a private army for hire that had been established in 1989 by Eeben Barlow, a veteran of the South African Defence Forces (SADF). Before the apartheid regime crumbled in South Africa, Barlow had served in 32 Battalion, also known as Buffalo Battalion. This infamous infantry unit played a key role in destabilizing South Africa's neighbours by supporting rebel movements and conducting its own military and sabotage operations. Barlow served as second-in-command in the early 1980s when the battalion was active in southern Angola, supporting UNITA. He later moved into military intelligence and joined the innocuous-sounding Civil Co-operation Bureau, where his job involved undermining ANC operations abroad. He is also reported to have set up front companies used to circumvent the international sanctions that were in place against South Africa.

To staff his army, Barlow hired former members of the SADF who had no place in the new South Africa, which was in transition to black-majority rule. Nelson Mandela eventually became the country's first black president on May 10, 1994. Between engagements, Executive Outcomes consisted of a skeletal administrative staff and a phone book. When contracts came, calls were made to men willing to take on work that was short-term, dangerous and extremely lucrative.

While the first few jobs in South Africa were kept secret—there were reports that Executive Outcomes had provided security consulting for diamond companies and training for the SADF—Barlow was upfront about the existence of the organization. It was registered as a company, distributed its own promotional videos complete with a corporate song, had a website and even gave prospective clients wine bottled under the

Executive Outcomes label. In the beginning, Barlow worked with fellow SADF veteran Lonny Keller, but Keller was replaced early on by Lafras Luitingh, another former soldier. Buckingham and Mann, also a former special services officer, had met Barlow previously and knew of his private army. When Soyo was seized, it was just a matter of calling him to see if he was interested in the job. It became the first major international contract for Executive Outcomes.

Buckingham's spokesman Michael Grunberg told me how Executive Outcomes came to be involved at Soyo: "It's a very simple story. Soyo is an oil port location. Overrun by UNITA. Oil companies were severely affected by their inability to continue their exploration work because all of their support capabilities at that particular location were cut off. Tony Buckingham, with Ranger Oil, had an expensive plant there. Ranger Oil—Tony's company Heritage had an interest in it—had an expensive plant there which was costing about $20,000 a day in leasing charges. And they couldn't get at it. They sent an emissary to UNITA to ask UNITA if they would please allow his company access to his equipment. . . . And the answer came back: 'No, Mr. Buckingham, we are not going to provide you with any help. Because if we do allow you to have access to your equipment, you are effectively supporting the economy of Angola.'

"So Tony, in his discussions with the other oil companies, said, 'What we should do is go and get it ourselves.' And the Angolan oil company [SONANGOL] asked the government, 'Why don't we get it ourselves?' And the government said, 'We haven't got the armed forces to do this, to release the oil companies' equipment from there. And that's why we're not going into Soyo. But why don't you go back and ask Buckingham if he knows a solution?'

"So the contact came back to Tony and Tony said, 'I'm sure I can find a solution.' And he turns to his business associate Simon Mann and says, 'Simon, what should we do?' And Simon says, 'It just so happens I know a chap in South Africa called Eeben Barlow who runs a company called Executive Outcomes that has people who used to work in the armed forces in Angola, and he might be able to help or give us some advice.'"

Barlow put together a proposal that was then shown to the Angolan government, said Grunberg. "They came back and said, 'You're on.' And therefore the government funded Executive Outcomes through Tony Buckingham's introduction." Executive Outcomes entered the annals of modern mercenary lore when it retook Soyo in a bloody battle that lasted only a few days.

Although Grunberg made a point of saying that the government had paid the mercenaries' bill, there is much controversy surrounding the question of where the money originated. The idea that private companies might be hiring their own armies is a sensitive issue, but it isn't inconceivable that the funding for Executive Outcomes came from some of the oil companies that were using Soyo. They could have channelled the money through SONANGOL accounts to make it look as though the government had paid the mercenaries.

In the spring of 2002, I travelled to South Africa to interview one of the mercenaries who had fought in the battle for Soyo. Our meeting took place at his home, which like many others in South Africa was surrounded by high walls, protected by motion sensors within the house and guarded by two vicious-looking dogs. A panic button was installed by the front door in case intruders made it past the concentric circles of security. The former mercenary asked not to be identified by name—there were reports that men who had worked for Executive Outcomes had received death threats for talking publicly about Angola—so for our purposes he will be called Kobus, a common South African name.

Kobus is one of life's hard men. This does not mean his demeanour was unpleasant in any way. He was a gracious host, open and helpful in his comments, and he even showed me his photo album of the operation. It's just that life for his generation of white South African males had been one of constant turmoil. When just old enough to understand the evening news, they were deluged with horror stories from the civil war in the Congo, reports of white missionaries being slaughtered in an orgy of mindless black violence. That, at least, was the version presented to the white community in South Africa. When they were old enough to fight, they were conscripted into the South African Defence Forces and ordered to take part in the severe repression of their fellow South Africans or sent off to undermine governments in neighbouring countries. Some believed in the cause and went willingly; others were bewildered but trusted in their government. Conscientious objection was a difficult option.

And then came the great change. The government that had sent them off to battle was replaced by one composed of the very people they had considered the enemy. Black governments in the neighbouring countries of Angola, Mozambique and, finally, Namibia were to be left alone so they could govern as they wished. That was difficult enough to absorb. But the biggest change, the one that would hit many of them personally, was that as apartheid-era fighters, they were no longer welcome in the South African army. Men who had spent the best years of their lives in an almost total state of war were out on the streets with few skills other than the ability to fight and kill. Disillusioned and angry, they were at a loss to see where they would fit in the new South Africa. When the call went out from Executive Outcomes in Pretoria in 1993, these men were willing takers. Where else could they earn the kind of money Barlow and Keller were offering for doing what they had been trained to do?

Kobus and about seventy other former SADF members, both black and white, signed contracts that paid them anywhere from a few thousand US dollars to $6,000 a month for a trained pilot. Although this does not sound like a lot of money for putting your life on the line, it was a fortune in South African terms because of the low value of the rand relative to the US dollar. A core group of them had worked together before, some even in Angola supporting UNITA and fighting the MPLA. They knew each other's strengths and weaknesses in battle and made an instant team. "We were recruited in South Africa with the objective of taking the port," said Kobus. "We were told the reason they wanted to retake the port was that the oil companies could not operate efficiently. They needed the harbour facilities and they had their workshops and all that there."

While Barlow and Keller supplied the men, Kobus said the actual operation was put together by Buckingham and his associate Mann—the two worked closely with Executive Outcomes to plan the assault. The mercenaries were ferried in small groups by plane from Lanseria Airport near Johannesburg to the Cabo Ledo training camp south of Luanda. There they met with some of the Angolan troops that would be taking part in the attack on Soyo. "To be working for your previous enemy was very strange," admitted Kobus. "There is this mistrust, suspicion. You are not sure how you are going to treat these guys and how they are going to treat you. But very quickly you realized these guys were happy to have us there. It's quite embarrassing for them to have to hire mercenaries to do their dirty work. And they were aware of it, so we didn't rub their noses in it or anything. We were in their back garden. Quite easy to be disposed of, so you watched your P's and Q's."

Once on the ground at the Cabo Ledo camp, it became evident that the recruitment process had been a little too hurried. Soyo had been seized by UNITA in mid-January and the mercenaries were aiming to retake it by mid-February. But in putting together the team, Barlow and Keller had included what Kobus calls "rabble": "Before we deployed, we had to put fifteen to twenty guys under house arrest. We couldn't take them with us. They were just totally useless. Why Eeben recruited them, I don't know. I think it was a case of getting the numbers up."

The house arrest was meant to keep the rejected soldiers from returning to South Africa and talking about the operation. It turned out to be an unnecessary precaution. Within a week of the landing of Executive Outcomes at Cabo Ledo, news of their arrival broke in the South African papers. The stories said the men were in Angola to assassinate Savimbi, a slant the mercenaries suspected had been put out by former colleagues in the SADF who still sided with the UNITA leader. Savimbi announced that if his fighters caught any of his former allies, he would deal with them harshly.

The attack began not at Soyo, but at the Quefiquena tanker storage facility on the Atlantic Coast, about 13 kilometres south of the supply depot. There, they would make their beachhead. The mercenaries had been flown the night before to the airfield in Cabinda, where Chevron held sway. At first light, they were transported by helicopter to Quefiquena. Even early in the day, the air was thick with humidity. The temperature would soar to close to 38 degrees Celsius by early afternoon. The soldiers hit the ground, cut through a security fence and came across a pickup truck just as it was accelerating away. The vehicle and its two occupants were shot to pieces. The battle had begun.

What followed were two days of chaos as the South Africans faced fighters whom they had trained and who were now using their own tactics against them. Executive Outcomes lost one man, who was hit by a grenade. When the helicopter arrived after the first day to evacuate the wounded, another fifteen or so mercenaries said they'd had enough and wanted to go home. After the helicopter took off, only thirty of the original complement were left on the ground.

The Angolan army arrived after the fight had started. Kobus was scathing in his comments about them. The barge carrying the reinforcements went sideways to the beach for the landing, which made it difficult for the soldiers and vehicles to disembark. One tank burned out its clutch trying to get up to the beach; another ran over a vehicle when the driver panicked. The third never got off the barge. As for the soldiers, "they were basically children who had been in uniform for three weeks. Each had a rifle and one magazine."

Once they had run UNITA out of Quefiquena, the South Africans put the Angolans into defensive positions to hold the tank facility while they themselves moved on to Soyo. UNITA had fled the depot and the mercenaries were able to walk in unopposed. Kobus said, "UNITA generally don't make a stand. Typical rebel guerrilla tactics: fight, take the place, hold it, but if you come and put up a good [fight], they'll relinquish their position." On the streets of Soyo they saw dead bodies being eaten by wild dogs. They were told these had been men who had been executed for refusing to join UNITA.

The mercenaries found that the facility at Soyo had been ransacked. "UNITA had chased the oil companies away and then they went about destroying everything," said Kobus. "They went to where the mainframe computers were and just shot at the computer screens. They vandalized everything. Burnt the generators out." The South Africans secured the area and prepared for UNITA to counterattack. Two more of their men died when they ran into an ambush.

Kobus said he discovered only after the men had arrived in Soyo that they had an objective other than retaking the facility. "There was a very expensive, very unique and scarce buoy that was anchored in the harbour of Soyo," he said. "That was all kept very, very hush. We were not told what the objective was and I only found out purely by chance after we had already secured the harbour." UNITA had not destroyed this particular piece of equipment. "I don't think they knew about it. Otherwise they would have destroyed it. It was within RPG [rocket-propelled grenade] range. They could have fired rockets at it."

Dyment says Ranger did not have any equipment at Soyo and had no relationship with Executive Outcomes. The actual owner of the piece of equipment remains a mystery, although it could have been any of the oil companies that used the Soyo base.

Ranger was involved with Buckingham in its partnership in the subsidiary Ranger Oil West Africa, and Buckingham was involved with Executive Outcomes. However, there were some indications that individual Ranger employees, if not the company itself, may have backed the operation. When Executive Outcomes ran into problems getting supplies at Soyo—the Angolan officer in charge had been selling his troops' rations to the locals—new supplies were sorted out for them in Luanda by Simon Mann and someone who introduced himself as a Ranger Oil employee.

The mercenaries set up their headquarters in the Hotel Soyo. Several oil companies sent representatives to assess the damage, but the depot was not reopened for general use. After the first month, Kobus said the mercenaries were offered bonuses by Tony Buckingham to stay until mid-April. During that period they had to vacate several times when they feared that UNITA forces had penetrated the Angolan army defences and were heading directly for the Executive Outcomes headquarters. In one of the evacuations, a boat owned by an unnamed oil company took the troops to an oil rig offshore, but the manager of the rig refused to let them board and they went south to Luanda. By mid-April, the buoy had been retrieved and the mission was declared a success. At least three Executive Outcomes men had been killed in the operation, as well as an unknown number of UNITA fighters and Angolan army troops.

The South Africans went home, where their money had been deposited in their bank accounts. (One of Barlow's conditions for accepting the contract was that he be paid in advance. How much he was paid is not clear. He has said that a second contract, involving about five hundred men for a period of eighteen months, cost the Angolan government US$20 million. But this was separate from the contract to retake Soyo.) The mercenaries warned the MPLA before leaving that the Angolans could not hold Soyo by themselves, and they proved to be right. A short time later the depot was overrun again by UNITA.

Soyo was the making of Executive Outcomes. The Angolan government was so impressed that it signed a second contract with the group to come back and train the Angolan army. Among the skills the mercenaries taught the Angolan soldiers was how to use air-burst explosions—deadly weapons that spread a cloud of flammable vapour and then explode, incinerating everything in the immediate vicinity. According to Grunberg, Buckingham also brokered this second contract. "He got the call in London, from I think the president's office in Angola, saying, 'Mr. Buckingham, we would like to have a meeting with you urgently to discuss ways in which you can help us on a more macro level.' He said, 'Well let me look in my diary and I'll come back to you on when it would be possible to have this meeting.' And they said, 'No, Mr. Buckingham, the president's jet is already waiting for you in London. Could you possibly go out there this afternoon? And the president will look forward to seeing you in the morning.' And that's exactly what happened," said Grunberg. He added that he saw a copy of the contract, which set out the services that Executive Outcomes would provide. They included training the army and providing combat support. Buckingham, through his interest in another

Canadian company, DiamondWorks Ltd., received a diamond concession after the diamond fields in the northeast were retaken by the army with help from the mercenaries. This was the mine I visited in the summer of 1998, shortly before the area was again overrun by rebels.

While the mercenaries were fighting and dying at Soyo, back at Ranger Oil in Calgary, the operation was treated as a non-event. Dyment says the board was kept fully informed about material events in Angola at all times. However, the events at Soyo were not considered significant, he said, because of the small part Ranger Oil West Africa played in the company's overall operations. The subsidiary, jointly owned with Buckingham's Heritage Oil, was helping the Angolans set up their own oil company by providing management and training to develop an oilfield. If the operation proved to be a success, Ranger would be awarded a share of the profits. Chairman of the board, Simon Reisman, says he does not recall ever having a discussion about Ranger Oil West Africa, Heritage Oil or the events at Soyo. In fact, he said he did not even know about Heritage Oil. "When I joined the board [in 1991] they were already in Angola," said Reisman. The directors discussed the general political situation in the country in the context of what it meant for the safety of their people and their ability to find and produce oil.

William Gatenby, who joined the board in 1992, backs Reisman's recollections of the directors' discussions about Angola. "Soyo was just a minor thing," he says. "Our biggest problem over there was that we did not find any oil." Gatenby pointed out to me that by 1993, after Pierce had died and major changes were made to the board, there were few long-term members left. They relied on management to fill them in on the company's far-flung operations. "In the final analysis, management runs most companies," Gatenby said.

Shareholders were similarly in the dark. In corporate releases by the parent company during this period, Ranger Oil West Africa was mentioned in passing, as was Heritage Oil. But the political situation in Angola was not accurately described in company accounts. A week after the Executive Outcomes team was deployed to retake Soyo, and more than a month after the oil facility had been seized, Ranger Oil issued its annual report for 1992. The report offered a dry account of the award of Block 4 to Ranger in 1991, of the completion of the seismic survey in 1992 and of the plans to drill test wells in 1993. The only hint that Angola might not have been as safe and stable as western Canada came in the last two lines of the section: "Contingency plans are being developed to drill the first well this summer, notwithstanding the unsettled political conditions prevailing in the country since the government elections in 1992. The Company continues to monitor the political situation."

Ranger is certainly not the only resource company loath to alarm its investors with the unvarnished truth. But the degree of disclosure is underwhelming given that the company's supply base had been seized by rebels and that a mercenary counterattack organized by its partner was underway as the report was signed off. Perhaps the company hoped the problem would go away and no one would be the wiser. Ranger's involvement was largely ignored by the Canadian press, and though the international media picked up on the presence of Executive Outcomes at Soyo, few details were given.

Dyment says that after Soyo, Ranger had had little to do with Tony Buckingham. "There was a lot of publicity and we obviously distanced ourselves from [Buckingham]," he said to me. "But, more importantly, there wasn't anything to go forward with. It wasn't a case of boy, we'd love to do business with Tony but he's got Executive Outcomes doing their thing. There just wasn't a business opportunity, nor did we see any merit in going forward." A short-lived joint venture between them in Pakistan proved to be a disappointment. However, they remained partners in Ranger Oil West Africa Ltd.

Ranger disappeared as a company in July 2000 when it was purchased for CDN$1 billion by Canadian Natural Resources Ltd., another Calgary energy firm. Its new owners stated that they had scrutinized the books and commissioned three independent evaluations before deciding to buy Ranger Oil. Yet when I questioned senior executives about the Soyo episode, they said they had never even heard of Heritage Oil. "We have no partners," one executive insisted, seeming not to know about Ranger Oil West Africa Ltd., which still existed at the time of the meeting. The executive said that Canadian Natural liked to work alone and get 100 per cent of the profits for 100 per cent of the risk. Ranger's distancing of itself from Buckingham had been effective.

Ultimately, Angola was a disappointment to the company. Ranger never found oil in large quantities. The 100-million-barrel field it thought it had located ended up producing only 8 million barrels. "It used up a lot of our resources, with minimum return," said Reisman. Several years after Soyo, Ranger took a US$71-million writedown on its Angolan operations. Its partnership with Tony Buckingham had been an expensive failure.

Eeben Barlow, on the other hand, had discovered that there was money to be made in the mercenary business. Under his stewardship, Executive Outcomes landed a number of other lucrative contracts before disbanding later in the 1990s. Barlow began raising horses at a ranch in South Africa that the locals jokingly referred to as Dallas.

Kobus, the former Executive Outcomes mercenary, gave up the trade. Deciding his life was worth more than $6,000 a month, he moved into private, non-lethal business.

As for Buckingham, he remains a figure of some mystery despite the amount of media coverage he has generated through his activities in Angola, Sierra Leone, Papua New Guinea, Uganda and the Congo. He has moved his home base from London to Guernsey, a tax haven in the Channel Islands, and moved his field of combat from Africa to the high seas. Although he still has interests in a number of resource companies, including Heritage Oil, when his name crops up in the media these days it is in association with the epic battles he wages against opponents with names like *Warlord* and *Predator* for prizes called the Champagne Mumm Admiral's Cup or the Rolex Commodore's Cup. While it is not clear whether he has completely retired from his former pursuits, he is spending a great deal of time captaining his Farr 40 yacht in competitions around the world. The only hint of his earlier adventures can be found in the name of his boat. It is christened *A Bit of a Coup*.

CHAPTER EIGHT

RAKESH SAXENA IN
SIERRA LEONE

IN THE SUMMER OF 1997, DESPERATION, OPPORTUNISM AND HAPPEN-
stance brought three men together to plan a mercenary invasion of Sierra
Leone. Each was smarting from recent failure and looking for redemp-
tion. The elected president of Sierra Leone, Ahmad Tejan Kabbah, had
fled the country after a coup in May 1997 and yearned to return to power
in the capital, Freetown. Tim Spicer, whose new private military company
Sandline International had just suffered a well-publicized fiasco in Papua
New Guinea, needed to notch up a success. And Rakesh Saxena, an
Indian financier on the run from Thai authorities and under arrest in
Canada, saw diamond concessions in Sierra Leone as a way to raise
money on the Vancouver Stock Exchange. Each thought a mercenary-led
counter-coup would be the solution to his particular problem. Spicer
would arrange it, Saxena would finance it and Kabbah would give it his
blessing. That was the plan before it went awry. Only one of the three
would eventually achieve his goal.

The summer of 1997 was one of tremendous upheaval and bloodshed
in the small West African country. It began in the early hours of May 25,
when several pickup trucks carrying soldiers dressed in civilian clothing
roared up to the gates of Pademba Road Prison near Freetown. The soldiers leaped out and used grenades to blast open the steel main doors.
Murderers, rapists, drug dealers and petty criminals were freed, along

with nine soldiers who had been implicated, but not convicted, of trying to overthrow the government. Among them was Major Johnny Paul Koroma, a thirty-four-year-old officer who had been trained in Britain. He quickly took command of the soldiers, leading them on to capture the presidential palace recently abandoned by Kabbah. Then they began looting Freetown.

Though it was the country's third coup since 1992, Sierra Leoneans found this one particularly hard to bear. Expectations for a lasting peace had been high following the 1996 election that had brought Kabbah and his Sierra Leone People's Party to power, ending years of military rule. Kabbah had been the unlikely victor in the election. Politics in this part of Africa generally revolved around Big Men, people who looked after a community in return for unquestioned support. Kabbah had no such constituency. He had spent two decades working abroad in various mid-level positions for the United Nations and had only returned to the country of his birth when he had retired in the early 1990s. Virtually unknown in Sierra Leone, he won the election when the more powerful parties realized their strength was too evenly matched to secure outright victory and made him the compromise candidate.

With his deep, resonant voice and aura of *gravitas*, Kabbah looked and sounded like a president. He was more the cautious bureaucrat than the charismatic leader, but he did have one thing that the real power-brokers found attractive: international connections that might lead to funding and support for Sierra Leone.

Since its independence from Britain in 1961, the country had gone steadily downhill as a result of a combination of government misrule and infighting between the Big Men who used violence to sustain their political and economic networks. Competition for resources caused widespread instability, and in such an atmosphere of uncertainty, the economy suffered. The government became reliant on foreign aid and loans.

In 1991, members of the Revolutionary United Front (RUF), a rebel group backed by Liberia, crossed the border into Sierra Leone and began a drive for the capital, intent on unseating a government they claimed had become corrupt and incompetent. The army beat the rebels to it. In 1992, army captain Valentine Strasser led a handful of men in a march toward the presidential palace. They wanted to protest a reduction in their rice rations. But when then-president Joseph Saidu Momoh saw them coming, he assumed it was a coup and fled. Strasser, a twenty-seven-year-old officer, assumed the presidency. Throughout his brief reign, the rebels continued their campaign of terror in the hinterlands. They forced captives to mutilate or murder family members or community leaders so that they would not be accepted back in their communities and would therefore have to join the rebel movement. Many of the captives were children.

Unable to defeat the rebels with his own ragtag army, Strasser decided to hire the South African mercenary group Executive Outcomes. He had been introduced to them through Tony Buckingham. Having just chalked up a success in Angola (securing the Soyo oil depot) the mercenaries were riding a wave of acclaim in certain quarters. In Sierra Leone, they quickly established calm in the areas where they were active, which happened to include the diamond-rich region of Koidu. Their presence in the country became controversial, however, when Buckingham gained a diamond concession for his company DiamondWorks Ltd. This led to charges that the mercenaries were selling their services for mineral concessions. The paper trail for the diamond concessions disappeared into a maze of companies registered in offshore financial centres, making it impossible to establish whether the accusations were valid.

Executive Outcomes was still in Sierra Leone when Kabbah came to power in 1996. Under pressure from the International Monetary Fund, which did not want its funds used to pay mercenaries, Kabbah ended the contract in January 1997. The South African outfit had been earning US$1.7 million a month for providing 115 mercenaries to lead missions against the rebels and train the army troops. Some of these men stayed behind, starting their own security companies or signing on with Lifeguard, an associated company that provided security at mine sites and embassies. But the main group of mercenaries departed, leaving behind a security vacuum. The brief stability they had brought to the country did not outlast their departure.

Although Kabbah's government was democratically elected, it suffered from many of the same problems as the military dictatorships that had come before it: its tenuous grip on power made it brutal. The US State Department, in its 1996 report on human rights practices, said security forces in Sierra Leone were responsible for extrajudicial killings, beatings, arbitrary arrest and detention, and illegal seizure. The report described prison conditions as life-threatening and said there were lengthy delays in trials and violations of due process. Over half of the 640 people being held in Pademba Road Prison near Freetown were awaiting trial. Though Kabbah was not blamed personally for many of the excesses of his government, he was increasingly seen as a feeble leader, unable to impose his own standards of honesty and sincerity on the people around him.

It was not the corruption of his government, however, that brought Kabbah's tenure to an end, but rather his tense relationship with the army. The recent history of his country made Kabbah distrust the military, whose ranks had been inflated through the recruitment of street children. He planned to reduce its numbers from eighteen thousand to three thousand and, in a complementary move, to give the Kamajors and other ethnic militias better arms and improved training. The Kamajors were the traditional hunters in southern and eastern Sierra Leone, and their leader, Samuel Hinga Norman, was deputy defence minister in Kabbah's government. Kabbah trusted the Kamajors far more than he trusted the army, and he saw in them a force that could protect his government. Hinga Norman began negotiating with Cape International, a company set up by former members of Executive Outcomes, to arm and train the Kamajors. When a faction within the army caught wind of what was happening, it decided to topple Kabbah's government.

In May 1997 the triumphant coup leaders issued a statement from their new headquarters at the presidential palace, criticizing the government for not living up to its promises and for paying the Kamajors more than the military. Koroma invited the rebels of the Revolutionary United Front to join the military junta and issued a decree banning the Kamajors. "We are the national army," said a spokesman for the coup leaders. "They are not, any more."

Sierra Leoneans signalled their displeasure with the coup by refusing to go to work or to send their children to school. Business activity ground to a halt, both in the urban areas and in the countryside, where soldiers and rebels who had joined in an uneasy alliance attacked and looted mining operations. Sierra Leone has been blessed—or cursed, depending on your point of view—with significant mineral resources, including diamonds, bauxite (the chief source of aluminum) and rutile (used to make paint). One of the first moves made by the army junta was to seize control of the diamond areas in the eastern part of the country near Kono. To hold Kono was to hold instant wealth. The alluvial gems found there could be literally scooped from the ground. It was rumoured that three children had found a 100-carat diamond tangled in the roots of a yam just before the coup. Expatriate mine workers either fled the country or sought refuge in armed encampments and let the army and rebels get on with their looting.

Kabbah, who had fled to Conakry, the capital city in neighbouring Guinea, watched helplessly as his country was ransacked. Though he had the moral support of elected leaders around the world, armed support was in short supply. In the days following the upheaval, the United States and Britain declared the coup illegal. But neither government was prepared to lend its armed might to reverse the situation. The United States briefly sent in the Marines to evacuate expatriate workers who had holed up in the Mammy Yoko beachfront hotel in Freetown. One can only imagine the surge of hope that Kabbah must have experienced when he heard that an aircraft carrier, the uss *Kearsarge*, had been diverted by the Pentagon to Freetown. The 1,200 members of the 22nd Marine Expeditionary Unit on board had the firepower and training to secure the Sierra Leone capital had they been so ordered. But Operation Noble Obelisk was not about restoring Kabbah to power. The United States was still smarting from the disaster in Somalia and was not about to entangle itself in another African conflict, especially when it had no immediate strategic interest in the area. It might have been a different story if Sierra Leone had had an abundance of oil rather than diamonds.

The *Kearsarge* stopped 30 kilometres off the coast and sent transport helicopters into Freetown to evacuate 2,500 people (450 Americans, 250 British citizens and 1,800 nationals from about 40 other countries). Then it hoisted anchor and steamed away. Further evacuations were conducted by the United Nations and Britain.

The only country prepared to come to Kabbah's aid was Nigeria, which already had troops in Sierra Leone on a military co-operation agreement. The Nigerians were hurriedly given a UN mandate through a regional grouping called the Economic Organization of West African States (ECOWAS) and told to hold the line. There was a certain irony in having forces from Nigeria, at that time a dictatorship led by Sani Abacha, fighting to restore a democratically elected government in Sierra Leone. Nigeria was considered a pariah state by other countries in the region, especially after the 1995 execution of activist Ken Saro-Wiwa and his Ogoni colleagues. Some of Kabbah's people feared and distrusted their African brethren, suspecting Nigeria of harbouring hegemonic ambitions. But since help was not forthcoming from any other major power, Kabbah and his men accepted Nigeria's offer. But they continued to cast around for other ways of winning back their country.

In the early days of his exile, Kabbah kept his spirits up with the thought that it would not be long before he returned to Freetown. Just days after his overthrow, he received a call from Tim Spicer, a decorated former member of the Scots Guards regiment who had recently become head of a private military company called Sandline International. "I rang President Kabbah in Conakry and said that if he needed us or thought there was anything we might do to help him or his government, the rightful government of Sierra Leone, we were on hand and willing to help," Spicer wrote in his memoir, *An Unorthodox Soldier*. Kabbah, still expecting some international power to come to his aid, turned the offer down. But as the days turned into weeks and then into months, Kabbah sank into depression. Callers at the villa where he was staying were told at almost every hour of the day that the president was sleeping. It was hard not to feel that the world had abandoned him. Kabbah began to reconsider Spicer's early proposal.

In the late 1990s, Timothy Simon Spicer became the poster boy for private military companies. A handsome man with a solid military background, he had been a spokesman for UN forces in Bosnia. As a result of that experience, he was comfortable speaking to reporters, and they were only too delighted to find someone from the shadowy world of mercenaries who was prepared to speak to them. Photos of Spicer appeared in all the major British newspapers accompanying interviews in which he defended the role of the modern-day mercenary. Though too slow, by his own account, to become a member of Britain's crack Special Air Services, Spicer had seen active service in the Falklands and Northern Ireland in addition to fulfilling more pedestrian teaching and guarding assignments at home.

As early as 1993 he was approached by Simon Mann, Tony Buckingham's associate and friend, to work for Executive Outcomes in Angola, but he turned the assignment down because the money wasn't good enough. Spicer stayed in the army for a few more years and then left to join a small financial institution in London at the invitation of another former Scots Guard.

Around the time he was realizing he was not cut out for a life in finance, Spicer received two offers for work in the private sector. The first was extended by Richard Bethell and Alastair Morrison, both former Scots Guards, who had set up a military consultancy called Defence Systems Ltd. The second came from Mann on behalf of Tony Buckingham, who wanted to know if Spicer was interested in setting up his own private military company. Buckingham had decided that Executive Outcomes would always attract unfavourable media attention because of the stigma of apartheid. His solution was to create a new company that would be free of any baggage but could use many of the same people. Buckingham would back it as a business venture.

In February 1996, Spicer started the as-yet-unnamed company and began casting about for business. Its ultimate ownership was obscured by an offshore registration, and Spicer himself seemed confused about who actually controlled it. Buckingham, whom Spicer variously described publicly as the company's "chairman" and its "patron," was the prime mover behind the operation. He accompanied Spicer on his first major sales mission to meet senior ministers from Papua New Guinea. The government there had lost control of the island of Bougainville to a secessionist group, and the ensuing battles had forced the giant Panguna copper mine to close. Because the mine supplied an estimated 45 per cent of Papua New Guinea's export revenues, the government wanted Sandline to retake it as soon as possible. During the negotiations, Spicer suggested his company would take part payment in mineral concessions if the government did not have the ready cash. The offer proved to be unnecessary, but it created a stir in the media when it came to light. It was proof that mercenaries were bargaining their services for mineral concessions.

Testimony before an official inquiry held in Papua New Guinea revealed many details of the operation. The contract to supply men and weapons to the government of Papua New Guinea and to retake the Bougainville copper mine was signed in January 1997. The government paid its first instalment, which went into an account on which Buckingham was one of the signatories. But the contract ended two months later when a faction within the government arrested Spicer and forced him to abort his mission. What is instructive about the entire episode, aside from its humiliating outcome, is that it exposed the modus operandi of Spicer and his backers. Although Sandline had signed the contract, it subcontracted the work to Executive Outcomes, using the controversial group while shielding it from publicity. Most damaging for Sandline's image as an upstanding private company was that Spicer had asked for and received blank-end user certificates for arms shipments from the Papua New Guinea authorities. Such certificates, which are supposed to indicate the final destination and user of arms, can be used to circumvent arms embargoes if they are signed while still blank. Sandline's actions had been improper if not illegal.

Photographs of a dishevelled Spicer under arrest by members of the
Papua New Guinea Defence Forces appeared around the world. It was
not the best advertisement for the new private military company. Spicer
was eventually freed without charge and, after testifying at an official
inquiry into the matter, was allowed to go home. In summing up his experience for his memoirs, he blamed the failure of the operation on the perfidious nature of the chief of defence staff of Papua New Guinea, General
Jerry Singirok. In Spicer's eyes, Singirok had agreed to the contract with
Sandline and then exposed it in order to engineer a constitutional crisis
from which he hoped to benefit. Payments made to Singirok by British
arms-dealing firm J. and S. Franklin, which were exposed by an Australian
journalist and later confirmed by the Australian joint parliamentary committee on foreign affairs, defence and trade, may have influenced his
behaviour. Spicer does not castigate himself or others for failing to do
proper due diligence and ensure that all parts of the Papua New Guinea
government fully supported the plan before the contract was signed.

Back home in April 1997, Spicer needed to find a job for Sandline that
would be more successful than the first. In this regard, the coup in Sierra
Leone could not have happened at a better time. Kabbah was interested
in Sandline's services, but such help was available only for a price. And the
dispossessed president was short of money.

This is when Rakesh Saxena, the Indian financier being detained in
Vancouver, entered the picture with an offer of funds. Most people who
have met Saxena describe him as an immensely likable man who can be
both affable and extremely generous when the spirit moves him. I did not
meet the troubled financier until after 1998, when a court order tightening
existing restrictions on his movements confined him to house arrest in his
upmarket condo across a small stretch of water from the lively Granville
Market area. By then his whirlwind existence in the financial capitals of the
world had come to an end. Our meetings over the next few years would
always take place at the dining table in the main room of his condo, which
functioned as both home and office. Saxena dressed casually, with open-
necked golf shirts and loose slacks. He was often barefoot. What use did

he have for shoes if he was rarely allowed out? His conversation always came in sharp bursts, his sentences filled with ideas and peppered with historical references. He talked of places he had lived and worked with a sense of humour that was contagious. It was easy to see how people became comfortable enough to trust him and rely on his financial judgment.

Saxena had come to Vancouver by a somewhat circuitous route. Born in India in 1952, he was educated in Britain, where his mother sometimes worked as an international lawyer specializing in the law of the sea. He showed an early flair with figures—his mother still believes he is a mathematical genius—but studied English literature at university. On campus he was a radical who organized left-wing demonstrations. He says the contacts he made with the left during that period stood him in good stead when they later became prominent political figures. Like many of his generation, he eventually joined the system he had once scorned, becoming a currency trader first in India and later in Hong Kong. But it was when he moved to Thailand at the end of the 1980s that he really hit the financial jackpot.

A chance meeting on a golf course with Kirkkiat Jalichan, the managing director of the Bangkok Bank of Commerce, led to Saxena's appointment in 1990 as an adviser to the small but prestigious bank. For a brief period, life was very good. Saxena worked hard at the bank on deals that seemed never-ending. And he partied hard after work. It was not unusual for him to drink six to eight pints of beer a day, followed by a couple of glasses of wine and half a bottle of Scotch. These were the days of the phenomenal growth of the countries known as the Asian Tigers, when opportunities seemed endless and everything was done to excess.

His golden sojourn in Thailand, however, came to a sudden end in early 1996 when the Bangkok Bank of Commerce collapsed under the weight of bad loans valued at US$3.2 billion. After sorting through the debris, Thai authorities alleged that the bank had loaned money to many of the sixty-two companies directed by Saxena, at least one of which had no assets and no employees. Although his name was never on the loan approvals to these particular companies, which totalled 1.6 billion baht, or CDN$88 million, Saxena was charged with conspiracy to commit fraud.

That was the official charge on which the Kingdom of Thailand sought his extradition from Canada.

But more serious denunciations were made behind the scenes by those seeking to bring Saxena to Thai justice. He had actually caused the Asian crisis, they whispered, because the bank collapse caused the Thai government to devalue the baht, which then ignited the financial fires that swept through Asia and beyond. In recounting this theory, the *Wall Street Journal* described the financier as the Mrs. O'Leary's cow of the financial firestorm. Saxena did not stick around to find out what the Thai courts would decide. He fled the country in May 1996, stopping briefly in Switzerland before moving on to British Columbia. In July 1996, he was arrested by the Royal Canadian Mounted Police at the luxury ski resort in Whistler, BC, while meeting with Thai authorities. A suitcase full of cash was at his feet.

Saxena has stoutly denied that he had anything to do with either the problems at the Bangkok Bank of Commerce or the broader calamity. He claims that Kirkkiat Jalichan and his cronies were just looking for a scapegoat when they put the Thai financial authorities on his tail. The BC Supreme Court did not agree and ruled in 2000 that there was enough evidence for Saxena to be sent back to Thailand to stand trial. He appealed that decision on the grounds that Thai figures would have him killed the moment he set foot in their country because he knows too much embarrassing information about them. Saxena was afraid enough for his life that once he arrived in Canada, he hired a twenty-four-hour-a-day surveillance team to keep watch. When evidence came to light in 1998 that he was preparing to purchase a false passport to leave Canada, he was placed under house arrest and his minders became his keepers. Under the first arrangement of its kind in Canada, Saxena was allowed to remain in his own home under the guard of a security team he paid for by himself. His lawyer successfully argued that this arrangement would save Canadian taxpayers money.

Though physically constrained to Vancouver since July 1996, Saxena was still able to do business around the world by telephone and over the Internet. Stories of small Canadian mining companies striking it rich in far-flung places whetted his appetite for Africa. Even after the Canadian firm Bre-X crashed in early 1997 when its fabled gold deposit in Indonesia was found to be non-existent, he still thought there was potential to make money on the Vancouver Stock Exchange with the right vehicle. Saxena found it in the marriage of a defunct dating service called First Impression Singles Network, which had a stock exchange listing, with a number of promising mining concessions in Sierra Leone.

Throughout its ninety-two-year history, the Vancouver Stock Exchange (which was rolled into the Canadian Venture Exchange in 1999) gained a well-deserved reputation as a bucket shop, where the emphasis was on gambling, not investing. It had been created to help raise money for Canadian junior mining companies whose speculative business was not solid enough to meet the stiffer listing requirements on the Toronto Stock Exchange, but it quickly adopted something of a casino atmosphere. Every now and then, a VSE company would make a substantial find and its stock would rocket into the stratosphere. But mostly the penny stocks represented extremely speculative investments. A certain number of the companies were only ever meant to be stock plays—more corporate effort was put into writing their glowing press releases than into prospecting for minerals. There was quick money to be made on the appearance of good news, and promoters would be long gone when reality brought the stock crashing down. In such an atmosphere, companies changed names and hands frequently, retaining their listing even if the original business had ceased to exist. Thus, a resource company could transmogrify into a dating service before reverting to a resource company and then becoming a high-tech business. Such was the case with First Impressions, which had started life in 1988 as Meadow Mountain Resources Ltd. before changing its name and the nature of its business.

Saxena and his Canadian business partner Paul L. Hammond bought First Impressions in the early 1990s, years before things began to turn sour for Saxena in Thailand. The owner of the dating service had decided to take his software and move elsewhere, leaving the new owners with a shell company that had a name and an exchange listing. It was not until early 1996 that Saxena took steps to reactivate First Impressions. A chance meeting between a small-time promoter from Kelowna, BC, and a visiting Indian businessman from Sierra Leone (neither of whom knew Saxena) set the wheels in motion.

According to Saxena, Mervan Fiessel, the promoter, and Samir Patel, the businessman, found themselves on the same flight to Kelowna in the British Columbia interior and, as people sometimes do when trapped in a small, confined plane for hours, got to talking. It emerged that Patel owned the rights to a bauxite concession near Port Loko in Sierra Leone, which he wanted to develop. He had the rights and he had connections—he was close friends with both Mining Minister Prince Harding and Presidential Affairs Minister Momodu Koroma. What he needed was the money.

Fiessel knew an opportunity when he saw one. He contacted a broker at Canaccord Capital Corp. in Vancouver, who called John L. Gray, owner of the consulting firm Barrington Financial Services Inc. Gray brought the key players together with Saxena. They met in a bar on Howe Street, the Vancouver equivalent of Toronto's Bay Street or Wall Street in New York, and worked out a deal that gave First Impressions an option to acquire the bauxite concession owned by Patel's Jupiter Export-Import Company Ltd. in exchange for shares worth CDN$18.5 million. To reflect its new line of business, First Impressions was to change its name to Global Explorations Corp. Although Jupiter was ostensibly owned by Patel, all its shares were held by Barrington Investment Holdings Ltd., a company registered in the offshore financial centre of Tortola, British Virgin Islands. Gray was given stock options in Global for his part in the deal. Canaccord was rewarded by becoming Global's agent for a private share placement. Fiessel would remain involved.

Global Explorations also entered into an agreement to buy 75 per cent of another Patel company, Jupiter Mining Corp., which held two diamond exploration concessions in the Kindia region of Guinea. And it announced, but never followed through on, a deal with a related company called West Shore Ventures Ltd. to buy all of the assets of Mano River Resources Ltd., a private Swiss company that held gold concessions in Sierra Leone, Guinea and Liberia. Diamonds, bauxite and gold—Saxena had wanted in on the African mining scene, and now he was there with a vengeance.

The bauxite mine was first on his list, and he needed someone with mining expertise to go to Sierra Leone, take a look at the property and make sure things were as promised by Patel. The terms of his bail agreement prevented him from leaving Vancouver, so he sent a team whose members included his partner Hammond, Kelowna promoter Fiessel, geologist Ron Lyle of Watts Griffis McOuat Mining Consultants and his then-security adviser Alan Bell, a former member of the British Special Air Services who ran the security firm Bell and Associates out of Toronto. The team flew to Africa and travelled to the mine site near the northern border with Guinea.

On May 24, 1997, they called Saxena and told him that everything looked fine and that the deal should go ahead. The next day brought the coup that sent Kabbah fleeing to Guinea. Saxena's foray into the mineral sector of Sierra Leone appeared to have ended before it had even begun. The team sought refuge at the Mammy Yoko beachfront hotel in Freetown, where they and other expatriate workers were subjected to a violent and prolonged attack by soldiers loyal to the coup leaders.

The exact details of how Saxena became involved in the mercenary counter-coup that was to follow have never been clearly established. The players involved in the operation to restore Kabbah to his palace in Freetown have all given conflicting versions of who approached who with the proposal. Michael Grunberg told a British inquiry headed by Sir Thomas Legg that Saxena contacted him on July 11, 1997, and told him that he represented a group of investors with mining interests in Sierra Leone who had been approached by Kabbah's people with a request for assistance. Saxena wanted Sandline to do a feasibility study and, depending on how that study went, he might be willing to finance further action. Grunberg said he passed the information on to Spicer, who went to Conakry later that same month to talk to Kabbah's ministers and draw up a plan of military assistance aimed at restoring the president to power. In this version of events, the Sierra Leonean government made the first move and approached Saxena, who then approached Sandline through Grunberg.

In his memoirs, Spicer gives a similar account but says it all took place in June, a month earlier than Grunberg said it did. But Spicer has contradicted himself in an interview by saying that Kabbah had asked him if he could help and that he had replied that he could but needed to know who would pay. Kabbah then purportedly asked to be put in touch with possible funders. This version of events makes it sound as though Kabbah took the initiative and approached Sandline before Saxena did. Yet elsewhere Spicer has said that he called Kabbah within days of the coup to offer Sandline's help.

In a letter to UK foreign secretary Robin Cook, written when the affair blew up in the British media, Spicer's lawyers said that the British ambassador to Sierra Leone, Peter Penfold, had suggested to Kabbah that he ask Sandline for assistance. It was Penfold, said the lawyers, who initiated the approach and encouraged the involvement of Sandline. This version has the British government, in the person of Penfold, making the first move.

Saxena had yet another take on what happened. He said his business partner Patel was approached separately by Hinga Norman, who was the deputy defence minister for Sierra Leone, and Bert Sachse, an Executive Outcomes representative. Hinga Norman told Patel that the government needed helicopter gunships, arms and training if his Kamajors were to fight the army and rebels. Sachse told Patel he should call Spicer if he wanted someone who could supply them.

It makes a difference which party initiated the plan. The impression Spicer and Grunberg tried to leave in their various versions is that they were reacting to a request from a legitimate government or business for their services. But the entire episode takes on a slightly more sinister tone if Saxena's version is correct and Sandline had been shilling for work. What makes Saxena's version plausible is that Spicer is known to have approached Jean-Raymond Boulle, another businessman with mining interests in Sierra Leone, to see if he would be interested in funding a mercenary operation. Boulle turned him down.

Patel passed the information he received from Hinga Norman and Sachse on to Saxena, including one important piece of intelligence: "He said they [the government] need money and if they get back in then we'll get more [mineral] concessions." Saxena says that he liked the sound of diamond concessions and decided to at least consider the opportunity. He called Sandline and was put in touch with Grunberg, who set the wheels in motion. This may be the call that Grunberg told the Legg inquiry about.

Sandline and Saxena agreed to initiate a two-part plan: Spicer would travel to Conakry to talk to the Sierra Leonean ministers-in-exile and assess whether a military operation was feasible and what it might cost. Saxena would wire Spicer US$70,000—$60,000 for what in military terms was called a commander's estimate, plus $10,000 to cover his costs. If Spicer's opinion was favourable, Saxena would then decide whether to back the mercenary-led counter-coup.

Spicer began to gather intelligence on the situation in Sierra Leone. He drew on information from former Executive Outcomes personnel who were still in the country as well as from the Lifeguard personnel who were guarding mine sites. After consulting with Sierra Leonean ministers, he decided that a US$10-million operation involving arms, helicopters and trainers would be sufficient to reinstall Kabbah in Freetown. Spicer flew to Vancouver to brief Saxena. But there, he met with a surprise.

"We were driving around the city when he stopped the car at a Royal Canadian Mounted Police station in order to 'check in,'" Spicer says in his memoir. It was at this point that the head of Sandline realized the man he was counting on for financial backing was fighting extradition to Thailand. Spicer had failed to do due diligence on his contract with the Papua New Guinea government, and he made precisely the same mistake with Saxena. But he decided to forge ahead with the plan regardless. Saxena was not "a proven villain" and had not yet been deported, "and since our dealings would be strictly on terms of money up front, there would be no chance of President Kabbah's plan being thwarted or collapsing as a result of any inaction by Saxena."

Grunberg, who was working with Spicer on the deal, said he knew at the time that Saxena had to report daily to the police but felt that it didn't make a difference. He pointed out that the government of Sierra Leone was prepared to talk to Saxena. As he said to me, "The electricity company was still prepared to sell him electricity. The local restaurant was still prepared to have him in there for a meal. And the government of Canada was still prepared to take tax. So why should we make a moral judgment?" Spicer and Grunberg did decide on one precaution: they would not commit more resources to the project than could be covered by advances from Saxena. That way they would not be exposed financially if funding suddenly fell through. "Financially, it's very simple," said Grunberg. "When you have a high-risk client, you don't commit resources until the client has paid you."

Saxena had his own doubts about Sandline because of its high-profile failure in Papua New Guinea, but he figured the Sierra Leone operation would be much simpler than the one they had attempted in the West Pacific. "It was a very limited operation," he said. "Really, what you needed were two helicopter gunships, a military planner and a couple of hundred AK-47s. It was not a high-tech operation of any kind." Besides, Sandline had something that both Kabbah and Saxena valued highly. "They said they'd have the British government's consent," said Saxena. "And that was critical."

Two events occurred in the latter half of 1997 that persuaded the main participants in the plan that they had the tacit support of the British government. The first was the publication of the main details of the plot on the front page of the Canadian national newspaper the *Globe and Mail*. The newspaper exposé quoted faxes between Saxena, Spicer and Patel, as well as an exchange between Saxena and Momodu Koroma, Kabbah's minister for presidential affairs. I was one of the reporters who wrote the story, and I had interviewed Kabbah by telephone to get his side. He denied that he was contemplating hiring mercenaries, pointing out that this went against a UN agreement that Sierra Leone had signed that outlawed the use of mercenaries. But the evidence was damning and, according to Spicer's testimony much later, extremely accurate.

The British High Commission in Ottawa alerted the Foreign Office in London of the details. But there the matter rested. No action was taken by the British authorities to ascertain whether the British private military company was in fact planning a counter-coup. A UN arms embargo on Sierra Leone had not yet been implemented, so the plot, while questionable, was not yet illegal. Still, the impending supply of mercenaries and weapons from Britain to an African hot spot should have attracted government notice. When the UN embargo was passed on October 9, no one thought to check whether a British mercenary company had followed through on its published plans to supply arms and men to Sierra Leone. The lack of official reaction encouraged the plotters to continue their preparations, secure in the belief that the British government knew and approved of what they were doing.

The second event that fed their confidence was the invitation extended to Kabbah and his entourage by British prime minister Tony Blair to attend the Commonwealth Heads of Government meeting in Edinburgh as his special guests. For Kabbah, who was growing weary of his life as an exile, this was a welcome break as well as a strong signal that Britain continued to back him as the legitimate leader of Sierra Leone. The trip from Guinea to Edinburgh must have been heartening. One minute he was cooling his heels in Conakry, seemingly forgotten by most of the world; the next minute he was being feted by the Commonwealth leaders in Scotland and being received by the Queen and Prince Philip at Holyrood Palace. The Kabbah entourage revelled in the luxury of the posh Caledonian Hotel and went to lavish dinners and glittering receptions. The British government also hosted a special conference for Kabbah in London on the restoration of democracy in his country. From Kabbah's standpoint, Britain had pulled out all the stops.

Was it any wonder then that he was practically glowing with delight at a reception where journalists mingled with heads of government? He stood off to one side, resplendent in a well-tailored suit, a smile playing across his handsome features as he watched Nelson Mandela, the star of the conference, work his special magic on the room. The drinks were

flowing and the canapés were piled high on tables in the ballroom filled
with the buzz of conversation. I introduced myself to Kabbah and raised
the subject of the Sandline contract. Recognition flickered in his eyes.
"So you are the journalist who called me in Guinea?" he asked. Before the
conversation could go any further, Kabbah's people burst into the room
and practically danced around their leader. They had just received news
that a peace deal calling for his restoration by the following April had
been reached in their absence.

The ECOWAS Six-Month Peace Plan for Sierra Leone bore the names
of two members of the military junta, of two representatives of ECOWAS
and of two witnesses from the United Nations and the Organization of
African Unity. It set out a series of steps that would be followed leading
to the return of democratic government in Sierra Leone. Kabbah and his
people were initially delighted but then grew skeptical. The agreement
had been reached without their involvement and appeared not to have
been signed by the real leader of the junta and its RUF allies. "The junta is
a notoriously slippery customer," Kabbah told his fellow heads of government when asking them later not to let up pressure on the coup leaders.
They responded with a strong verbal backing of Kabbah in the meeting's
final communique, but they gave no promises of military support.

Once back in Guinea, Kabbah came to the conclusion that the junta
leaders would not honour their agreement and decided to continue the
negotiations with Sandline and Saxena. The group agreed relatively
quickly on the scope of the operation—helicopters with teams of advisers to assist and support the Kamajors—and on the amount of money
involved—US$10 million. However, the route the money would take
became a bit of a sticking point. Sandline's official position was that it did
business only with legitimate governments. Thus, its deal should have
been a straight two-party agreement with the Kabbah government. But
the men behind Sandline had done enough business in Africa to know
that money had a habit of disappearing when passing through government hands—and Kabbah's government-in-exile was strapped for cash.
Sandline wanted its official deal to be with Kabbah, but it wanted Saxena

to send the money directly to it. Spicer says he talked to Kabbah and suggested, "Why don't you do a deal with Mr. Saxena of Blackstone Capital [an offshore company controlled by Saxena and registered in Belize], which I don't want any part of. Whatever you sort out between yourselves is up to you. You then give me the money or he gives me the money. I'd rather he gave me the money because I know damn well that some of it may well get creamed off in the process if it goes into your setup." Patel, meanwhile, was pushing Saxena to route the funds through Hinga Norman, deputy defence minister and head of the Kamajors.

The final deal was triangular, so that Sandline could preserve the pretence of working for the Kabbah government while receiving money directly from Saxena. The first contract involved the Sierra Leone government and Saxena's Blackstone Capital. In it, Saxena agreed to pay up to US$10 million in exchange for diamond concessions. Just what those concessions were remains a matter of speculation. Penfold described them to an official British inquiry as minor. Hammond, Saxena's former associate, told a Canadian reporter for the television program *The Fifth Estate* they represented 25 to 30 per cent of the country's land mass, but this would appear to be an exaggeration. Saxena said they were in the central part of Sierra Leone, near where another Canadian-registered company, Rex Mining, had operations, but not in the same area as the rich Koidu concessions belonging to DiamondWorks.

The second contract was between the Sierra Leonean government and Sandline International for the supply of personnel and military equipment to restore Kabbah to power. The two separate deals were really one, in that Saxena's $10 million would be going to Sandline. Saxena would get diamond concessions, Sandline would get the money, and Kabbah, if all went according to plan, would get his country back.

The contracts were officially signed by all parties on December 23, 1997. Kabbah signed end user certificates on January 15, 1998, for 2,500 assault rifles, 180 rocket launchers and 50 machine guns, along with ammunition and magazines. But by that date the deal was already starting to fall apart.

As in most failed relationships, the problems that would cause the Sandline-Saxena-Kabbah deal to collapse were evident from the start. The very first time that Spicer met Saxena in Vancouver, he was confronted with the fact that the financial backer of his counter-coup had severe legal problems. It should not have come as a complete surprise when by mid-January no funds had been advanced to Sandline.

Saxena's situation had taken a turn for the worse. Word had somehow reached the Canadian authorities that he was preparing to flee the country using the passport of a Yugoslavian killed in the Bosnia war. Saxena denied this was the case, but the courts decided against him and he was sent to jail—which is where Grunberg found him when he flew to Canada to find out what was happening with the money. Grunberg managed to secure US$1.5 million, a fraction of what was needed for the operation.

Saxena said it wasn't money troubles or his changed situation that made him pull in his horns at the beginning of 1998. "I could call out [of jail] for a couple of months," he told me, "but at that time a couple of things happened. It became obvious that the British government had retracted from their backing earlier. That's number one. And gradually it became obvious that you could not dislodge the Revolutionary United Front in a hurry. The plan which these people [Sandline] had made was not going to work." Saxena said he was getting information from Momodu Koroma, Kabbah's presidential affairs minister, as well as from contacts in Liberia and Guinea. "The $10-million plan was not working," he said. "Then Grunberg came back with an $18-million plan, and that was really out of the question." Sandline would have to tailor its involvement in Sierra Leone to its new, vastly reduced budget of $1.5 million.

In early 1998, the British press finally caught up with the Sandline story, when Eric Lubbock, Lord Avebury, was surfing the Internet and found the *Globe and Mail* piece that had run six months earlier, as well as a subsequent item in a US newspaper. He brought the story to the attention of the media and the British government. The media zeroed in on the government's implied support for a plan that contravened the October 9, 1997, UN arms embargo against all parties in Sierra Leone and a British Order in

Council that had been passed the following month. The *Observer* ran a piece on March 8 with the headline, "Britain holds talks with hired killers." Just how much backing the British government had given the counter-coup became the focus of two official inquiries launched in 1998. The evidence at those hearings revealed that High Commissioner Penfold had been solidly behind the plan to involve the mercenaries. What remained unclear was whether Penfold's blessing was an official sanction or merely a personal endorsement. Lost letters, cryptic conversations between officials at the Foreign and Commonwealth Office and conflicting accounts of key meetings made it impossible for either inquiry to firmly establish the facts. Was this an example of perfidious British foreign policy? Or had Penfold rashly promised support the British government would not or could not deliver?

I had met Penfold in January 1997 at a talk in London being given by Herb Howe, an American academic studying Executive Outcomes. The audience was an unusual combination of businesspeople, mercenaries, aid and development workers and journalists. With his grey hair and grey suit, Penfold appeared to be the quintessential British diplomat. He was about to leave to take up his new posting in Sierra Leone at the time and wanted to learn about the South African mercenaries who had made such a name for themselves in two African conflicts. Penfold had already met Buckingham the previous month at the DiamondWorks office in Chelsea. The two had chatted enthusiastically about their shared passion for car rallying. Penfold was due to drive his Land Rover from London across Europe and North Africa to Freetown. Buckingham was about to participate in the trans Euro-Asian race.

At Howe's lecture and in the heated exchange afterward, the veteran diplomat heard about the dark side of the company Buckingham was associated with, how Executive Outcomes had "pioneered" (Howe's words) the use of air-burst bombs in Angola. Although Sandline was not discussed at that meeting—it had yet to gain notoriety from the Papua New Guinea debacle—Buckingham and his links with both mining companies and mercenaries were dealt with in some detail. Penfold could be under no illusions about the men associated with Sandline and the way they operated in Africa. We spoke briefly at the end of the talk, and I wished him good luck in his new posting. Neither of us realized how much he would need it.

Penfold had barely taken up his post in Freetown when the government fell in May 1997. He bravely tried to negotiate with the coup leaders, but that proved fruitless. He then played a key part in the British and US evacuations of foreign nationals from the Mammy Yoko Hotel in Freetown. Without knowing whether he could actually deliver, Penfold told the junta that he would call in a US bombardment from nearby American naval units if they did not stop the attack on the hotel. His bluff worked and the attack halted temporarily, allowing the foreigners to escape.

Within the foreign service, Penfold had a reputation as a freelancer, someone who went his own way. His colleagues speculated that he had not made the mental transition from governor of the British Virgin Islands, a position in which he was constitutionally independent of the Foreign Office, to the post of high commissioner, in which he was expected to report to headquarters. In the evacuation of the Mammy Yoko Hotel, Penfold's penchant for acting first and asking for permission later worked. But when knowledge of the plans for a mercenary counter-coup in Sierra Leone broke, leaving Foreign Secretary Robin Cook with a black eye, there were dark whispers in Whitehall that this time Penfold had gone too far.

When Kabbah fled to Conakry, Penfold went with him and found himself holding the hand of the deposed president. They met two to three times a week—an unusual level of contact for a president and a foreign diplomat. Kabbah consulted Penfold on the makeup of his cabinet and on his chances of attracting financial and political support to regain power. He also discussed with him the plans for a mercenary attack. Penfold never met with Kabbah, Spicer and Patel all at once, but he was kept apprised of the plans by the president, Spicer and Rupert Bowen, a former diplomatic colleague who worked for DiamondWorks before moving to Sandline.

During the 1998 inquiries, the British government's official position was that Penfold had been acting on his own and had not kept head office sufficiently informed about the plans for the counter-coup. Penfold, who had been commended for his courage during the siege of Freetown, was hung out to dry. He insisted that he had done his best under the circumstances. Communications had been difficult and he had had little support at his one-man high commission, which was run out of a hotel room.

As the drama unfolded in London, the situation in Sierra Leone was at long last resolved. The military junta had not honoured the terms of the October 1997 peace agreement, which called for disarmament and demobilization to start in December. Nigerian-led forces launched a new offensive in early February 1998. True to Sandline's decision not to commit itself beyond its financial resources, the mercenaries' involvement in the decisive battle was minimal. Only fifteen of their men and one helicopter, formerly owned by Executive Outcomes, helped the twelve thousand Nigerian-led forces. On February 12, the troops secured Freetown. Ten days later, the 35 tonnes of weapons that Spicer had purchased with Saxena's money were delivered to the Nigerians at Lungi Airport near Freetown. On March 10, 1998, Kabbah returned to his capital. He was the only one of the three players in the deal who had got what he wanted— and not because of anything Spicer or Saxena had done. But his reinstatement did not end the bloodshed in Sierra Leone. Fighting continued throughout the rest of 1998 and escalated in January 1999, when the rebels retook parts of Freetown. In two horrible weeks of street fighting, somewhere between five thousand and six thousand people died from machete attacks, vigilante killings and executions. The world, which had turned its back on Kabbah once, was forced to take notice.

The United Nations sent an observer mission to Sierra Leone in June 1998. Initially, its numbers were kept to fewer than 300 and its task was to establish negotiations between all parties. When this approach did not stabilize the situation, the Security Council agreed to set up a new, larger mission of six thousand military personnel in October 1999. The following February, the mission was increased to 11,100 military personnel and

then boosted again to 17,500 in March 2001. The civil war that the outside world had once ignored had become the location for one of the
largest UN missions ever mounted. The UN's involvement had been
prompted partly by Nigeria's announcement in 1999 that it would withdraw its troops. The newly elected democratic government in Nigeria had
decided it could no longer afford the cost of military engagement in Sierra
Leone. The announcement caused neighbouring states, as well as the
United States, the United Nations, Britain and the Commonwealth, to
lend more serious support to peace talks, which resulted in an agreement
between the Kabbah government and the rebels in July 1999.

Britain committed a substantial amount of troops and money to
Sierra Leone in 2000 and began a training program for the Sierra Leone
army. "Britain will not abandon the people of Sierra Leone to the mercy
of murderous thugs," Foreign Secretary Cook vowed in October 2000,
seemingly forgetting what had gone before. Had such support been given
to Kabbah back in early 1997 when he really needed it, he might not have
turned to Saxena and Sandline. And he would not have had to sell diamond concessions to get military aid. But the belated support of the international community kept Kabbah in power.

Spicer's hopes for a decisive success for his new military company
were thwarted. The affair left a bitter aftertaste for the soldier-turned-
mercenary. As in the case of Papua New Guinea, he was forced to appear
before several official inquiries to defend his actions. Britain went out of
its way to make him look like a foolish adventurer. "I found the whole proposal quite mind-boggling," Foreign Secretary Cook testified before the
parliamentary inquiry. "Mr. Saxena is an Indian businessman, travelling
on the passport of a dead Serb, awaiting extradition from Canada for
alleged embezzlement from a bank in Thailand. As the person putting up
the funding for operations in Sierra Leone, I would have thought there
were at least some intelligent questions to be asked about his provenance."
Neither Spicer nor the other men involved in the Sandline deal had asked
those questions until it had been too late.

Spicer and Buckingham had had grand plans for Sandline when it had started out. But after two high-profile failures, the company sank into the shadows. Though Sandline still exists as a military company, Spicer is no longer involved. He left to start up his own anti-piracy venture.

Saxena's ambitions for Sierra Leone also went unfulfilled. The same day that the 35 tonnes of weapons that he had paid for arrived in Freetown, Kabbah repudiated the deal with Saxena for diamond concessions. According to Spicer, the president had become seriously annoyed with the financier for not delivering the promised funds. Saxena also had problems with Patel, who cancelled the contract between Jupiter and Global Explorations on the bauxite mine, citing financial non-performance on the part of his Canadian partner. Saxena was left with neither diamonds nor bauxite in the West African country, though he insists that the Sierra Leonean government would give him back the diamond concessions if he asked for them. He claims to have spent about US$30,000 a month to help sustain Kabbah and his people while in exile, plus the $1.5 million used to buy weapons and advice. There are no plans in the works to test his belief. Saxena no longer controls Global Explorations, the dating service–turned–resource company. The last he heard, its new owner was turning it into a high-tech venture. He remains under house arrest in Vancouver, awaiting the verdict of the Canadian minister of justice on whether he will be extradited to Thailand.

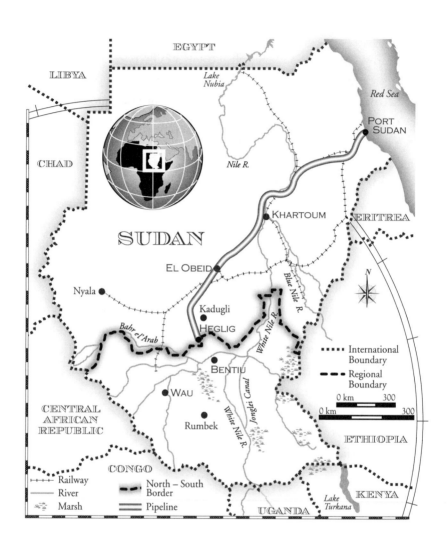

EGYPT

LIBYA

Lake
Nubia

Red Sea

CHAD

PORT
SUDAN

Nile R.

SUDAN

KHARTOUM

ERITREA

EL OBEID

Blue Nile R.

Nyala

Kadugli

N

Bahr el 'Arab

HEGLIG

White Nile R.

International
Boundary

Regional
Boundary

BENTIU

Jonglei Canal

0 km   300

WAU

0 km   300

CENTRAL
AFRICAN
REPUBLIC

Rumbek

White Nile R.

ETHIOPIA

CONGO

⊢⊢⊢ Railway
—— River
     Marsh

North – South
Border
Pipeline

Lake
Turkana

KENYA

UGANDA

CHAPTER NINE

TALISMAN IN SUDAN

JIM BUCKEE PACED THE HALLS OF TALISMAN ENERGY'S HEAD OFFICE IN Calgary, Alberta, muttering about what rebels in far-off Sudan were doing to his company's share price. The May 1999 annual general meeting had just ended, and the astrophysicist–turned–oil company president was visibly upset. For the first time in Talisman's history, he had been peppered with harsh questions when he had stood up to face the shareholders. And he wasn't used to public criticism. Until the company had gone into business in a war zone the previous fall, Buckee had been the darling of the Canadian oil patch. He had shaped Talisman from cast-off operations of British Petroleum and augmented its status from that of a small-time operator, pumping the equivalent of 30,000 barrels of oil a day in 1992, to a major player, on target to pump more than 400,000 barrels a day in 1999. However, since he had purchased a 25-per-cent share in the Greater Nile Petroleum Operating Company, a consortium of Sudanese, Chinese, Malaysian and Canadian companies pumping oil and building a pipeline across Sudan, he had confronted a public uproar. And it didn't make sense to Buckee. People were accusing the Sudanese government of conducting ethnic cleansing, but Talisman had invested in many other countries known for human rights abuses— Algeria, Indonesia and Peru, to name a few—without being similarly attacked. He did not see what was so special about Sudan. That blind spot would prove to be his undoing.

The first sign that May 4, 1999, was going to be a bad day came early that morning on the steps of the Palliser Hotel in Calgary. Talisman shareholders approaching the front doors of the ornate railway hotel were confronted by a line of tall, dark, dignified Africans from southern Sudan wearing placards that featured photos of mutilated and starving people. "This is what Talisman is responsible for," one protestor said to anyone who would listen. He pointed at the picture of a bloody body on his placard, his soft voice contrasting with the brutal violence depicted in the photo. Another protestor held a sign which simply said, "James Buckee is Adolf Hitler in Sudan." Talisman shareholders and employees quickened their pace to get by. Some snorted indignantly. Others averted their eyes.

While waiting for the meeting to begin, I overheard a conversation between two Talisman employees seated behind me which underlined their ready skepticism of the demonstrators and their claims. "There may be atrocities, but we're not responsible for them. Us drilling oil is not the reason," said the first. His colleague grunted in agreement and suggested that the protestors were making it all up, reusing photos from the Biafran war thirty years earlier. "I saw that guy before," he joked about the subject of one horrific picture. "He must have moved from Biafra to Sudan."

Few Canadians at the time were aware of the human catastrophe unfolding in Sudan, despite the efforts of international church groups, anti-slavery bodies and aid organizations to draw attention to the scale of the carnage and to Talisman's role in the conflict. An estimated two million people had lost their lives in the country's civil war, which had been raging off and on for almost five decades, ever since Sudan had gained its independence from Britain in 1956. Sudan is one of the many artificial constructs put together by Europeans in their scramble for Africa, lumping ancient enemies together under one national flag.

The fault line between the Arab world in the north and black Africa to the south runs through Sudan. For centuries, northerners pillaged the south for gold, black slaves, ivory and ostrich feathers, and southerners learned to fear their Arab neighbours. British rule, which began in 1899, deepened the divisions between the two groups. The Arabs, who quickly accepted British occupation, were rewarded with a modern infrastructure, a functioning civil service and education, and were allowed to maintain their Islamic religion and Arabic language. The black southerners, who kept up armed resistance for much longer, were punished and left largely uneducated, their economy undeveloped. Only a handful of Christian missionaries from Britain and the United States provided southerners with some education and health services, spreading English and Christianity among them. This further exacerbated the mutual distrust and misunderstanding between the two areas. When Britain prepared to withdraw from Sudan, it decided to lump the unequal parts together to form a single country.

Fearing domination by the northern Arabs, southern military officers mutinied in 1955. Though they were quickly suppressed, a broader-based uprising involving various southern tribal groups followed in 1956. Over the years, various northern governments attempted to resolve the impasse through negotiation, but none of the proposed deals gave southerners equal representation in the new Khartoum government, the civil service and all other positions of power. Southerners were particularly sensitive to northern attempts to impose the Islamic law of shariah throughout the country. This divine law of Islam dictates rules of personal and public behaviour and punishments that range from hand amputation for thieves, to death by stoning for women convicted of adultery. When the northern government announced a new drive to impose shariah in 1983, southern groups, including the Nuer and the Dinka, united under the banner of the Sudan People's Liberation Army (SPLA). The Sudanese government proposed a new round of peace negations with the south, but these never took place because General Omar Hassan Ahmed al-Bashir and his military officers, backed by the radical National Islamic Front, seized power in 1989. They ushered in a military dictatorship intent on dominating southern Sudan by force.

Not long after, the southern coalition began to fall apart when Riek Machar, the Nuer tribal leader, fell out with John Garang, of the larger Dinka tribe, over leadership of the southern forces. There were suspicions that the Nuer, following the example of some other southern groups, had transferred their loyalty to the northern government in a bid to gain advantage over rivals. This proved to be true when Machar signed a peace agreement with Khartoum in 1996 and assumed a government post.

Though the war was not about oil—oil was discovered only in 1979—it became a strategic asset for all sides in the conflict. As luck would have it, the area with the greatest potential straddled the rough political divide between north and south, putting the oil operations squarely on the front lines. Whichever side controlled the oil had the potential to generate revenues in the long term and to fuel aircraft, tanks and military vehicles in the short term. Parts of the oil fields became a no man's land as both the government and rebels laid land mines around installations to prevent anyone from using them. Southern rebel groups also fought among themselves for oil territory. When large-scale oil production became a possibility in the 1990s, Bashir used the Sudanese army and loyal militias to clear the area of southerners in order to allow oil companies access for exploration and development. Villages were bombed, huts and crops were burned and thousands of people were either killed or forced to flee their homes.

This latest armed attempt at southern subjugation was well under way when Buckee announced in 1998 that Talisman was planning to buy Arakis Energy Corporation, a small Calgary company whose only asset was a 25-per-cent share in the Greater Nile Petroleum Operating Company. Groups who were trying to publicize the human cost of the war in Sudan were appalled that an otherwise reputable Western oil company would go into partnership with a government engaged in what they labelled genocide. Church groups that held shares in Talisman took the opportunity at Talisman's annual meeting to challenge Buckee about his decision. As they posed one tough question after another, it became clear that they felt Talisman had gone beyond what was acceptable for a Canadian company. But they were careful to couch their complaints in terms that might appeal to all shareholders, not just to those concerned about the moral implications. Would this investment, with all its uncertainty and taint, not ultimately have a negative effect on the share price?

Buckee walked back and forth on the raised platform at the front of the rented ballroom, stopping every now and then to peer over his bifocals at those questioning his judgment. Stocky in build, with a shock of brown hair that had a tendency to fall over his forehead, Buckee looked like an aging schoolboy. Outwardly he seemed unperturbed, and his rebuttal touched on themes that would have been familiar to the Europeans who had taken part in the scramble for Africa a century ago. Cecil Rhodes and King Léopold II had claimed they were bringing the three C's—Christianity, commerce and civilization—to unenlightened savages, whose lives would be immeasurably improved by their presence. Buckee dropped the bit about Christianity—Sudan is officially an Islamic state—but talked of wealth leading to the development of all of Sudan, of oil money being used to build roads and hospitals in the south and of Talisman working with other governments to promote peace. While he did not use the actual words "constructive engagement," that was the policy he was outlining: changing the behaviour of a government from within. "We have done quite a lot of homework," he assured the gathering. "Khartoum is a very friendly, peaceful place. The operating area is also a peaceful, friendly place." It wasn't up to him to defend the Sudanese government, he said. It was, after all, a sovereign government. He used the word "tribal" repeatedly when describing the civil strife in Sudan, as if this explained away the brutality. "We're here for business. We do not take sides in the issue." It sounded good to those in the audience whose only source of information about that distant country was Buckee himself.

Before the meeting broke up, one last question was allowed. Peter Jolle, an African, stood up. His forehead scars identified him as a Nuer, from the second largest tribe in southern Sudan, the group that had recently transferred its loyalty to the northern government. The protestors outside were Dinka, opponents of both the government and the Nuer. That distinction was lost on most of the audience. They saw Jolle simply as a southern Sudanese who had come to Calgary to speak the truth. Talisman chairman

Peter Widdrington, grey-haired and suave, asked Jolle if he had the blue card that entitled him to ask a question in the meeting. This turned out to be a bit of prescripted drama. Talisman had paid for Jolle to come to the meeting from his home in Kitchener, Ontario, a fact that the audience did not know. Everyone listened with rapt attention as Jolle spoke out strongly in support of Talisman's involvement. He blamed the church groups for fuelling the war and insisted that Talisman's presence would help the people. "I like that," he said. "I support that." Employees and those shareholders who did not represent the churches lapped it up, applauding loudly. Here, finally, was someone to salve their consciences, someone to tell them they were doing the right thing. But even as this bit of theatre was being played out in a Calgary hotel, rival armies were mobilizing in southern Sudan to fight for control of the oil fields. Reports released later by the United Nations and by a Canadian observer mission would mark May 1999 as a month of particular savagery.

Buckee left the general meeting to face a second set of mostly hostile questions, this time from the media. He was self-assured, even cocky. He had told the shareholders, to great applause, that Talisman was working with the Canadian government on a joint initiative in Sudan. But when pressed for details at the press conference, he was surprisingly vague. "The drift is abolishing child soldiers," he said, adding later, "We wish them [the government] every luck." Questioned about the Sudanese government's bombing of a hospital run by a Norwegian relief agency in the south, Buckee appeared at first to justify the action. "The SPLA puts its camps next to Norwegian hospitals," he said. "This is another example of how there are always many sides of the story." Perhaps realizing he had gone too far, he added that Talisman challenged the government every time incidents like this occurred. "They [the government] are very concerned about the future of Sudan," he said. As for the widely published statement by Hassan al-Turabi, the radical cleric behind the Bashir regime, that the government planned to use oil revenues to buy weapons to wage war, Buckee said he had checked with al-Turabi and was told the statement was a total fabrication, a misquotation. He believed al-Turabi.

"The minister and the prime minister said proceeds will be used for the good of all people," Buckee said. He pointed to Nuer leader Riek Machar's participation in the northern government as proof that not all southern Sudanese were against the oil development. "He will be intimately involved," promised Buckee. Machar was his ace in the hole, a key player Buckee needed to make his investment in Sudan work.

Reporters at the press conference voiced skepticism. To many of them it looked as though Buckee had taken a massive gamble with the share-holders' money. It wasn't a question of whether the oil was there—that had been firmly established two decades earlier by US energy giant Chevron. It was everything *but* the oil. Buckee was investing in Sudan at a time when it remained on the outs with many governments in the Western world, most importantly the United States, not just because of its savage civil war, but also because it had put out a welcome mat for terrorists—the government had given refuge to Osama bin Laden and Carlos the Jackal as part of its open-door policy to those who opposed the West—and had refused to openly take Kuwait's side in the Gulf War. He was putting his faith in a government that had seized power in a military coup and in a warlord who was accused of barbarous acts. How the US government might react was an open question—they had already bombed a pharmaceutical factory in Sudan the previous fall, believing it was producing chemical weapons (mis-takenly, it turned out)—never mind the federal government in Canada, which had warned Talisman not to venture into Sudan.

After facing the shareholders and the media grilling, Buckee's day grew even worse. He received news that the SPLA had announced that Talisman's oil operations were a legitimate target in the civil war. The company's share price, which had jumped that morning after the announcement of positive earnings, promptly dropped. Buckee suspected that a plot had been hatched between the rebels and the human rights advocates who had tried their best to derail his annual general meeting. In his fury, he paced the corridors, subordinates trailing in his wake.

Taken all together, these negatives might have shaken the faith of most oil company presidents in the wisdom of drilling for oil in Sudan.

But not Buckee—at least not in public. He would maintain to the very end that the Sudanese oil operations were an excellent investment. In private, however, it turned out that he did have some concerns, although they appeared to be limited to the narrow impact on the company. "Jim's big worry is that some employee is going to wander off somewhere they shouldn't be and get shot," one of his aides confided that day in Calgary. Perhaps Sudan wasn't such a peaceful, friendly place after all.

When the Habub blows, filling the air with sand from the surrounding desert, it is hard to imagine a more unpleasant place than the Sudanese capital of Khartoum. Even when the full fury of the seasonal wind has abated, sand hangs in the air like a fine mist, coating skin, hair and clothing and creating a false twilight on the streets. Khartoum is a city constantly in danger of being reclaimed by the desert. The sun at midday is a dull silver disc in the sky.

Two months after the Talisman meeting in Calgary, I looked out from the air-conditioned sanctuary of the Khartoum Hilton on a scene seemingly unchanged since biblical times. Farmers worked their fields on the banks of the Nile by hand or with the help of an ox or donkey. The brown of the brick buildings was indistinguishable from the brown of the earth. Women covered from head to foot in flowing garments lent a dash of colour to the otherwise dun-coloured scene, flitting like butterflies between piles of rubble. Donkeys, ridden by giggling young boys or pulling carts, appeared to be the most common mode of transport.

A foreign ministry official assigned to me partly as minder and partly as watcher was anxious I not form the wrong impression of Sudan. To reach his current position he had had to make the long trek from his village in Darfur in the west to find work in the capital. He was proud of what Khartoum had to offer. "Don't think all of Sudan is like this," he said earnestly. "The rest is much poorer."

We took a drive around town so he could show off his city. The few modern buildings merely underlined how completely Khartoum had been bypassed by progress. In the general post-colonial decay, paint was faded and flaked. As the minder pointed out the presidential palace, the bridge the Chinese were building over the Nile and the broadcasting centre, I was making my own observations. A military tank was parked beside the television building. Communications facilities are always prime objectives in civil wars. If you control the airwaves, you are already one step ahead of your adversaries. More tanks sat near the approaches to a bridge across the Nile—another strategic target. Another tank was outside a military hospital. Contrary to the message Buckee had given shareholders, Talisman warned its employees to be on their guard in the capital because it was at least as dangerous as, if not more than, the oil fields in the swampy savannah around Heglig, 725 kilometres to the southwest. The company's eighty expatriate workers were split between the two locations. Company officials believed—wrongly, it turned out—that the high number of Sudanese troops and militia protecting the oil installations would deter attacks in the south. But in Khartoum, foreign employees stood out, making attractive kidnap targets for those southern rebels who dared infiltrate the city.

The shorthand used by the Western media has always made the conflict sound as if there were a clear dividing line between north and south, northerners and southerners. There is not. Some southern tribes have thrown their lot in with the government. Some northern tribes are bitterly opposed to the regime. It is a constantly shifting kaleidoscope of alliances. The faces on the streets of Khartoum are every shade, from the palest of the Arab northerners to the darkest of the black southern tribes. It isn't easy for the members of the regime to identify those who might pose a threat, and so everyone is treated with suspicion. A midnight curfew clears the streets of all but the most essential traffic. This is to stop people without travel permits from slipping into the city, explained the government-supplied driver. To move outside your area, a permit is required. There are checkpoints at major intersections, and at night men in camouflage emerge from the roadside darkness to ask for identity papers. Once they have established that the vehicle's occupants are entitled to be on the road, the soldiers wave the car through. "*Salaam aleikoum*"

("Peace be with you"), they say before giving the driver the nod and disappearing back into the blackness that is nighttime Khartoum.

When our tour was done for the day, the minder dropped me off at the hotel. Free from obvious surveillance, I hailed a rickety taxi and set out to meet Riek Machar, the southern warlord in whose hands the fate of the oil development supposedly lay. Machar had been installed by the Khartoum regime in a crumbling villa around the corner from the main government buildings. In exchange for throwing his lot in with the junta, he was given the title of president of the Co-ordinating Council of the Southern States and assistant to the president of the Republic—and the promise that his people would get a share of the oil wealth. Now he was trying to get the government to make good on the peace agreement he had signed with them and start building schools, hospitals and roads.

Visitors to the villa had to first pass through a large forecourt, where Nuer youths loitered, and then through a smaller antechamber, where people waited their turn for an audience. The routine was that you would file in, state your case and wait for Machar to render judgment. The atmosphere was that of an impoverished medieval court, with Machar as king.

When it was my turn, the curtain over the doorway was pushed back and I entered a once grand reception room. Overstuffed furniture bearing embroidered antimacassars lined the walls. A small air conditioner wheezed in the corner. Machar sat at one end of the room, fiddling with the laptop and cellular phone in front of him while listening to the conversation that was wrapping up as I arrived. Here was a thoroughly modern warlord.

I'd heard all the stories about Machar, how he was a descendent of a famous Nuer warrior-prophet and the only one of his father's thirty-one children to gain the most elusive of prizes for a poor Nuer youth: a university education in Britain. He had a master's degree from Strathclyde University in Glasgow and a doctorate from Bradford Polytechnic in Yorkshire. Instead of staying in England and joining the southern Sudanese diaspora, Machar returned to his homeland to lead his Nuer fighters in the civil war. It was his marriage to English aid worker Emma McCune in 1991 that turned the international spotlight on him and prompted intense media coverage in the form of television documentaries, newspaper features and literary treatments. Not all were positive. His fighters were accused of taking part in acts of barbarity, such as the 1991 Nuer attack on the Dinka village of Bor, which became known as the Bor Massacre. Two thousand people were thought to have died in that attack. Humanitarian groups who went to investigate the atrocity brought back horrific stories of disembowelled women, children tied together and shot through the head and bodies hanging from trees. Westerners looking for good guys with whom to identify in the Sudanese civil war are always left confused. There are none. Each group has proven itself capable of unspeakable acts, the savagery and brutishness of which make the observer recoil in horror.

It was with trepidation mixed with curiosity that I took a seat on Machar's sofa and accepted the cool drink he offered. He was dressed in a drab green outfit that gave him a vaguely military air. Fleshy but not fat, he was tall like most of the Nuer people. His seven-foot frame made him an imposing figure, even sitting down. He greeted me warmly and his voice was surprisingly mellifluous. In another country, in another life, he might have made a successful career in broadcasting. In Sudan, he was a warlord.

We talked of the oil fields and whether they were vulnerable to attack. Some of the most promising territory for oil lay in traditional Nuer territory, and Machar's militia, which he had named the South Sudan Defence Force (SSDF), had been given the responsibility of protecting it by the government. He saw his arrangement with Khartoum as a temporary step on the way to a lasting peace. "You cannot guard oil fields," he said. "Guarding the oil fields so that the business of finding and extracting oil could go on in the midst of war had been tried before. It failed."

He was referring to Chevron's attempts to develop the Sudanese oil. In 1984, five members of a Chevron seismic crew were specifically targeted and killed. Machar admitted that his people had laid mines around oil installations on his instructions, but he said they had done so before his supposed alliance with President Omar al-Bashir. The only lasting protection for the oil fields, said Machar, was peace. That was what he had been trying to engineer when he made his deal with the government. But the deal would only hold as long as he felt the terms were being honoured by Khartoum. And just before our meeting in the summer of 1999, he received news that government forces had entered his territory and were pushing his fighters out and away from the oil development.

"We have a problem of confidence," he said in a heavy voice. "It has been discovered recently when the South Sudan Defence Force and the Sudan army clashed south of Bentiu [a town at the centre of the oil fields]. The ssdf has been guarding the oil fields during the exploration, the drilling and all this. Now that production has started, the Sudan army decided to march to the oil field." Machar predicted there would be trouble if the government did not stop and recall the army from his lands. "You do not know what may be brewing," was his ominous prediction. "Guerrilla movements are not easily fought. They always get to the target. If Heglig [the southern centre of the oil operations] was vulnerable to us in the eighties and early nineties, why wouldn't it be vulnerable still? Whatever number of troops that you bring there, you cannot protect the oil fields. It is peace that can protect it." Our interview ended on that negative note. I left the villa thinking that Machar, like the Sudanese conflict, contained many contradictions: a southerner in the northern government, a warlord who talked peace, an educated man using modern technology reduced to primitive acts.

The day after the meeting with Machar, the foreign ministry minder picked me up with the promise of a special treat: we were to attend a graduating ceremony for officer cadets at the Omdurman soccer stadium. It was the tenth anniversary of the day the regime had seized power, and they were celebrating with a show of military might.

When we arrived, the stadium was packed. Out on the field, the cadets stood in neat rows under a blazing sun. Behind them, placards were arranged and rearranged by the crowd to spell out sayings from the Koran. On the shaded side of the stadium, dignitaries sat in upholstered chairs, chatting among themselves and offering each other the choicest dates from the silver dishes in front of them. A military brass band dressed in dusty red serge jackets lent an incongruous note to the proceedings. They played *Auld Lang Syne* on battered brass instruments while the placards behind them instructed true believers to desire peace but prepare for war. Far below, someone shouted incessantly into a microphone. Adding to the general din were the wives and mothers of the newly minted officers, grouped together at the far end of the stadium. In the heat-thickened air, their ululations rose and fell like the sound of cicadas on a hot summer day.

The temperature soared above 40 degrees Celsius, and the sun baked down on the graduating class for hours. Yet for those among them who were destined to protect their government's most valued assets—the oil fields and the pipeline—more trying conditions were to come. Many of them were students or university graduates. The regime had weighed the importance of an educated populace and oil and had come down on the side of oil. It was willing to sacrifice its intellectuals if that meant oil revenues would be protected. The Sudanese minister of defence explained in a television interview in 1997 how students were encouraged to join: "We made clear to the parents that any student who does not report for military service or military training will miss chances of going to university, going abroad or doing business in the country." Poorly trained and unprepared for the harsh life of a bush soldier, many would not live long enough to hold the government to its side of the bargain.

How did a reputable Canadian company like Talisman come to invest in a country plagued by war? To trace the roots of the acquisition, I went to see Lutfur Khan, the man responsible for the first Canadian involvement in Sudan's oil patch. Khan, a Pakistani Canadian, was the owner of State Petroleum, which merged with Arakis and was subsequently subsumed by Talisman.

There are three clocks on the wall of Khan's office in Vancouver. They display the time in Vancouver, Khartoum and Conakry—cities where Khan has interests in oil, gas and diamonds. Khan offered a fleshy handshake and led me on a tour of his photo gallery of family and friends. In one picture he was standing beside Sudanese president al-Bashir. Another had him with the cleric al-Turabi. He also had a picture of himself with former US vice president Al Gore, but he didn't explain the photo. The pictures caught him in chameleon-like changes of clothing as he blended with his surroundings. In some, he wore the flowing robes of northern Africa. In others, he was in Western business dress. On the day of the interview, he wore a beige golf shirt with matching slacks and tinted prescription glasses. He did not look like an oil man. Then again, some Calgarians would tell you there is no such thing as an oil man in Vancouver.

Khan dished out details of his background sparingly. He said the Khans are an old military family in Pakistan. He referred to the friends who introduced him to the Sudanese project, but despite gentle probing he never identified them by name. He simply said that he was told about the investment opportunity by friends of his father and decided to talk to the Sudanese representative in Washington. After a visit to the oil fields, which was arranged by the Sudanese government, he felt he could do business in Sudan. "My name cannot be taken out of the history of Sudan," he said proudly.

It was both a boast and a statement of fact: Khan was crucial in restarting the country's oil development and pipeline project after a long hiatus. Al-Turabi has said much the same thing. The Sudanese had been trying to get their oil on stream as far back as 1959, when the Italian oil company Agip was granted a concession near the Red Sea coast. Agip carried out seismic surveys and drilled some wells but was unsuccessful, as were most of the other Western oil companies that came to Sudan in its wake. Not until 1979 and after six years of exploration did Chevron Overseas Petroleum Inc. finally discover oil near Muglad, south of the Nuba Mountains. More Chevron discoveries followed in 1980 near Bentiu.

Sudan was the company's first major foray abroad and it was looking very promising. Chevron hired an American engineering firm to study the feasibility of a pipeline. A route was sketched from the southern oil fields near Bentiu to Port Sudan on the Red Sea, where an oil refinery capable of producing 20,000 barrels per day had been built by Royal Dutch/Shell and BP. Then-president Gaafar Mohamad Numeiry had laid the corner-stone of another refinery nearby, this one capable of producing 200,000 barrels per day. It was a joint venture between the Sudanese government, a French petroleum company and Triad Naft, a private company owned by Saudi Arabian arms dealer Adnan Khashoggi. Sudan was on the road to becoming an oil power.

But it all fell apart in 1983 when the south rebelled against the government's implementation of *shariah*. Caught in the crossfire, Chevron finally decided to abandon Sudan in 1991 in favour of more promising ventures in Kazakhstan. It had spent an estimated US$1 billion on the project and hadn't yet produced oil in marketable quantities. It sold its concessions to the Sudanese company Concorp for somewhere between US$23 million and $26 million—the final figure was never disclosed.

There has always been a question mark over why Chevron, having spent so much on the oil development, was willing to sell it so cheap. John McLeod, a Calgary-based petroleum engineer who ran the oil operation for Arakis from the beginning until 1997, speculates that Chevron management grew tired of the problematic project and was anxious to get rid of it. He and others also believe that Chevron's decision was made easier by an accelerated tax write-off from the US government worth about $550 million. Chevron would neither confirm nor deny that figure.

Within months of buying the concessions, Concorp flipped them back to the Sudanese government, which in turn went looking for foreign buyers. It was at this point that Khan and his Vancouver-based company, State Petroleum Corporation, came onto the scene. The company, which had some oil and gas wells in the United States, was small time by Chevron standards. But from the Sudanese government's point of view, Khan was exactly what they needed. He was an oilman, he was based in Canada—not the United States—and, most importantly, he was a Muslim. It was important to al-Turabi that Sudan's oil be brought to life by a true believer, and Khan fit the bill. Those who worked with him said he was a member of the Muslim Brotherhood, the same sect as al-Turabi, although Khan has denied he was a member. The aim of the movement, which began in Egypt in 1928 and has branches in more than seventy countries, is to establish Islamic states with a form of unity among them. According to Khan, he and al-Turabi got on famously: "The media has been projecting [al-Turabi] as a terrorist leader or something. I don't feel any terrorism in this man. He has a Ph.D. Very laid back."

Negotiations between Khan and the government stretched over several years, and by 1993 State Petroleum had acquired two of the five concessions that Chevron had given up. Khan already had the oil expertise he needed in the form of John McLeod, who had international operational experience. (McLeod now works for Heritage Oil, one of the companies that Tony Buckingham is associated with.) What Khan lacked was a source of money. Enter Terry Alexander, a silver-tongued Vancouver stock promoter who had a company called Arakis Energy with a listing on the Vancouver Stock Exchange and some gas wells in Kentucky. Khan found Alexander "very, very energetic, a go-getter type of guy." He says, "We negotiated a deal where we swapped our shares with Arakis shares—100 per cent of our ownership for a couple of million shares of Arakis." Arakis acquired State for shares with a deemed value of us$13 million.

Khan and Alexander seemed to be the ideal team. Khan was the fixer, the man who was trusted by the Sudanese government, and Alexander was the charismatic salesman who could interest investors in a remote oil project in a country riven by conflict. But even before the deal closed, the two men had a falling out. Their partnership would be troubled for the next four years, plagued by money and management problems. To begin with, they had to deal with security issues in Sudan. The Sudanese army set up a post at Heglig, with between three hundred and four hundred soldiers to guard the oil company's facilities. And every time a new well was drilled, a smaller post with six to ten soldiers was established nearby. "They had a tough life, those boys," says Ross Bailey, a Calgary security consultant who worked on contract for Arakis in the mid-1990s. "They [the army] provided them with a bag of milk or a bag of rice, and they fended for themselves for the rest of what they ate. If they wanted any kind of meat, they had to go get it." Despite the obvious military presence, the oil workers were nervous about working in a conflict zone. Bailey says there was a near-riot one day in 1995 when CNN, which was received at the camp by satellite signal, said the United States was thinking of closing its embassy in Khartoum. The workers, most of whom were from Alberta, demanded to be flown out immediately. It took a lot of coaxing from Bailey to calm them down. The United States did withdraw some of its diplomats in early 1996.

For security purposes, Arakis also established contact with the SPLA. Bailey hired two former RCMP staff sergeants, one of whom talked frequently with rebel leader Garang. Simon Kwage, a spokesman for Garang, says that a representative of Arakis approached the rebels during this period and told them the company would pay ransom if any of the oil workers were taken hostage, "and we told him, 'No, we are not sure we are going to take them alive for ransom. We are not going to take any hostages.'" In the end it was a moot point: the oil facilities were not attacked while Arakis was in charge.

Although security seemed to be under control, Arakis had other problems. Under Khan and Alexander's stewardship, the company was never able to raise the necessary funding for oil field development and pipeline construction. The best they could do was to get 10,000 barrels a day out of the ground and deliver it by rail and truck to the refinery at El Obeid. This was not what the Sudanese government had had in mind. In an effort to raise more funds, Alexander indulged in some unscrupulous financing involving offshore companies. Sharp movements in the share price in 1995 attracted the attention of securities regulators in British Columbia, who began an investigation that culminated in 1999 with a sizable fine for Alexander as well as a twenty-year prohibition on his acting as a director, officer or promoter of any BC company.

Mike Freeny of Chemex Inc., the US company that had brokered the sale of the Chevron concessions to Concorp, figures that although Arakis had a handful of dedicated oilmen in the field, management was more interested in using the concession for a stock promotion. "It's a shame, you know," says Freeny. "Arakis lost a tremendous opportunity, in my opinion, to become a substantial oil company. But their mentality was just to promote the stock and run." It's a familiar story, says Calgary oil analyst Ian Doig. He estimates that there were about 150 Canadian oil companies working abroad in 1999 and that about 50 per cent were there solely for the stock market play. While McLeod was a "good, honest oilman," according to Doig, other Arakis executives and board members were not what you would call at home in the oil patch. "About half those boys wouldn't know the difference between an oil rig and a grain elevator."

In an interview in early 1999, Alexander insisted Sudan had not been just another stock promotion. He put his mistakes down to ignorance and to enthusiasm for the project. Perhaps the fact that he was winding up his affairs in the wake of the BC Security Commission investigation at the time I spoke to him put him in a philosophical frame of mind. "I think about it almost daily still," he said. "It was a real passionate event in my life. Good, bad or indifferent, it changed me. As the desert changed people, the desert changed me too." Heglig, where Arakis based its operations, is a swamp for half the year and savannah the rest.

In 1996, realizing that Arakis could not live up to its commitments, the Sudanese government forced the company to relinquish 75 per cent of the project to the Chinese, Malaysian and Sudanese state oil companies, which split it 40–30–5, leaving Arakis with 25 per cent. Together, the four partners formed the Greater Nile Petroleum Operating Company Ltd. The Chinese National Petroleum Corporation held the presidency. Sudapet Ltd., the Sudanese state company, held the office of vice president. The general manager for upstream operations was from the Malaysian state company, Petronas Carigali Overseas SDN BHD, and the general manager for administration and services was from CNPC. Arakis supplied the general manager for the pipeline.

But the formation of the consortium did not solve Arakis's money problems. Alexander left in 1996 because of poor relations with Khan and the ongoing securities investigation. That left Khan and McLeod in charge, and their search for funds became intense. McLeod said that the way the consortium agreements were written, if a member did not come up with its share of the money, it was not ratioed down, which is typical of such agreements—it was out. That focused their minds: they would lose it all if they could not find investors. Because the United States had added Sudan to its list of terrorist states, Arakis could not get any of the us majors to buy into the project. And although European companies weren't bothered by us sanctions, they wanted control if they were to be involved. McLeod and Khan began to look to Canada for investors.

When they first approached Talisman, they were rejected. Buckee later told a reporter he thought the investment had a nasty odour. He was not referring to the activities of the Sudanese regime or even to the location of the project in the midst of a war zone, but to the stock market games played by the men who ran Arakis Energy. But Khan and McLeod took a Talisman team over to Sudan so they could see the project for themselves. Buckee recognized its enormous potential and changed his mind. In October 1998, Talisman purchased the company in a deal valued at CDN$277 million. Talisman came on board during the crucial last year of the pipeline construction and the completion of the oil centre at Heglig.

"I'm glad I'm out of it," Khan said as we wrapped up the interview. "It was an uphill battle from 1991 to 1998. I spent more time in Sudan than I spent with my family." He allowed a certain wistfulness in not seeing the project through to its completion. "I wish my company could have pulled it off."

I got the chance to see Heglig for myself in June 1999. The Sudanese government, with Talisman's approval, arranged for me to accompany a visiting delegation of Chinese officials and Iraqi politicians who were attending a commemoration ceremony of the oil installation. It was 4:30 a.m. when our weary group trooped out of the vip lounge at Khartoum airport to board a number of small planes. A Chinese employee of Greater Nile Petroleum was in charge of logistics. He ticked off my name on his passenger list and asked, "Are you coming to *our* oil field?"— reminding me that while Talisman was an important partner in the oil development, it was not in control.

Our Twin Otter plane, chartered from Canada's North Cariboo Air, took several hours to reach Heglig, passing over miles of featureless desert and then savannah before the swamp came into view. It was the rainy season, and from the air the oil camp was a small speck of twentieth-century technology in a vast flooded landscape. Lines cleared for seismic surveys stretched to the horizon. As the plane circled lower, details of the oil camp came into sharper focus. Portable cabins raised on concrete blocks were islands in a sea of red mud, connected by raised walkways. Beyond the mud, pools of water were held back by dykes.

As our small plane bumped to a halt on the gravel airstrip, a welcoming party of Chinese workers came into view. Along one side of the runway, several dozen workers wearing dress white coveralls and caps were holding aloft red and white banners. "Warmly Welcome Our Friends From All Over The World," read one. A second, much larger banner's message was written in English and Chinese: "Warmly welcome Chinese Government Special Envoy Zhou Yongkong and Members of Delegation to visit Sudan." The airstrip had been built by the oil companies but was owned by the Sudanese government, which used it as a base from which to launch bombing raids on the southern Sudanese. An ancient Russian military helicopter sat at the end of the runway. Beside it was a Toyota pickup with a machine gun mounted on the truck bed. A Lebanese journalist made the mistake of snapping a quick picture of the helicopter with his still camera. The camera was instantly confiscated and the film exposed. Around the perimeter of the airstrip, indeed around the entire installation, soldiers carrying AK-47s stood guard. We were clearly visiting an armed camp.

Although Heglig had been established by the Canadians, most of the workers currently at the site were Chinese. Most of the Canadians had departed for other installations in the south and in Khartoum, but there were still reminders of their presence. The shoulder patches of a group of unarmed guards sported the Canadian national symbol: a maple leaf. In the kitchen, a grizzled canteen cook from Canada showed off his newly made butter tarts and peanut butter cookies. The camp drivers betrayed their Canadian road safety training by dutifully buckling their seatbelts and using turn signals at the rough dirt intersections despite the absence of any other vehicles in the near vicinity.

China had supplied tens of thousands of workers to build the 1,610-kilometre pipeline from Heglig to Port Sudan on the Red Sea. It was one of many projects that the Chinese National Petroleum Corporation was involved in around the world as it searched for sources to satisfy China's surging appetite for oil. The Khartoum government had hoped to celebrate the first oil exports on June 30, the tenth anniversary of when they had seized power. They pushed the consortium members hard to meet that political deadline. But this proved to be disruptive and impossible. Time was lost as the contractors tried to figure out how they could speed up the work to have oil gushing out of the pipe at Port Sudan at the appointed time. Although the consortium did not meet the government's political deadline, the pipeline was completed in record time, and the spigots were turned on at the beginning of June 1999. It would take another three months and three and a half million barrels of oil to fill the pipeline's enormous length. Exports would not be physically possible until the end of August 1999. The Sudanese regime had to content itself with oil-related celebrations at a private refinery owned by the Sudanese company Concorp near Khartoum and with the commemoration ceremony at Heglig.

A television crew from China filmed the occasion as the official party stood and watched oil slosh into an open pit from a pipe decorated with a large red bow. Sudanese Energy Minister Awad Al-Jaz was moved to predict a great future for the oil development and the other oil projects to the southeast run by Total (of France), IPC (of Canada), Gulf (of Qatar) and the Chinese. "Hopefully, in a very short time Sudan will be one of the biggest producers in the world," he said. Given that Sudan's proven oil reserves as of January 2001 were only 262 million barrels, compared to Saudi Arabia's 264.2 billion or Iraq's 112 billion, this was an unrealistic boast. After the ceremony, I asked him about the security of the oil installations and of the giant pipeline that stretched diagonally across much of

Sudan. Al-Jaz was in no mood to entertain negative thoughts. He displayed the type of wilful blindness common to authoritarian regimes everywhere. "You are here with us in the field," he said haughtily. "We move around without having guns and without any kind of insecurity." Less than ten metres away a young soldier casually shifted his AK-47 off his shoulder.

Where he stood at Heglig, the energy minister was at the centre of concentric circles of security designed to protect the oil development. The armed soldier nearby formed part of the first circle. Then there were the soldiers around the installation. They were supplemented here and there by the men who wore civilian clothes but bore arms. Outside the camp gates was a military helicopter. Further out in the oil fields were army units, various militias and members of the Popular Defence Forces. Security, in all its forms, was the Sudanese government's contribution to the oil development. Talisman provided expertise, China provided manpower, and Sudan provided an army and loyal militias who not only protected the pipeline and facilities, but also aggressively cleansed the oil fields of people.

Talisman's involvement with the Sudanese regime did not escape the notice of the Canadian federal government or, more particularly, of Lloyd Axworthy, whose tenure as Canada's foreign minister had been marked by his efforts to establish the middle power country as a leader in humane foreign policy. I met with Axworthy in November 2001, after he had left politics to head the Liu Institute for Global Issues at the University of British Columbia, a job that allowed him to delve further into and be a leading proponent of the priorities he had set out as a politician. Freed from the constraints of cabinet solidarity, he spoke frankly about the government's response to Talisman and his failed attempt to call the company to account.

Axworthy's department had warned Talisman ahead of time not to invest in Sudan. One of the reasons for this was that officials knew that if the company was attacked in the conflict, it would call on Ottawa for help. "I was getting tired of reading in the newspapers that some executive was kidnapped in the jungle, knowing full well that they had been forewarned not to do it, where they were dumping arsenic in the river, and of course the natives are going to do something about it," said Axworthy. "And then you'd get some heartbreaking stories from their wives, please rescue them. Pull them out. My view was, hey, this is costing us a lot of money and time and effort for your lack of responsibility. I tried to establish that responsibility begets obligation." When Buckee, whom Axworthy describes as a "free-booting, old-line capitalist" went ahead anyway, the minister was amazed that the company could be so stupid—and so flagrant. After recovering from his initial shock, Axworthy tried to get Talisman to make the best of the situation by setting up a process to monitor human rights and to make other moves at transparency—constructive engagement, in other words. But the behind-the-scenes negotiations went nowhere. An angry Axworthy cast about for ways of shaming the company into re-examining how it was doing business in Sudan.

Talisman was weighing heavily on the foreign minister's mind in September 1999 as he prepared to make a scheduled speech at the UN during a special two-day session of the Security Council session on Africa. Though the official text of his speech made no mention of Sudan, minutes before he was set to speak one of his officials scribbled in the margin that Axworthy should say that Canada was worried about child soldiers in Sierra Leone and slavery in Sudan. The minister went one better, saying that the Security Council should intervene to help "the victims of genocide in Rwanda, widespread starvation in Somalia, pervasive terror in Sierra Leone, slave-trading in Sudan and senseless war between Ethiopia and Eritrea." Axworthy had barely sat down before Sudanese foreign minister Mustafa Osman Ismail angrily demanded a meeting.

The normally pleasant minister (Sudanese media have nicknamed him "Mr. Smile") launched into a heated exchange with Axworthy. Ismail speaks perfect English and his usually moderate statements made him the acceptable face of the regime in Khartoum. But he was anything but moderate with Axworthy. "How can you say that about Sudan?" he demanded. "You've never even been there." When it was his turn to speak at the UN meeting the next day, Ismail issued a public challenge to Axworthy: name one person who has been enslaved and the identity of his purchaser. Send a fact-finding mission to ascertain the "falsity" of the accusation, which he called "the worst insult that could be hurled at a country."

"It was an opening I couldn't resist," said Axworthy. Within a week, his officials had tracked down Ottawa consultant John Harker, who had previously offered to investigate humanitarian conditions in Sudan. Harker agreed to assemble a fact-finding team to fulfill a double mandate: he would investigate the allegations of slavery, and he would also look into the possible connection between oil development and human rights abuses. There was anger and determination in Axworthy's voice when he announced Harker's mission to the Canadian media in October 1999. "Canadians want assurances that the operations of Canadian enterprises are not worsening the conflict or the human rights situation for the Sudanese people," he told reporters. "If it becomes evident that oil extraction is exacerbating the conflict in Sudan, or resulting in violations of human rights or humanitarian law, the Government of Canada may consider, if required, economic and trade restrictions such as are authorized by the Export and Import Permits Act, the Special Economic Measures Act, or other instruments." He added that Senator Lois Wilson, a former moderator of the United Church, would act as Canada's representative in the flagging peace talks aimed at ending the civil war and report to him on their progress.

The very mention of possible sanctions caused Talisman shares to drop $2.55 to $40.95. Still, Buckee professed to be "delighted" with the government announcement and offered to give Harker and his team any support he could. That same day, the company issued a press release with the headline "Talisman applauds Canadian government initiative on Sudan." The company contacted Harker and offered him the use of its aircraft and facilities. This was not all window dressing. Talisman management genuinely believed it would be vindicated by an objective report—it felt that what the public was demanding of the company went far beyond its role and was more in keeping with what was expected of government.

Shortly before Harker and his team left for Sudan, a report on human rights abuses in the country was released by Leonardo Franco of Argentina, a special rapporteur for the UN. It made for horrific reading. In detailing a number of instances in which Sudanese people had been tortured and killed by the authorities, the report told of one group of bank robbers who had been sentenced to cross-amputation (amputation of the right hand and the left foot), followed by death by hanging, then crucifixion, all apparently in accordance with Sudan's penal code. Franco also included an account of a ten-day offensive launched in May 1999 to create a 100-kilometre swath of empty land around the oil fields just east of Heglig. Troops had swept through the area, attacking and killing civilians with Antonov bombers, helicopter gunships, tanks and artillery. An estimated six thousand homes were burned. While it had often been impossible in the past to positively identify the aggressors in Sudanese hostilities because of the bewildering array of militias and army factions, in this instance there was no such confusion. Only one side in the Sudanese civil war had access to air power: the government.

Franco was even-handed in his condemnation of abuse, pointing out that the government was not the only faction targeting civilians. He told of a group of rebels, thought to belong to the SPLA, who had attacked a team from the International Committee of the Red Cross in February 1999. The rebels had kidnapped six members of the team, eventually releasing two expatriates but killing four Sudanese nationals. The SPLA refused to take responsibility for the attack, claiming that the humanitarian team had been caught in the crossfire, and it wouldn't return the bodies.

Franco estimated that about 2 million people had been killed in the previous sixteen years of the civil war, and that an estimated 4.5 million people—or one out of every five of the country's 30 million inhabitants— had been internally displaced. He said that the increase in human rights abuses and military action in the oil fields was a direct result of militias' fighting over who would provide security for sections of the pipeline. His conclusion was unequivocal: "The economic, political and strategic implications of the oil issue have seriously compounded and exacerbated the conflict and led to a deterioration of the overall situation of human rights and the respect for humanitarian law, as well as further diminished the already slim chance for peace."

Harker read everything about Sudan that he could get his hands on before leaving Canada, including Franco's report. But in an interview later, he said he had kept an open mind. Much of what he read "was romanticized retelling of things that suited the purposes of the teller." However, he also felt "there's no smoke without fire." Whether any of it was Jim Buckee's fault also remained to be seen. Harker decided to visit the sites mentioned in Franco's report with his team of investigators.

On February 14, 2000, Harker released his findings to the public. In the end, he and his team had been able to confirm enough of Franco's information to reach several firm conclusions. First, they had found that slavery—or "abduction," as the Sudanese government preferred to call it—was indeed a persistent problem in Sudan. It was organized and was accompanied by violence, and the burden of responsibility for bringing the practice to an end rested on the government. Harker's team also determined that though the civil war was not fundamentally about oil, the resource had become a key factor in the conflict and was actually exacerbating it.

Talisman was clearly adding to the suffering of the Sudanese people. The report made mention of two particularly troubling events that had occurred at the Heglig oil installation. One was that government helicopters had used the installation's airstrip to launch offensives against southerners. The other was that eight Nuer who had gone to Heglig in search of work had been killed. Talisman could not say that these events had occurred outside the company's narrowly drawn sphere of influence. In writing his report, Harker borrowed a phrase from an earlier UN special rapporteur, Gáspár Biró, to explain why Talisman and other oil companies seemed blind to the reality of Sudan: "If the oil companies don't know what's going on, they're not looking over the fences of their compounds." It was an image that would resonate long after the mission itself became old news.

Though Axworthy had not asked Harker and his team to make recommendations, the report included several. The most crucial of them in
terms of what would happen next was that Canada should not impose
sanctions on Talisman. Senator Wilson made a similar recommendation
in her report, explaining that Canada would be excommunicated from the
Sudanese peace process if it initiated a sanctions program. Axworthy's
options were considerably narrowed.

While Harker and his team were busy in Sudan, Talisman chose to kick
its public relations campaign into high gear. Various groups involved in
the anti-Talisman campaign had been working hard. Some were trying to
shame the company into withdrawing from Sudan. Others were applying
pressure in Washington and Ottawa. Still others were trying to persuade
large investors to sell their Talisman stock. By late 1999, those pushing for
divestment began registering successes in the United States. The Texas
Teachers Retirement Fund sold its 100,000 Talisman shares in October,
and TIAA-CREF, the largest US pension fund for teachers, sold its 302,815
shares in December. In January 2000, the State of New Jersey Finance
Board divested its 780,000 shares, and CalPERS, the US$170-billion
California public employees' retirement system, followed suit. Though the
reasons they all gave for selling the stock were based on the performance
of the shares and not the company's ethics, this was mere semantics. The
shares were performing badly because of the negative publicity surrounding Talisman's Sudanese oil development.

Talisman decided to sign up public relations giant Hill & Knowlton
to help lobby the government and craft a communications strategy. In the
run-up to the Gulf War ten years earlier, Hill & Knowlton had been paid
$10 million to present Kuwait's case to the United States. The firm sent
seven women to testify before a congressional hearing in Washington
about atrocities committed by Iraqi troops, including the taking of dozens
of Kuwaiti babies out of incubators and leaving them to die. It was later
discovered that five of the seven witnesses had used false names and that
one was the daughter of the Kuwaiti ambassador in Washington. Hill &

Knowlton had also worked for the now defunct BCCI (Bank of Credit and Commerce International) after the bank was indicted in 1988 for laundering drug money. The PR firm had put together a campaign to demonstrate that the BCCI was not a criminal bank. But after the bank finally collapsed in July 1991, investigations found that it had been involved in criminal behaviour on a grand scale.

None of this dissuaded Talisman from employing the services of Hill & Knowlton. Buckee, in his inimitable fashion, told the media that Sudanese issues were taking up more time than they should and were distressing many Talisman employees. "We need to get somebody to start writing letters and things like that because we have better things to do," he said. Little wonder that one of the first bits of advice Hill & Knowlton gave him was to "put a sock in it." His blunt comments were not helping the company with its growing image problem. Under the PR firm's wing, Talisman started targeting government ministers thought to be more friendly toward its case than Axworthy. International Trade Minister Pierre Pettigrew was approached, as was Natural Resources Minister Ralph Goodale, a westerner who was more sympathetic to the concerns of the oil patch. Goodale later opened an investors' conference call that promoted Talisman, sparking outrage from the groups protesting the company's involvement in Sudan.

Talisman stressed the company's importance to the Canadian economy—it was the country's largest independent oil producer—and said the downward pressure on its share price was leaving it vulnerable to foreign takeovers. If sanctions were imposed, the result could well be the loss of yet another Canadian head office. "Be careful of what you are doing to your Canadian companies," was the message. "We [Talisman] have a major force here in the Calgary environment. And we have a lot of employees. We are offering tremendous opportunities for Canadians to work in a major head office. And if policy doesn't support the activities of what is becoming a really globalized energy business, then before you know it, you won't have one." The threat sent a chill through the federal cabinet, which was sensitive to the issue in the wake of a large number of foreign takeovers of Canadian companies. Talisman's lobbying ensured that Axworthy would not get the support he needed from his fellow ministers to take firm action against the company.

On February 14, 2000, the foreign minister faced the media again. Gone was the fire and determination he had displayed the previous October. He looked distinctly uncomfortable, sheepish even, as he raced through a statement that, boiled down to its essence, said the Canadian government would do exactly nothing. He would not be recommending sanctions against the company.

"The mistake I made, I got ahead of myself, was when I set up the Harker Commission and I said, 'Look, we'll do something about it.' And then I got the rug pulled out from under me because I didn't have the legislative authority I thought I did," said Axworthy. Government lawyers had told him he would be acting illegally if he tried to impose sanctions. "And I'm not sure I could have done it politically, because I got a lot of pressure around town."

For opponents of Talisman's involvement in Sudan, there was worse news to come: Axworthy had decided to open up a Canadian government office in Khartoum. It would enable Canada to observe the situation and respond as need be, he said. Any further action would be taken through the United Nations and the IMF. Axworthy held out hope that Canada would be able to raise the issue at the UN Security Council, where it then held one of the rotating, non-permanent seats. As he hurriedly left the press theatre and made for the door, one last question was put to him: Do you believe that oil is exacerbating the conflict as Mr. Harker says? "Yes," he replied. Upstairs in his office, Axworthy canvassed his advisers. "How did I do?" One staffer summed up the general feeling in the room: "It could have been worse."

Not much worse as far as the various special interest groups who had been campaigning against Talisman's involvement were concerned. "Lloyd Axworthy was the last hope," Stephen Lewis, a former Canadian ambassador to the United Nations who later became deputy executive director of the UN Children's Fund before being appointed UN special envoy for HIV/AIDS in Africa in June 2001, told a CBC interviewer. "When he commissioned the Harker report he made it absolutely clear that if Harker demonstrated that the oil was fuelling the war, and I think that was the phrase that was used, then obviously Canada would do something. And when Axworthy backed off and gave that lame excuse, that he would try to work with the government of Sudan, I think the NGO community, the activist community, the human rights community in Canada, felt terribly depressed, disbelieving that Axworthy could betray them in that way."

Far from punishing Talisman or the Sudanese government, Axworthy had actually given both a gift. Every government has its soft spots. For the regime in Sudan it was international acceptance. Declared a pariah state by the United States, which had removed its ambassador in February 1996, Sudan craved official contact with the rest of the world. Great Britain had restored diplomatic ties in November 1999. Egypt had followed suit that December. Now here was Canada, one of the regime's harshest critics, deciding to open its first embassy office in Khartoum. For the Sudanese regime, this development overshadowed the negative news contained in the Harker report.

Particularly disheartened were four humanitarian groups that had been working with Talisman to try to get the company to play a positive role in the Sudanese conflict. Unlike other humanitarian groups, which immediately chose to lobby shareholders to sell their Talisman stock, representatives from World Vision, Project Ploughshares, the United Church and the Steelworkers Humanity Fund wanted to try constructive engagement. They spent a great deal of time in the fall and winter of 1999 edging Talisman executives toward adoption of a three-point plan that would see the company backing its claims of having influence with the Sudanese government by including independent witnesses at meetings, being more transparent about the oil funds that were going to the Sudanese government and establishing independent monitoring of the company's human rights performance, to be paid for by Talisman. The talks were an uphill battle. At one meeting Buckee suggested to his disbelieving audience that the way to peace in Sudan was through sports. How about having baseball games between the opposing parties, he asked. "That's what he wanted to do," says Kathy Van der Grift, the Ottawa representative of World Vision and its representative in the talks. "He wanted to hold these sports tournaments. You know, attractive, southern young males, wouldn't that be the thing to do?"

Despite the bizarre suggestions from Talisman's chief executive officer, the groups still held out hope that their three-point plan would win acceptance from the company, mostly because Talisman would want to stave off government sanctions. But when the Harker report recommended that sanctions not be applied, the chance of Talisman's adopting the three-point plan disappeared.

Van der Grift says the turning point came at a meeting between Talisman and the four groups in early February 2000. They had been bargaining hard all morning when Buckee left to meet representatives of the government of Sudan over lunch. When he returned for the afternoon session his attitude had changed. He was no longer interested in making a deal. "We knew then it was game over," says Van der Grift. After thirty minutes, the meeting ended. What had happened? She believes that Buckee had seen a copy of the Harker report and knew that it was not recommending sanctions. The big stick that was being held over the company's head had disappeared.

The humanitarian groups blamed Axworthy for letting them down. He in turn felt unfairly targeted. "I was probably outright foolhardy," he says. "In the views of my senior officials, I should have just left it alone, taken a couple of bad hits from the human rights groups and then left it. But I didn't. I stuck my neck out and I got pretty badly bruised." The lesson both the human rights groups and the minister learned was that more lobbying should have been done in Ottawa to ensure all the right people were on side. Afterward, both sides seemed to lose heart. The four groups that had been negotiating with Talisman announced ten days after the report's release that they had given up that particular effort. Axworthy left politics. Talisman had won its wrangle with the government. But there was an even more demanding fight shaping up with the church share-holders and other critics who were not yet ready to concede defeat.

By the time of the May 2000 annual general meeting, the balance had shifted between the oil company and its detractors, with Talisman in the ascendancy. The line of tall, dark Africans wearing placards was back in place in front of the Palliser Hotel, but they had lost the shock value of the previous year. Their cries of "Shame! Shame! Dr. Buckee!" drifted away on the wind as shareholders and employees walked past, unheed-ing. Inside, there was more evidence of the Hill & Knowlton public rela-tions machine. Instead of downplaying its Sudanese operations, Talisman emphasized them. Scenes from Sudan were projected on the screen at the front of the darkened ballroom. An upbeat soundtrack of African drums played in the background. A shot of the oil installations in the endless, flooded plain of the south was followed by one of Africans scooping fresh water from a well. A World Food Program aircraft deliv-ering food supplies was shown, followed by a shot of happy Sudanese children waving. Then came photos of a school, a church and a clinic, with women lined up outside. A slide of a Mobil gas station appeared briefly and was gone. The message was not subtle. Talisman was bring-ing good things like water, education, health care and prosperity to Sudan. And, by the way, it was not the only Western company doing business there.

After the film, Buckee proudly reported spectacular results for the company. Production in Sudan had reached 208,000 barrels per day, and the company was planning further expansions. Buckee couldn't stop him-self from crowing a bit about the Axworthy debacle, but he controlled himself and phrased it diplomatically. "We were very pleased with the Canadian government's announcement in February endorsing construc-tive engagement," he said. What he did not mention, but what gave him extra cheer, was that Axworthy's attempt to have the issue raised at the UN Security Council had been stymied the previous month by opposition from the Arab League, the Organization of African Unity, and China, a permanent member of the Security Council and the senior partner in the

Great Nile Petroleum consortium. Before moving on to other business, Buckee added that the company had adopted the International Code of Ethics for Canadian Business—a voluntary code of ethics first developed by oil companies active in Nigeria.

Shareholders were then invited to ask any questions they might have. Archbishop Barry Curtis of the Anglican Church of Canada made the motion that an independent assessment of Talisman's human rights record be done within six months. A version of this resolution had been before the company for two years but had been held back from previous share-holders' meetings by of a technical point: the groups backing the proposal were beneficial rather than registered shareholders. After changing how their shares were held, the church groups now met the requirements.

Curtis's motion was seconded by Ken Sylvester, a trustee of the New York City Employees' Retirement System, which held 300,000 Talisman shares. Curtis pointed out that although the annual report had said that operations in Sudan were going from strength to strength, schools and hospitals were being bombed. Only the previous week, fourteen children had been killed when a school was directly hit. "What kind of strength does Talisman seek in Sudan?" Sylvester asked, and said that the company was in a state of denial about the atrocities being committed by the Sudanese government, its partner in the oil consortium. It was all very well for the company to sign the International Code of Ethics, but that meant it was supposed to live up to the values listed in the code, which included sharing the benefits of any project with all stakeholders. "As of this day," he said, "we have seen no compelling evidence that those beliefs, those values and those principles are being met."

Earlier, Sylvester had told journalists at a press conference that the fund he represented was a long-term investor but that the fund managers had qualms about keeping their money in a company that was accused of contributing to the war in Sudan. "Irresponsible companies present an investment risk to our funds," he said. In a practice first honed in the fight against apartheid, the fund managers would attempt to persuade Talisman to be more responsible. If that did not work, if the company management proved intransigent, then the shares would be sold. Sylvester held out hope that Talisman managers could be influenced. "We have just begun," he said. "We intend to pursue this issue."

Buckee let Reg Manhas, a smiling young lawyer and engineer who was the company's senior adviser on corporate responsibility in Sudan, respond. Manhas assured Sylvester and Curtis that Talisman was extremely disturbed by reports of bombing. The company certainly felt that the government of Sudan should both guarantee the security of all Sudanese and ensure an equitable distribution of oil revenues. As proof of its good faith, Talisman was talking to humanitarian groups about what could be done, and it had created a new department for corporate responsibility. The department had hired a Dinka man from southern Sudan as an adviser. Murmurings of approval came from Talisman employees and other shareholders.

Mindful that the company had flown in a southern Sudanese person the previous year to speak in support of the project, its critics produced one of their own at the 2000 meeting. Natalina Yoll rose to tell of her experience at the hands of the government. Her village was burned and looted, women raped, crops and cattle taken, and many people killed. She was crying by the end of her emotional presentation. "I am here to beg you, in God's name, in the name of all that is good and just, to stop your activities in Sudan. Please end your partnership with the brutal Sudan government. Please stop supporting the genocide of my people. Why should your future deprive my people of theirs?"

It was water off a duck's back. Chairman Peter Widdrington called for a vote on the motion put forward by the church and pension groups. It garnered only 27 per cent of shareholder support. When the company produced its own watered-down version, which had a one-year deadline and fewer conditions, it passed. After the vote, the meeting continued in a desultory fashion, with Buckee taking questions from shareholders, most of whom were representatives of the church groups and pension funds. He assured them that Talisman would not be a silent witness to human rights violations: "What is in our sphere of influence, what we can do, we will do."

He claimed that the government had stopped using the Heglig airstrip for military purposes. "We have influence with the government."

Although the churches' task force had not been successful in getting support for its proposal, the presence of Sylvester and Coleman represented a significant new stage in the campaign against Talisman's operation in Sudan. If they could not shame the company into withdrawing, they would go after its major institutional investors and try to persuade them to sell their shares. Buckee misread the signals he was being given at the meeting. He told reporters later that the divestment campaign by the church groups and pension funds had run out of steam and that anybody who wanted out had probably already sold their shares. "The remainder of the people are saying, 'We're holding your stock, do what you can. Or do more.' But as far as I can tell, the divestiture, per se, is quieting." In fact, it had only begun.

In an interview later in the Talisman boardroom, with its spectacular view of the Rocky Mountains, Buckee appeared calm, even introspective. At his side was Jacqueline Sheppard, vice-president of corporate affairs. She had played a key part in the Sudanese acquisition and was now charged with heading the corporate responsibility team. Petite and well groomed, she had fought her way to the top of an industry dominated by men. She had a hard carapace, developed no doubt in order to survive the constant battles she had faced. When she smiled, it was more a baring of teeth than a sign of warmth or humour. Axworthy referred to Sheppard as "the shark lady." In a neat reversal of roles, she played bad cop to Buckee's good cop. When he offered information, she cut him short. When he wanted to get a map to illustrate some of his comments, she said there wasn't time. And in the end, she stopped the interview after twenty minutes when a period of one hour had been agreed to.

I asked Buckee why he had purchased Arakis, knowing that there was a campaign against Western involvement in Sudan at the time of the purchase. Sheppard replied in his place by talking about slavery's long history in Sudan, how the practice had been embedded long before the discovery of oil in the country. She was attempting to lead the discussion away from

Talisman to the confusing inter-tribal conflicts that had caused much of the bloodshed. It took some effort to manoeuvre Buckee and Sheppard out of this conversational cul-de-sac. After repeated urging, Buckee answered the question.

"We were aware of their presence," he said, referring to the groups campaigning against any investment in Sudan. "But we also did our own homework and we were satisfied that there was sufficient uncertainty about their position that we could go ahead both from a security and reputational point of view." Arakis had been there for five years, with only one minor security instance, he said, "so we felt that it was a complex situation and prone to one-sidedness." Much of the criticism, he felt, was irrational. "There are lots of countries with strife and there are lots of other companies active in Sudan, as we subtly hinted in that movie." He added that more than half the countries in Africa had civil strife. "The vehemence that we have attracted seems disproportionate."

I moved on to the question of security. The actual policing of the oil fields, which had been both defensive and offensive, was carried out by the Sudanese army and government-backed militias. Had there been fatalities on the pipeline? Buckee admitted that people had died, "but they are always due to road accidents. Quite often the contractors have Chinese drivers, who are not very good drivers. Like two weeks ago, we had two dump trucks run into each other head on, both drivers killed. How you can do that, I'm not sure." I reminded him of a report of an attack on a rig the previous October in which five people were killed. Two subcontractors had died when the remote rig came under fire. Three soldiers coming to their defence had hit a land mine and were killed. "But that's not on the pipeline," said Buckee. Was this the astrophysicist in him being scientifically accurate, or was the oil company president being corporately evasive? It was hard to tell.

The people who had been killed in the attack had all been Sudanese. Scores of oil company workers can die, but if they happen to be African, it is never mentioned by the company or by the media. If a Canadian, American or British worker were to be killed, however, all hell would break loose. No one knows how many people have died building, defending or fighting for control of the Sudanese oil installations. Reports from the government and from the rebel militias are untrustworthy. The only people who could give a more or less accurate count—the oil companies—aren't keeping track. It is enough for them that their expatriate employees are safe.

In the interview, Buckee repeated his claim that no one actually lived in the oil fields, which is why, according to him, the government's scorched-earth policy had to be a myth. "It's a swamp," he said. "No matter what they say, nobody lives there." He ended the interview on an up note, saying that he hoped the company would eventually be vindicated for its involvement in Sudan. He hoped people would see "that in the long run, that development is good for the country and that our presence helps." If he was aware of the trouble brewing among some of the company's key investors, he gave no indication.

In these stories of corporate involvement in Africa, characters who do not seem to have any direct connection to the parties involved often emerge to play influential roles in the outcomes. Edmund Dene Morel, the British shipping clerk who campaigned vociferously against King Léopold and his cronies in the Congo, was one. In Talisman's case, Eric Reeves, a professor of English at Smith College in Northampton, Massachusetts, would turn out to be the company's most effective critic. Though the English department of a small, if prestigious, New England college might seem an unlikely place to find an expert commentator on the rights and wrongs of oil development in Sudan, Reeves pursued a dogged crusade to publicize the atrocities taking place on the other side of the world. He believed Talisman was complicit in the Khartoum regime's war against the southern Sudanese, and he sent out countless e-mails to that effect, wrote many newspaper commentaries and gave testimony before Congress. "I very much had E.D. Morel in mind as I campaigned against Talisman," says Reeves.

The professor stumbled into this activist role in January 1999 following a conversation with his friend Joelle Tanguy, the US executive director of Médecins Sans Frontières (Doctors Without Borders). Tanguy was in despair over the scant attention being paid to the unfolding tragedy in Sudan. How could an estimated two million people die and close to five million people be displaced without anyone's seeming to care? Now that oil was giving the various factions a new, attractive prize to fight over, the situation would undoubtedly get worse. Reeves, moved by his friend's anguish, decided then and there to take on the task of publicizing the role that oil companies were playing in the Sudanese conflict. He took a six-month sabbatical, and began working twelve to fourteen hours a day, scouring the Internet for recent developments in the far-off war and relaying what he had learned to his growing e-mail list of journalists, politicians, special interest groups and legislators. He had the eloquence one would expect from a lover of Milton and Shakespeare, and the analytical skills of a trained academic. It helped that he was no stranger to corporate finance. His father had been a stockbroker at Merrill Lynch for twenty-seven years, three of his brothers were still in the business and Reeves himself had held summer jobs on Wall Street. His knowledge would help him to decipher the next stage of the Talisman story.

Following on the heels of the company's May 2000 annual meeting were two more high-profile divestments: the New York State Common Retirement Fund and the New York City pension funds all sold their Talisman holdings, a total of US$16 million worth of stock. The men who ultimately controlled those funds—Alan G. Hevesi, comptroller for New York City, and H. Carl McCall, comptroller for New York State—sent a letter to nine hundred other public finance officers across the United States urging them also to divest. Hevesi's explanation was damning: "As long-term investors, we believe a company that is cavalier about its moral and social responsibility presents an unacceptable investment risk."

There had yet to be any divestiture by high-profile Canadian pension funds. Whether that was because of government rules limiting the proportion of foreign securities that pension funds can hold (forcing them to rely on the much smaller pool of large Canadian companies) or because humanitarian groups in the United States had more clout was unclear. In a late May 2000 e-mail sent out to a wide list of people, ranging from journalists to politicians, Reeves upbraided Canadians for their lack of will. "I've pretty much lost hope for action on Talisman by Canada," he said. "I've gotten very clear signals from several folks who know Axworthy's situation intimately that he can do nothing, given the position of the other ministries and [Prime Minister Jean] Chrétien. And Canadians seem unwilling to engage politically in the tough effort of divestment." When shareholders enquired, the funds gave similar responses. Royal Mutual Funds, part of the Royal Bank of Canada corporate family, defended its continued holding of Talisman shares, citing fiduciary duty. In a letter signed by E. Taylor of the customer service department, Royal Mutual said that Buckee of Talisman had pledged to respect the highest standards of business ethics in Sudan and that he supported the investigation of slavery. For good measure, the Royal Mutual employee said it was not the only fund with Talisman shares. AGF, Trimark, CI Funds, TD and the Ontario Teachers' Pension Plan Board were also shareholders. The Ontario Teachers' Pensions Plan Board defended its position, saying it was the pension manager's job to make sure there was enough money in the fund to pay teachers' pensions in future. "We do not have the legal authority to restrict investment on the basis of social or ethical criteria," Lee Fullerton, manager of communications for the board, wrote to a shareholder. "If teachers can agree on an ethical screen and the government changes the law, we'll act accordingly." Even a vote by the teachers federation to divest did not sway their pension fund managers.

The situation in the United States, however, was quite different. On September 14, 2000, Reeves exultantly wrote, "After months of relentless divestment pressure, all 186,000 shares of Talisman Energy in the pension plan accounts of New York City have been sold!" This, said Reeves, sent "the clearest possible signal that divestment efforts will pursue Talisman for as long as it is in Sudan." Two months later, after the company had posted record quarterly profits, Reeves gleefully reported that shares had nevertheless dropped on the news. "Sudan is the reason—and Sudan will continue to be the reason. Only mindless and vicious stubbornness on Jim Buckee's part puts Talisman shareholders in this distressed position." Talisman could not ignore the campaign against it forever, said Reeves, adding for good measure, "We will destroy your share price."

While the divestments were gratifying for the anti-Talisman campaigners, it was becoming clear that they had not brought the company to its knees. Talisman took advantage of its depressed stock price, announcing it would buy back 5 per cent of its shares (the maximum allowed by Canadian law in any one year) in 2000 and the same amount in 2001. This would, in effect, concentrate ownership of the company. If its critics no longer held shares, it was also true that their voices would no longer be heard at annual meetings.

The stalemate might have continued indefinitely had it not been for the emergence of a new and formidable Talisman opponent in the spring of 2001: the US Congress. A core group of representatives and senators had been actively working against the company for some time. Among them was Frank Wolf, Republican representative from Virginia. Wolf chaired the House appropriations subcommittee with authority over the Securities and Exchange Commission (SEC) and also co-chaired the House Human Rights Caucus. In January 2001, he had travelled to Sudan to witness at first hand the effects of the long-running war. When Secretary of State Colin Powell saw the video of Wolf's trip, he, along with National Security Adviser Condoleezza Rice and Secretary of Defense Donald Rumsfeld, decided to make Sudan a foreign policy priority. "There is perhaps no greater tragedy that is unfolding on the face of the earth today than the tragedy that is unfolding in Sudan," said Powell.

The violence in the country had continued unabated. A report in March 2001 by Gerhart Baum, a new UN special rapporteur on human rights, said that the situation had worsened in the previous year and that abductions, arbitrary arrests and forced displacements of people were on the increase. "The government is resorting to forced eviction of local populations and destruction of villages to depopulate areas and allow for oil operations to proceed unimpeded," reported Baum. He said that the building of new roads to facilitate oil exploration meant that more villages would soon be burned and crops destroyed. Like Franco before him, Baum said that all sides in the conflict were guilty of abuses. He asked them to stop the displacements and called for oil companies to minimize the negative effects of their operations. "It is a fact that oil is fuelling the war," Baum later told journalists in London. "It is not a religious war. Religion is misused. It is a power struggle."

Franklin Graham, son of evangelical preacher Billy Graham, also helped raise Sudan's political profile in Washington. Through a charity called Samaritan's Purse, Graham ran a hospital near Juba in southern Sudan. It had been bombed by the Khartoum government. When Graham was invited to give the prayer at the January 2001 inauguration of George W. Bush, he used the opportunity to lobby the president personally.

While the US administration had decided to focus on Sudan, its policy on the country was confused. Aid and money was being channelled to the south, but rebel forces were seizing what they could and forcing aid agencies to distribute food through them. The United States was also trying to encourage the northern government to negotiate peace. Meanwhile, in Congress, there were voices calling for tighter restrictions against Sudan. The Commission on International Religious Freedom recommended that capital market sanctions be imposed against companies doing business with the regime. Various lobby groups, including the umbrella organization known as the Sudan Campaign, whose members spanned the political, religious and racial spectrum in the United States, were pushing for further divestment efforts. Wolf sat on the board of advisers of the Sudan Campaign, along with Senator Sam Brownback, a Republican from Kansas, and representatives Gregory Meeks (D-NY), Eleanor Holmes Norton (D-DC), Donald Payne (D-NJ) and Tom Tancredo (R-CO). Reeves, in a January 2000 e-mail, said the group represented the type of commitment and muscle that had rarely been seen in the United States.

The first demonstration of this new muscle came in May 2001 in the form of a letter from Laura Unger, acting director of the Securities and

Exchange Commission, to Wolf in his capacity as chairman of the House appropriations subcommittee overseeing the SEC. Unger said the SEC, which regulates US stock markets, had decided to expand its role in order to ensure that foreign companies with listings in the United States were complying with its sanctions policy. Talisman trades on the New York Stock Exchange. It would now have to register filings electronically, just like US firms, making it easier for the public to access them. The SEC would also more closely review the registration statements made by Talisman. And there would be enhanced disclosure requirements. Unger said that the fact that a company was operating in a country under sanction was likely to be significant to an investor's decision whether to buy that company's shares. The commission had served notice that it would be watching Talisman—and other foreign companies in countries subject to US sanctions—much more closely. The move not only had political backing in the United States, it also had the tacit support of the major US oil companies, which were barred from doing business in Sudan. They did not like to see their Canadian competitor operating under different rules.

Providing Talisman fully disclosed everything that the SEC thought relevant, the higher level of scrutiny would not be fatal to the company. Much more threatening for it was a new bill called the Sudan Peace Act. Designed to strengthen US sanctions against Sudan and to prevent companies who were doing business there from raising capital on US markets, it had been introduced in 1999 in Congress; competing versions in the House and Senate could not be reconciled before the 2000 Congressional elections. When it was reintroduced in 2001, it was with extra teeth in the form of an amendment that stated, "The president shall exercise the authorities he has under the International Emergency Economic Powers Act to prohibit any entity engaged in the development of oil or gas in Sudan (1) from raising capital in the United States; or (2) from trading its securities . . . in any capital market in the United States." Talisman had circumvented the existing sanctions by structuring its Sudanese operations in such a way that it could assure regulators that none of the funds being raised on us markets were being used in Sudan. The new Sudan Peace Act removed this legal fig leaf. If passed by the Senate and signed by the president, it would force Talisman to give up its prized listing on the New York Stock Exchange.

Reeves, who had been advocating capital market sanctions for some time, practically shouted "Gotcha!" from his office in Northampton. "You don't use capital market sanctions unless you have a compelling case," he said. "The threshold should be very, very high." But if Talisman was not the perfect candidate for such treatment, he argued, what was? When Walter Kansteiner, the us assistant secretary of state for African affairs, said that the Bush administration would oppose the Sudan Peace Act because capital market sanctions were an unacceptable tool, Reeves was ready with his rejoinder. "The real issue takes the form of a question," he wrote. "Are there no circumstances sufficiently egregious, in which corporate complicity in genocidal destruction is so great, that both morally and politically we are obliged to restrict us capital market access? That is the real question and Mr. Kansteiner has simply failed to address it."

On June 13, 2001, the bill passed the Senate, but without the amendment that had given it teeth. Still, it frightened Buckee and the Talisman management team. They could not afford to ignore capital market sanctions. Talisman prized its listing on the New York Stock Exchange and was not about to lose it over Sudan. Buckee began to talk publicly about selling the Sudanese operations. "We want to remain in compliance with laws and we will," he said. "No asset is worth more than that."

The club that humanitarian groups had been looking for to beat Talisman into submission had finally materialized. But their optimism was short-lived. In July 2001, Federal Reserve Board chairman Alan Greenspan came out against using capital markets to sanction companies, saying that it would cause the United States to lose out to London, Frankfurt and Tokyo when it came to new financing and would undermine the long-term growth of the American economy. The Bush administration opposed the bill for the same reason, according to Kansteiner. He said that politicizing capital markets would set a dangerous precedent.

The bill was set to go to a House–Senate conference, where a final version would be worked out, when it was put on legislative hold by a Senate Republican who was not named. It was eventually revived, passed by Congress and signed into law minus the capital market sanctions by George Bush in October 2002.

The terrorist attacks on New York and Washington in September 2001 diverted the attention of the US administration from Sudan, although it continued to back ongoing peace talks in the region. Talisman, however, was not out of the woods. In November 2001, two prominent New York attorneys, who had previously won compensation from a group of European banks for survivors of the Holocaust who had been used as slave labour, filed a class suit against Talisman in US District Court. The plaintiffs—the Reverend John Sudan Gaduel and the Presbyterian Church of Sudan, plus three other individuals—charged that Talisman violated international law by participating in the Sudanese government's ethnic cleansing of areas of southern Sudan where the company was exploring for oil. "Talisman, a New York Stock Exchange company, cannot be allowed to profit from its partnership with a morally corrupt government," said Carey D'Avino, one of the two lawyers filing the suit. "Corporations cannot simply hire thugs to protect their operations and then feign surprise when the thugs commit a crime. At some point, respect for human rights and international law must not be sacrificed for the sake of the corporation's bottom line."

The suit cited the findings of numerous investigations, including Harker's and a subsequent report by Georgette Gagnon, a former Harker commission member, and John Ryle, a British journalist, which highlighted the atrocities being committed in the oil fields of Sudan. To support their case, the lawyers filed a document they said was a Sudanese government memo to its security officers in Heglig ordering that various military initiatives be taken in the oil fields "fulfilling the request of the Canadian company." The memo was dated May 7, 1999, two days before a brutal assault that had been outlined in graphic detail by Leonardo Franco. If validated, the memo could prove to be the smoking gun that would tie Talisman more directly to the atrocities committed by the Sudanese government.

David Mann, Talisman's spokesperson, said, "Obviously, Talisman believes in and respects human rights of all individuals around the world and we're disappointed to learn of this action." Talisman pronounced the accusations made in the lawsuit to be unfounded and said it would fight the case in court. The suit is expected to take many years to complete— if it isn't thrown out of court as the result of the Bush administration's current attempt to restrict the type of lawsuit that can be filed under the Alien Tort Claims Act.

In January 2002, Riek Machar, the southern Sudanese leader whom Buckee promised would be "intimately involved" in ensuring that the company's oil operations would benefit the local people, gave up all pretense of working with the Khartoum government and rejoined the southern rebels. He reintegrated his fighters with those of John Garang, who announced to the BBC, "We are one and the same again." Machar's decision should not have come as a complete surprise to Buckee, because Machar had sent him a letter the previous year complaining that the Sudanese government was not honouring its obligations under the peace agreement and that his people were being displaced "by the barrel of the gun." Nevertheless, it did not augur well for Talisman, which had already been hit by rebel attacks several times. In one instance, a supply convoy had been attacked and ten oil workers killed. In August 2001, rebels assailed Heglig itself and claimed to have damaged property and killed people. Talisman, however, said that it had been a failed attempt in which no one died.

Although the war on the ground continued to rage, peace negotiations mediated by the United States, Great Britain and Norway were actually starting to show promise. In July 2002, the Sudanese government and the rebels reached what was called the Machakos Protocol. It set out the initial building blocks for a post-war Sudan. Though it was a hopeful sign, the issues of power sharing and of where the border between north and south should lie were still to be settled.

For Talisman, this tantalizing prospect of peace had come too late. Although company officials continued to exude confidence, something had broken within the company. No single factor—the Canadian government's criticisms, the humanitarian groups' campaigns, the actions of Congress or, finally, the court case—had landed a killing blow, but the relentless attack had clearly worn Buckee down. On October 30, 2002, he announced that Talisman had reached an agreement to sell its Sudanese operations to India's Oil and Natural Gas Corporation (the final price was US$771 million, or CDN$1.1 billion). "The controversy surrounding this asset certainly played a part in our decision," Buckee told a news conference. "It was an excellent asset, but we felt that the controversy, for 12 per cent of our production detracted from the strength of our other assets. It is time for Talisman to turn the page." Buckee tried to put the best light on the sale by boasting that Talisman stood to make an after-tax profit of between CDN$275 and 285 million. To the end, he insisted that the company had done good things in Sudan.

The Oil and Natural Gas Corporation echoed the comments Buckee had made when Talisman had first purchased Arakis. "It is a good business deal at the given price," said Chairman and Managing Director Subir Raha. As for the political risk in operating in a conflict zone, Raha dismissed it: "We have had more sabotage here in India than in Sudan." But in India, the deal was already being questioned. A piece had run in Bombay's *Sunday Express* with the headline, "With $750 million, we rush in where the world fears to go—ONGC's oil project is terror-torn Sudan." Ernst & Young had apparently advised the company that the Talisman operations could be had at a discount because of US sanctions but that there were signs that the sanctions cloud would be lifted, especially in light of the Machakos Protocol.

Buckee had been aware of those promising signs but had told investment analysts during a conference call in October 2002 that "in the end, we had to weigh an improving political climate both in the United States and in the Sudan against having a fair, firm offer in hand right now from a significant and capable buyer." Industry analysts had acted mainly as cheerleaders for Talisman throughout the Sudan debacle, concentrating on the money the company was making by pumping cheap oil (the Sudan operations were Talisman's most profitable) and largely ignoring the conflict and the troubling ethical questions it raised. A few of the participants in the conference call congratulated Buckee on the deal and noted that the Sudan investment had been very profitable. Most of their questions focused on what Talisman would do with the money from the sale and what the company's plans were for the future. Buckee assured them that Talisman had no intention of replacing the Sudan operations with an equally controversial asset, "but as we've also said before, the rocks need to work before you worry about where it is, and that's a lot better than the other way around." No one asked whether Buckee had learned any lessons from the episode, a far more interesting question.

There are a number of adjectives that have been applied to Buckee over the years. He's been described as stubborn, too smart for his own good and myopic in the way that people focused on physical challenges can sometimes be. One human rights representative described him as "a cowboy who enjoys risks." Another called him "Mr. Magoo on his worst day." Those who remember that short-sighted cartoon character will recall that although he walked blindly into life-threatening situations, he always managed to stumble out of them intact, narrowly avoiding the thirty-storey drop or the train racing straight for him. Buckee was not so fortunate. He may have profited from the sale, but he also subjected his company to a bombardment of bad publicity that tarnished its image. In the end, he was forced to back down because of the negative effect it was having on the company's share price. For a proud man like Buckee, that retreat will rankle forever.

CHAPTER TEN

SALIM SALEH IN THE CONGO

ONE WOULD BE HARD PRESSED TO FIND A STORY SADDER THAN THAT of the Congo since the arrival of Europeans. From its inception in 1885 as the private preserve of rapacious King Leopold II of Belgium, the country has been a battleground for powerful interests seeking to enrich themselves at the expense of the Congolese. After Leopold and the giant trust companies, power in the Congo fell to dictator Mobutu Sese Seko, whose many crimes against his own people were ignored by the Western nations just as long as he promised to provide a bulwark against communism in Africa. Once communism crumbled, taking Mobutu's usefulness with it, his external support evaporated. The dictator's last years were characterized by spreading anarchy within his country, as rival militias vied for control of territory and resources that Mobutu could no longer securely hold. The ailing dictator fled the country in 1997 while a ragtag army of rebels, led by Laurent Désiré Kabila and supported by armies from neighbouring Uganda and Rwanda, marched across the country. But Kabila was no more effective than Mobutu in controlling the chaotic country. He lost the support of his original backers by allowing rebel groups hostile to the governments of Uganda and Rwanda to retain bases in the eastern reaches of the Congo and by sending his Rwandan advisers home. Less than a year after they had helped Kabila to power, President Yoweri Museveni of Uganda and President Paul Kagame of Rwanda decided that Kabila, too, would have to go. Their joint invasion in August 1998 ushered in a new period of strife. In the following four years, an estimated three million people would die.

Uganda and Rwanda hoped to repeat their 1997 success with a swift overthrow of the Congolese leadership. But this was not to be. Their assault rapidly drew other countries into the fighting: Angola, Zimbabwe and Namibia rallied to Kabila's side. Burundi joined Uganda and Rwanda. What had begun as a settling of political scores became an African world war.

But this war was not fought under the terms of the Geneva Conventions. At its heart was a corrosive desire for plunder. The armies of Uganda, Rwanda and Zimbabwe, the last in payment for services to Kabila, each occupied an area of the Congo and set about denuding it of its gold, diamonds, rare timber, coffee, copper, cobalt and coltan (a mineral used in mobile phones), terrorizing the population in the process. To these traditional forms of booty was added a lucrative new one: taxes, which joined the flow of riches leaving the country. A century after Cecil Rhodes showed how to use oppressive armed force to amass wealth, African leaders were following in his footsteps.

The foreign armies were not the only vultures feeding off the corpse of the Congo. They worked alongside and sometimes in concert with criminal groups, arms traffickers, diamond smugglers, rebel groups and companies that saw the potential for profit in a conflict zone. This chapter focuses on one individual who had links to many of the predatory groups mentioned above: Salim Saleh, a high-ranking officer in the Ugandan People's Defence Force and the younger brother of Ugandan president Yoweri Museveni. Saleh used his military and political connections to make money from the Congo war. He is an ambiguous figure, known both for his questionable attempts to amass great wealth, but also for his charity to war veterans, the poor and the disabled. His story is one of youthful promise curtailed by war, of the misuse of privilege and position, and of the corruption of members of the powerful elite. In short, it is the story of much of modern Africa.

Before anything more can be said about Salim Saleh and his role in the looting of the Congo, it must be acknowledged that he is a hero in his homeland of Uganda. Newspapers carry breathless stories about his activities. Cigarette vendors stare agog if his midnight blue Land Rover pulls up in front of their stall. Kids in the schoolyard want to be General Saleh when they play guerrillas versus the evil government forces—the Ugandan version of cowboys and Indians. In the spring of 2002, a rumour that he had died while on a trip to Europe spread a ripple of panic across the country. A soccer stadium was needed for the tearful crowds that turned out to welcome him home.

Saleh receives all this adoration from his countrymen despite the trouble he's been in. He was dismissed from active military service in 1989 for being a drunkard, a fact he readily admits. He broke the law to secretly acquire a state-owned bank when it was privatized and had to hand it back when the sale became public knowledge. And a military procurement contract he was expecting to earn a hefty commission on went sour when it turned out that the helicopters purchased in Belarus at great cost were duds. But more often than not, the man in the street in Kampala will defend Saleh, saying that he always apologizes when he is caught, and besides, everyone knows how generous he has been to fellow war veterans, widows, orphans, the sick and the poor. To many Ugandans, he is a mythological hero with human flaws, an African Robin Hood.

Salim Saleh was born in 1960. His family were originally nomadic cattle herders in southwestern Uganda, and cows were still central to their lives when Saleh's older brother Yoweri Museveni was born in 1944. Traditional members of the Banyankore Bahima ate only cattle-related products—consuming anything else was considered shameful. By the time Saleh came along, the family had converted to Christianity and most members had abandoned their traditional cattle worship.

Saleh was still in primary school when Museveni left Uganda in 1967 to attend university in Dar es Salaam, Tanzania, from which he graduated in 1970 with a degree in political science. Museveni espoused socialist ideals while at university and helped the members of the Front for the Liberation of Mozambique (FRELIMO), who were based in Tanzania, to raise money and publicize their cause. FRELIMO, in turn, gave him military training. In 1969, Museveni went to North Korea to receive further training before briefly returning to Uganda in 1970 to serve as a research assistant in the office of President Apolo Milton Obote, who had formed the first government after independence in 1962.

Obote's rule had been a troubled one, marked by infighting among members of the governing Uganda People's Congress and by accusations of corruption. One such allegation is interesting as far as the Saleh story goes: In 1966, Obote and his deputy army commander, Idi Amin, were accused in the Ugandan parliament of taking advantage of the chaos then enveloping the Congo to smuggle out gold, ivory and coffee. Parliament voted to set up a commission of inquiry and suspend Amin from his army post. Obote ended up overturning the decision and took no action against Amin, promoting him instead, two years later, to commander of the armed forces. In 1971, Amin overthrew Obote and began his infamous reign of terror, during which thousands of people were tortured and slaughtered for political purposes. Obote, who was out of the country attending a Commonwealth meeting when Amin struck, went into exile, as did Museveni. For the next eight years, Museveni—independent of Obote, with whom he'd had a falling out—used Tanzania as a base from which to organize resistance to Amin.

Saleh was sixteen years old and still in school when he went to visit his brother in Dar es Salaam in 1976. Museveni persuaded Saleh to join the Ugandan guerilla forces being trained by FRELIMO, which had gained power in Mozambique. Saleh would always regret his interrupted education, and would later say that his brother "abducted him from school." Museveni's version of events is that life was too dangerous in Uganda for his brother, who was "delighted at the prospect" of becoming a fighter. It was at this point that Saleh traded his given name, Caleb Akandwanaho (Akandwanaho means "God has been my defender") for his *nom de guerre*: Salim Saleh. It has stuck with him ever since.

Museveni decided to protect his young brother by keeping him out of combat during the successful Ugandan-Tanzanian operation to unseat Amin in 1979. Instead, Saleh acted as a liaison between Museveni's small force and the Tanzanians, who were backing a number of anti-Amin groups.

Obote became the leader of Uganda after Amin was ousted. But as he grew increasingly despotic, going so far as to rig elections in 1980, Museveni and his colleagues returned to the bush and launched a second guerilla war, aided by the Rwandans. Saleh was front and centre in this war, joining the guerrilla high command chaired by his brother and leading a number of successful attacks on behalf of Museveni's National Resistance Army (NRA). In January 1985, Saleh was asked by his brother to capture the Kahemba military barracks to secure rifles for the guerilla troops, who were perennially short of weapons. Museveni had already attempted the mission twice and had failed both times. Saleh succeeded in his first attempt. Twelve months later, after many more such missions, Saleh masterminded the operation that ended the guerilla war. He captured Kampala, and the legend of Saleh the glorious freedom fighter was born.

After being sworn in as president of Uganda on January 29, 1986, Museveni rewarded his younger brother for his exceptional military service by making him chief of operations for the army. Saleh was enormously popular with his troops. Not only did he have a reputation for bravery under fire, he didn't put on airs or treat himself to luxuries in the field. "If everyone is eating beans, he will eat beans, while the other [generals] would eat meat," says one former military man.

The Ugandan military, unlike many other African armies that act as repressive arms of despotic regimes, is largely respected, even revered, in its homeland. The National Resistance Army, which has since become the Ugandan People's Defence Force, is credited with saving the country from the bloodshed and chaos that went unchecked during the eight-year rule of Idi Amin and two successor regimes. Museveni ushered in a period of relative peace and prosperity. Uganda saw an increase in its economic activity, especially after Museveni invited back the Asian merchants and entrepreneurs Idi Amin had expelled.

Trouble, however, soon flared up in the north of the country, where the remnants of the former government's army continued to wage war. Museveni sent his brother to deal with it, and Saleh managed to add to his already illustrious legend. In one famous incident, Saleh got into a helicopter, flew to the rebel camp and suggested to the startled rebels that they think about negotiating a peace accord. He then got back into the helicopter and flew back to the government camp. Saleh has confirmed this story, saying that his initiative led to the first peace deal with the north. But after the incident, the high command charged him with risking the helicopter and endangering the life of the crew and a senior officer— Saleh himself. He was a hero and a renegade at the same time.

It was at this point in Saleh's career that his business proclivities began to come to light. He noticed that northerners in the conflict zone known as Acholiland were growing sim-sim (sesame) but were not marketing it. Saleh bought 300 tonnes of sim-sim, cleaned it up and sold it. When the peasants saw they could make money from their traditional crop, they began a more sustained cultivation of sim-sim and the harvest grew to tens of thousands of tonnes. Saleh's intervention also served the government's interest because the locals became more interested in making money than in fighting, helping to bring temporary peace to the region.

Peace, however, posed problems for Saleh the military hero. With no wars to fight, he began to drink heavily. This got him into trouble with his "boss," Museveni, who had been strongly influenced by his mother, a member of the puritanical wing of the Anglican Church and a teetotaller. He disliked drinking and he hated indiscipline. When, in 1989, Saleh's rowdy behaviour became too public to ignore, Museveni sacked him from his army post. Saleh told an interviewer that when he lost his job, he almost drank himself to death: "I was not educated. I had no other profession. The only job I had was military leader. I was twenty-nine years old." And to top it off, according to Saleh, he did not even receive a severance package. "My brother is a harsh man."

There is some debate about how total that sacking really was. One school of thought is that Museveni only removed his brother from an accountable position in the public eye and in fact continued to rely on his military expertise. Another, complementary school of thought is that Museveni had grown concerned about his brother's immense popularity with the army and wanted to shift him out of the limelight in case he was tempted to overthrow him. A third version, and the one that Saleh puts forward, is that the firing was exactly what it appeared to be: a complete severance from power as punishment for drinking and bad behaviour.

The evidence, however, argues against Saleh's version, because he was never completely out. When the Rwandans, who had fought alongside Museveni in his drive for power, returned home to fight their own war in 1990, Saleh was asked to be the liaison between them and the Ugandan army units sent to help them. That job lasted until the Rwandan war ended in 1994. At that point, Museveni decided to reduce the number of Ugandan troops from 100,000 to 60,000, and he asked Saleh, whom he had made chief of the reserves, to manage the 40,000 ex-soldiers. In April 1996, Saleh was named the president's adviser on defence and military affairs.

Meanwhile, Saleh was continuing to manage a burgeoning business career. The mid-1990s was a time of investment opportunity in Uganda. Museveni had obligingly cast aside his earlier socialist inclinations and embraced capitalism and the restrictive economic prescriptions of the International Monetary Fund and the World Bank. Those prescriptions included a massive privatization program and limits on the amount he could spend on the military. The United States and Britain threw their support wholeheartedly behind Uganda, which was being trumpeted as one of the few African success stories. Saleh decided to use his proximity to Museveni to increase his personal wealth. In return for making introductions and offering advice to businesses attracted to Uganda, he received commissions from or shares in the companies he helped. In this way, Saleh says he became part owner in about twenty different companies over a period of two years. The legend of Salim Saleh, big businessman, was born during this time. Though conventional wisdom was that he had his hand in just about everything in Uganda, this was not always true. Sometimes just his appearance at a company would start the rumour mill going. And such was the allure of the Saleh name that owners often decided it was better for business to keep mum than to deny that the famous general was their partner. Record keeping on corporate ownership in Uganda is sufficiently opaque that no one would really know for sure.

Saleh became involved in such diverse enterprises as a mattress factory, a maize producer, a security firm and a gold mine. This last venture involved Branch Energy, one of the stable of companies associated with British businessman Tony Buckingham. "My job was to locate pieces of land for them," Saleh told an interviewer. "I used to be a military officer in the area [the northeast corner of Uganda]. I had seen people picking gold out of the streams. So I told them to buy that land." Branch Energy invested US$7 million in the mine and was proceeding with more development when the government raised the ground rent so high that the project became uneconomical. Another business Saleh was involved in was Saracen Uganda, a security company associated with the now disbanded private military company Executive Outcomes of South Africa. Saleh owns 12.5 per cent of the shares. This particular connection would come in handy in the aftermath of the Congo war.

One British businessman, who did not want to be identified by name, explained to me how Saleh had helped his company: "Every company that wants to do work inside the country needs someone that can help make things happen. Salim never short-circuited anything, he didn't say, 'OK, I'll bribe this official.' He'd say, 'OK, if you need to file this particular application, this is the man to deal with. I'll introduce you to him.' You would have to spend weeks of somebody's time trying to find out who in the bureaucracy you need to file a permit with. And he would say, 'Go and see Jimmy' or Colin, or whatever his name would be. You need that type of person. Because otherwise the bureaucracy in these countries is in complete inverse proportion to their efficiency. And Salim is very good at that. He's just a savvy local guy who has used his visibility to his own financial advantage. And frankly, I don't blame him."

"I wanted on one occasion, for a particular reason, to have a meeting with the president. You cannot pick up the phone and call his private office or his political officer and ask for a meeting with him." Saleh arranged the meeting, saving the businessman months of dealing with junior officials and paying assorted bribes to gain access. Giving Saleh shares for his "priceless" work was well worth it, said the businessman. "To give someone 10 per cent of a company in a country or whatever it is, is inconsequential. I would rather have 90 per cent of whatever it is, of a [large] pie . . . than 100 per cent of something that is a crumb because I can't find the ingredients to bake it."

According to Saleh, fifteen out of the twenty companies he became involved in during these years turned out to be very profitable, but he was only a minority shareholder. Still, things seemed to be going well in his new endeavour as a businessman. It seemed so easy, he thought anyone could do it. There was really only one small cloud on this otherwise bright picture as far as he was concerned: his reputation as a successful businessman and his popularity with the troops meant that more and more veterans were showing up at his door asking for money. Saleh could not turn them away. He's said that the continuous stream of handouts started to have an impact on his bottom line. "That's when I mixed up business with humanism. If a man was injured with you and he needs money, you can't say no."

In certain societies in Africa, it is expected that once someone has attained high office in politics or the military, he will use his position to enrich himself and then share the riches with others. Power confers obligation on the office holder. If someone is "eating," as such enrichment is termed in Uganda, he is expected to invite others to share in the banquet. Grateful recipients tend to turn a blind eye to how the money is acquired, and they often aspire to attain a similar position so they can "eat" the government's money, too. Thus, corruption becomes more socially acceptable. Saleh says much of the corruption in Uganda was caused by the fact that public servants received poor salaries: "A police officer gets $75 a month. Do you think he's going to look after crime all the time? A teacher gets $50 a month. Do you think he's going to teach eight hours? That is 80 per cent of the so-called corruption in Uganda. The other 20 per cent is people like me who take advantage of their positions to make commissions."

How much money Saleh gave away is unclear. But even his harshest critics agree that he was extraordinarily generous. "If you go to Salim Saleh's house, you'll see poor veterans. He'll give them money and they walk away," says Charles Onyango-Obbo, former managing editor at *The Monitor*, an independent newspaper for which he wrote a column frequently critical of Saleh. "He steals money and then he shares it. He actually is Robin Hood." The stealing that Onyango-Obbo refers to is not so much the commission arrangements that Saleh had made up to 1996 as a series of deals that came afterward, as he sought other ways to make larger amounts of money through Uganda's newly inaugurated privatization program.

Museveni announced the massive privatization program in 1991, following the prescription of the IMF and the World Bank. Most of the 150 firms that the government had owned in 1987 were still in government hands. A list of 40 that were to be sold was published in 1992, but the process started slowly and it was not until 1995 that a minister was put in charge of the program, which by then involved 80 companies.

Privatization was not popular in Uganda. Concerns were raised that companies would fall into foreign hands and that Ugandans would lose control of their economy. The international financial institutions were adamant that the program go ahead, however, and so a total of ninety-three privatizations took place in the 1990s, one-third of them liquidations. Many of the small operations ended up in the hands of high-ranking military officials or government members. Three large privatizations were particularly controversial: the sale of ground-handling operations at Entebbe Airport, which ended the monopoly of Uganda Airlines Corporation, the sale of Uganda Grain Milling Corporation, and the divestiture of Uganda Commercial Bank. Saleh was involved in all three.

The privatization of the airport ground-handling operations was a tangled affair that started in 1993 when the Uganda Civil Aviation

Authority posted notice of business opportunities at Entebbe Airport. Two years later a company called Entebbe Handling Services was created, of which the state-owned airline Uganda Airlines held 50 per cent. Efforte Corporation, owned by Saleh and Israeli businessman Hezi Bezalel, held 20 per cent, Global Airlinks, owned by Sam Kutesa, the minister of state for investment and planning, held 20 per cent, and the rest was divided between Sabena SA, and the workers of both Uganda Airlines and the Civil Aviation Authority.

When the privatization minister decided to sell the Uganda Airlines shares in this company in 1997 in order to pay off the airline's debts, estimates of their value by three accounting firms ranged from US$3.75 million to $8.5 million. Efforte and Global Airlinks successfully bought the shares for the lowest estimate. A parliamentary committee questioned why the lowest estimate had been used and why the shares had not been sold on the open market to realize their true value. The committee also said it could find no proof that the full payment had been made. Furthermore, it noted that while the initial shareholders' agreement stipulated that Entebbe Handling Services was to remain in Ugandan hands, in the end foreigners owned more of it than Ugandans. The committee concluded that the privatization had been manipulated to benefit "a few politically powerful people." Parliament called for a review. It also censored Kutesa, whose daughter was married to the president's son. Kutesa was dropped from cabinet in 1999, only to reappear in the same job in 2001. No government action was taken on the ownership. Nevertheless, the problems with the deal cast a shadow on Saleh.

Uganda Grain Milling Corporation was put up for sale in 1996, and a Kenyan firm made the highest bid of US$5.3 million. Caleb's International, a company controlled by Saleh, was awarded the shares, despite a lower bid of $5 million. It then resold the shares to a firm called Greenland Investments. As part of that sale, Saleh made a profit and acquired a stake in Greenland Investments. While members of parliament complained that the sale of shares to Greenland violated the original sale agreement signed with the Ministry of Finance, again no government action was taken. But more questions were raised about the commercial activities of the president's younger brother.

The fact that Museveni did nothing about these two cases might have caused Saleh to believe he was home free. But then came his involvement in the privatization of Uganda Commercial Bank, the country's largest. That deal resulted in a backlash that even Saleh the war hero could not escape.

The bank was put forward for privatization in 1997, and a Malaysian firm called Westmont Land (Asia) BHD was the successful bidder at US$11 million. Under the purchase agreement, Westmont was not allowed to assign its shares for several years. However, just before the share sale was complete in early 1998, the company did just that, making a secret agreement with Greenland Investments, which was by then partly owned by Saleh. Rumours of the secret deal sparked a public uproar and an investigation by a parliamentary committee.

Before the committee could report its findings, Saleh made a public confession in December 1998. He defended his actions, saying that he wanted to keep Uganda Commercial Bank in Ugandan hands: "If my actions smacked of impropriety, it was impropriety caused by my feelings for, especially, the poor and the weak of this country, for whose protection and uplift I have toiled so much." Saleh said the only regret he had was that he had failed. "I now announce my withdrawal from the deal. Long live Uganda. Long live the spirit of the NRM [National Resistance Movement]."

Unlike Saleh's other questionable transactions, this one carried consequences. The government repossessed Uganda Commercial Bank (and later sold it to South Africa's Standard Bank Investments Corporation). Saleh was forced to resign immediately as presidential adviser on defence and military affairs, a position he had held for two years. He escaped legal sanction because the minister of ethics and integrity declared that although Saleh had been implicated in the scandal, he had not been actively involved, "but just gave money to other people to carry out the purchase." Sulaiman Kiggundu, a former governor of the Bank of Uganda and founder of the Greenland Group of companies, was not so lucky. He was tried for misuse of depositors' money in Greenland Bank, a subsidiary of Greenland Investments, in relation to the Uganda Commercial Bank deal. But Kiggundu was determined to go down swinging. Testifying in his own defence in July 2001, he said that Museveni had known about the purchase of the bank by Saleh and had agreed to it. Kiggundu also said that Museveni had rung him earlier to ask that he lend money to Saleh to buy Uganda Grain Milling Corporation. This was the first time the president had been directly linked to the corrupt privatization deals. Kiggundu was sentenced to six months in prison. No action was taken against Museveni.

However, the constant problems raised by his brother's business deals and the fact that mud was now being slung at him began to wear on the president. In March 1999, he gave an interview to *Time* magazine in which he called Saleh "a renegade fellow" and said he himself had nothing to do with his brother's business activities. "He's always doing his own things. I had sacked him from the army." He told *New African* magazine that Saleh's involvement in the scandal was "an act of stupidity." Nevertheless, Museveni pardoned him. For his part, Saleh said in *New African* that he realized that you can't be both in public office and private business at the same time. "I am repentant," he announced publicly. "I will start afresh."

After this latest apology, Saleh dropped out of sight. There were reports, which later turned out to be true, that he had gone back to school to complete the education that had been interrupted by war. He sat along-side teenaged boys to take his O-level exams in 1998 and passed every-thing but economics. He said he had failed this subject because he had presented his own theory of economics, which he calls "humanomics" and which involves adding a human side to economic theory. Later, in April 2001, he passed his A-levels. His studies were not just a matter of self-improvement: the Ugandan constitution demands ministers attain a certain level of educational achievement. Saleh had been in line for a ministerial post earlier in 1998, but his lack of qualifications had become an issue and he had withdrawn.

There was one other reason why Saleh was not getting into as much trouble at home anymore. He ,had found a whole new area on which to concentrate his money-making efforts: the Congo. In the final years of Mobutu's reign, the eastern part of the Congo had become a lawless land. The ailing dictator, who would die of prostate cancer in Morocco in September 1997, allowed rival militias, some headed by his own generals, to take control of large parts of the country. His thinking was that as long as they were fighting each other for regional dominance and local resources, they would not be challenging him. These militias did a booming business in cross-border trade with neighbouring countries and with various rebel groups fighting the governments of Uganda and Rwanda from bases within the Congo.

As early as 1996, when he was still presidential adviser on military and political affairs, Salim Saleh had gone before the Ugandan parliament and asked them to allow the Ugandan People's Defence Force to attack bases set up by Ugandan rebel groups in the Congo (then known as Zaire) and in Sudan. His request was based on a military concept known as the "depth factor," a measure of how vulnerable a nation is to invasion. The calculation involves the surface area of a nation and its circumference and is an indication of how quickly it can be overrun and occupied. The depth factor can range from very low for a country with a huge land mass like Canada or Russia, to very high for somewhere like Israel or Uganda, where the country is small and the neighbours numerous. In cases where the factor is high, the military pays more attention to hostile groups near the borders. Creating buffer zones by invading neighbouring countries—which is what Israel did with southern Lebanon—is one countermeasure.

Ugandan military strategists often cite the Israeli example when discussing how they chose to deal with the Congo. Mobutu had given sanctuary to Ugandan rebels, so in the interests of Ugandan national security, he had to go. This was accomplished in May 1997 when Laurent Désiré Kabila, backed by the armies of Uganda and Rwanda, marched his ragtag army across the country and took Kinshasa. When Kabila then turned on his erstwhile backers within months of taking power, he became the target of their 1998 assault.

Kabila had had a long history in this part of the world. A Maoist-turned-capitalist, he first came to public notice in the mid-1960s when he was second vice-president of the Supreme Council of the Revolution, fighting a succession of Western-backed governments in the Congo. Che Guevara, who for a brief period in 1965 led a band of Cubans to the Congo to help the anti-government forces, remarked in his diaries that Kabila had most of the qualities needed by a revolutionary leader but lacked the key ingredient: revolutionary seriousness. Guevara defined this ingredient as having an ideology to guide one's actions and a spirit of sacrifice to accompany it. Kabila seemed to be more noticeable during the period covered by Guevara's diaries for his absence. He was forever promising his comrade that he would be joining him at the front to fight, but he was somehow rarely able to leave the comfort and safety of Cairo in Egypt or of Dar es Salaam or Kigoma in Tanzania. Guevara and the Cubans eventually left in disgust at Congolese infighting, indiscipline and superstition. The revolution fizzled out when Mobutu, then commander-in-chief of the army, seized power on November 25, 1965, five days after the Cuban contingent had departed.

Kabila turned his attention to commercial enterprises, basing himself first in Tanzania and later in Uganda. He traded gold and coffee to Uganda, smuggled ivory on the side and kidnapped hostages for ransom. When he started organizing another revolution in the late 1990s, the Ugandans and Rwandans decided to back him.

Saleh had a personal connection to Kabila. At some point during the 1990s—the timing is uncertain—Saleh obtained a gold concession in the eastern Congo. Kabila told an interviewer from *Time* magazine that Saleh received the concession from the son of Mobutu and then travelled to Kinshasa after Kabila's victory to ensure that his claim was still secure. Museveni told the same interviewer that Kabila had invited Saleh to Kinshasa. Either way, one thing is clear: Saleh was already interested in making money from the Congo's resources before the Ugandan army, in concert with the Rwandan army, invaded the country for the second time in August 1998.

While planning this second invasion, Museveni and his old friend, President Paul Kagame of Rwanda, agreed they would install a president but maintain control over the eastern part of the country nearest their borders. Their plan was derailed when troops from Angola, Zimbabwe and Namibia defended Kabila. Still, by the time the dispute came to a stalemate in late 1998, Rwanda and Uganda had secured a large slice of eastern Congo, which was rich in gold, timber, diamonds, coffee and coltan. Uganda held the territory in the northern part of the area, while Rwanda held land to the southeast. Each set about exploiting the bounty.

By all accounts, the Rwandans were extremely organized, setting up transport systems to send resources and funds directly back to government coffers in Kigali. The Ugandans, on the other hand, were more ad hoc. It was thought that Museveni had not initially condoned the plunder of the Congo but had come around when he saw he could have a self-financing war. Raising defence spending any other way would contravene an agreement he had signed with the International Monetary Fund. If the army was paid with money taken from the Congo, or if senior officers paid themselves with bounty, the IMF would be none the wiser. Had the Ugandan military shown the same discipline as their Rwandan counterparts, it might even have worked. But Museveni had not reckoned with the independence and avarice of his generals—including his brother—who went into business for themselves.

For several months after the start of the 1998 invasion, the Ugandan government denied that its troops were even in the Congo. It was during this period that Ugandan journalist Charles Onyango-Obbo received a telephone call late one night. Saleh was on the line, and to Onyango-Obbo's ears he sounded quite drunk. Saleh admitted he had been drinking. "I'm celebrating," Saleh told him. "I'm in Kisangani." He urged the journalist to come and join him in the Congo city and make money. Onyango-Obbo declined the offer.

Saleh set about exploiting the Ugandan army's occupation through a network of companies he controlled or had created. His local accomplices included fellow army officers, Congolese rebel leaders, private entrepreneurs and his wife, Jovia Akandwanaho. Saleh counted among his international connections members of two Lebanese clans suspected of having ties to the guerrilla group Hezbollah, as well as Victor Bout, a Russian arms trafficker who has sold arms to some of the world's bloodiest regimes and rebel groups, including the Taliban in Afghanistan, Charles Taylor in Liberia and UNITA in Angola.

Saleh's entry point was transport. At one point he owned or controlled three airlines—Take Air, Planet Air and Air Alexander—whose aircraft were leased to the Ugandan army to fly troops and supplies into the Congo. The planes came back loaded with gold and timber and coffee. Even when the goods or minerals were obtained legally, there were huge profits to be made from their sale because Ugandan military officers did not have to pay import or export taxes. While helping themselves to the Congo's riches, Saleh and Jovia were also giving international criminals a hand in establishing themselves in the area. Planet Air helped Bout, the Russian arms trafficker, set up air services between the Congo and Entebbe Airport in Uganda by sharing flight times and landing slots with Bout's newly created Ugandan airline, Odessa. Planet Air also filed flight plans for Bout's aircraft, which were used to transport supplies and military personnel into the Congo, loading up with minerals such as coltan for the return journey. An equal-opportunity trafficker, Bout worked with both Rwandan and Ugandan groups. Saleh was far from the only military officer involved in the Congo plunder. A veritable free-for-all was taking place on the military side of Entebbe airport, and no records of the bulging commercial cargoes arriving from the Congo were kept.

Museveni publicly warned the army in late 1998 not to engage in business activities. But his most senior officers, including his younger brother Saleh, ignored him. Saleh was particularly interested in coltan, or colombotantalite, the black gold of the Congo, which when refined is made into the heat-resistant electronic components used in mobile phones, laptop computers and computer game consoles. Because no heavy equipment is needed to mine the ore—a pick and shovel will do—thousands of

Congolese rushed into the eastern areas where it could be found. War had destroyed almost all other means of making a living. The international price of coltan soared from US$30 a pound in January 2000 to $380 by the following December. While most miners digging in the bush saw very little return, some could still make a small fortune in a region where the average person lived on twenty cents a day. They sold their finds to middlemen who exported the coltan to world markets. One such middleman was a company called LA CONMET, which was based in Kampala, run by a Russian couple and thought to be owned by Salim Saleh. Even after the price of coltan collapsed after December 2000, to roughly US$7 per pound, LA CONMET was able to buy and sell the ore for a profit because labour costs in the Congo were so low. The company bought the Congo's coltan, trucked it to Entebbe Airport outside Kampala and then flew it to Kazakhstan, where it was processed. No taxes or customs duties were paid, which increased the company's profits.

Some of the finest hardwood forests in the world can be found in the Congo, and Saleh exploited them, too, through a company he was involved with called Trinity Investments. The wood was exported by truck to Kampala, then onward to the Kenyan port of Mombassa, where it was put on ships and delivered to world markets. Some of the logging was done illegally, and again, no taxes or duties were paid. Further illegal profits were made by levying taxes on the Congolese people and businesses. The revenues went to the operating expenses of rebel groups or for the personal profit of high-ranking officers rather than to maintain services for the local population. Trinity was heavily involved in this activity, demanding that companies pay their taxes in advance of importing or exporting goods. Because the activity was clandestine, no reliable figure is available for how much money was siphoned out of the Congo in this manner.

One method of tracking at least some of the wealth being taken from the Congo is to look at Uganda's gold and diamond exports during the Congo wars. Although Uganda has little or no gold production, its gold exports increased from a mere 0.2 tonnes in 1994 to 10.39 tonnes in 1999 before decreasing slightly to 9.82 tonnes in 2000. Diamond exports followed a similar trajectory. There were no records of diamond exports between 1987 to 1996, but in 1997 Uganda exported US$198,302 worth of diamonds. This amount rose to $1.8 million in 1999 before dropping slightly to $1.2 million in 2000 and then rising again to an estimated $3.8 million in 2001. These figures represent only the gold and diamond exports that were declared. There is no way of measuring the shipments that were smuggled, leaving no paper trail.

Diamonds held a special allure for the plunderers of the Congo. Widely available from artisanal miners, some of whom worked for nothing at the point of a gun, diamonds were easier to transport than timber, coltan or gold, and worth much more by weight than other illicit resources. The international diamond world, with its fierce code of secrecy, made it easy to dispose of illegal diamonds. Saleh's entry into this world came through another of his corporate vehicles, known as the Victoria Group, which purchased and exported gems from Kisangani, a regional centre on the Congo River. Diamonds from about two hundred small mines in the area were traditionally brought to the city and sold to comptoirs (diamond dealers), who then exported them to countries in the region or around the world. When the Ugandan and Rwandan armies captured Kisangani in May 1999, the diamonds were routed through dealers sanctioned by the military elites and their accomplices.

Although the Victoria Group was controlled by Saleh and Jovia, its actual operations were carried out by Congolese nationals working with Lebanese middlemen. The Congolese dealt with the miners, while the Lebanese had the diamond expertise and connections in the international trade. The Ugandan army supplied the military muscle to protect the group's activities. Khalil Nazeem Ibrahim, a Lebanese expat who once operated a restaurant in Kampala in partnership with Jovia, was most often mentioned to me as the driving force behind the Victoria Group operations. He marketed the gems from the Congo out of Kampala with the aid of Nami Gems, a diamond firm in Antwerp, Belgium. Khalil worked with a number of other Lebanese diamond traders who were suspected of having links to Hezbollah, the guerrilla group that blew up the US embassy in Beruit in 1983 and kidnapped Americans in Lebanon in the 1980s. The Victoria Group was able to export its gems from the Congo free of tax, representing another financial windfall for the group.

When the armies of Uganda and Rwanda turned against each other at Kisangani in 1999 and again in 2000, vying for total control of the lucrative diamond trade, the Victoria Group's operations were temporarily interrupted. Residents of the city, whose population had swelled to about one million during the war, suffered a series of bombardments over a number of days. Hospitals and schools were indiscriminately hit, and tens of thousands of people were forced to evacuate their homes. A local human rights group estimated that one thousand civilians were killed and three thousand wounded as ten thousand shells rained down upon the city.

The Ugandans lost both battles, leaving the Rwandans temporarily in control. Museveni reprimanded Brigadier General James Kazini for poor judgment in the final battle for Kisangani, saying he had ignored Museveni's written advice and had misdeployed Ugandan troops across a key bridge in the city. A week after delivering the reprimand, Museveni promoted Kazini to major general and made him army commander. The president disagreed with his general on tactics, but not on the ultimate goal.

The battles at Kisangani marked a watershed in the Congo war because they unmasked the real intentions of Uganda and Rwanda. Until August 1999, the two armies had co-operated while controlling separate areas within the Congo. After they came to blows in Kisangani they could no longer claim that the war was being waged to protect national security. The conflict was clearly about controlling the Congo's resources.

The Victoria Group moved its operations to Kampala in the wake of the battles. It continued to buy diamonds from Kisangani, but used couriers to bring them to the Ugandan capital. Evidence of this shift in tactics came to light after one of the couriers was robbed of US$550,000 as he made his way from the airport at Entebbe into Kampala. It turned out that Jovia was facilitating the smuggling of diamonds through Entebbe airport by personally instructing army officers to look the other way when a shipment came through.

Considering the scale of the pillaging being carried out by Saleh and a host of others, the free-for-all could not remain secret forever. Although war had made the country inaccessible to most outsiders other than the military groups and commercial predators, news of the great resource grab eventually began to trickle out to the rest of the world. As early as October 1998, Rwandan officials began complaining that Saleh was engaged in large-scale business activities in the Congo. According to the Rwandans, who were involved in similar activities themselves, Saleh was breaking the ground rules that the two countries had agreed upon regarding their armies' occupation of the country. It was after this that Museveni directed his generals not to go into business.

By July 2000, Kofi Annan, secretary-general of the United Nations, had grown sufficiently alarmed about reports emanating from the Congo that he appointed a panel of experts to investigate. The panel's first report, released in April 2001, was damning in the extreme. It not only backed up rumours of commercial exploitation by the Ugandan and Rwandan armies, as well as others, it also named the individuals and companies who were involved. Salim Saleh and Jovia Akandwanaho were singled out for criticism. "Khaleb [*sic*] Akandwanaho, alias Salim Saleh, and his spouse Jovia are at the core of the illegal exploitation of natural resources in areas controlled by Uganda and allies," said the report. "He is the younger brother of President Museveni (very popular in the army) and he pulls the strings of illegal activities in areas controlled by Uganda and allies. James Kazini is his executing arm and right hand." The report highlighted the activities of Saleh's corporate vehicles: the Victoria Group and Trinity Investments. And it went on to make the interesting observation that Jovia was thought to be more aggressive in business terms than her husband and had a special interest in diamonds: "According to very reliable sources, she is at the root of the Kisangani wars." The authors of this first report also attempted to tie Ugandan president Yoweri Museveni directly to the looting, but this was a strategic error. While those close to

the president, such as his younger brother, Saleh, and his army commander, Kazini, were deeply implicated, there was no hard evidence that
Museveni himself was involved.

The official Ugandan reaction to the expert panel's report was outraged denial. President Museveni, who enjoys a reputation with the
United States and Britain as one of the rare African success stories, was
stung by the criticism. He responded first through his spokesman, presidential aide Ruhakana Rugunda, who called the report biased and shallow and said it was based on hearsay and rumours. The government
planned to expose the flaws in the report, he said. While it was true that
Ugandan exports of gold and diamonds had skyrocketed in recent years,
this was due to free trade with the Congo and not because of illicit dealings, he said. A few days later, Museveni said the report was "shoddy, mali-
cious and a red herring!" He told a supportive group of members of parliament that he had spoken to his family members who were named in the
report, including Saleh, Jovia, and Museveni's first-born son, Muhoozie
Kainerugaba, and they had assured him that they were not doing business
in the Congo. Nevertheless, he intended to set up a judicial commission
of inquiry to investigate the issues raised by the panel of experts.

The Ugandan president then made two moves designed for international consumption: he threatened to withdraw completely from an international peace process meant to end the turmoil in the Congo, and he
pledged his support to work with US president George W. Bush to fight
terrorism. Though this was before the September 11 attacks on New York
and Washington, it was a reminder to the United States that Museveni's
Uganda provided a bulwark against the Islamic regime in Sudan to the
north, which had harboured Osama bin Laden and Carlos the Jackal
among others.

If Museveni had any harsh words for his younger brother Saleh over
the Congo imbroglio, they were spoken in private. Publicly, he stood by him.
As for the average Ugandan, it was difficult to tell whether the negative publicity had succeeded in making a dent in Saleh's reputation. Opinion polling
is a nascent industry in Uganda, and no survey addressed this specific

question. However, Kenya's Strategic Public Relations and Research published a poll in June 2002 on potential candidates for the presidency in the 2006 Ugandan election. It indicated that while 20.3 per cent of Ugandans would pick Museveni for another term as president, 5.1 per cent said without prompting that Saleh should get the job—this despite the fact that he had repeatedly said he was not interested in the position.

The United Nations condemned the bloodshed in the Congo, and the Security Council passed Resolution 1304, calling for the withdrawal of all "non-invited" troops, including those of Uganda and Rwanda. They had already agreed to a ceasefire during talks in Lusaka at the beginning of July, but no movement was forthcoming. The UN condemnation fell on deaf ears.

There is some debate in Uganda about how sincere Museveni was in setting up the commission led by Justice David Porter to investigate the allegations made in the UN panel's report. Comments by members of his immediate circle made clear that the aim of the commission would be to prove that there had been no exploitation of Congolese natural resources. Opposition politician Aggrey Awori, who campaigned against Museveni for president in 2001 on a platform that included withdrawing Ugandan troops from the Congo, said Museveni was just trying to whitewash everything. I spoke to Awori in the cafeteria of the Ugandan parliament, a cavernous building in which MPs bustle about looking busy although they have very little power in the country. Museveni's embrace of democracy is more tentative than his adoption of capitalism. Uganda officially remains a one-party state, and only members of the National Resistance Movement are allowed to run for president. Museveni is trying to change the constitution, which limits a president to two terms, so that he can run again in 2006. Critics say Museveni retains the military commander's need for absolute control. Though members of the opposition are allowed to hold seats in Parliament and use the forum to voice their criticisms of the government, this is seen as a containment strategy, as is the emergence of a critical press. Opposition MPs can let off steam without having any real access to power.

Awori told me he spent a month in the Congo investigating resource theft. "The top military men and their wives got into it in a big way," he said. "At one point there was practically a war at the airport in Entebbe between two of these wives over a planeload of precious timber that had just arrived from the Congo." He also witnessed how the military operated on the ground. When Ugandan or Rwandan troops occupied a gold mine, for example, they kept it producing and allowed local management to remain in place. The mine managers went along because they did not want to lose the mine altogether, even though the production was now going to foreign generals. "These people [the generals] came in and picked up where Mobutu left off."

Awori raised the problem of looting in a speech in Parliament, "where I got the usual denials." When the Porter Commission issued an interim report in November 2001, Awori's fears were confirmed: it absolved the president, his family and senior army officers of any wrongdoing. But as we parted, Awori expressed hope that so many questions had been raised by the UN panel of experts that even Museveni would have a difficult time explaining them all away: "In the course of the [Porter] inquiry, they found a lot of cracks—so many, he may now need Polyfilla." Surprisingly, Awori indicated that it was Museveni and not his younger brother that he was gunning for: "Salim Saleh is not the kind of man I would take to the International Criminal Court. He is a package of good and bad, and most of the bad things are done collectively."

The same month that Porter issued his interim bill of health for Uganda, the UN panel of experts published an addendum to its first report. In it were repeated the allegations against Saleh and the Trinity and Victoria groups, saying the two companies were still active. The addendum also made new allegations against Saleh, asserting that he was siphoning customs revenues at border points and receiving diamonds through Congolese rebel leaders. All mention of Museveni, however, was dropped. The experts concluded, "There is a link between the continuation of the conflict and the exploitation of the natural resources, in the case of Uganda. Influential government officials, military officers, and businessmen continue to exploit the security situation for their vested commercial interests."

A third report by the UN panel, delivered to the secretary-general of the UN in October 2002, accused Saleh and associates of being part of a criminal cartel exploiting the Congo's resources and of using the Ugandan army as its enforcement arm. This report highlighted the activities of Victor Bout and pointed to possible connections between the Lebanese diamond dealers and Hezbollah. It also said that Saleh, aided by the security firm Saracen Uganda, in which he held shares, was training paramilitary forces in the eastern Congo to protect his business operations as the war wound down and Ugandan troops were being withdrawn. Both Saleh and Heckie Horn, the former South African Defence Forces soldier who heads Saracen Uganda, have denied these charges. The report called for what is known as "smart" sanctions, which would target, among other things, the bank accounts and travel privileges of those accused of wrongdoing. It named fifty-four individuals, including Saleh, who should be subjected to these sanctions. As well, it listed eighty-five companies accused of violating international principles of business conduct.

I was in Uganda when the first UN report was released, and I witnessed the explosion of denials from the government about the activities of its officials and military leaders in the Congo. I went back in the summer of 2002, after the addendum but before the final panel report was released, to see what had been done about Uganda's involvement in the Congo in the interim.

Air travellers destined for Kampala land at Entebbe Airport, which is forty-five minutes southwest of the capital. Nairobi, my point of departure, was wilted and beaten brown by a punishing multi-year drought. Entebbe, located on the northern shores of Lake Victoria, was verdant in comparison. The road to Kampala passes through a succession of rolling hills covered with banana trees and flowering bougainvillea, interspersed with valleys of papyrus swamp. This had been a dangerous route, frequented by armed thugs who frequently killed their victims or left them naked and helpless by the side of the road after taking their cars, their clothes and their valuables. It was on this road that robbers relieved the diamond dealer from Kisangani of his US$550,000 in the summer of 2000. But those dangers, my driver happily informed me, were now a thing of the past. Two months previously, the government had launched Operation Wembley, which involved shooting potential robbers on sight. It had been a tremendous success in terms of reducing the rate of robberies, although it had attracted criticism from human rights advocates. New instructions were then given to the security agents to shoot only in self-defence. The week I arrived, Colonel Elly Kayanja, the commander of Operation Wembley, complained there was not enough room in detention centres to house all the suspects his men were now forced to bring in alive. Rush-hour traffic was the only problem we confronted on the trip in from the airport.

No one I spoke to during that visit expected that anything would happen to Saleh as a result of the UN panel reports. First and foremost, he was the president's brother, and Museveni would stand by him, I was told. The president owed him for foregoing his education and chalking up military successes all those years ago when they fought together in the bush. This was often cited as the reason why the president had not cracked down harder on Saleh years earlier when the scandals over his questionable role in several high-profile privatizations broke.

It was not just the president's personal feelings that would play a part in Saleh's protection. He was widely believed to be the second most powerful person in the land, his supposed resignation in 1998 merely a sham to disguise his continued role as the commander of the army. The evidence given to back up this theory was that Saleh continued to participate in meetings of the army high command, to attend high-profile military occasions, such as a visit by a Rwandan military delegation in the spring of 2001 during a delicate period for the two countries, and to play an official role in seeking a peace settlement with rebels in the north. In the summer of 2002 one Ugandan newspaper reported that Saleh was known to be giving direct orders to the military, even though officially he was only commander of the reserve force.

Then there was his popularity, with the public in general and the army in particular. The newspapers ran stories about how he broke up a fight between parliamentarians, how he secured the release of an abducted Congolese minister, how his Salim Saleh Foundation for Humanity was distributing relief supplies to hungry northerners, how he had left the safety of the army barracks in a rebel area up north to live among the villagers. Despite all the negative publicity written about him over the years, the Salim Saleh fan club in Uganda was both large and vocal. He appeared virtually untouchable. "They might find a fall guy," said veteran journalist Charles Onyango-Obbo, "but it won't be Saleh."

I wanted to talk to the man himself to get his version of events, but it wasn't easy to get in touch with him. He changed phone numbers frequently—a number that had worked only days before would turn out to be disconnected. Eleven phone numbers later, I finally reached the famous Ugandan hero. He amiably agreed to an interview about his business endeavours and said that an aide would come and fetch me from the hotel. True to his word, he dispatched Sarah, a lovely, soft-spoken young woman who identified herself as one of his research assistants. She brought me to his compound in the exclusive area of Munyonyo on the banks of Lake Victoria.

When we pulled up, a small group of people was waiting outside the guarded metal gates. Sarah said they were there to ask Afande Saleh (*afande* is a Kiswahili term of respect from subordinates) for money to pay school fees. On most days, there were about three hundred people at the gates, she said, but because the newspapers had reported that Saleh was in the northern town of Gulu helping to fight the rebels, the group that day was much reduced. Five or six Africans sat patiently in the shade of a vibrant orange bougainvillea bush, and one middle-aged European man with a battered briefcase looked uncomfortable as he stood apart in the equatorial sun. Sarah went off to make arrangements and left me to sit in a plastic lawn chair overlooking a broad sweep of lawn that ran down to the lake. Herons and egrets were stalking fish along the shore and a cool breeze was blowing off the water. For the first time in days I could not hear the noise and bustle of Kampala. The only sound was the occasional cry of a bird circling overhead.

Saleh received me in an upstairs living room with windows on two sides that gave views of the lake. It was comfortable but not ostentatious, with black leather sofas ranged along the walls and a muted grey carpet underfoot. The only art on the walls was a portrait of Saleh in military fatigues. His family was not in evidence. Apparently they lived elsewhere in Kampala, in another house he owned. If I had expected a display of wealth—a few ingots of gold, perhaps, or a small pile of diamonds—I was doomed to disappointment. Then again, space, comfort and quiet count as luxuries in Uganda, as they do everywhere.

The man who stood up to greet me was dressed in black slacks and a black t-shirt, its short sleeves exposing scars from wounds suffered during his days as a guerrilla in the bush. As is the case with so many rogues, he was charming, insisting we have a cup of coffee—grown on the slopes of Mount Elgon—and exchange small talk before we got down to business. Saleh had recently become involved in a coffee venture, which we discussed in much detail later. But first we talked of how he had come to be involved in business, and for that we had to start back at the beginning.

"I am a military officer who is accidentally doing business," explained Saleh before launching into a description of his past that made no reference to the Congo. Saleh avoided all mention of that country, preferring to concentrate on his earlier business activities and on his current project to sell Ugandan coffee to the world. When I asked whether the bad publicity surrounding his activities in the Congo would scare off the outside investors he needed to make his coffee project work, he was dismissive. "Fortunately, I have outlived it," he said of the furor caused by the initial findings of the UN panel of experts. He seemed to believe that the final report of the Porter Commission would exonerate him, as its interim report had done. "All those allegations will be disproved. The UN is too embarrassed to accept they were wrong. I'm looking at possibilities of suing them. But it will all fade away, especially if I persist with coffee." And with that, he ended our conversation.

Things did not turn out quite the way Saleh predicted. In May 2003, Museveni released the Porter Commission report that he had been sitting on since the previous November. He did so at the insistence of international donors who were growing increasingly concerned about the level of corruption in Uganda and what they called the "culture of impunity." Museveni was forced to comply because he depends on foreign governments and international financial institutions to supply half of his government's annual budget. Porter had taken some pains to present a picture sympathetic to Museveni, absolving the president of all wrongdoing in the Congo. But the evidence of large-scale looting by Ugandan army officers was so exhaustive it couldn't be ignored. As journalist Onyango-Obbo had forecasted, a fall guy was found: Brigadier General James Kazini, commander of the Ugandan troops in the Congo. Not only was Kazini involved with Victoria diamonds for his own benefit, Porter found, he allowed officers under his command to loot the Congo at will. The commissioner recommended that Kazini be disciplined.

Saleh, however, was not completely off the hook. He disobeyed a direct order from Museveni to stop doing business in the Congo, Porter said, and pretended to transfer control of one airline to his wife while remaining in charge. He broke Ugandan laws by naming his four-year-old son a director of that airline, claiming the child was a businessman. The penalty for this last act is normally two years in jail. Porter recommended that criminal charges be laid. As for Saleh's involvement with Victoria and Trinity groups, Porter gave a nuanced view. The commission could find no firm proof of his involvement, he said, and Saleh denied any connection under oath. Nevertheless, the evidence before the commission "is enough to raise the great suspicion of the secret participation of Salim Saleh." As for the charge that he had trained a paramilitary group, again there was no concrete evidence, but Porter concluded, "it is of course possible that there is some secret paramilitary group being organized and funded by Lt. General Saleh as the (UN) Panel described." In considering Saleh's overall role in the plunder, Porter said the commission was "not impressed by the denials of Salim Saleh, bearing in mind his involvement in air transport to and from the Democratic Republic of the Congo."

This was not the clean bill of health Saleh had expected, but whether Museveni will rein in his younger brother is another matter. The week after the Porter report was released, Museveni said publicly that no corrupt person was untouchable in Uganda, "[b]ut we must have proper evidence to act." He knew of course that such evidence is difficult to come by in a war zone, especially when the corrupt parties take steps to cover up their actions.

It is tempting to view Saleh as a good person who somehow stumbled down the wrong path, a man ruined by his brother's ambition and indulgence. But the cold, hard fact is that an estimated three million people died in the Congo because of the conflict that he helped perpetrate and that he benefited from.

As Sarah and I left Saleh's house and pulled up to the locked gates on our way out of the compound, I saw that the African supplicants were still there. So was the European man, who sounded distinctly shady when pressed by Sarah to explain his business. He mumbled a name and gave evasive answers about who he represented and why he wanted to see Saleh so badly that he was willing to sit in the sun for several hours. Sarah suggested he phone one of the general's other assistants and arrange a proper meeting. As we drove away, he was still standing at the gate.

I later told a Ugandan acquaintance about how peaceful Saleh's compound seemed and how I was tempted to take a stroll along the lake while waiting for him. He laughed uproariously and informed me that the shores of Lake Victoria are known to be infested with crocodiles. It would have been a short walk. What I thought I had seen at Saleh's villa in Munyonyo was only an illusion. The truth was submerged beneath the placid waters.

(C O N C L U S I O N)

PERFECTLY LEGAL,
PERFECTLY IMMORAL

THE MONTREAL-BASED ORGANIZATION ENTRAIDE MISSIONNAIRE
speaks for Catholic missionaries spreading the gospel and doing good
works throughout Latin America, Asia and Africa. Its members toil in the
hellholes of the world, where war, famine and disease make simple survival a daily struggle. Their aim is to help the powerless stand up to the
powerful. In the Congo, where more than three million people have perished in the war over resource riches, that means keeping track of atrocities. And there's no shortage of them: thirty people burned to death by
local militia at a wedding feast because one of the guests was suspected of
stealing a truckload of coltan, the mineral used in cell phones; three hundred people slaughtered and dumped in mass graves in Ituri in a vicious
fight over gold; one thousand civilians slain in the crossfire when the
Ugandan and Rwandan armies battled for the diamonds of Kisangani.
Like their counterparts in the time of King Léopold II, the missionaries
broadcast these horrific tales to the wider world, hoping that one day the
plunderers will be brought to book.

In late 2002, the co-ordinator of Entraide Missionnaire, Denis
Tougas, wrote Canadian foreign minister Bill Graham asking what he and
his Liberal government were going to do about eight Canadian companies
that a UN panel of experts suspected were helping to plunder the Congo.
Unscrupulous corporations form a crucial link between warlords and

world markets. The money they pay for access to gold, diamonds, coltan and rare timber buys arms and feeds troops. Would the minister launch an immediate investigation to see whether Canadian companies were feeding off the Congo's misery? It took Graham more than three months to reply, and when his response finally arrived, it wasn't encouraging. Yes, terrible things were happening in the Congo, he tut-tutted in his letter of late March 2003. Just terrible. And of course he took Tougas's concerns very seriously indeed. But the allegations against the companies had not been corroborated and were in fact being strenuously denied. A number of the companies had been in touch with Graham's officials, demanding that the minister get their names off the UN list. While he did not mention this last point to Tougas, he agreed that further investigations were merited—but not by Graham. This type of problem demanded international measures. Graham referred to a few vague possibilities for future action—perhaps France would take it up at the next meeting of the Group of Eight?—and signed off by thanking Tougas for sharing his "reflections" on the matter.

The exchange between the missionaries and the minister exemplifies the game of pass-the-buck that is played whenever accusations of multinational corporate misconduct are raised. National governments shrug off their responsibilities. Yet who else can oversee companies' behaviour if not the governments of the countries where they hold their annual meetings and pay their taxes? Those same governments, however, continue to insist that they are powerless and that the only way to see justice done is through international action. This response is meaningless because international bodies are subject to the will of their national members. And nothing will be done because there is a gaping hole at the international level in the laws that apply to corporations.

Companies have snuggled comfortably into this breach, confident in their claim that however dubious their activities, they are not breaking the law. In the Congo this means that a mining company can pay its taxes and fees to the local warlord, knowing full well that the money will be used to arm guerillas and kill more people. All perfectly legal.

All perfectly immoral. "It's just so frustrating," says the soft-spoken Tougas.

The good news—for everyone except the plunderers—is that the status quo will not hold. The mobs of anti-globalization protestors who chant outside the heavily guarded walls of almost every international meeting will ensure that. They are the physical manifestation of a much broader public unease with the role that multinational corporations play in the world today. A bout of similar demonstrations in the 1970s produced a raft of tougher environmental laws applying to business. This time around, the target is human rights, specifically the obligations of corporations. In the last five years there has been an explosion of interest in this topic, with everyone from the World Bank to military strategists weighing in. While the avalanche of studies and reports have produced diverse recommendations, the trend is clear: corporate bosses will, sooner or later, be held accountable for their actions in the world's troublespots.

To date, multinationals have reacted to charges of human rights abuses with anger and denial. When the UN panel of experts produced its Congo report criticizing eighty-five companies, including eight Canadian corporations, for fuelling the war, the initial response of those named was outrage, typically followed by a threat to sue. "All allegations included or implied within the report are categorically refuted," read a press release from First Quantum Minerals of Toronto. "First Quantum intends to pursue, by all means available, a full retraction of the allegations contained within the report." Barclays Bank, a British firm, says it took its ethical responsibilities extremely seriously "and apply high standards of business conduct across our operations worldwide." The president of Kinross Gold, another Canadian firm, assured me that all his company's dealings in the Congo were "by any standards, appropriate and defensible." He later called the mention of his company on the list "irresponsible commentary" that would hit its share price. Behind the scenes, other corporations' responses were less measured. Tougas says he received threats from one company, which he refused to name to me, for even mentioning its activities in the Congo to a government official.

Some corporate leaders and pension fund managers have defended their actions, not just in the Congo but elsewhere, by saying that they are required by law to put the interests of their shareholders—and thus profits—above all else. The sublime irony of this argument was shown when the Ontario Teachers' Pension Plan held on to its shares in Talisman Energy even though the Ontario Teachers' Federation, whose members are its beneficiaries, asked that the shares be sold after Talisman was accused of fuelling the war in Sudan. Governments could put a swift end to this defence by broadening the definition of a director's duties beyond the bottom line. Thirty US states have already moved in this direction by amending their laws to ensure that directors take the interests of stakeholders such as those in the surrounding community into account.

Those companies that have accepted that they have had a role in the perpetration of human rights abuses are making a public show of adopting a corporate code of conduct. While this is a recognition of sorts that they can no longer conduct business as usual, these codes are fatally flawed. They tend to make minimal commitments because they are written by the companies' own legal departments, who worry that they could be used in litigation. A survey done by the Organisation for Economic Co-operation and Development of 246 company codes of conduct discovered that only 17 per cent of mining companies and 35 per cent of oil companies even mentioned respect for human rights. As for the use of security forces, it was mentioned in only 3 per cent of mining company codes and 14 per cent of oil company codes. Yet these are the very companies that use armed security in many of their operations. Far too often, the codes are drawn up only after a public relations crisis or in the hope of averting looming legislation. But their most glaring weakness is that they are voluntary and contain no punishment for violations. Their inadequacy is demonstrated by the fact that two of the most comprehensive are those of Royal Dutch/Shell and Talisman Energy, two corporations that are now being sued in the United States for violating human rights in the area of their African operations.

The international codes that have been developed with the support of the wider business community suffer from the same weaknesses as the individual codes. The OECD, a Paris-based grouping of the richest industrialized countries in the world, produced its Guidelines for Multinational Enterprises in 1976. These are the guidelines that the UN panel of experts accused the companies of violating in their Congo operations. Canada is a signatory. Yet when Tougas of Entraide Missionnaire approached the Canadian custodian of the guidelines, who happens to be an official in Graham's department, he was told that the code was voluntary and there was no way of forcing companies to comply. Similar toothless efforts have been produced by the UN (the Global Compact) and by groups of governments and industry associations (the US-UK Voluntary Principles on Security and Human Rights).

Clearly, the voluntary route will not work. The only way to ensure that companies adhere to an international standard is to enact new laws that define what is acceptable behaviour and that stipulate penalties harsh enough to make corporate executives think twice. Their absence provides a loophole through which many of the worse perpetrators can crawl. The Belgian government, unlike Canada's foreign minister, decided to investigate the allegations made by the UN panel of experts and set up a fifteen-member commission. After interviewing many of the key corporate players and their accusers, the senators who constituted this commission delivered their report in February 2003. It reached the meek conclusion that while natural resources were being exploited in the Congo at the expense of the local population, there had been no evidence of "illegal acts" by any company. "I am bitter and even furious that we weren't able to publish a more precise and more convincing report which could have contributed to stop the plundering and thus the tragedy," said Senator Georges Dallemagne, one of the dissident members who refused to sign the report. The Belgian case drives home a crucial point. It shows how easy it has become for powerful businesses to avoid being called to account for their misbehaviour. The Congolese laws were too weak. Belgium's laws did not reach beyond its borders. And there was no international law that could be applied.

The suggestion that this void should be filled with legally binding international rules provokes a furious response from the business community. The International Chamber of Commerce, one of the main global lobby groups for business, has warned that even mentioning a possible treaty will cause corporations to halt whatever voluntary initiatives they have undertaken in the fear that these will be enshrined in law. This says a great deal about the depth of the corporations' commitment to their voluntary codes.

The corporate allergy to global governance laws also smacks of hypocrisy. The UN Conference on Trade and Development (UNCTAD) points out that corporations have pressed governments to negotiate a series of international laws enshrining their rights on overseas investments while at the same time fiercely resisting any attempt to define their obligations. On their behalf, governments have negotiated at least 1,700 bilateral investment treaties, set up the World Trade Organization and attempted to seal the Multilateral Agreement on Investment. This last agreement, negotiated by governments under the auspices of the OECD in Paris, fell apart under civil society pressure precisely because it gave corporations investment rights but no responsibilities in areas such as labour, human rights or the environment. UNCTAD surveyed these legally binding investment treaties and found there was a "conspicuous absence" of any mention of corporate governance, ethical business standards or the observance of human rights.

The current set of international laws governing human rights was written to regulate the behaviour of states in an era when corporations were not the global force they are today. The benchmark in this area is the Universal Declaration of Human Rights, adopted in 1948 by the UN General Assembly in the wake of the Second World War. It states that "every individual" and "every organ of society" (which would include corporations) is obliged to promote and respect the rights and freedoms it sets out. But it does not provide a direct way, either through a court or through specific laws, to enforce these obligations on "organs of society." Even the declaration itself is not legally binding, although it has been endorsed in other UN treaties that are. Some of the recent spate of research on corporate accountability has addressed the question of whether these laws can also be applied to business. At the moment, the answer seems to be "only partially." In its report "Beyond Volunteerism," the International Council on Human Rights Policy, based in Geneva, surveyed current legal sanctions and concluded that while international law does place some direct and indirect obligations on companies to observe human rights, these obligations are not always clear, and are difficult to monitor and hard to enforce.

Those advocating new global rules to curb corporate misbehaviour had their hopes raised briefly during talks on the creation of the new International Criminal Court. In early negotiations, it was suggested the court would be a forum where corporations could be tried. Those pushing the idea had a long list of likely defendants in mind: construction companies covering up mass graves in the aftermath of genocide; private military companies employed to fight rebels in Bougainville; coffee companies in Rwanda that stored arms for the perpetrators of the genocide; oil companies involved in mass population transfers and acts of violence; a radio station in Rwanda that urged its listeners to kill Tutsis. The French delegation at the talks pushed particularly hard to include corporate entities. However, some countries, including Switzerland, Japan, Belgium and Norway, refused to go that far. The United States said that it wasn't against the proposal in principle but that there wasn't time to work out an acceptable solution. The final treaty, reached in Rome in 1998, mentions only "natural persons." While this would still include individual corporate leaders, it would not cover their businesses. This omission opens an escape hatch for corporations, whose structures are so complex that criminal lawyers have a hard time tracking down which individuals are responsible for specific actions. The very fact that the discussion took place, however, indicated that the court's statute could be amended in future to bring corporations into its ambit. On a less promising note, the United States has withdrawn even its lacklustre support of the court, which could severely impact its effectiveness.

The lack of a comprehensive international law and of a court to enforce it does not mean corporations are getting off scot-free. While

national governments are generally loath to pass laws covering misde-
meanours on foreign soil because this infringes on another's national sovereignty, it has been done in the past. In the wake of the Lockheed bribery
scandal, the United States passed the Foreign Corrupt Practices Act of
1977 to prohibit bribery by US corporations abroad. Australia passed a law
targeting sex offenders no matter where the offences take place. But the
most important national legislation for this discussion is the Alien Tort
Claims Act in the United States. The law was first passed in 1789 to deal
with the Barbary pirates off the north coast of Africa, who were costing
countries and companies millions in lost cargoes and ransoms for captured crews. Under the law, foreigners could sue parties accused of violating the laws of nations, the prohibition of piracy being one such law. The
act was invoked only a handful of times in its first 190 years.

Then in 1980 it was catapulted into the legal limelight when lawyers
for a Paraguayan family living in the United States used it to sue a
Paraguayan police official accused of torturing and killing their son. That
suit opened the floodgates for a wave of suits by parties seeking redress for
everything from environmental damage to genocide. Not surprisingly,
many of those named in the actions were corporations. The law has been
used to sue Citigroup Inc. and a number of other banks for profiting from
apartheid in South Africa. Ford Motor Company faced charges of using
slave labour in its German subsidiary during the Second World War.
Union Carbide Corporation was sued for the 1984 toxic gas leak that
killed thousands in Bhopal, India. Royal Dutch/Shell was accused of con-
spiring with the Nigerian military government to violate human rights in
the Niger Delta, and Talisman Energy Inc. was accused of aiding and
abetting ethnic cleansing by the Sudanese government in southern
Sudan. The act is not a perfect tool. Many lawsuits fall at the first hurdle:
establishing that a US court has jurisdiction to hear the case and that the
United States provides the most convenient forum for the hearing. Still,
this law which was designed to thwart pirates has become a useful tool in
constraining their modern equivalent: the corporate buccaneer. Its very
success may prove its undoing. In May 2003 the Bush administration

moved to restrict the application of the Alien Tort Claims Act by inter-vening on the side of the defence in a human rights suit against California oil giant UNOCAL for its operations in Burma.

If the Bush administration succeeds, it will be a crushing blow to groups such as Human Rights Watch, which seeks to make multinationals accountable for their global actions. The United States is one of the few countries that even has such a law. Even if left untouched, the Alien Tort Claims Act is not enough. It is doubtful that the international community wants US courts to shape the new world order. A more inclusive group of countries will have to negotiate a new global rulebook if it is to have legitimacy.

Smart corporations have already recognized that a wind of change is blowing. Now they must accept that real change is required of them and abandon their resistance to global regulation. If they act now, they can help shape the new laws, although there are some drawbacks to allowing corpo-rate input. The failed Multilateral Agreement on Investment, which they helped draw up, contained only rights, with no obligations. Realistically, however, the process will not get off the ground without the business com-munity on board. Corporate leaders can join willingly, or their participa-tion could be forced by the sudden onset of a crisis of such magnitude and horror that the international community is forced to take action.

Doubters should keep Nuremberg in mind. The horrific discovery of the Nazi concentration camps produced such global outrage that the nations of the world responded with one voice. They drew up the Universal Declaration of Human Rights and created the current crop of international institutions. At the post-war trials in Nuremberg, corporate executives were tried alongside military officers for war crimes. The busi-nessmen accused of making poison gas for the concentration camps, of using slave labour in their factories and of other crimes were tried as indi-viduals, but the courts made clear in their decisions that they believed the corporations had violated international law. Those who advocate includ-ing corporations in the mandate of the new International Criminal Court hope to build on the Nuremberg decisions.

If corporations wait too long, there is a risk that a new Auschwitz or Bhopal will lead to an instant set of global rules that they had no hand in creating. It is in their best interest to help update the current set of outdated laws to reflect today's realities. They are global powers now, and with power comes responsibility. Laws developed while the world is in crisis mode by politicians seeking to reassure a panicky public will be far more onerous and arbitrary than ones they could negotiate in a calmer process. And there are benefits for corporations in having an agreed-upon rulebook covering their operations worldwide. It would provide that fabled level playing field they all claim to hanker for. And it would give them the legal certainty that only a comprehensive law can provide. The current legal free-for-all is a double-edged sword: it allows some companies to violate human rights without censure, including some of those who have used armed force to do business, but it also means that blameless companies have few ways of proving their innocence in court. The credibility of Anglo American, De Beers, Barclays Bank, and the eighty-two other companies on the UN roll of dishonour from the Congo has been irrevocably damaged. Guilty or innocent, the stain on their corporate honour remains.

ACKNOWLEDGMENTS

THIS BOOK COULD NOT HAVE BEEN WRITTEN WITHOUT THE INVALUABLE
support of the Reuters Foundation in the United Kingdom and the
MacArthur Foundation in the United States. It would not have seen the
light of day if Anne Collins had not picked it up for Random House
Canada and if Stacey Cameron had not persevered through the editing
process. My agent, David Johnston, was key to securing the deal. All of
them deserve special thanks.

Hundreds of people helped in my research, some at considerable risk
to themselves. There isn't the space to name everyone individually here,
but I hope they know I am grateful to them for taking the time to meet
with me and answer my questions.

The friends and colleagues who read drafts of each chapter provided
valuable advice, context and support. Whatever mistakes that remain are
mine alone. My thanks to Catherine Dowling-Smout; Phyllis Ferguson,
Jim Freedman, Georg Frynas, Sharon Hobson, Godfrey Hodgson, Don
Hubert, Roy MacLaren, Anne McIlroy, Guus Meijer, Colin Newbury;
Jeff Sallot, Deborah Scroggins, Craig Shaw, Bernard Simon, Edison
Stewart and Leah Wedmore.

I am indebted to Akin Akingbulu, Conor Christie, Badru Mulumba,

Douglas Okwatch, Abbey Onadipe, Ozonnia Ojeilo, Sonny and Vicki for making me feel welcome and keeping me safe during my travels in Africa.

Doug Sephton drew the elegant maps that add so much to the book.

Finally, and most importantly, I want to thank my husband, David Lord. He alone had to suffer through all the early drafts, and he was unstinting in sharing his extensive knowledge of Africa and providing his personal support. It will surprise him to hear me say so, but I am forever in his debt.

SOURCE NOTES

Making a Killing is based on original material, supplemented by official filings with securities commissions, company records, published works and academic research papers. Site visits and interviews with more than one hundred subjects were conducted between 1998 and 2003 in North America, Europe and Africa. Some of the earlier interviews were done in the field for my work as a foreign correspondent for the *Globe and Mail* newspaper.

The historical chapters relied on archival records in London and Brussels, published works and historical research papers. I made extensive use of the Public Records Office in London and Rhodes House Library at the University of Oxford. I also drew on collections lodged with the London School of Economics in London and the Royal Archives in Brussels.

This book is not intended to be a comprehensive list of all companies operating in the world that have used armed force. Such a compilation would be difficult if not impossible to put together given the secrecy that surrounds such operations. Instead, it follows the evolution of this type of corporate behaviour by examining ten specific incidents in detail. The following notes mention the principal texts used and, when they have not requested anonymity, the individuals who contributed to my understanding of the issue.

CHAPTER ONE: RHODES

The research for this chapter was done at Rhodes House, which is part of the Bodleian Library at the University of Oxford. Rhodes's own bound copy of the records of the British South Africa Company from 1891 to 1898 proved invaluable as it contained complete texts of speeches made to shareholders and full notes of each meeting, including the questions raised by shareholders.

The British South Africa Company, a 1939 corporate history by Dougal O. Malcolm, provides a longer-term picture of how insiders viewed Rhodes's achievements. A more objective view is presented by John S. Galbraith in his book Crown and Charter: The Early Years of the British South Africa Company (1974). Colin Newbury and Rob Turrell cast a critical contemporary eye on the company in separate papers written for the Journal of Imperial and Commonwealth History, Newbury's "Out of the Pit: The Capital Accumulation of Cecil Rhodes" (1981) and Turrell's "Rhodes, DeBeers and Monopoly" (1982).

Although there have been many biographies of Rhodes, the one I found most useful for factual information is Cecil Rhodes: The Colossus of Southern Africa (1967), by J.G. Lockhart and C.M. Woodhouse, which is based on unrestricted access to Rhodes's papers. Frank Johnson, who put together the Pioneer Column for Rhodes, reveals how the businessman was viewed by those who worked for him in Great Days: The Autobiography of an Empire Pioneer (1940). T.O. Ranger gives a graphic account of the impact on the locals of imperial expansion in Revolt in Southern Rhodesia 1896–7: A Study in African Resistance. And Zimbabwe: The Search for Common Ground since 1890, a compilation of articles drawn from the pages of Drum magazine, connects the past to the present. Thomas Packenham's The Scramble for Africa, 1876–1912 (1991), was invaluable for providing context in many of these early chapters. Finally, Phyliss Ferguson, my academic advisor during the period in which I held the Reuters Fellowship, helped immeasurably by guiding me through the Bodleian Library, with suggestions not just of where to look but also of what to look for. She ensured that the research started out on a good foot.

CHAPTER TWO: LÉOPOLD

Exterminate All the Brutes, a haunting examination of genocide in the Congo by Sven Lindquist published in English in 1992, first alerted me to the terrible toll exacted by King Léopold and the rubber companies. Adam Hochschild fleshes out this story in *King Léopold's Ghost: A Story of Greed, Terror, and Heroism in Colonial Africa* (1998). For a contemporary point of view, I used the writings of Edward James Glave: *Six Years of Adventure in Congo-land,* published in 1893, and "Cruelty in the Congo Free State," published after his death by *The Century Magazine* in 1897. Glave was only one of a number of adventurers who wrote about their experiences in the Congo. Others who helped paint a picture of what life was like on the ground include Guy Burrows, who wrote *The Land of the Pigmies* (1898) and *The Curse of Central Africa* (1903), and Edgar Canisius, in *A Campaign among Cannibals: The Rubber Regime* (1903). For the view of a Belgian officer serving in the Congo, I read *Le Nègre du Congo* (undated) by the infamous Leon Rom. The case against the rubber companies was eloquently made at the time by the shipping clerk E.D. Morel, whose prolific writings include *Red Rubber: The Story of the Rubber Slave Trade Which Flourished on the Congo for Twenty Years 1890–1910* (1919) and the newsletter for the Congo Reform Association.

Catherine Coquery-Vidrovitch looks closely at the corporate side in *Le Congo au temps des grandes compagnies concessionnaires 1898–1930* (1972), as does Robert Harms in "The World Abir Made," which appeared in *Business Empires in Equatorial Africa and African Economic History* in 1983. In *The Congo Rubber Atrocities,* which appeared in the journal *African Historical Studies* in 1971, Roger Anstey details specific incidents as told by the local people. Two chapters in the *History of Central Africa,* Vol. 2, *The Violence of Empire* (1983) by Phylis Martin and "Rural Society and the Belgian Colonial Economy" by Bogumil Jewsiewicki in the same volume provide more perspective. Finally, L.H. Gann and Peter Duignan give an overview of this period in *The Rulers of Belgian Africa 1884–1914* (1979).

CHAPTER THREE: SIR PERCY
Much has been written about Ernest Oppenheimer. The three books I found particularly useful for details of his life and business operations are *Oppenheimer and Son* (1973) by Anthony Hocking, *Ernest Oppenheimer and the Economic Development of Southern Africa* (1962) by Theodore Gregory and *The Story of De Beers* (1939) by Hedley A. Chilvers, which includes a foreword written by Sir Ernest.

Sir Percy Sillitoe was a more elusive figure. His autobiography, *Cloak without Dagger* (1955), was heavily edited by the British authorities before its release and suffered for this treatment. His son, Richard Sillitoe, kindly shared memories of his father and family tales about Sir Percy's work. Biographer A.W. Cockerill was generous with his knowledge. I relied heavily on Cockerill's book *Sir Percy Sillitoe* (1975) and the information he provided. However, I differed with him on his conclusion that the use of industrial diamonds by the Soviets was nothing more than a hoax dreamed up to persuade Sir Percy to work for De Beers.

For information on the Soviet need for and supply of industrial diamonds during the Cold War, I used *Diamonds of Siberia* (undated), edited by A.P. Burov and V.S. Sobolev; *Practical Uses of Diamonds* (1993) by A. Bakon and A. Szymanski; a series of papers published in *The Bulletin of the Atomic Scientists* on the development of the H-bomb, and *Atom Bomb Spies* (1980) by H. Montgomery Hyde. Hyde's *The Quiet Canadian: The Secret Service Story of Sir William Stephenson (Intrepid)* (1989) also revealed the approach made to Stephenson prior to the hiring of Sir Percy.

Information on the workings of the International Diamond Security Organization was gleaned from *Diamonds are Dangerous*, written by former IDSO operative J.H. du Plessis in 1960; *Burning Bright*, the autobiography of Edward Wharton-Tigar with A.J. Wilson in 1987, *The Diamond Smugglers* (1957), a rare non-fiction work by Ian Fleming; and two 1982 books by Edward Jay Epstein, *The Death of the Diamond* and *The Diamond*

Invention. When I contacted the De Beers archives in Kimberley for information on Sir Percy's force, they sent me photocopies of Epstein's works. "Flash" Fred Kamil tells his own story in *The Diamond Underworld* (1979).

The most useful information for this chapter came from records kept at the Public Records Office in London. These internal memos between civil servants and politicians, along with the correspondence with outsiders such as Sir Percy and Sir Ernest, reveal the inner workings of the security world, the fear of the West that the Soviets were smuggling diamonds for their H-bomb program, and details of the IDSO that Sir Percy provided to British authorities. The Public Records Office also contains the draft chapter and book proposal by Sir Percy.

The papers of Chester Beatty held by the London School of Economics shed light on the position of Sierra Leone Selection Trust and its suspicion of Sir Ernest. Further information on Sierra Leone diamonds and smuggling came from *The World of Diamonds* (1981) by Timothy Green, *West African Diamonds 1919–1983: An Economic History* (1985) by Peter Greenhalgh and *Tributors, Supporters, and Merchant Capital: Mining and Develoment in Sierra Leone* (1995) by Alfred Zack-Williams.

CHAPTER FOUR: UNION MINIÈRE

For the early history of the company, I drew on a corporate account published on the fiftieth anniversary of the company, *Union Minière du Haut-Katanga: Memorial 1906–1956.* Later years are covered from the corporate point of view in *La mangeuse de cuivre* by Fernand Lekime. Jean-Jacques Saquet gives an employee's view of the Congo Crisis in *De l'Union Minière du Haut-Katanga à la Gécamines.* The writings of Bruce Fetter, including *L'Union Minière du Haut-Katanga 1920–40: La naissance d'une sous-culture totalitaire* (1973) and "The Union Minière and Its Hinterland: A Demographic Reconstruction," published in *Études d'histoire africaine* in 1982, helped set the local context. Some earlier company newsletters found at the Royal Archives in Brussels flesh out the details in Cousin's corporate career.

The political situation at the time is described in detail in *The Assassination of Lumumba* by Ludo de Witte, published in English in 2001.

His work prompted a Belgian parliamentary investigation, whose report was a goldmine of information on the manoeuvring behind the scenes by the Belgian government and the leaders of Union Minière. It is also the source of many of the quotations from cables between company managers in Katanga and head office in Brussels. Contemporary accounts were provided by former British ambassador Ian Scott in *Tumbled House: The Congo at Independence* (1969), Conor Cruise O'Brien, who gave an insider's view of the UN action in *To Katanga and Back: A UN Case History* (1969); Rajeshwar Dayal gave a slightly different UN view in *Mission for Hammarskjöld* (1976) former Belgian foreign minister Paul-Henri Spaak, who wrote on his dealings with UMHK in *The Continuing Battle: Memoirs of a European, 1936–1966* (1971); and Thomas Kanza, a Congolese diplomat, who wrote *The Rise and Fall of Patrice Lumumba* (1978). Through the newsletters of the Centre de Recherche et d'Information Socio-Politiques and their separate writings, Jules Gérard-Libois and Benoit Verhaegen provide detailed accounts of the Congo Crisis. A general history was provided by Catherine Hoskyns in *The Congo since Independence* (1965). A US view was provided by Madeleine Kalb in *The Congo Cables: The Cold War in Africa—From Eisenhower to Kennedy* (1982), Smith Hepstone in *Rebels, Mercenaries, and Dividends: The Katanga Story* (1962) and John Gunther in *Inside Africa* (1955).

The Public Records Office in London again furnished interesting insights into what insiders were telling British officials about company activities. The John F. Kennedy Library in Boston, Massachusetts kindly provided a copy of the cable that Jules Cousin sent to the president.

CHAPTER FIVE: LONRHO
For three widely differing views on Tiny Rowland, I read Richard Hall's *My Life with Tiny* (1987), Tom Bower's *Tiny Rowland: A Rebel Tycoon* (1993), and *Tiny Rowland: The Ugly Face of Neocolonialism in Africa* (1993), by a team from Executive Intelligence Review, a conservative publication backed by Lyndon LaRouche, Jr. All have certain drawbacks.

Further information on Lonrho was provided by Suzanne Cronjé in *Lonrho: Portrait of a Multinational* (1976) by company records and newspaper accounts, and most importantly by the British Department of Trade inquiry into the workings of the company which took place after the attempted boardroom coup in 1973.

For information on the war in Mozambique, I referred to *Destructive Engagement: Southern Africa at War* (1986), edited by David Martin and Phyliss Johnson; *Beggar Your Neighbours: Apartheid Power in South Africa* (1986) by Joseph Hanlon; and the chapter on Mozambique written by John S. Saul in *Civil Wars*.

Alex Vines detailed Rowland's payments to RENAMO in his contribution to *The Mozambican Peace Process in Perspective* (1998).

This research was supplemented by extensive interviews in London, Mozambique and South Africa with those who worked for Lonrho, representatives of the Mozambican government, former diplomats, rebel leaders and former members of the South African Defence Forces who were active in Mozambique. Some have requested that their names not be used. Particularly helpful were Alex Vines, Joseph Hanlon, John Hewlett and Alves Gomes, even though not all of them agreed with my analysis. Josie Rowland, Tiny's widow, kindly met with me to discuss her husband and his business dealings.

Again, memos from the Public Records Office added to my understanding of prevailing views. They were particularly revealing on the sanctions-busting by British oil companies and Rowland's response. I covered the last Lonrho annual general meeting attended by Rowland in my work for the *Globe and Mail*.

CHAPTER SIX: SHELL

For basic corporate information on the company and its history in Nigeria, I used the 1997 corporate publication *A Century in Oil: The Shell Transport and Trading Company 1897–1997* by Stephen Howarth, and a more objective look at the oil industry, *Seven Sisters* by Anthony Sampson (rev.ed., 1993). Two Harvard Business School publications, *Royal Dutch/Shell in Transition* (1999) and *Royal Dutch/Shell in Nigeria* (2000), supplemented this information.

For Shell's work on scenarios, I relied on the writings of various former members of the scenario team, including Pierre Wack, who wrote "Scenarios: Uncharted Waters Ahead" for the *Harvard Business Review* in 1985. A series of interviews with Betty S. Flowers, published online by Robbie Davis-Floyd under the title *Storying Corporate Futures* for the Institute for Advanced Interdisciplinary Research in 1996, were invaluable in this regard. I also interviewed a current member of the team at Shell headquarters in London.

For Shell's operations in Nigeria, I visited its headquarters in Port Harcourt and was taken on a tour of its operations. Shell's numerous corporate publications on its operations and its community development program supplemented what I was told. *Oil in Nigeria: Conflict and Litigation between Oil Companies and Village Communities* (2002), written by Jedrzej Georg Frynas, provides key information for the basis of community unrest. Frynas further shared his knowledge in a separate interview. Karl Maier casts a journalist's eye on the situation in *This House Has Fallen: Midnight in Nigeria* (2000). Human Rights Watch provides details of specific incidents in *The Price of Oil: Corporate Responsibility and Human Rights Violations in Nigeria's Oil Producing Communities* (1999). And Ike Okonta and Oronto Douglas give a passionate view in *Where Vultures Feast: Shell, Human Rights, and Oil in the Niger Delta* (2001). For more details on the Umuechem incident, I referred to the *Conclusions of the Government of Rivers State on the Report of the Judicial Commission of Inquiry into the Umuechem Disturbances* (1991). Austin Onuoha, who later worked in Umuechem, provided additional information. I am indebted to Abiodun Onadipe, Ozonnia Ojielo and Akin Akingbulu, who accompanied me for part of my time in Nigeria and added to my understanding of their country and its people.

CHAPTER SEVEN: RANGER

The key texts for information on the Angolan conflict and the role of oil were *Angola's War Economy: The Role of Oil and Diamonds* (2000), edited by Jakkie Cilliers and Christian Dietrich; *Angola from Afro-Stalinism to Petro-Diamond Capitalism* (2001) by Tony Hodges; *Angola: Struggle for Peace and Reconstruction* (1997) by Inge Tvedten; and *Angola: Arms Trade and Violations of the Laws of War since the 1992 Elections*, published in 1994 by Human Rights Watch. Karl Maier provides insights from the ground in 1996's *Angola: Promises and Lies*. Jon Lee Anderson paints a picture of the oil industry in his piece "Blood and Oil," published in the *New Yorker* magazine in 2002.

For published information on the role of private military companies in Angola, I referred to *An Unorthodox Soldier: Peace and War and the Sandline Affair: An Autobiography* (1999) by Tim Spicer, *Bloodsong: An Account of Executive Outcomes in Angola* (2002) by Jim Hooper and the chapter written by Kevin O'Brien in *Mercenaries: An African Security Dilemma* (2000), edited by Abdel-Fatau Musah and J. Kayode Fayemi. Two newspaper items—"The Mellow Mercenaries," by Jeremy Harding, published in *The Guardian* in 1997, and "The Private War of Tumbledown Tim," published in 2000 by *The Sunday Times*—were also helpful. A former member of the Executive Outcomes team in Angola provided invaluable insight into their operations on the ground.

I made extensive use of documents filed with the Alberta Securities Commission for corporate information on Ranger Oil and Heritage Oil. The Heritage Oil website provided some of the most detailed information on the relationship between the two companies.

This published information was supplemented by extensive interviews with former Ranger Oil executives and directors, including Gordon Bowman, Fred Dyment and Simon Reisman; with those associated with Buckingham, including Michael Grunberg, Tim Spicer and Simon Mann; and with analysts and companies in the oil industry. Tony Turton, an academic who once served with the South Africa Defence Forces, was extremely helpful in explaining the personal history and outlook of some former soldiers.

CHAPTER EIGHT: SAXENA
The chapter on Saxena sprang out of a collaborative effort with two talented former colleagues at *The Globe and Mail*, Karen Howlett and Alan Robinson. Our articles were discovered on the Internet by a British peer whose outcry sparked two official inquiries in the United Kingdom into what came to be

called the Sandline Affair. The reports of those two inquiries, plus a third in Australia investigating the activities of Sandline and Executive Outcomes in Papua New Guinea, yielded valuable material in the testimony of key players. Other published works consulted include the chapter written by Abdel-Fatau Musah specifically on Sierra Leone in *Mercenaries: An African Security Dilemma* (2000); *Once a Pilgrim: The True Story of One Man's Courage under Rebel Fire* (1998) a book written by former soldier Will Scully about his adventures as a corporate security guard in the country at the time of the coup; and Tim Spicer's *Unorthodox Soldier.* Articles from the *Wall Street Journal* provided background facts on Saxena's early career.

Most of the material for this chapter came from interviews with the key players. I visited Rakesh Saxena three times at his condo in Vancouver, where he was under house arrest. I interviewed Sierra Leone president Tejan Kabbah twice—once while he was in exile in Guinea, and later at the Commonwealth Heads of Government meeting in Edinburgh. I spoke to his minister for presidential affairs, Momodu Koroma, when the scandal first broke. I also met with Michael Grunberg and Tim Spicer for their side of the story.

Documents on file with the British Columbia Securities Commission provided background information about some of Saxena's companies. Leaked correspondence between Saxena, Spicer and Koroma provided more details. Sources within the wider diamond community were generous with their information but did not want their names to be used.

CHAPTER NINE: TALISMAN
This chapter is largely based on original material which I first gathered for newspaper articles for *The Globe and Mail* and for a 1999 magazine piece called "Into Africa" for *Report on Business Magazine.* This was supplemented by further interviews as the situation developed, some in Sudan, which I visited in 1999 to see the oil operations in Heglig and speak to people in Khartoum. It was during that visit that I interviewed warlord Riek Machar and spoke to the Sudanese ministers for foreign affairs and energy. I attended two Talisman general meetings and interviewed its

president, Jim Buckee, several times. Sudan-based Talisman employees were also helpful but asked not to be identified.

In building up my knowledge of Sudan, I was helped immeasurably by a seminar series at Oxford University conducted by Wendy James and Douglas Johnson. Early history was taken from Alan Moorhead's books *The Blue Nile* (1962) and *The White Nile* (1960). Some key books covering later developments include *Inside Sudan: Political Islam, Conflict, and Catastrophe* (1999) by Donald Petterson, *Requiem for the Sudan: War, Drought, and Disaster Relief on the Nile* (1995) by J. Millard Burr and Robert O. Collins, and *Emma's War: Love, Betrayal and Death in the Sudan* (2002), by Deborah Scroggins. This last author was also generous with her advice and knowledge in the early stages of my research.

Details of the early days of Arakis Energy in Sudan were provided by company insiders Terry Alexander, Lutfur Khan and John McLeod in interviews. This information was supplemented with documents the company had filed with the BC Securities Commission and the Alberta Securities Commission. *Fuel for War*, a television documentary by CBC journalist Carol Off, which aired March 26 and 27, 2001, contained valuable interviews with key players in the Talisman saga.

John Harker, who was sent to Sudan by Canadian foreign minister Lloyd Axworthy to investigate the impact of Talisman's operations, was an important source of information, both through his mission report and in interviews afterward. Axworthy added to my understanding of the political response in an interview following his departure from politics. My thanks are also due to oil industry analyst Ian Doig, who provided one of the few independent takes on the Alberta oil patch. Eric Reeves supplied constant updates on the state of play in both Canada and the United States. Finally, the Sudanese Peoples Liberation Front was happy to provide its take, both on Arakis and later on Talisman.

CHAPTER TEN: SALEH

Key information for this chapter was provided by three separate reports published in 2001 and 2002 by the United Nations panel of experts sent to the Congo to investigate reports of plundering by neighbouring countries. Without their work, the details of the looting would never have been uncovered. The report of the judicial commission of inquiry set up by President Museveni of Uganda confirmed many of the panel's charges when it was released in May 2003. Their material was supplemented by reports published by a number of brave civil society groups and academic researchers who continued to collect information in the midst of the conflict. Two were particularly useful in that regard: *La guerre des alliés et le droit à la paix*, published by Groupe Justice et Libération, and *Network War: An Introduction to Congo's Privatised War Economy*, written by Tim Raeymaekers in 2002 for IPIS (International Peace Information Service) in Antwerp. Denis Tougas, whose Montreal group Entraide Missionnaire has close links to partners in the Congo, was generous with information about the situation on the ground.

For an insider's view of Uganda and its political leaders, I turned to *Sowing the Mustard Seed: Struggle for Freedom and Democracy in Uganda* (1997), written by its president Yoweri Museveni; *Uganda since Independence: A Story of Unfulfilled Hope* (1992) by Phares Mutibwa; and *Museveni's Long March from Guerrilla to Statesman* (1998) by Ondoga ori Amaza. These books also provide details of Saleh's part in the guerrilla war. His activities during the privatization of state companies are detailed in "Corruption and Cronyism in Uganda's Privatization in the 1990s," written by Roger Tangri and Andrew Mwenda in 2001 for *African Affairs*. Two other works were particularly useful in setting the scene in the Congo: "Sovereignty and Personal Rule in Zaire," published in 1997 in *African Studies Quarterly*, by William Reno, and *In the Footsteps of Mr. Kurtz: Living on the Brink of Disaster in Mobutu's Congo* (2001) by Michaela Wrong. The information about Kabila's early days as a revolutionary was taken from *The African Dream* (1999) by Ernesto Che Guevara.

Two magazine items were particularly useful in providing details of Saleh's later activities: "Erstwhile Friends Slide from Partnership to Acrimony," a 1999 *Time* magazine piece which included interviews with Museveni and Kabila Sr., and "The Rise and Fall of Salim Saleh," published in the *New African*. For spot news coverage, I made frequent use of items from *New Vision* and the *Monitor*, both based in Kampala. The key interview for this chapter was with Salim Saleh at one of his homes in Kampala. I also interviewed opposition politicians Aggrey Awori and Cecilia Ogwal for a different view of the Ugandan political scene. Journalists Badru Mulumba, Charles Onyango-Obbo and Simon Kaheru helped me understand their country.

CONCLUSION

This chapter was based on the research done for the previous chapters and on a growing body of work being done on the related issues of corporate accountability, the economics of war and the liability of multinational corporations.

Conversations I had with Denis Tougas of Entraide Missionnaire over the course of my research were instrumental to this chapter. He supplied copies of his December 5, 2002, letter to Canadian foreign minister Bill Graham, and of the minister's response, which Tougas received on March 28, 2003.

Information on the Belgian senate commission was taken from the Belgian senate's website and from a news report that was carried on the UN's Integrated Regional Information Network on February 22, 2003. The UN panel of experts report is the final version S/2002/1146, dated October 15, 2002.

The responses of Canadian companies came from a Reuters report on October 22, 2002, personal e-mails and information from Canadian government officials, who asked not to be named.

The two key works I used for corporate accountability are the 2001 *Overview of Issues* and the 2002 report of the Canadian Democracy and Corporate Accountability Commission, which was co-chaired by Edward Broadbent and Avie Bennett. Also useful were two reports published by the United Nations Commission on Trade and Development (UNCTAD), *Social Responsibility* (2001) and *The Social Responsibility of Transnational Corporations* (1999).

The economics of war is a growing field of study. Paul Collier at the World Bank has written extensively on this subject, helping to broaden the discussion of the causes of war to include not just grievance but also greed. His *Doing Well out of War* (1999) is a useful document in this area. The International Peace Academy in New York and the Norway's FAFO Institute for Applied Social Science have jointly and separately published a series of reports that I found extremely useful. Of particular note are *Economic Agendas in Armed Conflict: Defining and Developing the Role of the UN* (2002), *Controlling Resource Flows to Civil Wars: A Review and Analysis of Current Policies and Legal Instruments; Private Sector Actors in Zones of Conflict: Research Challenges and Policy Responses* (2001) and *Options for Promoting Corporate Responsibility in Conflict Zones: Perspectives from the Private Sector* (2002). The 2002 OECD publication *Multinational Enterprises in Situations of Violent Conflict and Widespread Human Rights Abuse* provides a slightly different take on this issue.

The sources used for the possible legal response to multinationals included *Beyond Volunteerism: Human Rights and the Developing International Legal Obligations of Companies*, published in 2002 by the International Council on Human Rights Policy; Andrew Clapham's "The Question of Jurisdiction under International Criminal Law over Legal Persons," in *Liability of Multinational Corporations under International Law* (2000), edited by Menno T. Kamminga and Saman Zid-Zarifi; and "Transnational Corporations and Environmental Damage: Is Tort Law the Answer?" written by Michael Anderson for the *Washburn Law Journal* in 2002.

Much of the information on the Alien Tort Claims Act and its uses was taken from the opinion of Justice Allan G. Schwartz of the US District Court of the Southern District of New York, published in March 2003, in which Schwartz decided that the act would apply in the suit against Talisman. The information on the Barbary pirates is from "America and the Barbary Pirates: An International Battle against an Unconditional Foe" by Gerard W. Gawalt, available online from the Library of Congress.

Many of those active in this field of research provided information on current research and a sounding board for ideas. Special mention must be made of Mark Taylor of FAFO and Philippe Le Billon of the Liu Centre.

SELECT BIBLIOGRAPHY

Anderson, Jon Lee. "Oil and Blood." *The New Yorker*, August 2000.

Anderson, Michael. "Transnational Corporations and Environmental Damage: Is Tort Law the Answer?" *Washburn Law Journal*, 7 May 2002.

Andrew, Warwick. Transcript of Proceedings of the Commission of Inquiry into the Engagement of Sandline International. Boroko, PNG: National Judicial Staff Services, Supreme Court, 1997.

Anstey, Roger. "The Congo Rubber Atrocities: A Case Study." *African Historical Studies*, vol. 4, no. 1 (1971).

Armon, Jeremy, Dylan Hendrickson, and Alex Vines, eds. "The Mozambican Peace Process in Perspective." *Accord: An International Review of Peace Initiatives*, no. 3 (1998).

Arnold, Guy. *Mercenaries: The Scourge of the Third World*. London: Macmillan, 1999.

Aspen Institute. *Beyond Grey Pinstripes*. New York: Aspen Initiative for Social Innovation through Business, 2001.

————. *Business Leaders Dialogue*. New York: Aspen Initiative for Social Innovation through Business, 2001.

————. *Where Will They Lead? MBA Student Attitudes about Business and Society*. New York: Aspen Initiative for Social Innovation through Business, 2002.

Aubert, Marie-Hélène, Pierre Brana, and Roland Blum. *Le rôle des compagnies pétrolières dans la politique internationale et son impact social et environnemental*. Paris: Assemblée Nationale, 1999.

Ayittey, George B.N. *Africa in Chaos*. London: Macmillan, 1998.

Bakon A., and A. Szymanski. *Practical Uses of Diamond*. Trans. P. Daniel. New York: Ellis Horwood, 1993.

Bayart, Jean-Francois, Stephen Ellis, and Béatrice Hibou. *The Criminalization of the State in Africa*. Oxford: James Currey, 1999.

Berdal, Mats, and David Malone, eds. *Greed and Grievance: Economic Agendas in Civil Wars*. Boulder, Col.: Lynne Rienner, 2000.

Berenbeim, Ronald. *How Effective Are Corporate Codes in Combating Corruption?* London: Transparency International, 1999.

Berman, Jonathan. "Boardrooms and Bombs: Strategies of Multinational Corporations in Conflict Areas." *Harvard International Review*, vol. 22, no. 3 (2000).

Beshir, Mohamed Omer. *The Mercenaries of Africa*. Khartoum: Khartoum University Press, 1972.

Bethe, Hans. "Sakharov's H-Bomb." *Bulletin of the Atomic Scientists*, vol. 46, nos. 8–9 (1990).

Bilton, Michael. "The Private War of Tumbledown Tim." *The Sunday Times Magazine*, 2 July 2000.

Birmingham, David, and Phyllis Martin, eds. *History of Central Africa*, 3 volumes. London: Longman, 1983.

Blake, Robert. *A History of Rhodesia*. London: Eyre Methuen, 1978.

Bower, Tom. *Tiny Rowland: A Rebel Tycoon*. London: Mandarin, 1994.

Braeckman, Colette. "Carve-up in the Congo." Trans. Barbara Wilson. *Le Monde diplomatique*, October 1999.

———. "Congo: A War without Victors." Trans. Barbara Wilson. *Le Monde diplomatique*, April 2001.

Bread for the World. *Principles for the Conduct of Company Operations within the Oil and Gas Industry*. Stuttgart, Germany: Bread for the World, 1999.

British Petroleum. *Conflict and Security*. London: BP, 2003. <www.bp.com>

British South Africa Company. *Reports 1891–1898*. London: BSAC, 1898.

Brittan, Victoria. *Death of Dignity: Angola's Civil War*. London: Pluto Press, 1998.

Burgess, P.H.E. *Diamonds Unlimited*. London: Adventurers Club, 1960.

Burov, A.P., and V.S. Sobolev, eds. *Diamonds of Siberia*. London: Industrial Distributors Sales, n.d.

Burr, J. Millard, and Robert O. Collins. *Requiem for the Sudan: War, Drought, and Disaster Relief on the Nile*. Boulder, Col.: Westview, 1995.

Burrows, Captain Guy. *The Curse of Central Africa*. London: R.A. Everett, 1903.

———. *The Land of the Pigmies*. London: C. Arthur Pearson, 1898.

Campbell, Bonnie. *Canadian Mining Interests and Human Rights in Africa in the Context of Globalization*. Montreal: International Centre for Human Rights and Democratic Development, 1997.

Canadian Democracy and Corporate Accountability Commission. *The New Balance Sheet: Corporate Profits and Responsibility in the 21st Century*. Toronto: The Commission, 2002.

———. *An Overview of the Issues*. Toronto: The Commission, 2001.

Canisius, Edgar. *A Campaign among Cannibals: The Rubber Regime*. London: R.A. Everett, 1903.

Cassel, Douglas. "Human Rights and Business Responsibilities in the Global Market Place." *Business Ethics Quarterly*, April 2001.

Catma Films. *The Drilling Fields*. Prod. Poonam Sharma. Dir. Glenn Ellis. Channel 4, London. 23 May 1994.

Cawthra, Gavin. *Brutal Force: The Apartheid War Machine*. London: International Defence and Aid Fund for Southern Africa, 1986.

Chabal, Patrick, and Jean-Pascal Daloz. *Africa Works: Disorder as Political Instrument*. Oxford: James Currey, 1999.

Chambre des Représentants de Belgique. *Rapport de la Commission d'enquête Parlementaire visant à déterminer les circonstances exactes de l'assassinat de Patrice Lumumba et l'implication éventuelle des responsables politiques belges dans celui-ci*. Brussels: Chambre, 2001.

Chapleau, Philippe, and François Misser. *Mercenaires SA*. Paris: Desclée de Brouwer, 1998.

Chilvers, Hedley A. *The Story of De Beers*. London: Cassell, 1939.

Christian Aid. *The Need for Legally Binding Regulation of Transnational Corporations*. New York: Christian Aid, 2002.

Cilliers, Jakkie, ed. *Dismissed: Demobilization and Reintegration of Former Combatants in Africa*. Halfway House, South Africa: Institute for Defence Policy, 1995.

Cilliers, Jakkie, and Christian Dietrich, eds. *Angola's War Economy: The Role of Oil and Diamonds*. Pretoria, South Africa: Institute for Security Studies, 2000.

Cilliers, Jakkie, and Peggy Mason, eds. *Peace, Profit or Plunder? The Privatization of Security in War-Torn African Societies*. Halfway House, South Africa: Institute for Security Studies, 1999.

Clarence-Smith, W.G., ed. "Business Empires in Equatorial Africa." *African Economic History*, 12 (1982).

Clapham, Andrew. "The Question of Jurisdiction under International Criminal Law over Legal Persons." In *Liability of Multinational Corporations under International Law*, ed. Menno T. Kamminga and Saman Zia-Zarifi. The Hague: Kluwer Law International, 2000.

Clarke, S.J.G. *The Congo Mercenary: A History and Analysis*. Johannesburg: South African Institute of International Affairs, 1968.

Cockerill, A.W. *Sir Percy Sillitoe*. London: W.H. Allen, 1975.

Collier, Paul. *Doing Well out of War*. Washington, DC: World Bank, 1999.

Colvin, Ian. *The Rise and Fall of Moise Tshombe: A Biography*. London: Leslie Frewin, 1968.

Coquery-Vidrovitch, Catherine. *Le Congo au temps des grandes compagnies concessionaires*. Paris: Mouton, 1972.

Couzens, Tim, ed. *Zimbabwe: The Search for Common Ground*. Harare, Zimbabwe: NatPrint, 1992.

Cronjé, Suzanne Ling, and Margaret Cronjé Gillian. *Lonrho: Portrait of a Multinational*. Harmondsworth, UK: Pelican, 1976.

Cuvelier, Jeroen, and Tim Raeymaekers. *European Companies and the Coltan Trade: Supporting the War Economy in the DRC*. Antwerp: International Peace Information Service, 2002.

Daum, Juergen. "How Scenario Planning Can Significantly Reduce Strategic Risks and Boost Value in the Innovation Chain." *The New Economy Analyst Report*, 8 September 2001.

Davidson, Basil. *The Search for Africa: A History in the Making*. Oxford: James Currey, 1994.

Davis, James R. *Fortune's Warriors: Private Armies and the New World Order*. Toronto: Douglas & McIntyre, 2000.

Davister, Pierre. *Katanga, enjeu du monde*. Brussels: Éditions Europe-Afrique, 1960.

Dayal, Rajeshwar. *Mission for Hammarskjöld: The Congo Crisis*. London: Oxford University Press, 1976.

de Geus, Arie. Interview. *Emerald Insight*, May 2001.

———. "The Living Company." *Harvard Business Review*, March–April 1997.

Delpelchin, Jacques. *From the Congo Free State to Zaire (1885–1974): Towards a Demystification of Economic and Political History*. Dakar, Senegal: Codesria, 1992.

Detheridge, Alan, and Noble Pepple. "A Response to Frynas." *Third World Quarterly*, vol. 19, no. 3 (1998).

De Witte, Ludo. *The Assassination of Lumumba*. Trans. Ann Wright and Renée Fenby. London: Verso, 2001.

Dietrich, Christian. *Hard Current: The Criminalized Diamond Economy of the DRC and its Neighbours*. Ottawa: Partnership Africa Canada, 2002.

Donaghy, Greg, ed. *Documents on Canadian External Relations*, vols. 16 (1950) and 17 (1951). Ottawa: Department of Foreign Affairs and International Trade, 1996.

Dorney, Sean. *The Sandline Affair: Politics and Mercenaries and the Bougainville Crisis*. Sydney, Australia: ABC Books, 1998.

Douma, Pyt S. *Political Economy of Internal Conflict: A Review of Contemporary Trends and Issues*. The Hague: Netherlands Institute of International Relations, 2001.

du Plessis, J.H. *Diamonds Are Dangerous*. New York: John Day, 1960.

Duffield, Mark. *Globalization and War Economies: Promoting Order or the Return of History?* Birmingham, UK: University of Birmingham, 1999.

Executive Intelligence Review. *Tiny Rowland: The Ugly Face of Neocolonialism in Africa*. Washington: EIR, 1993.

Fetter, Bruce. *L'Union Minière du Haut Katanga 1920–40: La Naissance d'une sous-culture totalitaire*. Brussels: CEDAF, 1973.

Epstein, Edward Jay. *The Death of the Diamond*. London: Sphere, 1982.

———. *The Diamond Invention*. London: Hutchinson, 1982.

Fairclough, Gordon. "Baht and Sold: Did Mr. Saxena Kill a Bank and Trigger the Asian Contagion?" *The Wall Street Journal*, 7 May 1999.

Falvey, R.E., and P.J. Lloyd. *An Economic Analysis of Extraterritoriality*. Nottingham, UK: Centre for Research on Globalization and Labour Markets, 1999.

First, Ruth. *The Barrel of a Gun: Political Power in Africa and the Coup d'Etat*. London: Allen Lane; Penguin, 1970.

Fleming, Ian. *The Diamond Smugglers*. London: Jonathan Cape, 1957.

Flowers, Betty S. Interview. *International Journal of Futures Studies*, vol. 1 (1995–97).

Frynas, Jedrzej Georg. *Oil in Nigeria: Conflict and Litigation between Oil Companies and Village Communities*. London: Lit Verlag, 2000.

————. "Political Instability and Business: Focus on Shell in Nigeria." *Third World Quarterly*, vol. 19, no. 3 (1998).

Frynas, Jedrzej Georg, and Scott Pegg, eds. *Transnational Corporations and Human Rights.* New York: Macmillan, 2003.

Gaddis, John Lewis. *The United States and the Origins of the Cold War.* New York: Columbia University Press, 1972.

Galbraith, John S. *Crown and Charter: The Early Years of the British South Africa Company.* Berkeley: University of California Press, 1974.

Gann, L.H., and Peter Duignan. *The Rulers of Belgian Africa, 1884–1914.* Princeton, NJ: Princeton University Press, 1979.

————, eds. *Colonialism in Africa 1870–1960,* 5 vols. Cambridge: Cambridge University Press, 1969.

Gawalt, Gerard W. "America and the Barbary Pirates: An International Battle against an Unconventional Foe." Washington, DC: Library of Congress, n.d. <www.loc.gov>

Gérard-Libois, Jules. *Katanga Secession.* Trans. Rebecca Young. London: University of Wisconsin Press, 1966.

Gérard-Libois, Jules, and Benoit Verhaegen, eds. *Congo 1960.* Brussels: Centre de Recherche et d'Information Socio-Politiques (CRISP), 1961.

Germani, Hans. *White Soldiers in Black Africa.* Cape Town, South Africa: Nasionale Boekhandel Beperk, 1967.

Gibbs, David N. *The Political Economy of Third World Intervention.* Chicago: University of Chicago Press, 1991.

Glave, Edward James. "Cruelty in the Congo Free State." *The Century Illustrated Monthly Magazine,* September 1897.

————. *Six Years of Adventure in Congo-land.* London: Sampson, Low, Martson, 1893.

Global Reporting Initiative. *Sustainability Reporting Guidelines.* Boston: GRI, 2002.

Goncharov, G.A. "American and Soviet H-Bomb Development Programs: Historical Background." *Physics–Uspekhi,* no. 39 (1996).

Green, Timothy. *The World of Diamonds.* London: Weidenfeld and Nicolson, 1981.

Greenhalgh, Peter. *West African Diamonds 1991–1983: An Economic History.* Manchester, UK: Manchester University Press, 1985.

Gregory, Theodore. *Ernest Oppenheimer and the Economic Development of Southern Africa.* London: Oxford University Press, 1962.

Groupe Justice et Libération. *La Guerre des alliés et le droit à la paix.* Kisangani, DRC: Groupe Justice et Libération, July 2000.

————. *La Guerre du Congo: Des pratiques mafieuses.* Kisangani, DRC: Groupe Justice et Libération, 1999.

Guevara, Ernesto Che. *The African Dream: The Diaries of the Revolutionary War in the Congo.* Trans. Patrick Camiller. New York: Grove, 1999.

Gunther, John. *Inside Africa.* London: Hamish Hamilton, 1955.

Hall, Richard. *My Life with Tiny: A Biography of Tiny Rowland.* London: Faber and Faber, 1987.

Hampson, F.J. "Mercenaries: Diagnosis before Proscription." *Netherlands Yearbook of International Law,* vol. 22 (1991).

Hanlon, Joseph. *Apartheid's Second Front: South Africa's War against Its Neighbours.* New York: Penguin, 1986.

————. *Beggar Your Neighbours: Apartheid Power in South Africa.* Oxford: James Currey, 1986.

Hanson, Philip. *Trade and Technology in Soviet-Western Relations.* New York: Columbia University Press, 1981.

Harden, Blaine. *Africa, Dispatches from a Fragile Continent.* London: HarperCollins, 1993.

————. "The Dirt in the New Machine." *New York Times Magazine,* 12 August 2001.

Harbottle, Michael. *The Knaves of Diamonds.* London: Seeley Service, 1976.

Harms, Robert. "The End of Red Rubber: A Reassessment." *Journal of African History,* vol. 16, no. 1 (1975).

———. "The World Abir Made: The Maringa-Lopori Basin 1885–1903." *African Economic History*, vol. 22 (1983).

Harvard Business School. *The Brent Spar Incident: A Shell of a Mess.* Boston: HBS, 1997.

———. *Royal Dutch/Shell in Transition (A).* Boston: HBS, 1999.

———. *Royal Dutch/Shell in Nigeria (A).* Boston: HBS, 2000.

———. *Royal Dutch/Shell in Transition (B).* Boston: HBS, 1999.

Hempstone, Smith. *Rebels, Mercenaries, and Dividends: The Katanga Story.* New York: Frederick A. Praeger, 1962.

Hirsch, Daniel, and William Matthews. "The H-Bomb: Who Really Gave Away the Secret?" *Bulletin of the Atomic Scientists*, vol. 22, nos. 1–2 (1990).

Hochschild, Adam. *King Leopold's Ghost: A Story of Greed, Terror, and Heroism in Colonial Africa.* New York: Houghton Mifflin, 1998.

Hocking, Anthony. *Oppenheimer and Son.* New York: McGraw Hill, 1973.

Hodges, Tony. *Angola from Afro-Stalinism to Petro-Diamond Capitalism.* Oxford: James Currey, 2001.

Hodgson, Godfrey. *Lloyds of London: The Risky Business, Colorful History, and Turbulent Future of the World's Most Famous Insurance Group.* New York: Viking, 1984.

Holt, P.M. *A Modern History of the Sudan.* London: Weidenfeld and Nicolson, 1961.

Hooper, Jim. *Bloodsong: An Account of Executive Outcomes in Angola.* Johannesburg, South Africa: Galago, 2002.

Hopkins, A.G. *An Economic History of West Africa.* London: Longman, 1973.

Hoskyns, Catherine. *The Congo since Independence.* London: Oxford University Press, 1965.

Howarth, Stephen. *A Century in Oil: The "Shell" Transport and Trading Company 1897–1997.* London: Weidenfeld and Nicolson, 1997.

Human Rights Watch. *Angola: Arms Trade and Violations of the Laws of War since the 1992 Elections.* New York: HRW, 1994.

———. *Famine in Sudan, 1998: The Human Rights Causes.* New York: HRW, 1999.

———. *The Oil Diagnostic in Angola: An Update.* New York: HRW, 2001.

———. *The Price of Oil: Corporate Responsibility and Human Rights Violations in Nigeria's Oil Producing Communities.* New York: HRW, 1999.

———. *Uganda in Eastern DRC: Fueling Political and Ethnic Strife.* New York: HRW, 2001.

Hyde, H. Montgomery. *The Atom Bomb Spies.* London: Hamish Hamilton, 1980.

———. *The Quiet Canadian: The Secret Service Story of Sir William Stephenson (Intrepid).* London: Hamish Hamilton, 1962.

Ibeanu, Okechukwu. "Oiling the Friction: Environmental Conflict Management in the Niger Delta, Nigeria." *Environmental Change and Security Project Report*, no. 6 (2000).

International Council on Human Rights Policy. *Beyond Volunteerism: Human Rights and the Developing International Legal Obligations of Companies.* Geneva: ICHRP, 2002.

International Peace Academy. *Options for Promoting Corporate Responsibility in Conflict Zones: Perspectives from the Private Sector.* New York: IPA, 2002.

———. *Policies and Practices for Regulating Resource Flows to Armed Conflict.* New York: IPA, 2002.

International Peace Academy and FAFO Institute for Applied Social Science. *Economic Agendas in Armed Conflict: Defining and Developing the Role of the UN.* New York: IPA; FAFO, 2002.

———. *Private Sector Actors in Zones of Conflict.* New York: IPA; FAFO, 2001.

Isenberg, David. *Soldiers of Fortune Ltd.: A Profile of Today's Private Sector Corporate Mercenary Firms.* Washington, DC: Center for Defense Information, 1997.

Jewsiewicki, Bogumil. "Rural Society and the Belgian Colonial Economy." In *History of Central Africa*, vol. 2, ed. David Birmingham and Phyllis Martin. London: Longman, 1983.

Johnson, Frank. *Great Days: The Autobiography of an Empire Pioneer.* London: G. Bell and Sons, 1940.

Joye, Pierre, and Rosine Lewin. *Les trusts au Congo.* Brussels: Société Populaire, 1961.

Kalb, Madeleine. *The Congo Cables: The Cold War in Africa from Eisenhower to Kennedy.* New York: Macmillan, 1982.

Kamil, Fred. *The Diamond Underworld.* London: Allen Lane, 1979.

Kanfer, Stefan. *The Last Empire: De Beers, Diamonds, and the World.* New York: Farrar, Straus, Giroux, 1993.

Kanza, Thomas. *The Rise and Fall of Patrice Lumumba.* Rochester, Vt.: Schenkman, 1994.

Kaplan, Robert D. *The Ends of the Earth: A Journey at the Dawn of the 21st Century.* New York: Random House, 1996.

Keegan, John. *War and Our World.* The Reith Lectures 1998. London: Hutchinson, 1998.

Kennan, George F. *Russia and the West.* New York: Mentor, 1960.

Kennes, Erik. "Le Secteur minier au Congo: 'Déconnexion' et descente aux enfers." In *L'Afrique des Grands Lacs: Annuaire 1999–2000,* ed. F. Reyntjens and S. Marysse. Paris: L'Harmattan/CERGLA, 2000.

Khalid, Mansour, ed. *The Call for Democracy in Sudan: John Garang.* London: Kegan Paul International, 1992.

Kunert, Dirk. "Africa: Soviet Strategies and Western Counter-Strategy." *Southern African Forum,* 1981.

———. *The Kremlin, the World Revolutionary Process and African National Liberation Movements.* Halfway House, South Africa: South African Institute of International Affairs, 1977.

Le Billon, Philippe. "The Political Ecology of War: Natural Resources and Armed Conflict." *Political Geography,* vol. 20 (2001).

Le Billon, Philippe, Jake Sherman, and Marcia Hartwell. *Controlling Resource Flows to Civil Wars: A Review and Analysis of Current Policies and Legal Instruments.* New York: International Peace Academy, 2002.

Lefever, Ernest W. *Crisis in the Congo: A UN Force in Action.* Washington, DC: Brookings Institution, 1965.

———. *Uncertain Mandate: Politics of the UN Congo Operation.* Baltimore: Johns Hopkins University Press, 1967.

Legg, Thomas, and Robin Ibbs. *Report of the Sierra Leone Arms Investigation.* London: HMSO, 1998.

Lekime, Fernand. *La mangeuse de cuivre: La saga de L'Union Minière du Haut-Katanga 1906–1966.* Brussels: Hatier, 1992.

Lindquist, Sven. *Exterminate All the Brutes.* Trans. Joan Tate. New York: New Press, 1992.

Lituin, Daniel. *Empires of Profit: Commerce, Conquest and Corporate Responsibility.* New York: Texere, 2003.

Lockhart, J.G., and C.M. Woodhouse. *Cecil Rhodes: The Colossus of South Africa.* London: Hodder and Stoughton, 1963.

Macdonald, Bill. *The True Intrepid: Sir William Stephenson and the Unknown Agents.* Surrey, BC: Timberholme, 1998.

Maier, Karl. *Angola: Promises and Lies.* London: Serif, 1996.

———. *This House Has Fallen: Midnight in Nigeria.* New York: Public Affairs, 2000.

Malan, Mark, and Jakkie Cilliers. *Mercenaries and Mischief: The Regulation of Foreign Military Assistance Bill.* Halfway House, South Africa: Institute for Security Studies, 1997.

Malcolm, Dougal O. *The British South Africa Company: Incorporated by Royal Charter.* London: Herbert Fitch, 1939.

Manning, Patrick. *Francophone Sub-Saharan Africa 1880–1995.* Cambridge: Cambridge University Press, 1988.

Martin, David, and Phyllis Johnson, eds. *Destructive Engagement: Southern Africa at War.* Zimbabwe: Zimbabwe Publishing House for the South Africa Research and Documentation Centre, 1986.

Martin, Phyllis. "The Violence of Empire." in *History of Central Africa,* vol. 2, ed. David Birmingham and Phyllis Martin. London: Longman, 1983.

Metz, Steven. *Reform, Conflict, and Security in Zaire.* Carlisle Barracks, Penn.: Strategic Studies Institute, US Army War College, 1996.

Michaels, Marguerite. "Erstwhile Friends Slide from Partnership to Acrimony." *Time,* 30 March 1999.

Mining Minerals and Sustainable Development. *Breaking New Ground.* London: MMSD, 2002.

Misser, François. "Economy: The Democratic Republic of the Congo." In *Africa South of the Sahara 2001.* London: Europa Publications, 2001.

Misser, François, and Olivier Vallée. *Les gemmocraties: L'économie politique du diamant africain.* Paris: Desclée de Brouwer, 1997.

Mitchell, John, ed. *Companies in a World of Conflict: NGOs, Sanctions and Corporate Responsibility*. London: Royal Institute of International Affairs, 1998.

Mockler, Anthony. *The New Mercenaries*. London: Sidgwick & Jackson, 1985.

Moorehead, Alan. *The Blue Nile*. London: Hamish Hamilton, 1962.

———. *The White Nile*. New York: Harper & Row, 1960.

Morel, E.D. *Red Rubber: The Story of the Rubber Slave Trade Which Flourished on the Congo for Twenty Years 1890–1910*. Manchester, UK: National Labour Press, 1919.

Musah, Abdel-Fatau, and J. Kayode Fayemi, eds. *Mercenaries: An African Security Dilemma*. London: Pluto Press, 2000.

Museveni, Yoweri Kaguta. *Sowing the Mustard Seed.: The Struggle for Freedom and Democracy in Uganda*. London: Macmillan, 1997.

Mutibwa, Phares. *Uganda since Independence: A Story of Unfulfilled Hope*. London: Hurst, 1992.

Newbury, Colin. *The Diamond Ring: Business, Politics and Precious Stones in South Africa, 1867–1947*. Oxford: Clarendon Press, 1989.

———. "Out of the Pit: The Capital Accumulation of Cecil Rhodes." *Journal of Imperial and Commonwealth History*, 10 (1981).

Noer, Thomas J. "New Frontiers and Old Priorities in Africa." In *Kennedy's Quest for Victory: American Foreign Policy 1961–63*, ed. Thomas G. Paterson. London: Oxford University Press, 1989.

Nyaba, P.A. *The Politics of Liberation in South Sudan*. Kampala, Uganda: Fountain, 1997.

Obasanjo, Olusegun. *My Command: An Account of the Nigerian Civil War 1967–1970*. London: Heinemann, 1980.

O'Brien, Conor Cruise. *Memoir: My Life and Themes*. London: Profile, 1998.

———. *To Katanga and Back: A UN Case History*. London: Hutchinson, 1962.

Okonto, Ike, and Oronto Douglas. *Where Vultures Feast: Shell, Human Rights, and Oil in the Niger Delta*. San Francisco: Sierra Club Books, 2001.

Oliver, Roland, and, J.D. Fage. *A Short History of Africa*. London: Penguin, 1995.

Olorunsola, Victor A. *Soldiers and Power: The Development Performance of the Nigerian Military Regime*. Stanford, Conn.: Hoover Institution Press, 1977.

Ondoga ori Amaza, Godfrey. *Museveni's Long March from Guerrilla to Statesman*. Kampala, Uganda: Fountain, 1998.

Organisation for Economic Co-operation and Development. *Multinational Enterprises in Situations of Violent Conflict and Widespread Human Rights Abuses*. Paris: OECD, 2002.

———. *The OECD Guidelines for Multinational Enterprises, Background and Issues Paper*. Paris: OECD, 2001.

———. *The OECD Guidelines for Multinational Enterprises, Policy Brief*. Paris: OECD, 2001.

Owen, Edgar Wesley. *The Trek of the Oil Finders*. Tulsa, Okla: American Association of Petroleum Engineers, 1975.

Pakenham, Thomas. *The Scramble for Africa 1876–1912*. London: Abacus, 1991.

Panter-Brick, Keith. *Soldiers and Oil: The Political Transformation of Nigeria*. London: Frank Cass, 1978.

Paterson, Thomas G., ed. *The Origins of the Cold War*. Toronto: D.C. Heath, 1974.

Pearson, John. *The Life of Ian Fleming*. London: Jonathan Cape, 1966.

Pegg, Scott. "Corporate Armies for States and State Armies for Corporations: Addressing the Challenges of Globalization and Natural Resource Conflict." Paper presented at the annual meeting of the American Political Science Association, Washington, DC, September 2000.

———. "Corporations, Conscience and Conflict: Addressing NGO Reports on the Private Sector Role in African Resource Conflicts." Paper presented at the annual meeting of the International Studies Association, New Orleans, La., March 2002.

Petterson, Donald. *Inside Sudan*. Boulder, Col.: Westview, 1999.

Pratt, David. *Sierra Leone: The Forgotten Crisis*. Ottawa: David Pratt, 1999.

Ranger, T.O. *Revolt in Southern Rhodesia 1896–7: A Study in African Resistance*. London: Heinemann, 1967.

———, ed. *Aspects of Central African History*. London: Heinemann, 1989.

Raeymaekers, Tim. *Network War: An Introduction to Congo's Privatised War Economy*. Antwerp, Belgium: International Peace Information Service, 2002.

Reno, William. "Shadow States and the Political Economy of Civil Wars." In *Greed and Grievance: Economic Agendas in Civil Wars*, ed. Mats Berdal and David Malone. Boulder, Col.: Lynne Rienner, 2000.

———. "Sovereignty and Personal Rule in Zaire." *African Studies Quarterly*, November 1997.

———. *War, Debt and the Role of Pretending in Uganda's International Relations*. Copenhagen: Centre of African Studies, 2000.

———. *Warlord Politics and African States*. Boulder, Col.: Lynne Rienner, 1998.

Richards, Paul. *Fighting for the Rain Forest*. Oxford: James Currey, 1996.

———. "Rebellion in Liberia and Sierra Leone: A Crisis of Youth?" In *Conflict in Africa*, ed. Oliver Furley. London: Tauris, 1995.

Rivers State, Nigeria. *Conclusions of the Government of Rivers State on the Report of the Judicial Commission of Inquiry into the Umuechem Disturbances*. Nigeria: Rivers State, 1991.

Roberts, Brian. *Cecil Rhodes: Flawed Colossus*. London: Hamish Hamilton, 1987.

Rom, Leon. *Le Nègre du Congo*. n.p., n.d.

Royal Dutch/Shell. *Business and Human Rights: A Management Primer*. London: Shell, 1998. <www.shell.com>

———. *People and Connections: Global Scenarios to 2020*. London: Shell International, 2002.

———. *SPDC Submission to the Oputa Commission*. Port Harcourt, Nigeria: Shell Petroleum Development Company, 1998.

Rubin, Elizabeth. "An Army of One's Own." *Harper's Magazine*, February 1997.

Sampson, Anthony. *Black and Gold: Tycoons, Revolutionaries and Apartheid*. London: Hodder & Stoughton, 1987.

———. *The Seven Sisters: The Great Oil Companies and the World They Shaped*. New York: Viking, 1975.

Saquet, Jean-Jacques. *De l'Union Minière du Haut-Katanga à la Gécamines*. Paris: L'Harmattan, 2000.

Scott, Ian. *Tumbled House: The Congo at Independence*. London: Oxford University Press, 1969.

Scroggins, Deborah. *Emma's War: Love, Betrayal and Death in The Sudan*. New York: Pantheon, 2002.

Scully, Will. *Once a Pilgrim: The True Story of One Man's Courage under Rebel Fire*. London: Headline, 1998.

Sebunya, Crespo. "The Rise and Fall of Salim Saleh." *The New African*, March 1999.

Select Committee on Foreign Affairs. *Second Report*. London: HMSO, 1999.

Selvin, Peter S. "Jurisdictional Reach: Liability of Foreign Corporations Based on the Activities of Their US Subsidiaries." *Los Angeles Daily Journal*, 24 July 2001.

Shearer, David. *Private Armies and Military Intervention*. Adelphi Paper 316. New York: Oxford University Press for the International Institute for Strategic Studies, 1998.

Sillitoe, Sir Percy. *Cloak without Dagger*. London: Cassell, 1955.

Simpson, Chris. "Analysis: Rwanda, Uganda's Friendship Tested by Congo War." IPS, 13 August 1999.

Smillie, Ian, Lansana Gberie, and Ralph Hazelton. *The Heart of the Matter: Sierra Leone, Diamonds and Human Security*. Ottawa: Partnership Africa Canada, 2000.

Soyinka, Wole. *The Open Sore of a Continent: A Personal Narrative of the Nigerian Crisis*. Oxford: Oxford University Press, 1996.

Spaak, Paul-Henri. *The Continuing Battle: Memoirs of a European, 1936–1966*. Trans. Henry Fox. London: Weidenfeld and Nicolson, 1971.

Spicer, Tim. *An Unorthodox Soldier: Peace and War and the Sandline Affair*. Edinburgh: Mainstream Publishing, 1999.

Stavenhagen, Rodolfo. *Structural Racism and Trends in the Global Economy*. Geneva: International Council on Human Rights Policy, 1999.

Steinhardt, Ralph G. "Litigating Corporate Responsibility." *Global Dimensions*, 1 June 2001.

Stengers, Jean. "The Congo Free State and the Belgian Congo before 1914." In *Colonialism in Africa 1870–1960*, vol. 1, ed. L.H. Gann and Peter Duignan. Cambridge: Cambridge University Press, 1969.

Stevens, Christopher. *The Soviet Union and Black Africa*. London: Macmillan, 1976.

Stockwell, John. *In Search of Enemies: How the CIA Lost Angola*. London: Andre Deutsch, 1978.

Stokes, Eric. *The Political Ideas of English Imperialism*. Oxford: Oxford University Press, 1960.

Stoppard, Anthony. "Corporate Bribery on the Rise." IPS UN Journal, vol. 10, no. 87 (2002).

Swanson, Philip. Fuelling Conflict: The Oil Industry and Armed Conflict. Oslo: FAFO, 2002.

Schwartz, Allan G. Opinion 01 Civ. 9882 (AGS). New York: United States District Court, Southern District of New York, 19 March 2003.

Talisman Energy. Corporate Social Responsibility. Calgary: Talisman, n.d. <www.talisman-energy.com>

Tangri, Roger, and Andrew Mwenda. "Corruption and Cronyism in Uganda's Privatization in the 1990s." African Affairs, no. 100 (2001).

Tarabrin, E.A., ed. USSR and Countries of Africa. Moscow: Progress Publishers, 1977.

Taisier M. Ali, and Robert O. Matthews, eds. Civil Wars in Africa: Roots and Resolution. Kingston, Ont.; Montreal, Que.: McGill-Queen's University Press, 1999.

Taylor, Mark. Emerging Conclusions. Oslo: FAFO Institute for Applied Social Science, 2002.

Thomas, Gerry S. Mercenary Troops in Modern Africa. Boulder, Col.: Westview, 1984.

Thomas, Hugh. The Slave Trade: The Story of the Atlantic Slave Trade, 1440–1870. New York: Simon & Schuster, 1997.

Thomson, Janice E. Mercenaries, Pirates, and Sovereigns: State-Building and Extraterritorial Violence in Early Modern Europe. Princeton, NJ: Princeton University Press, 1994.

Tshombe, Moise. Quinze mois de gouvernement du Congo. Paris: La Table Ronde, 1966.

Turrell, Rob. "Rhodes, De Beers and Monopoly." Journal of Imperial and Commonwealth History, vol. 10, no. 3 (1982).

Tvedten, Inge. Angola: Struggle for Peace and Reconstruction. Boulder, Col.: Westview, 1997,

Tylden, G. The Armed Forces of South Africa. Johannesburg, South Africa: Trophy Press, 1982.

Uganda. Final Report of the Judicial Commission of Inquiry into Allegations of Illegal Exploitation of Natural Resources and other forms of Wealth in the Democratic Republic of Congo 2001. Uganda: Ministry of Foreign Affairs, 2002.

Union Minière. Union Minière du Haut Katanga 1906–1956. Brussels: Editions L. Cuypers, 1956.

United Nations. The Nine Principles of the Global Compact. New York: UN, 1999.

———. Responsibilities of Transnational Corporations and Other Business Enterprises with Regard to Human Rights. New York, UN, 2002.

———. Rome Statute of the International Criminal Court. New York, UN, 1999.

United Nations Conference on Trade and Development. Social Responsibility. Geneva: UNCTAD, 2001.

———. Social Responsibility of Transnational Corporations. Geneva: UNCTAD, 1999.

United Nations Panel of Experts. Addendum to the Report of the Panel of Experts on the Illegal Exploitation of Natural Resources and Other Forms of Wealth of the Democratic Republic of the Congo. New York: UN, 2001.

———. Final Report of the Panel of Experts on the Illegal Exploitation of Natural Resources and Other Forms of Wealth of the Democratic Republic of the Congo. New York: UN, 2002.

———. Report of the Panel of Experts on the Illegal Exploitation of Natural Resources and Other Forms of Wealth of the Democratic Republic of the Congo. New York: UN, 2001.

US Department of State. "Uganda." Country Reports on Human Rights Practices 2000. Washington, DC: Bureau of Democracy, Human Rights and Labour, 2001.

———. Voluntary Principles on Security and Human Rights. Washington, DC: Bureau of Democracy, Human Rights and Labour, 2000.

Valahu, Mugur. Ci-Git le Katanga: Voici: Le cirque Katangais. Paris: Nouvelles éditions latine, 1963.

van Creveld, Martin. On Future War. London: Brassey's, 1991.

Vandervort, Bruce. Wars of Imperial Conquest in Africa, 1830–1914. Bloomington: Indiana University Press, 1998.

Vellut, Jean-Luc. "Mining in the Belgian Congo." In History of Central Africa, vol. 2, ed. David Birmingham and Phyllis Martin. London: Longman, 1983.

Wack, Pierre. "Scenarios: Unchartered Waters Ahead." Harvard Business Review, September/October 1985.

Ward, Halina. Corporate Accountability in Search of a Treaty? Some Insights from Foreign Direct Liability. London: Royal Institute of International Affairs, 2002.

———. *Governing Multinationals: The Role of Foreign Direct Liability*. London: Royal Institute of International Affairs, 2001.

Wassermann, Jacob. *Bula Matari: Stanley, Conqueror of a Continent*. Trans. Eden Paul and Cedar Paul. New York: Liveright, 1933.

Watts, Phil. *Big Issues for Business: A Personal Perspective*. Stockholm: ICC Sweden, 2000.

Weinberg, Samantha. *Last of the Pirates: The Search for Bob Denard*. London: Jonathan Cape, 1994.

Weissman, Stephen. *American Foreign Policy in the Congo 1960–1964*. London: Cornell University Press, 1974.

Wharton-Tigar, Edward, with A.J. Wilson. *Burning Bright: The Autobiography of Edward Wharton-Tigar*. London: Metal Bulletin Books, 1987.

Wrong, Michela. *In the Footsteps of Mr. Kurtz: Living on the Brink of Disaster in the Congo*. London: Fourth Estate, 2000.

Yachir, Faysal. *Mining in Africa Today: Strategies and Prospects*. London: Zen Books, 1988.

Yalichev, Serge. *Mercenaries of the Ancient World*. London: Constable, 1997.

Young, Crawford. *The African Colonial State in Comparative Perspective*. New Haven: Yale University Press, 1994.

Zack-Williams, Alfred. "Kamajors, 'Sobel' and the Militariat: Civil Society and the Return of the Military in Sierra Leonean Politics." *Review of African Political Economy*, no. 73 (1997).

———. *Tributors, Supporters and Merchant Capital: Mining and Underdevelopment in Sierra Leone*. London: Avebury, 1995.

Newspapers and Periodicals
The East African (Nairobi)
The Financial Times (London)
The Globe and Mail (Toronto)
The Mail and Guardian (Johannesburg)
The Monitor (Kampala)
The New York Times (New York)
The New Vision (Kampala)
The Observer (London)
The Sunday Times (London)
The Wall Street Journal (New York)
West African Mail (Liverpool)
Time Magazine (New York)

Unpublished and Archival Sources
The Royal Archives, Brussels.
Beatty, Chester A. Papers. London School of Economics, London.
Selection Trust Archives. London School of Economics, London.
Foreign & Commonwealth Archives. The Public Records Office, London.
Alberta Securities Commission Records, Edmonton.
British Columbia Securities Commission Records, Vancouver.

INDEX